GREAT BRITISH GARDENERS

About the Author

Garden historian Vanessa Berridge was launch editor of *The English Garden* magazine and now writes widely on gardens for newspapers and magazines. Her other books include *The Princess's Garden: Royal Intrigue and the Untold Story of Kew* (Amberley, 2015), and *Kiftsgate Court Gardens: Three Generations of Women Gardeners* (Merrell, 2019), winner of the 2019 Garden Media Guild Garden Book of the Year award. She lives and gardens in Gloucestershire, where she is county organiser for the National Garden Scheme.

GREAT BRITISH GARDENERS

FROM THE EARLY PLANTSMEN TO CHELSEA MEDAL WINNERS

VANESSA BERRIDGE

AMBERLEY

To Chris

First published 2018
This edition published 2021

Amberley Publishing
The Hill, Stroud
Gloucestershire, GL5 4EP

www.amberley-books.com

British Library Cataloguing in Publication Data.
A catalogue record for this book is available from the British Library.

ISBN 978 1 3981 0331 3 (paperback)
ISBN 978 1 4456 7241 0 (ebook)

Typesetting and Origination by Amberley Publishing.
Printed in the UK.

Contents

PART III
The Great Designers

PART IV
The Industrial Age

PART V
The Flower Garden

Introduction

The British have always been a nation of gardeners. We have a temperate climate, ample rain, a reasonable amount of sunshine, and few extremes of temperature. There are variations even within our small island: our western shores are warmed by the Gulf Stream, while the east of the country benefits from continental air currents, making the former wetter and the latter drier. But wherever we are in Britain, we can be outside and putting a fork into the earth almost every day of the year.

Our gardens evolved over the centuries. The Romans introduced a wealth of Mediterranean plants to these shores, and mosaics at Fishbourne villa in Sussex hint at gardening there. Medieval monks kept the flame alive in their monastery gardens, growing medicinal herbs, as well as vegetables and fruits, often planting species brought back by crusading knights. The literature of Chaucer and Shakespeare is full of references to cultivated flowers and fruit, evoking the idea of the cottage garden, often seen as the embodiment of British gardening.

Land is also political: landowning represents power and control, so how the land is gardened informs the cultural voice of the nation. The gardeners who designed gardens for royalty and the aristocracy helped manipulate both the landscape and its ornamentation to present a particular political viewpoint. That continues to be true today, when those who garden organically and with wildlife in mind are making a political point about the kind of society they want to live in. Designers at the Chelsea Flower Show all convey social and economic messages in the gardens they build.

Many gardeners in this book were very aware of their political roles. There are designers, nurserymen, private gardeners and garden writers. Most have worked or designed for other people, often for the royal family and the aristocracy. The few who have simply created their own personal paradises have written about their gardening philosophies to inspire others. All have been acutely aware of carving out a particular niche in the gardening world.

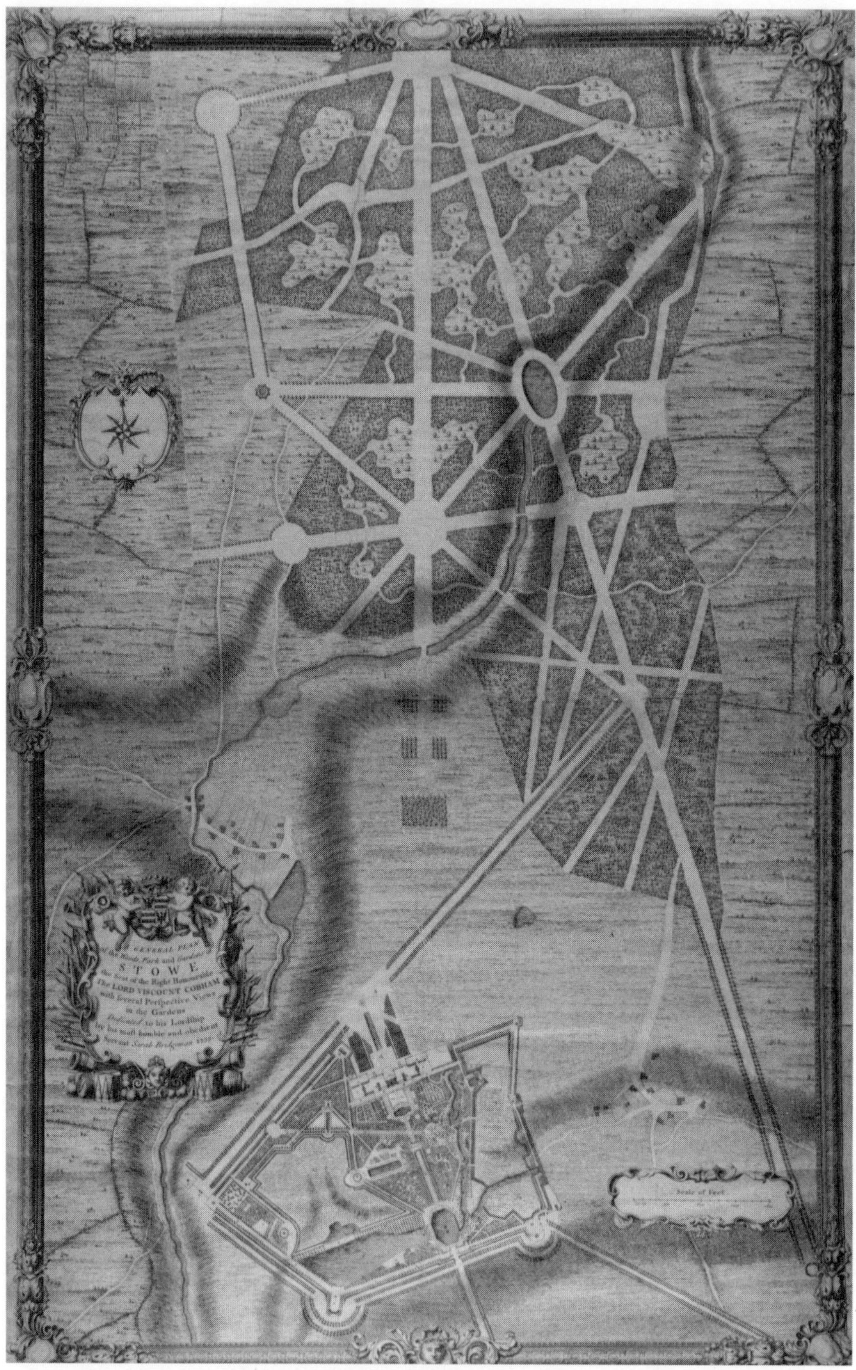

General plan of Lord Viscount Cobham's Stowe, 1739, 'Dedicated to his Lordship by his most humble and obedient servant Sarah Bridgeman'. (Courtesy Stowe House Preservation Trust/Stowe School)

Notably, it is only after exploring the lives of fifteen gardeners that we reach our first great woman gardener, not born until 1843. Gertrude Jekyll was one of a number of supremely gifted amateurs after the mid-nineteenth century who turned professional, driven primarily by deep enthusiasm for their craft, but also to earn a living. More women feature in the last two sections of the book. Equally significantly, almost all of the twentieth-century gardeners, both women and men, were born into the comfortable middle class or above. Over the last century and a half, when social mobility has supposedly been improving, garden design seems to have become instead the preserve of the already affluent; it is no longer a career path from gardener's boy to landowning and social success, as it was for 'Capability' Brown, Sir Joseph Paxton and William Robinson. True, John Brookes cut his teeth with three years in the Nottingham Parks department, but he had been educated at a public school, and studied gardens in southern France first. Women gardeners who have followed in Gertrude Jekyll's footsteps have come from backgrounds similar to hers, a number of them university graduates. Had Paxton been alive today, he would have been designing Chelsea Show gardens, but no contemporary Chelsea designer has followed a career path comparable to his.

***

My challenge when selecting great British gardeners was to know where to start, whom to leave out, and where to finish. My list is necessarily personal and partial, and readers may well disagree with my choices and want to suggest additions and/or exclusions. I have tried to choose practising gardeners, designers and plantspeople who reflected the age in which they lived, and also helped to reimagine gardening, botany and design at that period. This book is not a comprehensive history of British gardening – for that, I suggest you read Jenny Uglow's excellent *A Little History of British Gardening*, updated with new additions in 2017. My account is focussed more on the individuals, their lives and their personal aspirations, but, in every case, the gardeners' lives are set against their historical background.

So whom to choose? There were unassailable candidates: the Tradescants, father and son, royal gardeners and early overseas plant collectors, foreshadow the work of enterprising British plant hunters from the late eighteenth century onwards. 'Capability' Brown changed the face of the British landscape in the second half of the eighteenth century. His successor, Humphry Repton, partner of John Nash, and a bridge between Brown and the more manicured gardens of the nineteenth century, was also never in doubt. Nor were Gertrude Jekyll, the painter turned gardener who taught us how to use colour in the flower garden, nor Vita Sackville-West, poet, novelist, columnist and creator with her husband, Harold Nicolson, of Sissinghurst, the National Trust's most visited garden. Nearer our time, Beth Chatto, advocate of the right plant in the right place, has clearly earned her place here.

The sixteenth century seemed the obvious place to begin, a time of intellectual ferment, when printing increased the accessibility of learning. I could have opened with the Cambridge-educated physician William Turner, known as the father of English botany and author of the scholarly *A New Herball*, published in 1551. Instead, I have begun with a roguish barber-surgeon, John Gerard, whose *Herball*, published in 1597, remained a mainstay for gardeners and botanists into the early years of the nineteenth century. Moreover, the previous year Gerard had published what is believed to be the first complete catalogue of plants in any garden, either public or private.

From Gerard, it was really plain sailing for a couple of centuries, with the gardeners falling neatly into place, although some may be surprised by the appearance of Thomas Fairchild, a little-known nurseryman from Hoxton, who was the first hybridiser. As printed records increase, so, too, do my exclusions, and I regret having to omit Sir Joseph Banks, botanist, founder of the Royal Horticultural Society, and first director of the Royal Botanic Gardens at Kew; and Kew's two Victorian directors, Sir William Hooker and his son, Sir Joseph, who rescued the garden from a period of obscurity (William) and became a major plant hunter (Joseph). My excuse for leaving out this trio is that they were essentially botanists rather than gardeners. Kew is represented, though, through the earlier work there of three major garden designers, Charles Bridgeman, William Kent and 'Capability' Brown.

William Nesfield and Sir Joseph Paxton carry the high Victorian flag, the former the master of formal parterres, the latter the creator of the great glasshouses which enabled plants introduced from hotter climes to thrive in Britain.

Coming closer to our own time, I have chosen Russell Page to hold the fort for the landscape designers of the early post-war years. And, among contemporary garden designers, I have plumped for international garden designer Tom Stuart-Smith, who has won multiple gold medals at the Chelsea Flower Show for his gardens combining naturalism and modernity in the years when he is not there judging the efforts of others.

Between them, I hope that these gardeners and the others I have selected will give some account of the challenges they faced in their own times. All have been practising gardeners, who have loved plants and planting, and have known how to create places of beauty, both large and small. Gardening is an integral part of our island history, and to understand that we need to know about the people who have had their hands in British soil and who have helped fashion the landscape we too often take for granted.

PART I

THE EARLY PLANTSMEN

CHAPTER 1

John Gerard (1545–1612)

In 1597, as Elizabeth I's reign drew to its close, John Gerard, botanist, gardener and member of the Company of Barber-Surgeons, published a book entitled *The Herball, or General Historie of Plantes*. It was not the first nor the most original herbal to be published in England, it was riddled with errors, and its author has been accused of plagiarism. But at 1,400 pages, it was far more extensive than its predecessors and was intended as a practical guide for gardeners (especially women). It became a classic of English botany, largely because of Gerard's charmingly individual style, and remains over four hundred years later a living, breathing book. His pen portraits of plants still spring off the page with a relish for language shared by his greater contemporaries William Shakespeare, John Donne and George Herbert. This was the gift which established Gerard's Herball in its pre-eminent position.

A copy was owned by the great naturalist Sir Joseph Banks, and the Herball was used into the early nineteenth century. In 1806, Richard Weston, an agricultural and horticultural writer, recorded that 'at this day the book is held in high esteem, particularly by those who are fond of searching into the medicinal virtues of plants'.[1]

So, although this roguish barber-surgeon has had his detractors, he is a fitting character with whom to begin this history of British gardeners. Gerard did much to advance the knowledge of plants when botany was still in its infancy in England. By looking at his life, as that of the other gardeners in this book, we can better understand the historical period he inhabited.

Gerard was gardening and botanising at a time of exploration, both intellectual and geographical. The early Tudor humanists, Thomas More, Thomas Linacre, Hugh Latimer and John Colet, had created a new intellectual climate in England. They were part of a Europe-wide scholarly exchange, similar to the nexus of botanists to which Gerard and his continental colleagues belonged two generations later. Linacre founded

Frontispiece of *The Herball or Generall Historie of Plantes* by John Gerard. (Courtesy of the Library of Congress)

the College of Physicians, which in 1586 selected Gerard to establish and curate a physic garden; he held the post until about 1603 or 1604.[2]

The development of printing in the vernacular rather than in Latin made learning more widely accessible. Tyndall's English translation of the Bible, proscribed initially, was the foundation stone of the King James Bible, published within a decade of Gerard's Herball. The 1590s saw the publication of Edmund Spenser's *The Faerie Queene* and the first performance of Shakespeare's *The Merchant of Venice*, *Romeo and Juliet* and *Henry IV Part 1*. As Gerard compiled his Herball, John Donne was composing his *Songs and Sonnets*. The virile young poet is not so much in love that he is unaware of contemporary events, such as the opening up of the New World to colonists and commercial opportunities. He encourages adventurers to travel abroad and leave him and his mistress alone to enjoy themselves. 'Let sea-discoverers to new worlds have gone,' wrote Donne.

Gerard was an enterprising individual, who, like John Tradescant the Elder, invested £25 in the Virginia Company, set up by London merchants to promote the first permanent settlement. The Company of Gardeners was among the London livery companies which invested in the Virginia Company in its early days, seeing prospects for plant hunters in the colonisation of the New World.[3]

England in the late sixteenth century was becoming part of an interconnected world, leading to the arrival of exotic plants as well as ideas. The Reverend William Harrison, domestic chaplain to William Brooke, 10th Baron Cobham, wrote that 'it is a world to see how many strange herbs, plants, and unusual fruits are daily brought unto us, from the Indies, Americas, Taprobane [Sri Lanka], Canary Isles and all parts of the world'.[4]

Gerard himself sent an assistant, William Marshall, as ship's surgeon, to go plant hunting in the Mediterranean. The fig tree or ficus was one of Marshall's discoveries, as Gerard describes in the Herball. 'A port town in Morea, where my servant William Marshall ... did see not onely great store of those trees made of its leaves ... whence he brought me divers plants thereof in tubs of earth, very fresh and greene for my garden, where they flourished at the impression hereof.'[5] Gerard's description of this fig tree could have been read by John Milton, who echoes it in *Paradise Lost*, Book IX (ll.1101-05), writing of the fig leaves behind which Adam and Eve hide after eating from of the Tree of Good and Evil.

***

John Gerard was born in Nantwich in Cheshire in 1545. He clearly received a grammar school education, given that his Herball is sprinkled with Latin tags, and some Greek, and indicates familiarity with Terence, Caesar, Cicero, Virgil, Sallust, Horace, and Ovid.[6] There are signs that he took an early interest in plants; he describes, for instance, vaccinea as growing 'upon the hils in Cheshire called Broxen hils, neere unto Beeston castle, 7 mile from the Nantwich'.[7]

Gerard left Cheshire before he was seventeen to be apprenticed to a barber-surgeon, Alexander Mason, with a large London practice. Medicine was stratified in the mid-sixteenth century, with physicians at the top, prescribing drugs, and apothecaries at the bottom administering them to patients. (The apothecaries, indeed, were suspicious of the physicians trespassing on their domain by asking Gerard to establish a physic garden.)[8] The barber-surgeons came somewhere in the middle.

The United Company of Barber-Surgeons received its charter in 1540, laying down for the first time technical standards for surgeons. A grounding in Latin was essential for Gerard's seven-year apprenticeship, during which he followed a prescribed course of reading, including Galen and Paulus Aeginata, a seventh-century Byzantine Greek physician, later quoted by Gerard. He was admitted to the Company of Barber-Surgeons in 1569, rising eventually to master of the company in 1607, five years before his death.

There is little record of Gerard's activities for the next eight years or so, although we know that by 1577 he had married and settled in Fetter Lane, Holborn, then a fashionable London suburb. During those years, he travelled across northern Europe, although whether as a botanist, private traveller, or ship's surgeon is not known. In his Herball, he records his observations of plants as he travelled overland from Narva to Moscow. In describing the bay tree he says, 'I have not seen any one tree thereof growing in Denmarke, Swevin, Poland, Livonia, or Russia, or in any of those colde countries where I have travelled.' His account of the abies (or 'firre tree') suggests that he ventured even further: 'They are found likewise in Pruse, Pomerania, Lieseland, Russia, and especially in Norway; where I have seen the goodliest trees in the worlde of this kinde.'[9]

He botanised around London (Hampstead Heath was a favourite spot), in Kent, Surrey and Essex, and in Cheshire, Staffordshire, and Lancashire. On more than one 'simpling' expedition, he was accompanied by Matthias de l'Obel, a qualified physician from Lille and an ardent botanist, after whom that cascading summer annual, lobelia, is named. This Protestant exile spent about five years in London from 1569, returning again in the late 1580s and subsequently becoming botanist and physician to King James I. Together, de l'Obel and Gerard found the red-flowered prickly poppy at Southfleet in Kent, and de l'Obel also sent Gerard two figures of the ginger plant, accompanied by a letter in Latin explaining how they had come into his possession.[10] Poley, or polium*, wrote Gerard, 'are strangers in England, notwithstanding I have plants of that Poley with yellowe flowers, by the gift of L'Obelius'.[11]

During his first visit, de l'Obel collaborated with the French-born Pierre Pena, a physician from Aix-en-Provence, on *Stirpium Adversaria Nova*, published and dedicated to Elizabeth I in 1570. The book argued that botany, like medicine, must be based on thorough, exact observation.

It paid tribute to botanists of the ancient world, such as Theophrastrus, Dioscorides and Pliny, and to their own, older contemporary, the Flemish physician and botanist Rembert Dodoens, whose major botanical work, *Stirpium historiae pemptades sex*, formed the basis of Gerard's Herball.

De l'Obel almost certainly met Gerard through the tightly knit medical world, the power base for professional plantsmen in England and Europe in the late sixteenth century.[12] The Society of Apothecaries, the College of Physicians and the Barber-Surgeons Company were key botanical players. Take, for example, the Cambridge-educated physician William Turner, whose *A Newe Herball*, published in 1551, was the first original scientific herbal written by an Englishman and published in English. Gerard almost certainly owned a copy, as he commended 'that excellent work of Master Doctor Turner' in his Herball.[13] The book, the third part of which was dedicated to the Company of Barber-Surgeons, was intended for all members of the medical profession. 'How many surgianes and apothecaries are there in England,' asked Turner, 'which can understand Plini in Latin or Galene and Dioscorides, where as they wryte ether in Greke or translated into Latin?'[14]

No British universities had departments devoted to the study of plants, nor did they have botanic gardens, unlike in Italy where such gardens were established in Pisa, Padua and Florence in the mid-sixteenth century. The first botanic garden at a British university wasn't founded until 1621 at Oxford, although Gerard encouraged his patron, William Cecil, Lord Burghley, Elizabeth's chief minister, to set one up in Cambridge.[15]

The main collectors of plants for their rarity rather than medicinal qualities were aristocrats such as Burghley, in his gardens on the Strand and at Theobalds in Hertfordshire, and Lord Zouche. The latter took a strong interest in the New World (he was a commissioner of the Virginia Company) and developed a physic garden at his home in Hackney, Middlesex, which de l'Obel superintended during an extended visit to England. Gerard himself received plants from Zouche; for example, *arabis* or candie mustard, which 'groweth naturally in that Pannonia which is nowe called Austria, in untoiled places, and by high waie sides: in Crete or Candia, in Spaine and Italie, and such like hot regions, from whence I received seedem by the liberalitie of the right Honorable Lorde Edwarde Zouche at his return into England from those partes, flourish in my garden'.[16]

***

Gerard's dedication of the Herball to Burghley suggests that he began working for Elizabeth's chief minister in about 1577 as superintendent of his London and Hertfordshire gardens: 'Under your Lordship I have served, and that way imployed my principall studie, and almost all my time now by the space twenty years.'[17]

Burghley's gardens are recorded by German Paul Henzner, who visited on the day of Burghley's funeral in 1598. He saw 'the summer-house, in the lower part of which, built semicircularly, are the twelve Roman emperors in white marble, and a table of touchstone; the upper part of it is set round with cisterns of lead, into which the water is conveyed through pipes, so that fish may be kept in them, and in summer time they are very convenient for bathing'.[18]

Gerard would have had a hand in acquiring and planting the variety of trees which Henzner also admired. And, side by side with his work for Burghley, he continued to foster his own garden in Fetter Lane, Holborn. There, he grew 'all manner of strange trees, herbes, rootes, plants, floures and other rare things, that it would make a man wonder, how one of his degree, not having the purse of a number, could ever accomplish the same'. These are the words of George Baker, Master of the Barber-Surgeons and chief chirurgion to Elizabeth I, in his introductory commendations to Gerard's Herbal.[19]

Baker had clearly seen Gerard's Fetter Lane garden, and in 1596, Gerard published a catalogue of more than 1,000 plants, both indigenous and exotic, that he grew there. Dedicated to Burghley, this twenty-four-page pamphlet is believed to be the first complete catalogue of any one garden, either public or private, ever published. Appended is a signed and dated Latin note (June 1596) from de l'Obel, confirming that he had visited Gerard's garden and that Gerard had indeed grown all the plants listed. This catalogue, like the Herball, published the following year, had a lasting impact on British botany. William Aiton, founding curator of the physic garden at Kew, used Gerard's catalogue to confirm the first recorded use of many imported plants when compiling his own catalogue at Kew (*Hortus Kewensis*) in 1789.[20]

The fact that de l'Obel, a distinguished botanist with a European reputation, attested to the accuracy of Gerard's plant catalogue indicates that, at this point at least, Gerard was generally respected in his field. He corresponded with Flemish botanists such as Charles de l'Escluse (who wrote a seminal treatise on tulips) and Rembert Dodoens, and exchanged plants with Jean Robin, botanist to the French kings, and first curator of the Jardin des Plantes in Paris. Robin sent Gerard crocuses, epimediums, nasturtiums, geraniums and a datura.

At home, Gerard received plants from all levels of society, from aristocrats to apothecaries. Plants came from two merchants, John Franqueville and Nicholas Lete of the Levant Co. The latter gave Gerard a yellow gilly flower from Poland, 'which before that time was never seen nor heard of in these countries', and also Beta rubra or Red Beete. 'There is likewise another sort hereof that was brought unto me from beyond the seas by that courteous merchant master Lete.'[21]

Gerard's friends moved in court circles: in 1594, he visited Dr John Dee, the queen's astronomer, and he knew Lancelot Browne, physician to the queen (and father-in-law of William Harvey, discoverer of the circulation of the blood), both of whom wrote introductory commendations to Gerard's Herball. Almost every page instances gifts of friendship, such as the tribute to an apothecary who gave him *cipredium* or ladies' slipper. 'I have a plant thereof in my garden which I received from Mr Garret, Apothecary, my very good friend.'[22]

All this suggests that Gerard was convivial, but there are hints that he could be peppery. He was fined in 1606 for abusing a fellow examiner of the Barber-Surgeons' Company, having the previous year been 'discharged of the office of second Warden and upper governor of this Company'. Apparently, he paid the fine, but subsequently asked for it to be remitted.[23]

Gerard's Herball, despite its many references to his own botanising expeditions and to plants received from friends and contacts, was not entirely original. To be fair, Gerard never pretended it was, admitting the influence of previous foreign-published herbals, including *Stirpium historiae pemptades sex*, Rembert Dodoens' seminal work of 1583. He also referenced William Turner and Henry Lyte, a landowner and amateur botanist, who had translated another work by Dodoens in 1578.

Gerard's Herball was published by the queen's printer, John Norton. Norton had earlier commissioned a translation of Dodoens' *Pemptades* from a Cambridge-educated physician, Dr Robert Priest, who died without completing the task. 'Doctor Priest, one of our London Colledge, hath (as I heard) translated the last edition of Dodoneaus, which meant to publish the same; but being prevented by death, his translation likewise perished,' wrote Gerard in the introduction to his Herball.

Not so: there has always been more than a suspicion that Gerard got hold of a copy of Priest's unfinished work, and that it formed the basis of his Herball, despite Gerard's claim that his text was based on his observations of both indigenous plants and on 'others which I have fetched further, or drawen out by perusing divers Herbals, set foorth in other languages'. This does seem to be an attempt at obfuscation, ignoring the extent of his debt not only to Priest but also to Dodoens. 'Lastly,' he concluded, 'myselfe one of the least among many, have presumed to set foorth unto the view of the world, the first fruits of these mine own labours.'[24]

In compiling the Herball, Gerard adapted Dodoens' classification of plants, choosing instead to follow the style of de l'Obel in *Stirpium adversaria nova*. Dodoens' system was broadly based on the economic uses of plants, but also grouped together some genera of flowering plants. De l'Obel, by contrast, divided plants by the character of their leaves, while his notions of genus anticipated the binomial system introduced by Linnaeus in the eighteenth century.

There were problems from the beginning: Norton bought in a job lot of woodblocks which had been used to illustrate a German herbal published in 1590, and Gerard was set to caption them. He was quickly at sea, and his 'very good friend', the Lime Street apothecary James Garret, told Norton that Gerard was getting it wrong. An anxious Norton called on de l'Obel to oversee the work. De l'Obel corrected more than a thousand errors before Gerard lost his temper and accused him of having forgotten his English (unlikely as de l'Obel had been re-settled in England for over a decade).

What really cooked Gerard's goose (certainly for twentieth-century botanical scholars) was his concluding story of the 'Barnakle tree'. A common contemporary myth had it that there was a tree which produced barnacle geese, which Turner had also mentioned in his herbal of 1551, having heard it, he said, on good authority. But Gerard went further and said, 'what our eies have seene, and hands have touched, we shall declare. There is a small Ilande in Lancashire called the Pile of Foulders, wherein are found ... the broken trunks or bodies of old and rotten trees ... whereon is found a certaine spume or froth, that in time breedeth unto certaine shells ... which in time commeth to the shape and forme of a Bird.'[25]

It's a colourful description, but it encapsulated Gerard's weaknesses for his sternest critics. It 'removes what little respect one may have felt for him as a scientist', wrote botany historian Agnes Arber.[26] 'It is hard to acquit him of almost all the sins of which a man of letters or of science can be guilty,' thundered Canon Charles Raven, Regius Professor of Divinity and Master of Christ's College Cambridge (and grandfather of the now more famous Sarah).[27] Gerard, however, was not alone: as late as 1678, the august Royal Society published an eye-witness account of barnacle geese emerging from shells attached to a piece of driftwood on a Scottish island.[28]

Other commentators have been more forbearing. Robert Jeffers, trained at Wisley and the Royal Botanic Gardens, Edinburgh, believed that Gerard was standing on the shoulders of giants, but that his work was not constructed on a direct translation of any previous work. 'It would be unwise to infer that Gerard intended any discourtesy to other authors,' he wrote, adding 'that Gerard must have possessed a knowledge of plant unrivalled by any contemporary Englishman, and the testimony of George Baker ... and close friends support that conclusion.'[29]

Jeffers points out that men such as Baker and Lancelot Browne were presumably prepared to give Gerard the benefit of the doubt by agreeing to write commendations for the Herball. So, too, was l'Obel, although relations in future were strained between the two men, and indeed he criticised Gerard in a later work.

***

Whether a plagiarist or an adaptor, Gerard brought a fresh, distinctive, and, above all, English voice to the study of botany. Unlike earlier herbalists, he wrote for a broad audience, not just for the medical profession. He emphasises that women are important members of his audience. 'I list not to be over eloquent among gentlewomen, unto whom especially my works are most necessary.'[30]

Contemporary readers 'found in Gerard's Herball a work which stimulated their fondness for flowers better than any other work had so far done in the English language'.[31] There is an attractive particularity about his descriptions, evoking his botanising expeditions and the people he meets. Look, for instance, at 'the cypresse tree' which 'groweth also at Greenwich, and at other places: and likewise at Hampstead in the Garden of Master Waide, one of the Clarkes of hir Maiesties Privy Counsell'. Or at his delightful evocation of the 'the wilde field violet', which 'has long leaves, riseth forth of the ground from a fibrous roote, with long slender branches, whereupon do growe long smooth leaves. The flowers growe at the top of the stalks, of a light blew colour. Of which kinde I have found another sort growing wilde neere unto Blackheath by Greenewich, at Eltham parke, with flowers of a bright reddish purple colour.'[32] These are a few examples of Gerard's jewel-like prose among countless others in the 1,392 pages of his Herball.

The Herball (and Gerard, for that matter) was well served by an accomplished editor. Dr Thomas Johnson, an apothecary and more skilful botanist than Gerard, corrected and extended it in 1633, producing the 1,634-page, so-called *Gerard emaculatus*, which is the edition generally used and quoted from. So immediately popular was Johnson's Gerard that another edition was produced within three years. Johnson doesn't pull his punches in his address on Gerard, accusing him of being less than frank about his debt to Priest and Dodoens: 'I cannot commend my Author for endeavouring to hide this thing from us.' Nevertheless, Johnson does admit that Gerard 'was neither wanting in pains or good will'.[33]

Later in life, Gerard was given a lease by Queen Anne, wife of James I, on a 'garden plot or piece of grounde' adjoining Somerset House, for 'his singular and approved art skill and industrie in planting nursing and preserving plants hearbes flowers and fruits of all kind'. He was asked to present 'yearlie to our owne use onely at the due and proper seasons of the yeare a convenient proportion and quantitie of herbes flowers or fruite renewing or growing within the said Garden plot'.[34] Gerard also remained close to the Cecils, parting with the interest on this royal lease to Robert, Earl of Salisbury, son of Lord Burghley, in November 1606. Nothing further is known of his life and family, other than that he died in February 1612 and was buried at St Andrew's Holborn. His grave is unmarked.

Gerard may not have been a great taxonomist, but he was clearly an excellent plantsman, who had enjoyed the patronage of both a powerful politician and the royal family. As Baker wrote in his commendation at the beginning of the Herball, 'I do not thinke for the knowledge of plants, that he is inferior to any.'[35] This practicality, allied to Gerard's literary gifts and enhanced by Johnson's superior botanising skills and accuracy, gave impetus to the study of botany, and made the Herball a foundation stone of British gardening.

CHAPTER 2

The Tradescants: John Tradescant the Elder (c.1570–1638) and John Tradescant the Younger (1608–1662)

If you visit the Ashmolean Story gallery at Oxford University's museum, you will see three portraits. One is of Elias Ashmole, who gave his name to the museum three and a half centuries ago. The other two are of John Tradescant the Elder and his son, also John, original owners of the Ark, the 'Closet of Rarities' which was the foundation of the Ashmolean Museum's collection.

You could argue that, by right, the museum should be called the Tradescantianum Museum. Ashmolean rolls more easily off the tongue, but the name wasn't the stumbling block. Every picture tells a story and these three portraits tell several. There is the be-wigged Elias Ashmole, city lawyer and smooth operator, wearing his Garter ribbon. This son of a Lichfield saddler, fuelled by ambition and ability, rose through an Oxford education to royal circles, and was made Windsor Herald by Charles II in June 1660 within a month of the monarchy's restoration.

That portraits of the Tradescants were painted at all is a mark of their eminence. Both were gardeners to aristocracy and to royalty, and were allowed to emblazon their South Lambeth home with a coat of arms, which had not been officially registered. A Walberswick-based cousin of the gardeners was less successful when he applied for arms in 1661; he was dismissed as 'ignoble' and 'no gent'. By the beginning of the seventeenth century, gardeners were pushing out frontiers of knowledge, finding for themselves or importing plants from across Europe, Asia and the New World; their expertise was valued by the highest echelons of society. The Tradescants' botanical garden at South Lambeth was visited by aristocracy, royalty and overseas travellers from 1630 onwards.

Tradescant the Elder by Wenceslaus Hollar. (Courtesy Rijksmuseum)

Tradescant the Younger by Wenceslaus Hollar. (Courtesy Rijksmuseum)

These callers came not just to see the gardens, but also the remarkable collection of natural history, art and other curiosities that the father and son had built up over many years. Peter Mundy, a well-travelled employee of the East India Company, described the Ark as a place 'where a Man might in one daye behold and collecte into one place more curiosities then hee should see if hie spent all his life in Travell'.[1]

Both Tradescants were primarily men of the soil, however, and chose to identify themselves as such in their portraits. The elder Tradescant wears a simple black cap and gown, with a wide, white collar, which makes him look rather scholarly. This is offset by the piratical gold loop in his left ear, hinting that this now elderly gardener was once a man of action. He looks out over his thick beard with beady, shrewd eyes from a frame adorned not with heraldic devices but with the produce of his gardens: parsnips, turnips, onions and fruit. His son, also bearded, appears less confident than his entrepreneurial father. He is seen in a garden, left hand on his spade, and clad in a loose white shirt, open almost to his waist, beneath a costly, embroidered velvet coat. It is as if he has just come in from planting, and quickly shrugged on a coat in which to be painted.

The contrast between the worldly lawyer and the hands-on gardener is striking. Small wonder, then, that Ashmole ran rings round the unfortunate younger Tradescant, who, when 'distempered' (drunk), was persuaded to sign a deed of gift bestowing his unique collection of curiosities on Ashmole after his death. Sober, Tradescant regretted his mistake, but the damage was done. He wrote Ashmole out of his will, but Ashmole took Tradescant's widow, Hester, to court in a case heard by the Lord Chancellor, the Earl of Clarendon. Backed up by two knighted advocates and King's Sergeants, Ashmole won without difficulty – especially as he had legal entitlement, if not moral right, to the collection. It was to remain in Hester's hands until her death some sixteen years after her husband, during which time she acquired more rarities. Ashmole moved in next door, and set up a commission to keep an eye on her. His badgering was too much in the end: she was found drowned in the garden pond in April 1678, her death probably suicide.

A sad end to the Tradescant story, even if the curiosities did eventually find their way to the university for which the Tradescants had themselves intended them. It seems hard that Ashmole's name rather than that of the Tradescants stands above the Ionic portico of the museum. As one of their biographers has said, these two men were, by modern analogy, 'responsible for establishing and maintaining the seventeenth-century equivalents of the Royal Botanic Gardens at Kew and a museum such as the Victoria and Albert'.[2] And the story of the Tradescants is a colourful one of derring-do, of two adventurous men prepared to journey dangerously in pursuit of their aims. The elder Tradescant attached himself to several doomed political missions, while his son travelled with would-be colonisers in Virginia.

***

The first sighting of Tradescant in 1609 is in a letter of complaint to William Trumbull, the British Resident in Brussels, about the red tape which entangled Tradescant on a journey to the Low Countries. He thanks Trumbull for his help, but says that 'your good Will and labours hath not effected what you desired to dooe for they have put me upon the Rack'.[3] His wish to be remembered to 'Mr Lasells', one Edmond Lascelles, formerly Groom of the Privy Chamber, suggests that Tradescant was already moving in court circles.[4] The next sighting comes the following year when he went to work at Hatfield House, for Robert Cecil, 1st Earl of Salisbury and James I's chief minister. Tradescant must already have made his name as a gardener, as Cecil would only have employed the tried and tested.

But where Tradescant came from is unknown. He was probably of Dutch ancestry, which may explain why he moved so freely through the Low Countries buying plants for his various masters. It seems likely, however, that he was born in Suffolk about 1570 and received a basic, but not grammar school, education, as his knowledge of Latin was slight: he uses Latin plant names, but spells them phonetically. In 1607, he married an Elizabeth Day at Meopham in Kent, and an only son, also John, was born the following year. All else about his early life is a mystery.

At Hatfield, he was paid a generous £50 per annum, employed for the most part as a supervisor rather than to wield a spade himself. He was sent on frequent plant-buying trips to the continent before Cecil's death in May 1612, although he continued to work for Cecil's son, William, until about 1614. His portrait is carved into a newel post in Hatfield House.

Lists in the Hatfield archives indicate the volume of plant material bought by Tradescant on successive trips to France and Low Countries. On one trip, he met Jean Robin, the French king's chief botanist, and his son, Vespasien. Their friendship lasted until Jean's death in 1629, with the two men often exchanging plants and seeds. While in Russia in 1618, Tradescant dried the amber-coloured berries and sent seeds of what was probably the yellow cranberry, *Rubus chamaemorus*, to Robin.[5]

On Cecil's behalf, Tradescant brought back vines and possibly 'a small Ozier' from Saint-Omer in Flanders, ideal for making 'incomparable networks', fruit trees and bushes from Delft, 800 tulip bulbs from Haarlem, and fritillaries, jonquils and the Provence Rose, 'the most double of any we have'.[6] In Paris, he also acquired exotics which would need over-wintering in England: oleander, myrtle, pomegranates and orange trees.[7]

Tradescant was a supremely talented fruit grower. His work was admired by the apothecary and royal botanist John Parkinson. Parkinson's magnum opus on plant cultivation, *Paradisi in Sole Paradisus Terrestris*, was published in 1629 and was dedicated to Henrietta Maria, the so-called Rose and Lily Queen, for whom both Tradescants later worked. Parkinson and Tradescant became friends, and in his own copy of Parkinson's *Paradisi*, Tradescant recorded his plant acquisitions, including those received from the Robins.[8]

Parkinson paid tribute to Tradescant's ability at growing plums, writing that 'the choysest for goodnesse, and rarest for knowledge, are to be had of my very good friend Master John Tradescante, who hath wonderfully laboured to obtaine all the rarest fruits hee can heare of in any place of Christendome, Turky, yea or the whole world'. And, as well as buying trees for employers, Tradescant also sold trees to the growing nursery trade in London.[9]

In Oxford's Bodleian Library is a book illustrated by sixty-six watercolour paintings of many different varieties of fruit, known as 'Tradescant's Orchard'. Found originally among Ashmole's papers, it has been dated by a Bodleian scholar to the 1620s or 1630s when Tradescant was building up his acclaimed fruit collection at South Lambeth, and was possibly designed as a sales catalogue. Whether or not the volume was commissioned by Tradescant, it reveals the variety of fruit trees available by the third decade of the seventeenth century, and the buoyancy of the trade in which he played a leading role. Illustrated are cherries, plums, damsons, apricots, nectarines, peaches, pears and grapes.[10]

After leaving Hatfield, Tradescant worked for eight or nine years at St Augustine's, Canterbury, a former monastery and the estate of Edward, Lord Wotton. During that time, the younger Tradescant was enrolled as a scholar at King's School, Canterbury, where he acquired the superior education which enabled him to help his father compile *Plantarum in Horto*, the list of some 770 plant varieties in their South Lambeth garden, published in 1634.

Tradescant's fame spread during his Canterbury years, and his gardens were visited by botanists and scholars. His cultivation of melons, a newly understood art, was of particular interest to a reformed pirate, Sir Henry Mainwaring, who wrote about his visit in 1620 to Lord Zouche, employer of Gerard's plant-hunting companion, Matthias de l'Obel. 'I went on Saturday to Canterbury to see my Lord Wotton's Garden and to confer with his Gardner for I do much desyre that your Lordship should eate a Muske Melon of your own at Dover Castell this year.'[11]

***

Despite his commitments at Canterbury, Tradescant went off on three extended trips which were anything but horticultural in purpose. In 1618, he attached himself to a diplomatic mission, led by Sir Dudley Digges, to the Tsar of Russia, Michael Fedorovich. The aim was to lend money to the tsar for his war with Poland, while at the same time opening up a trade route through Russia to Persia, and even as far as China. The mission was unsuccessful, but Tradescant was clearly involved in early seventeenth-century diplomacy and trade.

There was one positive result, apart from the treasures he brought back for garden and museum: his diary of the journey, now in the

Bodleian Library, gives a rare insight into the mind of this shrewdly observant gardener. He emerges as a practical man, prepared to turn his hand to anything on-board ship. The acquisitive collector, gardener and plantsman exist side by side: he preserved, for instance, the skin of a strange bird which came on board ship and died, 'whose like I yet never saw, whos case I have reserved'.[12]

His comments are specific and perceptive, underpinned by his familiarity with both horticulture and agriculture, and written using spelling idiosyncratic even by the phonetic standards of his day. 'The land, so muche as I have seene, is for there arable, fine gentill land of light mould like Norfolk land, without stones. Ther maner of plowes is like owre but not so neat, muche lik to Essex ploughes with wheels but the wheels very evill made.'[13] Elsewhere, he comments on 'littill trees that they make hoops of, which the Inglishe say they be wilde cheryes, but I cannot believe it. It is of that kind, but is like a chery in leafe, and beareth a bery less than our Scarbis [probably sorbus], bery somewhat blackishe, but not ripe at my being theare.'[14]

Tradescant's account of his Russian voyage is rich in this kind of detail, as he looks at red, black and white currants, three or four sorts of vaccinium, red bilberries, angelica, lysimachia, geraniums, saxifrage and sorrel. An important discovery was the Muscovy rose, still listed in his garden in the 1656 catalogue drawn up by his son. A fascinating detail emerges from his description of the rose, which he says is 'much like oure sinoment rose; and who have the sense of smelling, say they be marvelus sweete'.[15] Having no sense of smell must have been a significant handicap for a gardener, prompting, suggests his biographer Prudence Leith-Ross, his endless searches for the rare and exotic to compensate.

And this was not Tradescant's only adventure during his Canterbury years. At the end of 1620, this restless man enlisted as a 'gentleman volunteer' with an expedition, commissioned by James I, to tackle Mediterranean piracy.[16] The mission was humiliating for its leader, Sir Robert Mansell, as the pirate ships eluded his blockade of the harbour at Algiers: he returned to England with nothing more to show for a year's work than a few freed Christian captives and a couple of captured ships. But Tradescant spent three months botanising in the Mediterranean, stepping ashore on the Balearic island of Formentera and on the mainland of Spain, and seeing acres of gladioli growing wild on the Barbary coast of north Africa. Listed in his 1634 plant catalogue were several plants he probably found on this Mediterranean jaunt: a wild pomegranate tree, four types of cistus (or rock rose), two *Smilax*, a turpentine tree (*Pistacia terebinthus*), a yellow restharrow (*Ononis speciosa*) and Spanish sorrel. He also collected items for his museum, including shoes from Spain, north Africa and Turkey; jet given to children in Turkey to protect them from witchcraft; a Spanish tambourine and a pair of sharp Barbary spurs.[17]

***

Life would change dramatically for Tradescant in about 1624, when he caught the eye of the charismatic Duke of Buckingham. A favourite of James I and then his son, Charles I, Buckingham had acquired immense wealth and power, along with almost universal dislike. Buckingham was eventually murdered in 1628 by John Felton, a disaffected veteran of one of Buckingham's spectacular military disasters.

Tradescant was employed initially as a gardener at New Hall, Buckingham's Essex estate, possibly to supervise the planting of 1,500 oaks, a present from James and Charles, and of 2,000 walnut trees, a gift of the Earl of Northumberland.[18] In 1624, Tradescant was paid £124 14*s* for a tree-buying trip to the Low Countries (perhaps for limes for the avenue at New Hall), but he fulfilled many other roles for his magnetic master. (For a salacious take on Tradescant's varied tasks, read Philippa Gregory's spirited fictional account, *Earthly Joys*.)[19] Gregory almost certainly exaggerates the level of intimacy between the duke and his garden master, but many of Tradescant's responsibilities were not usually those of the gardener. For instance, in 1625, he was paid £20 to take his lordship's extensive wardrobe to Paris when Buckingham went to bring back Henrietta Maria as Charles's bride. Never one to lose a plant-gathering opportunity, Tradescant also met up again with the Robins, who were tipped £20 for 'divers plants'.[20]

Tradescant accompanied Buckingham to the Low Countries in 1625 on another tree-buying expedition. Then, in 1627, his engineering skills acquired as a gardener were employed militarily when the Duke of Buckingham sailed to La Rochelle to relieve the besieged Protestants. In an anonymous account of the expedition, Tradescant was described as 'the Dukes gardiner now an Ingeneere and best of all this true and most Deservinge'.[21] The whole thing was a shambles: the Protestants gave no support to Buckingham's forces, and Buckingham dithered, making elementary strategic errors, then withdrawing under full enemy fire. Tradescant was a lucky survivor: fewer than 3,000 men returned out of an original force of almost 8,000.

When not digging military redoubts, Tradescant botanised, bringing back (according to botanist Thomas Johnson in his 1633 edition of John Gerard's Herball) *Artimisia maritima*, while Parkinson lists *Matthiola sinuata*. In Plymouth on his return, Tradescant spotted a botanical freak in a widow's garden: *Fragaria vesca* var. *muricata*, also listed by Johnson.[22]

By the time of Buckingham's untimely (some would say overdue) death, Tradescant was financially independent, and able to lease a house with a two-acre orchard and a one-and-a-quarter-acre field in South Lambeth. There, he set up in business, opening his museum, which quickly acquired the name of the Ark, and working on the garden. From 1629, he began to record his new plant acquisitions in the back of his copy of Parkinson's book. Thomas Johnson visited Tradescant at South Lambeth several times, recording in July 1632 that he had seen '*Geranium Indicum noctu odoratum*, lately brought into this Kingdom by his industry'. Johnson also writes about snakeweed 'that was brought from Virginia, and grew with Mr John Tradescant at South Lambeth'.[23] Within three years, both house and garden had become one of the sights to be seen in London (at the price of 6*d* a head), its fame spreading abroad. The collections at the Ark were used, for instance, by the great naturalist John Ray, for identification purposes, viewing there the dodo, a penguin and a Brazilian blackbird.

The successful Tradescants held leases on four houses in Vauxhall and Lambeth, and kept several servants as well as a paid curator for the collection. Although nearing sixty and running a business concern, Tradescant still had appetite for the job of keeper of the gardens, vines and silkworms at Oatlands Palace, favourite home of Queen Henrietta Maria. From his salary of £100 a year he had to meet the cost of labour and maintenance materials. He seems to have planted 162 wall fruit trees and a further 314 other fruit trees, and supervised other improvements, including a new bowling green for which he was paid an extra £100.

***

As for the younger Tradescant, he was trained as a gardener, and became a freeman of the Worshipful Company of Gardeners in 1634 at the age of twenty-six. When his father died in 1638, Tradescant junior was away on the first of two, possibly three, trips to Virginia, 'to gather up all raritye of flowers, plants, shells, &c'. On this occasion, Tradescant brought back some 200 previously unknown plants.[24]

The younger Tradescant had married a Jane Hurte in 1628, but she died in 1635, and was buried at St Mary-at-Lambeth, leaving him with a daughter, Frances, and a son, another John, who died in 1652. His second wife, Hester Pooke, whom he married in 1638, was related to the de Critz and de Neve artist families whose portraits of the Tradescants are in the Ashmolean.

There are mixed reports from the time about how successfully the younger Tradescant followed in his illustrious father's footsteps. His voyage to Virginia at the time of his father's death was under King Charles's auspices, and, on his return the following year, he took over the job at Oatlands, and at the same salary of £100 per annum, so he too appears to have enjoyed royal favour.

Others, however, were less complimentary: one John Morris, Master of the Windmills, seems to have respected the younger Tradescant's skill as a gardener, listing him with Thomas Johnson and Parkinson as the 'three great men of our native botanists'. But he also described him as 'unschooled and clearly uncivilised', without 'one single vein of his father's testicle'. A Danish plant collector wrote scathingly that 'I have heard that he was an idiot'.[25]

For a royal employee, storm clouds were gathering, as Charles I's attempt to impose personal rule on the country led to the outbreak of civil war in 1642. Tradescant chose this moment to make a second voyage to Virginia, at the cost of £6 each way, plus extra charges for freight. This time he didn't take the king's shilling, but botanised for himself. No record in Tradescant's own hand has survived of his trips to Virginia, but his success in collecting can be plotted through references made by Parkinson in his second book, *Theatrum Botanicum* (1650), and in the museum catalogue *Musaeum Tradescantianum*, which Tradescant published in 1656.

There were difficulties with identification, as Tradescant was a gardener rather than a botanist, unlike Gerard, Johnson and Parkinson. Nonetheless, it appears that he brought back – against considerable odds – plants which still grow in our gardens today. These included Virginia creeper, American sycamore, tulip tree, swamp cypress, maidenhair fern, Michaelmas daisies and *Tradescantia virginiana*, the spiderwort that bears the family name.[26] He was also collecting for the South Lambeth museum: exhibits listed in the 1656 catalogue included 'many rare and beautiful Indian birds', an Indian girdle, 'a Virginian habit of Beares-skin', and 'an Indian dish made of excellent red earth, with a Nest of Snakes in the bottome'.[27]

Tradescant may have made a third visit to Virginia in 1654, when his name was listed on what turned out to be a fraudulent land claim for 500 acres south of James River. This trip would have been in the middle of his protracted, three-year project to produce a complete catalogue for the museum, but he made no reference to it in his somewhat poignant preface. Encouraged by friends 'that the enumeration of these Rarities ... would be an honour to our Nation', he started work. But, he added, 'my onely Sonne dyed, one of my Friends fell very sick for about a yeare, and my other Friend by unhappy Law-suits much disturbed'. He was then further held up by the illustrator, Wenceslaus Hollar, who was too busy to finish the plates.

This catalogue listed over 1,700 plants, a huge expansion of the 770 plants in his father's *Plantarum in Horto*, published twenty-two years earlier. The emphasis was on plants for physicians and apothecaries, although he continued to grow decorative flowering plants favoured by his father. Tradescant must have required great skill to maintain such a range of plants, indigenous, European and exotic. Exceeding his father as a plant hunter, he seems to have adopted a more scientific approach, which anticipated the work of the Royal Society, founded later in the century.

An extraordinary compendium of objects also appears in the catalogue, listed under headings as various as birds (eggs, beaks, feathers, claws, whole birds); fossils; exotic fruits; 'Materialls of Dyers and Painters'; mechanical objects; 'Warlike Instruments'; and gold, silver, copper and lead medals. It is an enigma how the Tradescants collected such a vast miscellany, although some clue is given by the list of 109 'Principal

Benefactors', arranged in order of precedence. These include Charles I and Henrietta Maria, the Duke of Buckingham, Archbishop Laud, Lady Wotton, Sir Dudly Diggs (*sic*), several merchants and Mr Nicolas, Secretary to the Navy.

Also listed is one Elias Ashmole Esq. Ashmole, himself a collector, had taken to plant hunting later in life, hence the dual appeal of the Tradescant family and their collections. His systematic lawyer's mind assisted the spade-wielding Tradescant as he compiled this detailed catalogue, and, to ensure that the Tradescants were further in his debt, Ashmole paid for the catalogue's publication. When John Tradescant died in April 1662, Ashmole moved in on the collections.

Ashmole had the famous garden maintained until his death in 1692, after which it passed through a series of hands. By 1749 the garden was derelict, according to the account of a visiting member of the Royal Society. As for the collection – Ashmole handed it over to Oxford University in 1683.

Over the centuries, the university cared less for the museum's founding exhibits than it should have done, and a visitor today will see a thin representation of that rich catalogue of 1656. The centrepiece, however, is Powhatan's tanned deerskin cloak. This allegedly belonged to the father of Pocahontas, the Indian princess who married an English sailor and died and was buried in Gravesend. This is probably apocryphal, but it seems right that this legendary embroidered hanging remains at the heart of a strange and remarkable collection.

All three John Tradescants are buried in the churchyard at St Mary-at-Lambeth, appropriately now the home of the Garden Museum, redeveloped and extended in 2017. The poetic inscription on the tomb, probably anonymous, but attributed by some to John Aubrey, neatly sums up the Tradescants' achievements:

> Know stranger as thou pass, beneath this stone
> Lye John Tradescant grandsire, father, sone
> The last died in his spring, the other two
> Lived till they had travelled art and nature thro'
> By their choice collections may appear
> Of what is rare in land in sea and air
> Whilst they (as Homer's Iliad in a nut)
> A world of wonders in one closet shut
> These famous Antiquarians that had been
> Both gardeners to the Rose and Lily Queen
> Transplanted now themselves, sleep here, and when
> Angels shall with their trumpets waken men
> And fire shall purge the world, these hence shall rise
> And change this garden for a Paradise.

PART II

A GROWING CONCERN

CHAPTER 3

George London (d.1714) and Henry Wise (1653–1738)

Gardeners often have dress circle seats in the theatre of history. Close relationships with royal and aristocratic patrons mean that over the centuries they have witnessed, if not actually participated in, great affairs of state. Tradescant the Elder accompanied the Duke of Buckingham on his ill-fated expedition to relieve the Huguenots in Bordeaux. Later in the seventeenth century, George London, also gardener to aristocracy and royalty, was embroiled in an equally dangerous intrigue by his patron Henry Compton, Bishop of London, at Fulham Palace.

The sixth and youngest son of the Earl of Northampton, Compton was an Anglican clergyman with éclat, and a cavalry officer in his youth. He was also a well-respected plantsman, 'one of the first that encouraged the Importation, Raising, and Increase of Exoticks, in which he was the most curious Man in that Time, or perhaps will be in any Age', according to the George London-trained gardener Stephen Switzer in his book *The Nobleman, Gentleman, and Gardener's Recreation*.[1] George London, previously apprenticed to Charles II's gardener, John Rose, was taken on by Compton in 1675 to tend his large collection of newly imported plants at Fulham Palace. Like Tradescant before him, London juggled several balls, working simultaneously for the Earl of Arlington at St James's Park and as a consultant on at least two other gardens.[2] But, again, like Tradescant, his day job doesn't seem to have stopped him engaging in other, more unconventional, activities for his master.

Compton educated James II's daughters, Mary and Anne, but was later suspended by James for failing to discipline one of his clergy for preaching an anti-Catholic sermon.[3] He was one of the 'Immortal Seven', signatories to the letter sent in June 1688 to William of Orange, inviting him to seize the British throne from his father-in-law, James II.

In the tense months that followed, Compton whisked Princess Anne away from her father's palace in an escape plan cooked up between him and the formidable Sarah, Duchess of Marlborough. The two women and

The Old Gate at Melbourne Hall, Derbyshire, an estate on which both London and Wise worked for many years.

a lady-in-waiting fled down a back stairs (which Anne, even in her haste, noticed needed repainting) and were taken to Nottingham where Anne was greeted rapturously.[4] It was a hazardous enterprise – the Protestant princess would have made a valuable bargaining counter for the Catholic king – so presumably muscle was needed in case the coach was stopped. So Compton enlisted London, described by Switzer as being 'of a healthy, strong Constitution'.[5] The gardener no doubt dined out on this tale in later years, as he tended the royal gardens at Hampton Court and Kensington, and ran his successful Brompton Park nursery, now the site of the South Kensington museums.

George London and Henry Wise, his younger partner in the Brompton Park nursery and royal gardener, are almost always spoken of in the same breath. Between them, they dominated Stuart gardening for almost forty years. They were the first garden designers with a country-wide clientele whom they serviced from their metropolitan base. To get a sense of their achievements, you need to imagine one of today's top garden designers running his design practice while working as managing director of a major plant nursery. This is what London and Wise did, in the process training the next generation of gardeners, Stephen Switzer and Charles Bridgeman.

Rising from humble origins, both London and Wise were immensely wealthy by their deaths. The estate of the thrice-married London, who died in 1714, included farms at Kingston and Thames Ditton, near Hampton Court Palace where he had laboured for so many years, and an interest in lead mines in Wales. Substantial sums of money were left to his children and grandchildren, and £10 to Henry Wise for a mourning ring.[6] When Wise died in 1738, he had estates in Warwick and Surrey, and a fortune of as much as £200,000 to be divided between his rather younger wife, Patience, and the few survivors of his ten children.

That London and Wise are not better known today is in part due to 'Capability' Brown, who within fifty years of Wise's death had swept away most of their French-inspired formal design schemes. The politics of the Hanoverian succession blew a chill wind across London and Wise's gardens as the newly formed Britain sought to construct a new cultural identity for itself.

***

The civil wars of the 1640s had put paid to the kind of flower and fruit gardening the Tradescants had undertaken for their masters. The younger Tradescant saw the outbreak of the first civil war in 1642 as a good moment to slip off to Virginia, while John Evelyn, diarist and garden writer, also spent some of these years travelling round French and Italian gardens. When peace returned in the 1650s, Tradescant continued to build up his collections at South Lambeth and Evelyn began work on his garden at Deptford. The pastoral poetry of Andrew Marvell, ardent republican and tutor to the daughter of a Parliamentary general, indicates that gardens still played an important actual and symbolic role in English life: *The Garden* provides an image of the type of verdant fruit and flower garden such as the Tradescants would have made at Hatfield and Oatlands Palace.

When Charles II was restored to the English throne in 1660, he introduced a different style of gardening. He had spent much of his exile at the court of his first cousin, Louis XIV, and French formalism would be the chief influence on English gardens, and indeed on its major exponents,

London and Wise, until the Hanoverian succession some fifty years later. At Versailles, André Le Nôtre laid out a rigidly geometrical garden with canals, fountains and sandy walks radiating out from the palace to represent the centralisation of power in the monarch's hands. Charles did something similar at Hampton Court, with the Long Water and the *patte d'oie* of paths leading out from the palace. It was less grandiose and costly than Louis's plans for Versailles, for the pragmatic Charles was all too aware that his grip on power was less total than that of his cousin.

Charles initially employed André Mollet, formerly gardener to his mother, Henrietta Maria, but he then turned to Le Nôtre-trained John Rose. Rose is familiar from the picture showing him kneeling to present a pineapple (then a very exotic fruit) to Charles II. George London's origins and date of birth are unknown and there is no extant portrait of him. Equally obscure is how London came to be apprenticed to Rose, who sent him to France to hone his skills with Le Nôtre. By 1675, London was back in England and working for Bishop Compton, described by Switzer as his 'Great Encourager'.[7] At the same time, he was beginning to build up a portfolio of gardens on which he consulted.

In 1681, George London founded Brompton Park, a hundred-acre nursery in South Kensington. His partners had variously worked for Queen Catherine of Braganza, the Earl of Bedford and the Earl of Essex at Cassiobury, and all these gardeners were aware that a multitude of trees would be needed for large-scale projects then in train. An early major commission was for parterre gardens, canals and fountains in the fashion of Le Nôtre at Longleat in Wiltshire. Eighteen letters, dating from 1685 to 1711 and preserved in the archives at Longleat, show the attention to detail of both garden consultant and aristocrat. One letter, for instance, has London apologising to Lord Weymouth for sending him a married gardener – marriage clearly being regarded as a distracting drawback.[8]

London's nursery business prospered, and Henry Wise became a partner in 1687, after the retirement or death of London's original partners. The nursery furnished both designers with plants for estates which included royal palaces, Longleat, Melbourne, Chatsworth and Blenheim, among others. The value of its plants was estimated by Switzer in the 1710s as being 'between 30 and 40000l., perhaps as much as all the Nurseries of France put together'.[9] The size of the operation can be seen from plant lists: take, for example, the requirements of Melbourne Hall, in Derbyshire, a major project of Wise's for several years from 1699, and the best surviving example of an early eighteenth-century French-style garden. One consignment of plants which went from Brompton to Melbourne, mainly by water, included 1,000 Dutch elms at 3*d* each, 600 limes at 1*s* each, 2,000 hornbeams, plus honeysuckles, jasmines, roses and sweet briar, and tulips, narcissus, crocus, snowdrops and hyacinths in their thousands.[10] The partners provided a full construction and maintenance service and long-term consultancy, as well as initial garden design and provision of plants. 'Brompton,' said John Evelyn, staunch supporter and advocate of both London and Wise, 'was the greatest work of the kind ever seen, or heard of, either in Books or Travels.'[11]

London had both ceremonial and practical roles for the new monarchs after the Glorious Revolution of 1688. He was appointed a page of the back stairs to Queen Mary, and, more importantly, master gardener and deputy superintendent of royal gardens at a salary of £200 a year. The superintendent was William Bentinck, 1st Earl of Portland, a favourite of William III, whom London accompanied to France in 1698 after the Treaty of Ryswick between England and France. Like Tradescant before him, London used a diplomatic mission for horticultural purposes, encountering again the eighty-five-year-old Le Nôtre at Versailles, and visiting Chantilly, Fontainebleau, and Vaux-le-Vicomte.

London joined a uniquely impressive team supporting William and Mary in their architectural and gardening projects. Sir Christopher Wren was first a colleague of London's; later, Wren and Wise worked together on Blenheim, Hampton Court, Chelsea Hospital and Kensington Palace. In Wren's company, London was a bystander to another moment of royal legend: Peter the Great's wrecking of Sayes Court, which the tsar rented from John Evelyn during a visit to England in 1698. The gigantic Russian, with a taste for horseplay, was pushed at one point through a holly hedge in a wheelbarrow – the hedge seems to have come off worse than Peter. Wren and London travelled to Kent to review the damage, and London recorded that 'all the grass work is out of order, and broke into holes by their leaping and Shewing tricks upon it ... all that ground which used to be cultivated for eatable plants is all overgrown with weeds and is not manured or cultivated by reason the Zar would not suffer any men to worke when the Season offered'.[12]

London's sympathy for Evelyn was well rewarded. As the friend of royalty and secretary of the newly founded Royal Society, Evelyn was in a position to recommend London and Wise, which he did fulsomely in a long advertisement in *The Compleat Gard'ner*, his 1693 translation of a French gardening book.

London and Wise worked together on the garden of the renamed Kensington Palace, which William bought as Nottingham House in 1689. He commissioned a Dutch-style garden, described by Wise's biographer, David Green: 'The grounds ... were immediately laid out according to the royal taste, which being entirely military, cut yew and variegated holly were taught under the auspices of London and Wise to imitate the lines, angles, bastions, scarps and counterscarps of regular fortifications.' Again, the nurserymen offered a full service, over-wintering tender citrus trees from the palace at Brompton Park.[13]

At Hampton Court Palace, both brain and brawn were required from London and Wise. 'The first worke I did at Hampton corte,' wrote Wise, 'was in ye Privie garden and sum in ye Wilderness gravelling and turfing, begun May 15th 1699. Begun on ye Grate Avenew ye 2...'[14] This was the chestnut and lime avenue in Bushy Park, designed originally as part of a magnificent approach to the palace from the north. William and Mary built on the distinctly French flavour given Hampton Court by Charles II, and extended Mollet's *patte d'oie* into the park. The Privy Garden on the riverside of the palace was probably initially laid out from designs drawn up by a French Huguenot, Daniet Marot, who had worked for William on the water gardens at his Dutch palace, Het Loo. London made the Fountain Garden on the east front to Marot's plans.

William lost interest in Hampton Court after Mary's death in 1694 from smallpox, aged only thirty-two. He spent the next few years embattled against France, but, in the late 1690s, William commissioned from London and Wise the chestnut avenue, and the reworking of the Privy Garden to give Wren's new wing an appropriate setting.

The garden was integrated with the palace by an orangery, from which William could see barges on the river. This required two changes of level and, in 1701, the transplanting of all the plants from there to the 'Wilderness' on the other side of the palace.[15] The work progressed smoothly and was almost finished when William died in 1702, thrown to the ground by his horse stumbling on a molehill. Having vanished beneath Victorian shrubberies and lawns, the Privy Garden was restored in the 1990s and replanted with box-edged parterre beds filled with hollies, phillyreas, roses, standard loniceras, junipers and variegated rhus. The beds were surrounded by grass à l'angloise, designed to display the excellence of English turf.[16]

This intricate style of gardening had its detractors even before the landscape movement changed English taste. Joseph Addison surely had London and Wise in his sights when he wrote in *The Spectator* in 1712: 'As our great Modellers of Gardens have their Magazines of plants to dispose of, it is very natural for them to tear up all the Beautiful Plantations of Fruit Trees, and contrive a Plan that may most turn to their own Profit, in taking off their Evergreens, and the like Moveable Plants, with which their Shops are plentifully stocked.'[17]

Brompton Park no doubt supplied the bushes for London and Wise's most famous extant work: the maze at Hampton Court, commissioned by William III in about 1700. Trapezoidal and covering a third of an acre, it is the UK's oldest surviving maze. Originally hornbeam, it was subsequently replanted in yew, and is a multicursal or puzzle maze, into which Harris leads some tourists in Jerome K. Jerome's *Three Men in a Boat*. 'You keep on taking the first turning to the right,' he says. 'We'll just walk around for ten minutes, and then go and get some lunch.' They are lost for hours.

***

When Anne succeeded William in 1702, London was passed over in favour of his younger partner. Wise had married Patience Banckes in 1695, some twenty years his junior and the daughter of the royal master-carpenter.

Wise bettered London by becoming superintendent of the royal parks and gardens, and ranger of Richmond Park. His fee was a colossal-sounding £1,600 a year, but out of that he had to pay staff, provide his own equipment, and bear the cost of restoration projects, and the importing of dung and earth to improve the soil. From this royal appointment, he probably, like London, took home about £200 a year.

Wise's origins were as shadowy as London's, although he may have come from Oxfordshire. He seems to have been better educated, and owned a considerable library, including gardening classics such as Gerard's *Herball*, Parkinson's *Paradisi in Sole Paradisus Terrestris* and John Evelyn's *Silva*, as well as the Whig philosopher John Locke's treatise on education. He surfaces first as a student of London, becoming, like his master, primarily a good practical gardener rather than an original designer. London appears not to have been slighted by Wise's winning the favour of the queen, whose first horticultural move was to rip up William's box bushes, complaining she detested the smell.

The London and Wise partnership continued until London's death in 1714. The surviving fragments of their garden plans include, for example, a small George London plan for a parterre at Hodsock Priory in Nottinghamshire (now a renowned snowdrop garden). At the other end of the scale are the huge and intricate plans for Chatsworth which the partnership remodelled for the newly created 1st Duke of Devonshire at the end of William III's reign. Two massive parterres were created there, one costing about £120, the other £500, fabulous sums for the time.[18]

It may have suited both partners that Wise should bear the brunt of running the nursery at Brompton and the royal gardens, while London travelled around the country, visiting other important gardens on which they were employed. He would ride fifty or sixty miles a day, taking five or six weeks to perform each circuit of gardens in the north and west of England. His northern itinerary for 1701, for example, included gardens in and around York, Lumley Castle, Rokeby, Burley-on-the-Hill and Newby Hall, as well as Melbourne in Derbyshire. Although Switzer suggests that London was not much of a botanist, he does commend him for his industry, and his skill in the cultivation of fruit – like John Tradescant before him.

Together, London and Wise translated a French gardening book, *Le Jardinier Solitaire* by Louis Liger. The 786-page book was published in 1706 as *The Retir'd Gard'ner* and contained plans for a garden London and Wise designed at Nottingham for a French marshal, Count Tallard, captured by Marlborough at the Battle of Blenheim. These displayed the geometric formality of French-inspired English gardens in the early 1700s as described by London and Wise. There is, they said, 'one oblong Quarter of Grass-work, which we call a Fund of Grass, upon which many Varieties of Works are cut out, as Angles of several Forms, Squares, Circles, Semi-circles, Ovals, and Branch-works; all which compos'd together the French call Gazon coupe, and we Cut-works in Grass'.[19]

London and Wise were not just designing 'Cut-works in Grass'. Volume I contained 'the Methods of Making, Ordering and Improving a Fruit and Kitchin-Garden', and, in their preface, they wrote that they believed 'Flowers, no less than a Fruit or Kitchin-Garden, will divert and imploy those Persons, who having disingag'd themselves from the World, have resolv'd to pass the rest of their Days in Retirement, amidst the innocent Pleasures of Country Life'.[20]

They used the book to plug their own business: 'To succeed well herein, I advise the buying of Trees only of Persons of an establish'd Reputation, who you may be sure will give you the Kinds you ask for; for nothing can be more vexatious to any Man, who has a fine Plantation to make, than at length to himself impos'd upon in the Kinds he thought to have.'[21]

The Retir'd Gard'ner was published by Jacob Tonson, a bookseller of lowly birth who founded the Kit-Cat Club in the 1690s with a piemaker, Christopher Cat. The club, originally a publishing venture, developed into a gathering of intellectuals and politicians, whose members included Sir John Vanbrugh, William Congreve, Joseph Addison, Richard Steele and Robert Walpole. Its members were mostly Whigs, who over the next few decades would begin to change the political and physical landscape of Britain. Wise was rubbing shoulders with Vanbrugh, the architect of Blenheim, Castle Howard and of several of the early follies at Lord Cobham's garden at Stowe in Buckinghamshire.

Blenheim was Wise's greatest commission, where he worked with Vanbrugh and Nicholas Hawksmoor on the palace given by the nation to the Duke of Marlborough after his triumphs in the War of the Spanish Succession. Most of Wise's work was subsequently erased by 'Capability' Brown, but his influence is still felt: an outline for the projected garden was essential before the foundations of the palace could be dug and vast quantities of earth removed. Brompton was the only nursery equipped to cope with such an undertaking. Just one bill for plants came to £1,400, and included 202 peaches and nectarines at 2*s* each, 200 pears at 1*s* each, 2,219 large espalier limes at 1*s* each and 5,900 of hornbeam, privet and sweet briar 'for the Inner line of the woodwork, at 1½*d*'. Hedge yews were graduated according to their intended positions: so 957 were needed at 4½ft, 2,612 at 4ft, 2,086 at 3½ft, 3,303 at 3ft and 399 at 1½ft. The operation was overseen by Wise, who had his own key to the estate; he paid the labourers himself, gaining about a shilling for every pound spent.[22]

Throughout Anne's reign, Wise also worked at all the royal palaces, including Hampton Court, St James's, Greenwich, Kensington and Windsor Castle. The court painter, Sir Godfrey Kneller, portrayed Wise as a comfortable, prosperous man, well but not extravagantly dressed in full wig, silk cravat and buttoned-up coat. He has sharp, intent eyes, and a large nose which overhangs a firm, rather narrow mouth. This is a man, you feel, who is used to giving orders.

Proximity to the court had its downside, as Wise discovered when the close friendship between the queen and the Duchess of Marlborough turned sour, resulting in a complete rupture between the two women. The duchess, always tricky about money, stopped work on Blenheim five months after her break with the queen. Wise, either through luck or judgement, had been paid most of what he had been owed and fared better than many. Work later recommenced, although money remained an issue between Wise and the Marlboroughs, with Wise eventually pulling out of the contract. He wrote to the duchess in September 1716 that 'I have Just now writ to my Foreman att Blenheim to discharge all the Men & Teams & to Come away'.[23]

***

The Hanoverian succession in 1714 marked the changing of the horticultural guard. The style of garden created by London and Wise was dismissed in a gardening book written in 1728 and dedicated to George II. Gardener Batty Langley wrote in his *New Principles of Gardening* that there is nothing 'more shocking than a stiff regular Garden; where after we have seen one quarter thereof, the very same is repeated in all the remaining Parts, so that we are tired, instead of being further entertain'd with something new as expected ... These regular gardens were first taken from the Dutch, and introduced into England in the time of the late Mr London and Mr Wise.'[24]

Henry Wise had retired only a year before Langley published his book. He was not dismissed on George I's accession, but he slipped down the pecking order with the appointment in 1715 of Sir John Vanbrugh to the newly created role of Surveyor of the Gardens and Waters. He remained on the royal gardening staff, but had constantly to defend the management of the royal gardens during the previous two reigns. It was detailed, unrewarding work, which must have made the ageing gardener long for retirement to one of the estates that he had bought during his palmy years.

Wise handed over the running of the Brompton Park nursery after London's death to William Smith and Joseph Carpenter, who were conspicuously less successful, both dying in debt to Wise. He retired to the Priory in Warwick, to be wheeled through his formal garden as his former pupil, Charles Bridgeman, began to design serpentine walks and informal planting at Queen Caroline's Richmond Gardens and at Lord Cobham's Stowe. Wise died at Warwick in December 1738 and was buried in St Mary's, Warwick, his tomb emblazoned with the coat of arms for which he had applied in 1719.

Their sometime critic Joseph Addison nevertheless appreciated the attainments of London and Wise. 'I think there are as many kinds of gardening as of poetry,' wrote Addison in *The Spectator* in 1712. 'Your makers of parterres and flower gardens are epigrammatists and sonneteers in this art; contrivers of bowers and grottoes, treillages and cascades are romance writers. Wise and London are our heroic poets.'[25]

CHAPTER 4

Thomas Fairchild (1667–1729)

Illustration from Thomas Fairchild's *The City Gardener*. (Courtesy of the Library of Congress)

Next time you come home from the garden centre with trays of brightly coloured annuals, spare a thought for an eighteenth-century nurseryman who was the founding father of modern flower gardening. Most of the plants you will have bought are likely to be hybrids, and, although the term 'hybridisation' wasn't actually used until 1845, Thomas Fairchild anticipated its coinage by more than 120 years. An observant and skilled gardener, Fairchild was eager to extend the range of plants he sold in his already well-stocked nursery at Hoxton, two miles from the City of London. So in the summer of 1716, he took pollen from the wild carnation *Dianthus caryophyllus*, and brushed it with a feather on to the stigma of a sweet william, *Dianthus barbatus*. He had to wait until the following spring to discover that he had been successful in producing the first man-made hybrid. This little pink came to be known as Fairchild's Mule; sterile like most hybrids, it was named after the cross between a horse and a donkey.

The discovery of hybridisation in time allowed plantsmen to produce an almost boundless variety of flower colours, shapes and sizes. For Thomas Fairchild, the sight of his new flower, which combined the double blossom of the carnation with the clusters of tiny flower heads of the sweet william, was a vertiginous moment. Fairchild lived at a period when scientists and thinkers were freeing themselves from the fetters of medieval superstition. The Royal Society was founded in the 1660s, bringing with it an interest in scientific exploration and an openness to new ideas at the dawn of the Enlightenment. Nevertheless, even members of the Royal Society were God-fearing Christians, who tried to place any new discoveries they made in the context of a world created in seven days by the Almighty.

Fairchild was familiar with advances in knowledge of plant sexuality and reproduction, and had also studied the effect of the circulation of sap on the grafting of trees. Grafting was acceptable (it had been carried out over a century earlier by John Tradescant), but acknowledging and then tinkering with the sexual reproduction of plants would have seemed blasphemous to Fairchild's contemporaries, as well as to Fairchild himself. Certainly, when the Mule was presented for Fairchild by a fellow at a meeting of the Royal Society in February 1720, the dried specimen was described as an accidental cross which Fairchild had chanced upon in his nursery, not as a hybrid that he had deliberately engineered. The meeting was not a *coup de foudre*. Few of the fellows really understood the implications of Fairchild's hybrid, but one did: Richard Bradley, a botanist, arguably the first horticultural journalist, and a friend of Fairchild. He foresaw that a 'curious Person may by this knowledge produce such rare Kinds of Plants as have not yet been heard of'.[1] Philip Miller, head gardener at the Chelsea Physic Garden, recognised the potential of Fairchild's Mule. Miller mentioned it in his *Gardeners Dictionary*, which became a textbook of garden-makers.

Fairchild's experiment was a harbinger, even if it was well into the nineteenth century before hybridisation became accepted practice; until then, nurserymen were nervous about exhibiting hybrids at horticultural shows, for fear of being thought ungodly.

Fairchild's concern at what he had set in motion may explain why, on his death in 1729, he left £25 to his local church of St Leonard, Shoreditch, for a sermon to be preached in perpetuity on the Tuesday of Whitsun week each year. The themes laid down reflect his life's work as a nurseryman, for he stipulated that the preacher should speak either about 'The Wonderful World of God in the Creation' or about 'The Certainty of the Resurrection of the Dead proved by the Certain Change of the Animal and Vegetable Parts of the Creation'.[2] Thomas Fairchild was hedging his bets.

***

His portrait suggests that he was a man able to balance different points of view. He appears both thoughtful and cheery in his short wig, a practical, down-to-earth sort of chap, with a half-smile playing about his lips and the plans of a garden open in front of him.

Thomas Fairchild was born in 1667 in Aldbourne, Wiltshire. His father, John, a tenant farmer, died within a year of his birth, bequeathing his estate worth a meagre £54 12*s* to his widow, and £20 to his only son. Half of it was to pay for the transfer of John's copyhold (tenure) into his son's name; the other £10 would be given to Thomas when he reached twenty-one, possibly providing the seed corn to start his nursery.[3] We can date the beginning of his involvement in the nursery to around 1691: in the introduction to his book, *The City Gardener*, published in 1722, he writes that 'I have upwards of thirty Years been placed near London, on a Spot of Ground, where I have raised several thousand Plants, both from foreign Countries, and of the English Growth'.[4]

He and two half-brothers and a sister were probably schooled in a room above the church porch in Aldbourne, Fairchild leaving the village at fifteen for an apprenticeship with a City of London clothmaker, Jeremiah Seamer. By then, Fairchild had acquired sufficient education for him later to write *The City Gardener*, which opened up gardening to a whole new stratum of society.[5]

Also in *The City Gardener*, Fairchild writes that he had been a gardener 'for about forty years', suggesting that even as an apprentice clothmaker he had gardened. He would have completed his apprenticeship in 1690, although, for some reason, he didn't become a Freeman of the Clothworkers' Guild until 1704, choosing to do so on the same day that he became a Freeman of the Gardeners' Company.

By 1691, he was working at the Hoxton nursery, probably first as an employee, becoming within a few years the sole proprietor. It has been estimated that a sum of between £500 and £1,000 would have been needed to set up as a master nurseryman in the 1690s, so it remains unknown how Fairchild raised the capital, even if he had sold the Aldbourne copyhold left to him by his father.[6]

But manage he did, and by 1703 he controlled the nursery, described by John Harvey in *Early Nurserymen* 'as one of the most influential nurseries in British gardening'.[7] Fairchild did not reach the regal heights attained by his older contemporaries, London and Wise. But the royal gardeners' nursery at Brompton Park was just the largest and wealthiest of many founded in the late seventeenth and early eighteenth centuries. Britain, a nation from 1707 and a victor in the War of the Spanish Succession, was growing in prosperity, its international trade in plants and other goods burgeoning. The fascination with plant collecting and gardening was filtering down from royalty and aristocracy to the increasingly affluent middle class, and nurseries such as Fairchild's serviced this developing market.

The fact that a Wiltshire copyholder's son raised sufficient capital to buy his own nursery, became a leading practitioner of his profession for almost forty years and attended the hallowed meetings of the Royal Society indicates that British society was in transition after the ferment of the civil wars. Fairchild was a new type of professional man, a tradesman who had acquired on the job, rather than through formal teaching, an expertise which was respected and required by his many clients.

His Hoxton location was ideal, close to the City of London but freer from the polluting effects of sea coal on which Fairchild dwells at length in *The City Gardener.* Fairchild's was one of several nurseries in what had been an area of market gardens, which had enriched and fertilised the London clay soil. The other nurseries were owned by friends and colleagues of Fairchild's, one of whom, Benjamin Whitmill, was such an admirer that he christened his son Fairchild in 1723. All would subsequently write about their chosen profession: Whitmill published *The Gardener's Universal Calendar* in 1726, arguing for the higher calling of gardeners in comparison with the military: 'It certainly redounds more to the honour and satisfaction of a gardener that he is the preserver and pruner of all sorts of fruit trees than it does to the happiness of the greatest general that he has been successful in killing mankind.'[8]

Another nurseryman and close friend, John Cowell, dedicated his 1730 book, *The Curious and Profitable Gardener*, to the wife of the prime minister, Sir Robert Walpole. In it, he gives a snapshot of the contemporary interest in tender imported plants. He praises bananas and hopes that his book 'may invite those Gentlemen who have Dealings in Jamaica, and other Parts of the American warm Countries, to bring over, as occasion may offer, some of these Plants. Which I the rather believe they will do, since many Nobleman and Gentleman with us have good Conveniences for their keeping.'[9]

Fairchild's profession was developing rapidly, with a lively exchange of both plants and ideas between nurseries and gardens. Cowell helps us to see the world in which Fairchild was working when he writes that 'from the seed of the Papa [papaya], which I gave to the Physick Garden at Chelsea, were raised two Plants, one of which produced Flowers, which proved to be Female: but the other Plant which was raised there at the same time, was sold or given away to a Gentleman at Parson's Green, that produced only Male Flowers; and so the Female Plant brought no Fruit'.[10] This short passage indicates that nurseries such as Fairchild's and Cowell's supplied new plants to botanical gardens like Miller's Chelsea Physic Garden. It also shows that by 1730 the sexual reproduction of plants was generally accepted, and that the horticultural world was gradually swinging round to an understanding of hybridisation.

Fairchild's nursery was just half an acre, according to his rates book, although he expanded his operations in 1725 by taking on another two acres about fifteen minutes' walk away. London and Wise's Brompton Park nursery dominated the trade for the largest trees and shrubs, but Fairchild grew pretty much everything else. He sold Tradescant's sycamores, imported from Virginia sixty or seventy years earlier, and was successful at cultivating tulip trees (*Liriodendron tulipifera*). In 1710, he is recorded as receiving bladder senna from the Caucasus, and was one of the first people in England to grow a banana tree, as well as hellebores, then 'so rare, that they are scarcely to be seen, unless at Mr Fairchild's at Hoxton'.[11] His vineyard was stocked with more than fifty grape varieties.

Richard Bradley praised Fairchild in his *Philosophical Account of the Works of Nature*, published in 1721, the year before Fairchild's *The City Gardener*. He wrote:

> I esteem the collections [of fruit] we have now in England to exceed all the Nurseries in Europe, for profitable and useful varieties; particularly the curious garden of Mr Thomas Fairchild at Hoxton, where I find the greatest collection of fruits that I have yet seen, and so regularly disposed both for Order in time of ripening and good pruning of the several Kinds, that I do not know any person in Europe to excel him in that particular; and in other Things he is no less happy in his Choice of such Curiosities, as a good Judgment and Universal Correspondence can procure.[12]

Fairchild, however, was far from being a one-trick pony. Elsewhere, Bradley recommends that gardeners should raise flowers from seeds, adding that 'there can be no greater Motive to encourage our Gardeners to this undertaking, than directing them to ... Mr Fairchild, where they may observe wonderful Collections of Flowers, viz. Ranunculas, Bulbose Iris, &c, lately raised from Seminaries discreetly made by those Artists'.[13]

Fairchild bought stock from the Dutch, whose skilled nurserymen traded with the Americas and the Far East. He also imported the latest technology from the Low Countries, installing a line of greenhouses along a south-facing wall, as can be seen from the frontispiece of *The*

City Gardener. There, he could nurture his own tender exotics, as well as over-wintering plants for gardens he supplied.

Through the plant collector and later renowned illustrator Mark Catesby, Fairchild acquired American plants. Catesby made his first journey to Virginia in 1712, following that with further visits over the next few years to America and also to Jamaica and the Bahamas. Fairchild carefully recorded the plants and seeds he received from Catesby, listing 'Mr Catesby's new Virginian Starwort' (*Aster grandiflora*) and Virginian Purple Sun Flower (probably *Echinacea purpurea*) among his collections.[14] Catesby's expeditions were sponsored by, among others, the physician Sir Hans Sloane, patron of the Chelsea Physic Garden and later founder of the British Museum. It was two-way traffic: Fairchild supplied Catesby with English plants suitable for settlers to grow in the new colonies to remind them of their home country.[15]

Catesby's watercolours of plants and birds now grace a thousand placemats sold by heritage trading companies. His original paintings illustrated the book on which he spent twenty years, *Natural History of Carolina, Florida and the Bahama Islands*. Some of these illustrations were used by Linnaeus to help with his classification of plants, while many of the originals, bought by George III in 1768, remain in the Royal Collection.[16] After Catesby returned to London in 1726, he settled in Hoxton and worked for Fairchild at his nursery, staying on until 1733, some four years after Fairchild's death. That this accomplished illustrator chose to give his services to Fairchild is a tribute to the nurseryman. In return, Fairchild left his friend a guinea to buy a mourning ring. Catesby subsequently worked for another eminent nurseryman, Christopher Gray of Fulham, whose catalogue used Catesby's illustrations and promoted the supply of plants discovered by the illustrator.[17]

For plant lovers, Fairchild's nursery was the place to visit. Among his callers was Peter Collinson, later a Quaker trader who supplied the aristocracy and royalty with plants from the American plantsman John Bartram for more than forty years. In the early years of the eighteenth century, the adolescent Collinson was brought by his garden-loving grandmother to admire the exotic plants in Fairchild's hothouses.[18]

Three letters sent by Fairchild to Richard Bradley for his *Monthly Register* list the plants in flower from April 1722 to March 1723, and show that Fairchild grew many different trees, shrubs, herbaceous plants and bulbs. It is also a considerable advance on a similar list drawn up by Henry Wise for Brompton Park nursery in around 1700. That list started in February and ended in September, while Fairchild's list is year-round: he has twenty species blooming in December 1722, and almost as many in January 1723. Among plants listed for that month are snowdrops, but also 'Black Helebore with white Flowers ... Winter Aconite, Mezereon ... Candy-tuft Tree ... blue Star Hyacinth ... Wall Flowers'.[19] The nursery must have been remarkable at any time of year.

***

Fairchild applied himself to many other gardening-related pursuits, including the affairs of the Gardeners' Company. This company was a Johnny-come-lately and poor relation of the other medieval City guilds. It wasn't until 1605 that the company received its first royal charter and only in 1659, in the closing days of the Commonwealth, were its members recognised by the City Corporation and given the freedom of the City. Despite its considerable power in controlling the large market gardens and nurseries around the City, its members didn't have their own livery (that wasn't granted until 1891), nor the right to vote in Parliamentary elections unlike other City liverymen. In 1722, Fairchild was one of seven members of the Gardeners' Company who attempted to vote, although their votes were discounted.

Fairchild was also a prominent member of the Society of Gardeners, which was set up in the early 1720s by Philip Miller, and held its meetings in Chelsea, conveniently close to Miller's Physic Garden. Christopher Gray, Catesby's future employer, was another member of a group which concerned itself with attempting, pre-Linnaeus, to establish more coherent plant classification and identification. In 1730, the year after Fairchild's death, the society published a *Catalogus Plantarum*, which aimed to list all plants currently sold in nurseries and to streamline their nomenclature. It was also a practical manual for gardeners, with advice on soil, growing conditions and propagation methods. Stephen Bacon, Fairchild's nephew and heir, was one of the signatories to the catalogue. Given that the catalogue ran to only one edition, it seems likely that Fairchild was instrumental in its compilation, and that the project lost impetus after his death.[20]

In style, the catalogue bears some similarity to Fairchild's *The City Gardener*, published in 1722. Fairchild's own book provides a telling insight into the mind of this ingenious man (as he was described by Bradley), and presents a captivating portrait of contemporary London. The book was dedicated not, like that of his friend John Cowell, to a member of the political establishment, but to the governors of Bethlem and Bridewell hospitals, respectively an asylum for the mentally ill and a workhouse. The dedication implies the concern of this successful businessman with those less fortunate than himself, and this is borne out by his stipulation in his will that he should be buried in the Poor's Ground of St Leonard's church in Hackney. He writes that he has been encouraged to write the book 'that every one in London, or other Cities, where Sea-Coal is burnt, may delight themselves in Gardening'.[21]

Fairchild's thoughts ran much on the problems caused by sea coal, so called because it was imported from Newcastle through the London docks, and to distinguish it from charcoal. 'From the Observations I have made in the London Practice of Gardening, I find that every thing will not prosper in London; either because the Smoke of the Sea-Coal does hurt to some Plants, or else because those People, who have little Gardens in London, do not know how to manage their Plants when they have got them.'[22]

Fairchild laid his cards on the table at the outset: the book was going to be a manual, not for the patrons of nurserymen/designers such as London and Wise (Wise was still alive at this point), but for the merchant class and below. These increasingly well-heeled people flocked to Fairchild's and other nurseries around London to acquire new plants. 'We may consider that then our judicious Traders in the City have as much Reason to hope for the Enjoyment of the Pleasures of his Life, as the Persons of Quality, which are in the highest Stations.' This new interest can be spotted, said Fairchild, just by looking around the city and seeing how 'my Fellow-Citizens ... in the midst of their Toil and Labour [make use] of every favourable Glance of the Sun to come abroad, and of their furnishing their Rooms and Chambers with Basons of Flower and Bough-pots, rather than not have something of a Garden before them'.[23]

Only seventy pages long, the book was packed with information on what to grow and where. 'The English Box will grow well, and be very ornamental,' he writes. 'The Italian Ever-green Privet will thrive well ... The Ilex or Ever-green Oak will grow, and make a handsome Appearance,' as will the 'Laurus or common Bay ... but the Laurel, Philirea, Alaternus, and others of our hardy Greens, will not do so well in London.'[24]

Fairchild, a plantsman to his finger-tips, encouraged his readers to fill their gardens with flowers and ornamental trees and shrubs, and opposed the still prevailing fashion. 'The plain way of laying out Squares in Grass Platts and Gravel Walks, does not sufficiently give our Thoughts an Opportunity of Country Amusements; I think some sort of Wilderness-Work will do much better, and divert the Gentry better than looking out of their Windows upon an open Figure.'[25] A wilderness in a London square, he suggests, will provide a habitat for birds as well as being easier on the eye.

His plant lists delightfully evoke eighteenth-century London, for, where he could, he pointed out where they grow. 'Bladder Senna, and Citissus' flourish in Lincoln's Inn Fields; syringa (lilac) grows well in Soho Square; pears thrive in the Barbican, Aldersgate Street and Bishopsgate Street, as does a vine in Leicester Fields. He also recommended a plant that the younger John Tradescant brought back from Virginia. 'John Tradescant's Starwort ... grows likewise very well in the closest Places, and will thrive well in Pots, if it be discreetly managed.'[26]

Fairchild's knowledge of plants, their shapes, colours and best growing conditions, resounds through every page, the names themselves a kind of prose poetry. He suggested a wonderful array of flowers: 'Annual-Stock, Venus Looking-Glass, Venus Navelwort, Candy-Tufts, small blue-Convolvulus, Flos-Adonis, Cyanus, Dutch-Poppy, Garden-Poppy, China-Pinks, Lupines, Nigilla Romana, Sweet-scented Peas, wing'd Peas, Heart-Ease, or Viola-Tricolor; these being properly intermix'd, will afford a considerable Ornament to the Border.'[27] This enticing list of herbaceous plants must have been a revelation to Londoners in the third decade of the eighteenth century, and still charms a twenty-first-century gardener.

Fairchild was a man on a mission. St James's Park, he had heard, was as pleasant a public place to walk as 'in any Country on this side of Italy'; indeed, the French king has nothing to show as fair. It is, he wrote, 'of a large Extent, and disposed in handsome Walks of Lime-Trees and Elms ... and there is an agreeable Beauty in the Whole'. This principle, he argued, could be adopted to the advantage of other Londoners: 'The Quantity of Ground, which now lies in a manner waste in Moorfields, might undoubtly be render'd very agreeable, was it to be adorn'd after the same manner, and be as delightful to the Citizens, as St. James's Park is to the Courtiers.'[28]

This is the public-spirited Fairchild who dedicated the book to two institutions for London's disadvantaged, and who left £10 in his will to the charity children of St Leonard's parish. The other main stipulation – that a sermon should be preached in his memory each year after Whitsun – is still honoured, now in nearby St Giles Cripplegate. Almost 290 years after Fairchild's death, the occasion is attended by liverymen of the Company of Gardeners, the procession up the aisle led by the bearer of the company's ceremonial spade.

Garden-fresh though it is, *The City Gardener* is probably now read by few apart from the most devoted students of eighteenth-century history and gardening. When Fairchild died in 1729, probably unmarried and without children, he left his nursery to his nephew, Stephen Bacon, little more than a teenager. Stephen died within a few years, and the nursery was closed down and dispersed in 1740, just eleven years after Fairchild's death. Fairchild deserves more recognition for his signal achievements, as a nurseryman and early hybridiser.

The precise spot where he was buried, among the poor of St Leonard's parish, is not now known, but the annual sermon honours a man whose life and work reveal the dynamism of English society from the late seventeenth century onwards.

CHAPTER 5

Philip Miller (1691–1771)

Believed to be a portrait of Philip Miller, but there is some doubt.

On Saturday 22 October 1749, John Wesley took a rare break from preaching to visit the Chelsea Physic Garden. He wrote in his journal: 'I spent an hour observing the various works of God in the Physic Garden at Chelsea. It would be a noble improvement if some able and industrious person were to make a full and accurate inquiry into the use and virtues of all these plants; without this, what end does the heaping them thus together answer, but the gratifying of an idle curiosity?'[1]

When the Methodist leader visited, Philip Miller had been gardener at the Chelsea Physic Garden for over quarter of a century. In that time, he had turned what had been the Apothecaries' rundown medicinal garden into a centre of botanical excellence, recognised across Europe and in the New World. Miller was a man of sharp observation and scientific bent. He exchanged plants and corresponded with the foremost botanists and plantsmen of his age, becoming part of what the Swedish botanist Carl Linnaeus called his 'Commonwealth of Botany'.[2] Miller was also the author of the *Gardeners Dictionary*, which went into eight editions in his lifetime. John Rogers, a nineteenth-century horticulturalist who met the aging gardener just before his retirement, wrote that the *Dictionary* was 'the first bright beam of gardening issuing from the dark cloud of ignorance in which it had previously been enveloped; but having once broken through, it has continued to shine with increasing splendour for the last century. It may be almost said to have laid the foundation of all the horticultural taste and knowledge in Europe'.[3]

Wesley's visit to the Chelsea Physic Garden was surely somewhat cursory. Far from being 'heaped together', the vegetable works of Wesley's maker had been planted according to a very clear system and for greater purpose than to 'gratify an idle curiosity'. Presumably Wesley didn't make the acquaintance of Philip Miller during his brief stopover, as few gardeners have been more 'able and industrious' than Miller. But, then, the very fact that the preacher had been drawn to explore the Chelsea Physic Garden signals the garden's fame and prestige.

***

Philip Miller was born in Deptford in 1691, the son of a Scottish market gardener, adding Miller to the ranks of the Scots resented for their domination of British public life in the mid-eighteenth century. According to John Rogers, 'Miller was looked upon with jealousy by many English gardeners, on account of his father being a Scotchman; and he is supposed to be one of the Northern lads mentioned by Switzer ... as having invaded the Southern provinces.'[4]

Pehr Kalm, a Swedish naturalist and pupil of Linnaeus, wrote that Miller père 'began to instruct his son ... in the art from his earliest years [and] spared no expense in also causing his son to have a sufficient education in various languages and other sciences, which profit and adorn a man'. The boy also learnt about ornamental and kitchen gardening, and read widely, all serving to help him in the extensive correspondence he maintained throughout his professional life.

The market gardening business prospered, giving the young Miller the financial freedom to travel through England, and then in Flanders and Holland. 'As agriculture had so near a connection with horticulture therefore he kept at the same time an observant eye on everything which occurred in rural economy, particularly the cultivation of ploughed lands,' Kalm added.[5] Later, Miller wrote at length in his *Gardeners Dictionary* about the best methods for sowing wheat, and saw the practice of horticulture and agriculture as two sides of the same coin.

Rogers recounts that Miller worked briefly for his father before establishing himself as a florist and ornamental shrub nurseryman at St George's Field, Southwark. There, apparently, Miller was a victim of his own success, so much enriching the ground on the rented property that his landlord was on the point of either raising the rent or turning Miller out altogether.[6] Fortunately, Miller had caught the eye of Sir Hans Sloane.

A replica of a statue of Sloane by Michael Rysbrack stands today in the Physic Garden, tribute to its major benefactor. The Apothecaries' Garden was originally established in Chelsea in 1673 on a three-and-a-half-acre plot rented from the local landowner, Charles Cheyne. The garden enabled the city company's students to learn about medicinal plants, and its riverside creek provided the Apothecaries with a mooring place for their ceremonial barge.

Various gardeners and managers were employed in the garden's first fifty years, one of whom, John Watts, himself an apothecary, was paid £50 a year. He exchanged plants with the professor of botany at Leyden, a leading European botanical centre, and was visited in August 1685 by John Evelyn, the gardener and diarist, who was impressed by the Physic Garden's 'collection of innumerable rarities'.[7]

Despite Evelyn's commendations, Watts was more interested in his own plant collection at Enfield. Five years later, Watts's fellow apothecary James Petiver was writing that 'the Physick Garden is but slenderly stocked ... and is at a low ebb'. The cost of maintaining the Physic Garden became a worry to the Apothecaries, as did finding the right man to run the garden: no gardener is mentioned by name between 1714 and 1722.[8]

Hans Sloane restored the garden's fortunes and established Miller's career. Born in Ireland in 1660, Sloane studied medicine in France, then worked in a London practice. A wealthy man thanks to his marriage to a planter's widow he met while a physician in Jamaica, Sloane was elected a fellow of the Royal Society and the College of the Physicians in the early 1700s. He became physician to the royal family, and was made a baronet by George I in 1716. When he died, aged 92, his great collections, left to the nation and valued at £80,000, formed the nucleus of the British Museum.

Some decades earlier, in 1712, Sloane had bought the manor of Chelsea, including the land on which the Physic Garden stood. Fascinated by medicinal plants and natural history (he wrote a *Natural History of Jamaica*), Sloane proved the struggling garden's saviour. In 1722, he handed the land over to the Apothecaries Company, requiring them to pay a nominal rent of £5 a year. His other proviso was that fifty dried specimens grown in the same year should be supplied annually to the Royal Society in London – an arrangement which led to the Society eventually receiving more than 3,000 plants from Chelsea.[9]

Sloane recommended Miller to the Apothecaries as head gardener, having had Miller brought to his attention by Patrick Blair, a scientist and author of *Botanick Essays* (1720). In a letter of November 1721 to Sloane, Blair described Miller as having 'such an easy and familiar way of expressing his thought, such a delight for improvement and so much exactness and diligence in the making of observations that I look upon him to go onward with a curiosity and genious superior to most of his occupation'.[10]

The opportunity Sloane gave Miller benefited not just the gardener, but botany and horticulture in general. 'To this good and great man, who proved both his friend and patron, the foundation of Miller's future fame may be considered in great measure indebted,' wrote Rogers in *The Vegetable Cultivator.*[11]

Miller spent the rest of his life living either in or next to the Chelsea Physic Garden. Around 1730, he married Mary Kennet, and the couple had a daughter and two sons, both of whom became botanists. While his father travelled round the country advising landowners on their estates, Philip the younger tended the Physic Garden, later dying while plant hunting in the East Indies. His brother, Charles, studied at Cambridge, and became the first curator of the Cambridge Botanic Garden on its foundation in 1762.

The family lived for a time above the greenhouse, a brick building with large windows, before occupying a house in adjacent Swan Walk. In later life, Miller must have returned to the greenhouse, for after his resignation in 1771, the Apothecaries' minutes state that Miller's successor was to be provided with lodgings in Chelsea, 'until such time as Mr Miller has quit his apartments in the greenhouse'.[12]

Miller repaid Sloane's trust. Within two years of his appointment, Miller published *The Gardener's and Florist's Dictionary*, a two-volume octavo work dedicated to Sloane. Writing the book gave him 'an opportunity publickly to acknowledge the many obligations I lie under your person. As it was your generous gift of the Physic Garden to the Worshipful Company of Apothecaries that encouraged the supporting of that Garden for the improvement of Botany and so consequently was the Occasion of my being employed in a service so agreeable to my natural inclinations.'[13]

Miller soon made his mark on the wider botanical world. A friend of Fairchild's, he built on his older contemporary's discovery of hybridisation (he mentioned Fairchild's 'Mule' in the *Dictionary*): he observed that insects are the agents of pollination, giving a paper on the subject in 1751. He constructed at Chelsea two hothouses and a greenhouse, where he grew pawpaw, melons and pineapples fine enough for Sloane to present them to George II. 'We have in flower several exotics in vast perfections,' Miller wrote to Blair in the mid-1720s, 'and I doubt not that we shall be able to manage the most tender plants in ye world with these stoves.'[14]

Miller demonstrated his abilities in a paper he gave to the Royal Society in 1728 on 'A Method of raising some Exotic Seeds', which had previously been considered impossible to cultivate in England. 'Two years afterwards,' wrote Rogers in *The Vegetable Cultivator*, 'Miller made known the present popular mode of causing bulbous plants to flower in water.'[15]

Among Miller's correspondents was Herman Boerhaave, professor of medicine and botany at Leyden, with whom Miller became friendly during a visit to the gardens of Holland in 1727. Boerhaave was one of the most respected teachers of medicine in Europe, and ran Leyden University's botanic gardens from 1709. The visit set up plant exchanges between Chelsea and Leyden: Boerhaave sent cleome seeds from Ceylon and *Watsonia meriana* from the Cape of Good Hope to Miller. In return, Miller passed on the lily thorn, discovered by Mark Catesby on Providence Island in 1726. *Watsonia meriana* still flourishes at the Physic Garden today.[16]

The Reverend Gilbert White, author of the *Natural History of Selborne*, owned two editions of the *Dictionary*. The naturalist parson followed Miller's advice on growing cucumbers and melons, although the latter required a visit by the parson to the Physic Garden in June 1750 to see the process for himself. The result was 'fine, large, beautiful fruit, just like Miller's'.[17]

There are glimpses in Miller's letters of the hands-on botanist, out searching for new plants, and injuring himself in the process. He wrote to Blair that a dozen young myrtles had been despatched from the garden, but he had been unable to pack them himself having hurt his leg 'a-herborising by water'.[18]

Miller's correspondence with both gardeners and collectors enabled him to acquire rare plants and seeds from around the world. Between 1731 and 1768, the number of species in cultivation in Britain doubled, with plants drawn mainly from the Cape of Good Hope, the East Indies and North America.[19] At the Physic Garden, the number of species grown rose from 1,000 to 5,000 in the years from 1730 to 1770.[20]

***

An important plant source for Miller was a Quaker farmer, botanist and plant collector from Pennsylvania. Virtually self-educated, John Bartram had a scientific bent, and his thirst for plant collecting took him across the swamps, woods and plains of the Eastern States, from Lake Ontario to Virginia and to the Carolinas and Florida.[21] Bartram was sponsored by a syndicate organised by another Quaker, Peter Collinson, a London cloth merchant and trader with the American colonies, and in particular with Pennsylvania, whose fast-growing population provided a ready market for his cloth.[22] Through these trading links Collinson contacted Bartram, and the first consignment of two plant boxes arrived at the London docks in January 1734.

Philip Miller joined the funding syndicate, along with Sir Hans Sloane, Dr John Fothergill (another Quaker), the Duke of Richmond, and Lord Petre, creator of a magnificent estate in Essex. Correspondence between Collinson and Bartram reveals the difficulties of transporting the plants and seeds safely across the Atlantic, especially a century before the invention of the Wardian case.* Nevertheless, over more than thirty years, some 2,000 species arrived in Britain, and Miller cultivated plants from all thirteen of the American colonies at the Physic Garden.[23] These included phlox, helianthus, ceanothus, balsam fir and *Magnolia grandiflora* which Bartram spotted in South Carolina. Morning glory, rudbeckia, Turk's-cap lily and *Verbena bonariensis* were other American introductions. Seeds were also offered by Miller and Collinson to trusted nurserymen to ensure the further spread of these new plant species into gardens across England.[24]

Some subscribers fell by the wayside, with Collinson informing Bartram in 1743 that 'only Philip Miller and the Duke of Richmond, who love new things, continue to contribute'.[25] Collinson appreciated Miller's support and dedication, writing in 1764 that 'Mr Miller ... has made his great abilities well known by his works as well as his skill in every part of gardening and his success in raising seeds produced by a large correspondence. He has raised the reputation of the Chelsea Garden so much that it excels all the gardens of Europe for its amazing variety of plants of all orders and classes and from all climates.'[26]

Miller also designed gardens, recognising that the landscape movement was revealing Britain as newly independent of the horticultural influences of the Italian, French and Dutch. In 1733, he wrote:

> But it is very lately that the truly magnificent taste in gardening has flourished in these northern parts of Europe, for although in King Charles the Second's reign there was great spirit amongst the nobility and gentry of England for planting and gardening, which spirit was greatly heighten'd in King William's reign, during which time most of the large gardens in England were laid out and planted, yet we find the taste at that time extended little farther than to small pieces of box-wood, finish'd parterres and clipp'd greens, all of which are now generally banished out of the gardens of the most Polite Persons of this age, who justly prefer the more extended rural designs of gardens which approach the nearest to nature.[27]

His wide-ranging expertise made him a useful adviser. Lord Petre planted, according to a letter from Collinson to Bartram, 'about ten thousand Americans' (trees and shrubs from America) at his Thorndon estate; it may well be that some choice specimens found their way from there to Chelsea in exchange for Miller's guidance on their cultivation. When Petre died aged just twenty-nine in 1742, his collections were dispersed, and the Duke of Bedford sent Miller to Thorndon to value thousands of rare trees and buy any he thought suitable for Woburn Abbey. Since 1740, Miller had been paid twenty guineas a year by the duke 'for inspecting my Gardens hot houses, pruning the trees, etc. and to come to Woburn at least twice a year and oftner if wanted'.[28] His advice was sought, too, by the 2nd Earl, later the 1st Duke, of Northumberland, Hugh Percy, to whom Miller dedicated three editions of the *Dictionary*. Miller recommended as head gardener to Northumberland one of his promising pupils, William Forsyth (after whom forsythia is named), eventually his own successor at the Chelsea Physic Garden.

Miller's hobnobbing with nobles, combined with increasing testiness as he grew older, helped alienate him from his fellow gardeners and collectors, who observed that '[w]hen the greatest lords drove out to their estates, he [Miller] often drove out with them in the same carriage'.[29] Miller had a couple of epistolary spats with Bartram, criticising the over-lengthy plant descriptions of the American, who replied defensively (and with a drop of acid):

> I am obliged to thee, for thy good advice, to contract my descriptions. I own, the leaves, acorns, and especially the cups, are very material in ascertaining the different species of our Oaks; yet the description of the bark, and form of growth, are useful helps, in our mature Oaks. I can often discover our different species of Oaks, one from another, by their form of growth, half or a whole mile distant; and I am sure he must be very sharp-sighted that can know them, at half that distance, by their leaves, acorns, and cups, all together.[30]

Collinson warned Bartram not to fall out with Miller, 'our Great Botanist', over the classification of American birch trees: '[P]ray run not the risque of harming thy Little finger for a Paper Birch.'[31] Known also as 'the dictator of English Gardening', Miller was prickly, even in his early days as secretary of the Society of Gardeners.

Thomas Fairchild, Christopher Gray, the illustrator and plant hunter Mark Catesby, and other London nurserymen and gardeners, were also members of this society, which met regularly at Newhall's Coffee House in Chelsea. The society was founded to systematise plant names and 'to compare such Things as should be received from abroad, with those already in the English Gardens, and to discover where the real Difference (if any) lay'.[32] Members brought boxed specimens to meetings and, fuelled by wine and ale, compared, discussed and classified them in a register.

The resulting *Catalogus Plantarum* was published just once in 1730 as a handbook for nurserymen and a practical guide for gardeners. The short-lived society broke up acrimoniously, but Miller used his notes on its discussions in his *Gardeners Dictionary*.

The first edition was published in 1731 and as mentioned earlier, it went into seven more editions in Miller's lifetime, growing in size along with the number of plant introductions. The eighth edition, published in 1768, weighs eight kilos, contains 333 folio sheets and measures 430 x 90mm, in comparison with the 215 sheets of the 1731 edition.[33] 'As the number of plants now cultivated in England, are more than double those which were here when the first edition of this book was published, the mentioning of them, together with their culture, could not well be avoided in a work of this nature,' wrote Miller in his preface to the 1768 edition.[34]

The *Dictionary* was the first comprehensive practical handbook about gardening, covering vegetable, fruit and flower gardening, how to choose trees and when to prune them, and including instructions on building greenhouses and stoves. There were sections on vineyards and wines, and passages about the most economical way of sowing wheat. All was the fruit of Miller's own experience, as he himself stressed: '[T]he author's situation in life rendered him capable of being well informed of the progress made in the art [of gardening], by his great correspondence both at home and abroad ... he has been careful not to publish any thing imparted to him, until he was fully satisfied of the facts by experiments.'[35]

This authoritative work was all the more remarkable given that Miller was compiling the *Dictionary* while running the Chelsea Physic Garden, maintaining his correspondence, and advising landowners country-wide. He also produced an abridgement in several editions and the less expensive *Gardeners Kalendar* in fifteen editions.

Four hundred subscribed to the first edition, clear indication of Miller's influence within a decade of starting work at the Physic Garden. Subscribers included aristocrats and their head gardeners, the collector of the King's Customs at Plymouth, the treasurer of St Bartholomew's Hospital, Astronomer Royal Edmund Halley, the Professor of Modern History at Oxford, and the Vice-Master of Trinity College, Cambridge, as well as at Boerhaave at Leyden, George Clifford (Linnaeus's boss) at Amsterdam, and the Governor of California.[36]

Collinson, who had his own botanical garden at Mill Hill, also admired Miller's *Gardeners Dictionary*, filling his seventh edition with marginal notes and inscribing the eighth edition, published in the year of Collinson's death, as 'The Gift of my old friend, the author'.[37] He also recommended the *Dictionary* to Bartram, telling him that it was 'a Work of the greatest use'.[38] Both George Washington and Thomas Jefferson used the *Dictionary* when creating their estates at Mount Vernon and Monticello, Washington preferring it to political or classical works.[39]

The editions of the *Dictionary* also reveal Miller's struggles with the most contentious issue for eighteenth-century botanists: plant classification.

In the earlier editions, Miller used the elaborate method of French botanist Joseph Pitton de Tournefort, who identified plants by the form of their flowers and fruit, rather than by their sexual parts as Linnaeus was to do in his binomial system. Names such as Acacia, Malus, Pulsatilla and Ananas, derived by Miller from Tournefort, are still current, witness to the influence of Miller's *Dictionary*.[40]

Linnaeus and Miller met in July 1736 when Linnaeus visited Sir Hans Sloane (who found the Swedish botanist a bore) and then spent three days at the Chelsea Physic Garden. It was, it seems, a tricky occasion, with Linnaeus more interested in dried specimens than live plants, to the disgust of Miller, who told his coffee house friends that 'the botanist of Clifford's doesn't know a single plant'.[41] Linnaeus heard of the insult and realised he would have to tread carefully to get hold of the North American plants he wanted for the garden he curated for George Clifford in Amsterdam. Both Sloane and Miller were sceptical of Linnaeus's revolutionary ideas, but Oxford's professor of botany was less so, and gradually the binomial system became generally accepted. Miller explains his position in the preface to his eighth edition, describing himself in the third person:

> In the last edition of this work, the author adopted in a great measure the system of Linnaeus, which was the prevailing method of ranging plants then in use among botanists; but as many of the plants which were treated of in the Gardeners Dictionary, were not to be found in any of Linnaeus's work then published, Tournefort's system was also applied to take in such as were not fully known to Dr Linnaeus but since that time the learned professor having made great additions to his works ... the author has now applied Linnaeus's method entirely, except in such particulars, where the Doctor not having had an opportunity of seeing the plants growing, they are ranged by him in the wrong classes.[42]

This passage gives a measure of the man. There is a slightly waspish tone, but Miller also emphasises that anything mentioned in the *Dictionary* must be based on actual evidence, rather than hearsay. This is what made Miller an outstanding botanist and gardener, but it didn't always endear him to his contemporaries, notably his fellow members of the Royal Society. He became a member in 1730, proposed by Collinson, among others, but often criticised the quality of the papers submitted.

Miller's argumentativeness occasioned his downfall when he found himself up against his *de facto* employers, the Apothecaries Company. In 1750, he had been praised by the company's committee for 'his great diligence in settling a correspondence and producing seeds and plants from various parts of the world'.[43] Nineteen years later, however, a new committee decided on a more thorough look at the garden that had become so famous under the guidance of Miller. It was time, they thought, to make an inventory of all the plants, marking each one with a stick. Now in his seventy-ninth year, Miller was not prepared to co-operate, especially when books from the garden's library, many of which Miller had himself collected, were removed to the Apothecaries' Hall. Arguments also broke out about whether certain plants belonged to Miller or to the garden, culminating in Miller tendering his resignation in November 1770.

Miller retired to live nearby, close to Chelsea church, and was supplied 'occasionally from the Garden'. He died just a year later, in December 1771, and was buried in Chelsea churchyard in a grave unmarked until 1810 when fellows of the Linnaean and Horticultural Societies put up a memorial.[44]

It was, perhaps, time for a man of nearly eighty to retire, but, for Miller, life without his garden and his daily activities was not worth living. John Rogers sums up a man to whom medicine, botany, horticulture and agriculture are all indebted. Miller, said Rogers, possessed 'that zeal in his profession which first urged him forward in the career of improvement, raised him to the zenith of his fame … [H]e laid open to his brother gardeners the knowledge he himself possessed; and the whole tenor of his labours seemed to say, to one and to all, "Go thou and do likewise."'[45]

PART III

THE GREAT DESIGNERS

CHAPTER 6

Charles Bridgeman (1680–1738)

Midway on the A40 between Burford and Northleach, a small brown acorn sign points to Lodge Park. A die-straight road leads to a building designed in 1632 as a deer-coursing lodge, its large first-floor balcony probably the first grandstand in England. From there, John 'Crump' Dutton, owner of nearby Sherborne House, and his hard-living friends would bet on their dogs chasing deer down the mile-long, walled course, with the finishing post directly below their grandstand. As the Great Room of the lodge is a double cube, a style favoured by Inigo Jones, it was once thought that the scaled-down Cotswold stone version of the Banqueting House in Whitehall was the work of the illustrious architect. Dutton hired out Lodge Park to others willing to pay, so it was in effect an early corporate hospitality facility.

All this is intriguing enough: a window onto a vanished world, as deer-coursing was superseded by racing and fox-hunting within a century of the lodge's construction. But, for a garden historian, there is a further jewel behind the lodge: an intact Charles Bridgeman landscape, with some of the 4,000 or more trees proposed by the designer still extant. It was identified by the discovery in the late 1990s of Bridgeman's plan among his other drawings in Oxford's Bodleian Library. The garden designer visited Lodge Park twice, in 1725 and 1729, and was paid £70 for supplying Dutton with 'a plan for my New Park'. He put in place his trademark features: a serpentine canal, a ha-ha to separate a small wilderness garden from the park, and long, straight avenues of trees. Unusually, this landscape has not disappeared beneath later work by Bridgeman's successors, William Kent and 'Capability' Brown. Where Bridgeman visited, Kent followed, but at Lodge Park, Kent had no hand in the landscape, contenting himself with designing the tables which are on view in the lodge.[1]

Bridgeman worked on many great gardens, including Claremont, Stowe, Rousham, Richmond and Kensington, and left traces of his style on all. The subsequent achievements of Kent and Brown have

View from the portico of Stowe house by Jaques Rigaud. (Courtesy Stowe House Preservation Trust/Stowe School)

often obscured Bridgeman's contribution. Stowe, the eighteenth century's garden *sans pareil*, is a case in point. It was a collaborative effort, created over more than four decades by two nobles, using the services of three garden designers (Bridgeman, Kent and Brown) and two architects (Vanbrugh and Gibbs).

Bridgeman was a pivotal figure. In a case of nominative determinism, he was a bridge between the highly structured, architectural and French-influenced garden design of the late seventeenth century and the more naturalistic and relaxed style of Kent and Brown in the mid-eighteenth century. Horace Walpole pays extended tribute to Bridgeman in his *History of the Modern Taste in Gardening*, written in 1770. Walpole dismisses London and Wise for stocking 'our gardens with giants, animals, monsters, coats of arms and mottoes in yew, box and holly' until '[a]bsurdity could go no farther'. The tide then turned:

> Bridgman, the next fashionable designer of gardens, was far more chaste … he banished verdant sculpture, and did not even revert to the square precision of the foregoing age … though he still adhered much to strait walks with high clipped hedges, they were only his great lines; the rest he diversified by wilderness, and with loose groves of oak, though still within surrounding hedges … But this was not till other innovators had broke loose too from rigid symmetry.[2]

Walpole, in his inimitable style, deftly sums up Bridgeman's significance as a transitional figure between two contrasting gardening styles.

***

Of this future royal gardener's personal life nothing is known until May 1717 when he married Sarah Mist, the daughter of a Westminster paviour, in the chapel at Gray's Inn. Charles and Sarah had at least seven children, of whom four survived infancy. His eldest son was sent to Westminster and then Christ Church College, Oxford, before becoming a member of the Inner Temple. Charles Bridgeman called himself 'Esquire' as a symbol of his professional status, and moved with his wife and family into a house in Westminster. He owned a house on the Harley estate north of Oxford Street, and a pub, the Bell Inn, at Stilton in Huntingdonshire, which he left to his eldest son on his death in 1738.[3]

The first professional sighting of Bridgeman is in about 1709, when he worked for London and Wise at Brompton Park nursery alongside Stephen Switzer, and drew up a plan of the grounds of Blenheim Palace.[4] Bridgeman's many surviving drawings show he was an accomplished draughtsman, the detailed plan of Lodge Park being just one example. Unlike London, Wise, Fairchild and Miller, Bridgeman wrote little, apart from a report on the state of the royal gardens for George II, and one on the drainage of the Fens, so we cannot hear his voice or read his thoughts on garden design. The 1725 *Report on the Present State of the Fens* suggests, however, that Bridgeman had technical ability as well as being a designer.

Others wrote about him, building up a portrait of a clubbable man who mixed easily with both Tories and Whigs without offending anyone. He was friendly with artists such as John Wootton and Sir James Thornhill, the latter describing Bridgeman in a poem of 1721 as

> A maker of Vistas, & much he's commended,
> This man can make water for miles altogether,
> They say he'as made Mountains that reach God knows whither.[5]

Other boon companions were the poet Matthew Prior, who left Bridgeman a 'Buste of Flora', and the gardener-poet Alexander Pope, who described Bridgeman as being 'of the Virtuoso-Class', a 'man of taste' and 'honest Bridgeman'.[6] Pope, having seen Bridgeman's work at Stowe, recommended him as garden designer to Henrietta Howard, mistress of the future George II, for her house at Marble Hill, Twickenham. Bridgeman visited the house with Mrs Howard and Pope in the summer of 1724.

Pope and Bridgeman planned visits together to Wimpole Hall, where Edward Harley, 2nd Earl of Oxford, gave the latter the run of his library: the garden designer visited many times in the early 1720s, looking at 'Rarities' and 'fine books'.[7] Bridgeman enjoyed familiarity with respected artists, and his networking led in 1726 to his election as a member of the exclusive St Luke's Club of Artists. The antiquarian George Vertue, another member, said St Luke's was one of the 'Tip top Clubbs of all, for men of the highest Character in Arts & Gentlemen Lovers of Art'. Bridgeman appears in several group portraits with other St Luke's members and virtuosi.[8]

A portrait of Bridgeman by William Hogarth reveals him to have a pleasant, open expression and dark, bright eyes, which glance away from the onlooker. Unlike Wise, his predecessor as royal gardener, Bridgeman has chosen to be painted in a simple rather than full dress wig, and in a plain jacket and loosely tied white cravat. He appears to be a man who concentrated on the job at hand.

Bridgeman's meteoric rise as a garden designer enabled him to command large sums: he was paid, for instance, sixty guineas in 1726 by Sir John Curzon for consulting on the gardens at Kedleston in Derbyshire. In that year, Bridgeman became 'Chief Gardiner' to the royal family in partnership with the elderly Henry Wise, perhaps at the suggestion of Henrietta Howard, or his Stowe colleague, Sir John Vanbrugh, Comptroller of the King's Works. The following year, Wise and Bridgeman produced for the new king, George II, *A State of the Royal Gardens, from the Revolution to the Year 1727*, a weighty account of all that had been spent on the gardens over the previous forty years. When Wise retired in 1728, Bridgeman took over as sole royal gardener, his notice of appointment signed by Sir Robert Walpole, his client at Houghton, and other courtiers. Out of his salary of £2,220 per annum or £15 per acre, he was expected to pay teams of men, and to work across the royal gardens at Hampton Court, St James's, Kensington, Newmarket and Windsor. This was a job with many facets, not all of them glamorous. At Windsor, Bridgeman had to provide 'the several Working Tools & Materials', to cultivate the fruit plantation 'with Dung as often as is necessary', while the evergreens in the Privy Garden at Hampton Court were to be 'stak'd Tyed up Pruned & Clipped'. He was also responsible for the 'Carriage of the Kings Sumer Fruit from the several gardns. daily by relays of Men on foot to the Court'.[9]

Bridgeman seems to have been largely concerned with maintenance, rather than with design, and certainly he changed little of the existing layout at Hampton Court, St James's or Windsor. But at Kensington Palace, and at Queen Caroline's personal fiefdom, Richmond Gardens, Bridgeman did rather more.

George II was a frugal man, little interested in gardens, which may be why he asked Wise and Bridgeman to account for his Stuart predecessors' expenditure on the royal estates. His wife, Queen Caroline of Ansbach, was a different proposition, and Bridgeman and then William Kent were to find her a sympathetic patron. Possibly the most intellectual royal consort in British history, Caroline had grown up in an enlightened and cultured court and had corresponded with the German philosopher and mathematician Leibniz until his death in 1716. Once in England, she befriended intellectuals such as Isaac Newton, Robert Boyle, a founder of the Royal Society, and the Anglican theologian Samuel Clarke, a regular contributor to her seminars on metaphysics.[10]

Caroline invested large sums in Richmond Gardens, now the riverside part of the Royal Botanic Gardens at Kew. Her endeavours were dismissed as 'childish silly stuff' by her husband, unaware that as a result she was in debt on her death in 1737 'to the amount of 20,000l'.[11] She employed Bridgeman from the mid-1720s at the garden, where he created walks of chestnut, walnut and elms, as well as a straight canal, rectangular pond, serpentine walks and a mound.[12] Bridgeman, Walpole suggests, grew in confidence at Richmond, able to move away from the formality of his teachers, London and Wise. 'As his reformation gained footing, he ventured farther, and in the royal garden at Richmond dared to introduce cultivated fields, and even morsels of a forest appearance.'[13]

As ever, Kent was hard on Bridgeman's heels at Richmond. Bridgeman's elms formed the backdrop to the quirky buildings Kent designed for Caroline, loaded with symbolism to press home her political message as she attempted to Britannify the very German Hanoverian monarchy. A generation later, 'Capability' Brown demolished both Bridgeman's avenues and Kent's buildings and smoothed out the contours to create the more naturalistic landscape familiar to Kew visitors today.

At Kensington, Bridgeman and Kent also worked in consort. Bridgeman's concept for the gardens was 'astonishingly grandiose', according to Roy Strong. Although Bridgeman's avenues have been replanted several times since the eighteenth century, an aerial view of the palace and gardens today bears a striking resemblance to a map by John Rocque from about 1756. Work began in 1730 on damming ten oblong ponds (made for Queen Anne) to create the Serpentine, in which Strong sees Kent's hand as well as Bridgeman's, its treatment of water in conspicuous contrast with the formality of the Round Pond. 'If to Bridgeman we owe the gradual dissolution of the old symmetry in favour of the serpentine line, to Kent we owe the deployment of the garden as fundamentally a vehicle for the creation of pictures.'[14]

***

Royal patronage was valuable, but so too was aristocratic support. Bridgeman spent time at Blenheim, where the redoubtable Sarah, Duchess of Marlborough, described him in a letter to Bridgeman's wife, Sarah, as 'honest and meant to do justly in every thing'.[15] He drew up a plan of the grounds at Blenheim for Wise, but made no major changes there apart from removing 'a few English Elms and Hedges'. It is with other gardens he is more closely associated.[16]

Designers such as Bridgeman and Kent, and after them Brown and Repton, routinely travelled remarkable distances. Much of Bridgeman's life was spent in the saddle as he worked more or less simultaneously at several royal palaces and lodges, and at Eastbury in Dorset, Claremont in Surrey, Rousham in Oxfordshire, and Stowe in Buckinghamshire.

An early major project, of which little now remains, was Eastbury, carried out in conjunction with Sir John Vanbrugh. The ambitious garden, with canal, glade, mounts and paths was surrounded by a ha-ha, a sunken ditch which obscures the division between formal garden and park, as explained by Walpole. '[T]he capital stroke, the leading step to all that has followed, was [I believe the first thought was Bridgman's] the destruction of walls for boundaries, and the invention of fossès – an attempt then deemed so astonishing, that the common people called them Ha! Ha's! to express their surprize at finding a sudden and unperceived check to their walk.'[17]

By the early 1720s, Bridgeman was working at Claremont in Surrey for the Duke of Newcastle, who had bought the estate in 1714 from Vanbrugh, both members of the Whig sympathisers' Kit-Cat Club (Claremont appears in a group portrait of the club members).[18] A future prime minister and fabulously wealthy, Newcastle turned Claremont over half a century into one of the most famous landscape gardens in Europe, employing a sequence of top designers. Vanbrugh originally laid out the garden in a V-shape (for Vanbrugh) with two main avenues, designed imposing walls for the duke's six-acre vegetable garden, and built several garden follies, of which the Belvedere, a meeting place for the Kit-Cat Club, is the sole survivor.[19] Bridgeman overlapped with Vanbrugh, creating a serpentine walk still known as Bridgeman's Walk, although now a third of the length since the estate was broken up in the early twentieth century.[20] His pièce de résistance, however, was the three-acre Amphitheatre, which remains the centrepiece of the garden, used for fêtes champêtres and open-air theatre. '[T]he fine Amphitheatre at Claremont [was] the Design of the very ingenious Mr Bridgeman,' wrote Stephen Switzer, while Newcastle referred to it as 'dear Bridgemans Hill'.[21] Bridgeman's drawing for the Amphitheatre and Round Bason survives in Sir John Soane's Museum, and indicates that the original design was for terraces of turf carved out of a hillside, with no additional planting, and overlooking what was then a round lake.[22] 'The whole is a place wherein to tarry with secure delight, or saunter with perpetual amusement,' wrote Thomas Whateley in his *Observations of Modern Gardening*, published in 1770.[23]

Bridgeman could spot what Timothy Mowl calls the 'latent geometry in an existing natural topography and then harden and emphasise it with avenues and planting' and embrace the house within the wider landscape.[24] This is true above all of Stowe in Buckinghamshire, where Bridgeman consulted for twenty years: his first recorded payment of £1 2*s* 6*d* was made to him by Lord Cobham in 1714, aptly the year of the Hanoverian succession.[25]

Richard Temple, 1st Viscount Cobham, who helped stage-manage that succession, was a leading Whig who fell out in the early 1730s with the Walpole-led wing of the party. One of Marlborough's generals, he was ennobled by George I, but his wealth, like that of many Whig leaders, came from trade – in Cobham's case, from his wife's brewing fortune. Owning land, therefore, and making a political statement on it, was crucially important. At Stowe, Cobham transformed a brick Caroline house into a Palladian mansion and replaced the previous century's terracing and fancy topiary with a garden that would break new frontiers. It would establish its creator as one of the political elite.[26]

By the time Cobham called Bridgeman to Stowe, Britain had only been a nation for seven years, since the Act of Union between England and Scotland in 1707. This union triggered a century-long struggle to define a national political and cultural identity. In the early 1770s, Britain was an embattled offshore island, still reeling from the civil wars of the seventeenth century. By 1759, it had acquired a world-wide empire through successive victories over the French and other enemies in the Seven Years War.

As the nation sought to define itself, the battle was played out between such gardens as Stowe, and the royal gardens at Kew and Richmond. The landscape movement, at Claremont, Chiswick and Stowe, expressed on the land the political views of the ascendant Whig aristocracy. Cobham's ambitions at Stowe resulted in the creation of perhaps the most outstanding garden in the history of British gardening. The gardens were always designed to be seen by the visiting public, following a set route which pressed home Cobham's political message. To that end, in 1717, Cobham opened an early visitor centre. The New Inn was leased to a series of innkeepers to feed and water the general public, who were admitted to the gardens only when the Temple family were away from home.

Bridgeman's work at Stowe demonstrated his talent for coping with difficult terrain. The architects, Vanbrugh and James Gibbs, were responsible for the ornamentation of the landscape, while Bridgeman took on the practical design and layout.[27] According to George Vertue in 1735, Vanbrugh 'was most concerned in the direction of Ld Cobhams [Gardens] or rather buildings because Mr Bridgeman Gardiner to the King had the direction & disposition of the Gardens'.[28]

It was a tall order for a young designer early in his career, especially as Stowe's awkward site lay mostly to the west of the house, bounded by roads and leaning slantwise across a valley. Added to that was the problem of creating the right setting for buildings erected by Vanbrugh and Gibbs, a Tory who began working for Cobham after Vanbrugh's death in 1726. Appropriate to Cobham's martial past, Bridgeman created a military redoubt of a landscape, with framing avenues of trees, roundels of trees on the perimeter like watchtowers, and a surrounding ha-ha. He imposed a formal geometry which linked walks and vistas, and used Vanbrugh's temples as focal points. A bird's-eye view of his 1720 layout shows diagonal paths which radiate out from the Rotunda, set on a mound (another of Bridgeman's favourite features). The layout is formal, with many straight lines, but it is already a departure from the straitjacket of the French style, for it is not symmetrical and serpentine walks are cut through groves of trees.

Stowe was an extraordinary achievement. By 1724, the politician and writer Lord Perceval was reporting that the gardens had already 'gained the reputation of being the finest seat in England'.[29] 'Bridgeman laid out the ground and plann'd the whole, which cannot fail of recommending him to business,' added Perceval.[30]

***

Bridgeman was satisfied enough with his work at Stowe to invite the French illustrator Jacques Rigaud to England in 1733 to draw perspectives of the landscape. These engravings still adorn the walls of Stowe School, providing an account of the gardens before the arrival of Kent or Brown.

The drawings had not been published when Bridgeman died from dropsy (oedema) in 1738. His probate inventory shows that he was the 'Proprietor of the Views of Lord Cobhams Seat and Gardens engraved on fifteen Copper Plates the Value thereof uncertain'. He also left implements and equipment to the value of £230 1*s* 9½*d* at the various royal gardens and household goods, divided between his houses in London's Broad Street and at Hampton Court Palace, worth £2,000, as well as the pub in Stilton.[31]

It was not a fortune for a man who had been so conspicuously successful, and indeed his widow, Sarah, found herself in financial straits. She published the *Views of Stowe* the year after her husband's death at four guineas a set, the price Cobham paid when he bought two sets. Sarah seems unlikely to have recouped Bridgeman's original outlay on the engravings of £1,400. Instead, she had to apply to the Lords of the Treasury for outstanding payments due to her husband of £5,541 12*s* 8½*d*, writing that 'your Memorialist and her family [had been] left in very narrow Circumstances'. By 1743, she had managed to obtain £5,000 from the Board of Works, but was less successful with Sarah, Duchess of Marlborough. The latter had kept a very careful note of all expenses incurred during the construction of Blenheim and its gardens, and eventually threatened a lawsuit if Bridgeman's widow continued to pester her.[32]

Sarah's final years were an unhappy coda to the triumphs enjoyed by Bridgeman, who was acclaimed on his death in an obituary notice in *Read's Weekly* as 'well skill'd in the Art of Gardening'.[33] Sarah's plight seems all the poignant given that her husband's achievements were subsequently to be in large measure obscured by Kent and Brown. 'Perhaps, for his lasting reputation, it was ultimately a disadvantage to have wealthy landed clients who had the means and whim to follow developing garden fashions,' Penelope Hobhouse has written.[34]

Walpole's Whig interpretation of gardening, *The History of Modern Taste in Gardening*, proposes a trajectory of improvement from the reactionary conservatism of London and Wise to the heroic revolutionary William Kent, with Bridgeman as 'a hesitant reformer' along the way, only able to relax his formal approach once 'other innovators had broke loose too from rigid symmetry'.[35] Garden design historian Tim Richardson, writing in the twenty-first century, takes a more positive view of Bridgeman's contribution. 'He was the person who made the hard decisions at the outset ... who found the most favoured natural spots and engineered everything around them ... subsequent designers rarely changed the basic structure created by Bridgeman.'[36]

'Consult the Genius of the Place in all,' wrote Alexander Pope in his *Epistle to Burlington* (1731), a moral essay on the appropriate use of wealth. Creating a landscape garden while bearing both art and nature in mind was, Pope suggested, the duty of men such as Burlington and Cobham, whose garden he extols in the poem:

> Parts answ'ring parts shall slide into a whole,
> Spontaneous beauties all around advance
> Start ev'n from Difficulty, strike from Chance
> Nature shall join you; Time shall make it grow
> A Work to wonder at – perhaps a Stow.[37]

The poem suggests that Bridgeman had helped put Stowe on the map, aesthetically and politically. Bridgeman, at Claremont, Stowe and Rousham, provided the perfect launching pad for the mercurial genius of William Kent, who would within a few years eclipse the older man.

CHAPTER 7

William Kent (1685–1748)

After Bridgeman, wrote Horace Walpole, 'appeared Kent, painter enough to taste the charms of landscape, bold and opinionative enough to dare and to dictate, and born with a genius to strike out a great system from the twilight of imperfect essays. He leaped the fence, and saw that all nature was a garden.'[1]

Walpole admired William Kent as embodying the Whig cultural project, and as a designer who achieved where, in his view, the more timorous Bridgeman had failed. In our own time, garden design historian Tim Richardson has written that 'Kent can be considered the greatest individual exponent of the landscape garden because he clearly had the ability to visualize the entire garden in his head before he started working, just as a great composer might with a symphony'.[2]

Not all Kent's contemporaries would have agreed with either Walpole or Richardson: William Hogarth, son-in-law of Sir James Thornhill, the court painter displaced by Kent, pilloried him and his friends and patrons, Lord Burlington and Alexander Pope, in a series of engravings. Spiteful Lord Hervey, chief confidant of Queen Caroline, described him as 'a man much in fashion as a gardener, an architect, a painter and about fifty other things, with a very bad taste and little understanding, but had the good luck to make several people who had no taste or understanding of their own believe that they could borrow both of him'.[3] Hervey was surely skating on thin ice, for Kent was then in good odour with the queen, the real power behind George II. Kent was variously described by his contemporaries as 'a soft and civil companion' (playwright John Gay), as having a 'civil and obliging manner' (antiquarian George Vertue, with a pen often as unforgiving as Hervey's), and 'by no means a Respecter of Persons, but using sharp speeches to the Greatest' (poet and gardener Alexander Pope).[4]

The quick-silver Kent was, as biographer Timothy Mowl has written, 'a fourth-rate artist with a modest colour sense, a poor grasp of Baroque

Rousham, Venus's Vale. (Author's collection)

composition and a lamentable inability to capture a good portrait likeness'.[5] Kent himself had a sneaking suspicion he wasn't much of a painter, which is why, when the opportunities arose, he turned to architecture, interior design, furniture design, and, most significantly, gardens. There, his genius was given full rein, as at Rousham, in Oxfordshire, Kent's crowning achievement and still gloriously intact today. Architectural historian Christopher Hussey had no doubt where Kent should be placed: 'As the founder, in effect, of the art of naturalistic landscape architecture, Kent deserves a place in the national hierarchy of creative genius.'[6]

***

Kent was born William Cant in Bridlington in late 1685 and was baptised on 1 January 1686. His father, also William, was a successful joiner, and the family, which included a younger sister, lived in Bridlington High Street. Kent's education was limited, given his apparently scant knowledge of Latin and Greek, and his erratic spelling, syntax and punctuation, blotchily appearing in his bold but unformed hand in his adult correspondence. It is possible that he was dyslexic. Mowl suggests that Kent gained a more important education as he gazed out from his school at the west front of Bridlington Priory. The Decorated Gothic style helped shaped Kent's 'Gothick' vision, and through him that of men such as Horace Walpole later in the eighteenth century.[7]

Kent may have been apprenticed to a coach or house painter, but, according to Vertue, when he early on 'demonstrated his youthful inclinations to drawing', wealthy Yorkshire patrons 'recommended him to proper persons in London', to finance his studies and send him to Italy.[8]

By 1709, he had changed his name from Cant to Kent, and had set sail for Rome. Kent's was an unusual apprenticeship for a gardener, as he spent almost a decade in Italy, sponsored initially by a Yorkshire gentleman, Sir William Wentworth. He subsequently picked up two further patrons, Burrell Massingberd of Lincolnshire, and Sir John Chester of Chichely in Buckinghamshire, and by 1713 was probably on about £70/80 a year.[9] Writing to Kent in May 1713, Massingberd sent him 20 guineas from himself and £20 from Chester, 'in order for your support in Rome, and mentioning ye hopes we had of your becoming a great Painter if you continue ye same dillegence I left you inclined to'.[10] Kent acted as a kind of artistic agent to Massingberd and Chester, sending to England works of art he had acquired for them, and advising Massingberd on building a classical summer-house. The latter had hopes of Kent becoming 'Raphael Secundus', but when these proved illusory, he may have questioned whether the painter was worth the £560 Chester and he had lavished on him over Kent's Roman years, especially as Kent all but ignored them when he returned to England in late 1719.

By then, Kent had been adopted by a Whig aristocrat nine years his junior. Richard Boyle, 3rd Earl of Burlington, saw in Kent a gift which he believed might help him realise his dream of becoming 'the noble Maecenas of Arts', as George Vertue termed him.[11] Burlington realised that Kent's personal qualities, as much as his professional gifts, would endear him to royalty and aristocracy.

Kent did not waste his ten years in Rome: he studied under Giuseppe Chiari, a pupil of Carlo Maratta; won second prize in an annual painting competition run by the Accademia di S Luca; and was paid fifteen golden scudi for a still-extant ceiling fresco in San Giuliano dei Fiamminghi. Kent would also have familiarised himself with the work of Claude Lorrain and Nicolas Poussin, painters who helped inspire the Whigs' vision of landscape.

Travelling through Italy, Kent absorbed influences from austere classicism to the glorious ornamentation of Roman Baroque, later evident in his florid interior design and furniture work. In 1714, he accompanied Thomas Coke, future Earl of Leicester and heir to Holkham in Norfolk, on the young man's Grand Tour in northern Italy. Kent's sketchy diary mentions his appreciation of the Medici garden of Pratolino, one of his few references to gardens during his Italian years. Coke later became a patron of Kent's, but most important to him was the Earl of Burlington, whom Kent met first in Rome and then again in Genoa as he travelled home to England in 1719.

Born in 1694, Burlington succeeded his father as 3rd Earl at the age of ten, inheriting vast wealth and estates in Ireland, Yorkshire, Chiswick and London. Appointed a Privy Councillor by George I, Burlington was more interested in the arts than in day-to-day politics: he saw it as his mission to provide the ruling Whig oligarchy with a suitable artistic setting by invoking republican Rome in its architecture, and an anti-French naturalism in its gardens. In his thinking, Burlington was influenced by the Whigs' artistic creed, *Characteristicks of Men, Manners and Opinions, Times*, published between 1708 and 1712 by the aristocratic philosopher Anthony Ashley Cooper, 3rd Earl of Shaftesbury. 'The horrid graces of the wilderness represent nature better and are more engaging than the formal mockery of princely gardens,' wrote Shaftesbury. He advocated an irregularity in English gardens which would represent Britain's new constitutional monarchy and British liberties, as opposed to the strict formality of gardens embodying the autocracy of Louis XIV.[12] The English would follow nature, rather than seek to dominate it, and subsequent writers would also see this link with the English constitution. Writing eighty years later in defence of 'Capability' Brown, Humphry Repton claimed that 'the neatness, simplicity, and elegance of English gardening' were a visual symbol of the English constitution, itself 'the happy medium betwixt the liberty of savages, and the restraint of a despotic government'.[13]

Burlington was intoxicated by Shaftesbury's vision. On two curtailed Grand Tours to Italy in 1714 and 1719, Burlington only brushed the surface of classical architecture, while his enthusiasm for Palladio was based on a wet afternoon in the Veneto during which he missed seeing all but a few of the master's buildings. Burlington's imperfect knowledge but messianic view of Palladianism acted as a straitjacket on Kent's architectural work.[14]

Kent arrived in London in December 1719, his journey probably financed by Massingberd. Burlington was an adept at spotting talent, having under his wing at various times Alexander Pope, John Gay and George Frederick Handel, as well as Kent. Kent had left England as an obscure 'limner' during the reign of Queen Anne, her government led by Tories. He returned a fully fledged painter in the pay of a generous and well-connected patron, just as the new Hanoverian dynasty and the controlling Whig elite were attempting to build a cultural platform.

Recommended by Burlington, Kent began working for George I. His first royal commission was to decorate the Cube (or Cupola) room at Kensington Palace, a job which should have gone to Sir James Thornhill as Serjeant Painter to the Crown. Kent worked at the palace for the next six years, painting several state rooms and, most memorably, the King's Staircase. The perspective is wrong, but the 'mural masquerade' is entertaining and populous, with a cast of some forty-five characters, many of them servants. It includes the king's dwarf and his two Turkish servants, Mohammed and Mustapha.[15]

Kent became Master Carpenter in 1725, then Master Mason and deputy to the Surveyor-General, ending in 1739 as Principal Painter to the Crown. He was, wrote Vertue, assisted 'above any artist living,' as Lord Burlington had 'promoted him on all occasions to everything in his power, to the King, to the Court Works, and Courtiers'.[16]

A portrait painted by William Aikman between 1723 and 1725 shows Kent as the confident court painter. His face, with its high-domed forehead, is as sleekly smooth as David Cameron's, with keen button brown eyes and full rosy-red lips. He wears a red silk turban with gorgeous red shoes to match, and holds a paint brush and palette, his spotless working garb a rich silk-lined loose overcoat, a silk waistcoat pulling slightly across a corpulent stomach, and velvet trousers. He was a bon viveur, a bachelor who enjoyed cooking his own food (Pope asked him for his recipe for steak) and inclined, according to one contemporary observer, to 'give his orders when he was full of claret'. Known as the 'Signior', he ran to fat: 'The greatest news I have to tell you is that the Signior is in perfect tranquillity,' wrote Pope to Burlington in 1736, 'enjoying his own Being, and is become a happy but plumper copy of General Dormer.'[17]

Kent's friendship with Burlington was deep and lasting: in a letter to Burlington in November 1732, Kent speaks of those who share a vision, 'living and loving together, as you and I do'.[18] He also remained friendly with Pope, working with him on his celebrated garden at Twickenham. Although in his will Kent left money to a supposed mistress, actress Elizabeth Butler and her two children, he didn't live with her, never married, and seems to have been happier in the company of men.

***

Embraced by the Whig establishment initially as much for his jovial bonhomie as for his talent, Kent was employed continuously until his death. At Sir Robert Walpole's Houghton in Norfolk, he designed the stone plinth within the staircase well for a massive bronze gladiator presented to Walpole by the Earl of Pembroke. Beyond is the Stone Hall, an extravagant creation which aligned Walpole with the Roman emperor Marcus Aurelius. A decade later, Kent created the soaring black and white Marble Hall for Coke at Holkham, five miles away.

But it was as a garden designer that Kent's true brilliance displayed itself, acknowledged by Walpole: 'The pencil of his imagination bestowed all the arts of landscape on the scenes he handled.'[19] Chiswick House was an early project. There, he improved on a stolid garden where before 1719 Burlington had laid out a *patte d'oie* or goose's foot radiating out from the Jacobean house. When this was demolished in 1725, Burlington built his not entirely authentic neo-Palladian villa, which Pope described as being small enough to dangle on a watch chain.[20] Kent painted the villa's interiors and redesigned the garden, turning a Bridgeman-designed canal into a naturalistic lake, and adding a Doric column and Ionic temple, a miniature version of the Pantheon in Rome, to be glimpsed through trees. He also made a simple exedra of yew, set with busts, planting cedars of

Lebanon on the lawn. His original design for an exedra of triangular topped niches was adopted not here but at Stowe as the Temple of the British Worthies.

Copies of Kent's irreverent sketches are positioned around Chiswick's gardens today. In one, Lord Burlington holds forth to Kent in front of his new villa, while a dog lifts his leg on his lordship. In another, Kent urinates against the wall of the garden, his dog keeping him company nearby, while, in a third, rabbits dance across the landscape. These whimsical touches prick the bubble of Burlington's pompous conception, which by 1738 had caused him debts of over £200,000.

Meanwhile, Kent added to a fifteenth-century house at Esher (of which one tower now remains) for the future prime minster Henry Pelham. A 1737 John Roque map shows that Kent laid a wide lawn down to water, planted groves of trees and designed several garden buildings, all now vanished. 'At Esher,' wrote Walpole, 'Where Kent and Nature vied for Pelham's love, the prospects more than aided the painter's genius.' Elsewhere, he wrote, 'where objects were wanting to animate his horizon, his taste as an architect could bestow immediate termination. His buildings, his seats, his temples, were more the works of his pencil than his compasses.'[21] Pelham chose to be painted, accompanied by his secretary, with Kent's Fishing Temple in the background.

Kent's achievements at Esher recommended him to Pelham's brother, Lord Newcastle, another future prime minister. At Newcastle's nearby Claremont, he opened up the prospects from the house by levelling Vanbrugh's terraces, turned Bridgeman's round pond into an irregular lake and made an island temple and a cascade in its middle. He surrounded both lake and Bridgeman's amphitheatre with cedars, silver spruce, Scots pine and laurel. 'The pond I conclude looks very well,' wrote Newcastle in 1738 to his head gardener.[22]

***

In 1719, Caroline of Ansbach, Princess of Wales, hosted a garden conference at Richmond, attended by Alexander Pope. Garden design was then dominated by Charles Bridgeman's geometric effects, which Caroline obviously liked well enough to appoint him as royal gardener after her husband's accession to the throne in 1727. Bridgeman initially laid out Caroline's pleasure grounds at Richmond, but she turned to Kent to design two bizarre garden buildings. The Hermitage (1732) and Merlin's Cave (1735) were intended as part of the ideological battle between the royal and aristocratic gardens, as the Hanoverian consensus began to disintegrate.

Lord Cobham, an architect of the Hanoverian succession, led a breakaway group of Whigs antagonistic to the Whig government. They believed that Robert Walpole's Caroline-backed regime was corrupting the early Hanoverian ideals by concentrating too much power in the hands of one individual: supposedly the king, but in fact Walpole. The Excise Crisis of 1733 proved a flashpoint, as Walpole sought to impose duties which Cobham and his ilk believed threatened an Englishman's right to privacy. Caroline and George's eldest son, Frederick, Prince of Wales, whom his parents detested, proved a perfect figurehead for the disgruntled Whig faction, while mother and son, at odds, used their gardens in the iconographical war.

Kent was a foot soldier on both sides. The buildings he erected for Caroline were razed by 'Capability' Brown, so for knowledge of them we have to rely on contemporary engravings. The Hermitage was a hut-like construction, with rusticated walls and an incongruous classical pediment. It was peopled with marble busts, still in the Royal Collection, of Enlightenment figures: Robert Boyle, founder member of the Royal Society, flanked by Isaac Newton and Whig philosopher John Locke, and by two contemporary divines, Samuel Clarke and William Wollaston. Merlin's Cave, which looked like Big Ears' toadstool, was thatched, its interiors featuring wax figures of Elizabeth of York and Elizabeth I. Both buildings were symbolic: the former establishing Caroline as a figure of the Enlightenment, the latter an attempt to Anglicise the German monarchy and associate the queen herself with past English queens.

Caroline freed Kent's imagination from Burlington's anodyne neo-Palladianism and encouraged his tendency to the Gothic, which he displayed at Esher, Stowe and Rousham.[23] Another key influence on Kent was in evidence at one of Kent's most important, though sadly no longer extant, gardens. 'Mr Pope undoubtedly contributed to form his taste,' argued Walpole. 'The design of the prince of Wales's garden at Carlton-house was evidently borrowed from the poet's at Twickenham.'[24]

Pope's Twickenham garden, full of decorative effects and symbolism, included a shell temple, an obelisk and elaborate grotto, and possibly looked something like Sir Roy Strong's heavily ornamented and narrative garden at The Laskett in Herefordshire today. Another enchanting Kent sketch reveals the friendship between poet and designer. The two men stand looking at a fantastic domed temple, Kent's arm round the shoulder of the much smaller Pope, while Pope's dog, Bounce, looks on.

Pope's garden was just five acres, the right size to inspire the Prince of Wales in his twelve-acre London garden, where the eye needed to be drawn inwards rather than borrowing from surrounding landscape. At Carlton House, Kent framed a lawn with plantations of trees, created mirrored exedras with busts, planted groves of trees, built a bagnio (or bath house) in the style of Chiswick House, and planted a wilderness. Statues around the garden associated the prince with British legends – Alfred the Great, supposed founder of the English constitution, and medieval hero the Black Prince. The result, a garden both naturalistic and full of symbolism, had a major impact on aristocratic gardening, as a contemporary letter shows.

It was written in 1734 by Sir Thomas Robinson to his father-in-law, the Earl of Carlisle, creator with Sir John Vanbrugh of the baroque palace and garden at Castle Howard in Yorkshire:

> There is a new taste in gardening just arisen, which has been practised with so great success at the Prince's garden in Town that a general alteration of some of the most considerable gardens in the kingdom is begun, after Mr. Kent's notion of gardening, viz. to lay them out, and work without level or line. By this means I really think the 12 acres the Prince's garden consists of, is more diversified and of greater variety than anything of the compass I ever saw ... The celebrated gardens of Claremont, Chiswick and Stowe are now full of labourers, to modernise the expensive works finished in them, even since everyone's memory.[25]

The implication of Robinson's remarks is that where the prince led, Newcastle, Burlington and Cobham followed, but in reality Kent worked on all these gardens simultaneously, bringing his freshness of vision to temper the harder lines of Bridgeman's layouts.

***

William Kent worked throughout the 1730s at Stowe, contributing to grounds which were, in the words of agricultural writer Arthur Young in 1771, 'the admiration of all that viewed them, not only for their real beauty, but the scarcity of other improvements of the same kind'.[26] Kent's first building, erected in 1731, was the Temple of Venus, which stands on a Bridgeman bastion overlooking the Eleven-Acre Lake. But Kent's major achievement, on which he worked between 1733 and 1739, was the Elysian Fields, a landscape he developed from Bridgeman's work a decade earlier. Here, Cobham moved from his broader philosophical vision to make party political points, establishing his faction of the Whigs, rather than Walpole's crew, as the true inheritors of classical values and British constitutionalism. The Temple of Ancient Virtue contains statues of a Greek general, legislator, poet and philosopher, while nearby was the ruined Temple of Modern Virtue, which featured a headless statue representing Walpole. Across the Alder River running through the fields is the Temple of British Worthies, designed as Robinson was writing the letter quoted above, and similar to a plan sketched out by Kent for Chiswick. The sixteen busts placed within the curved screen include Whig heroes Elizabeth I, the Black Prince, John Milton, Cromwellian hero John Hampden, William III, and a Walpole enemy, Sir John Barnard, a successful London businessman. Behind this row of solemn worthies is a memorial to 'Signor Fido' who was, the legend has it, 'An Italian of good Extraction' but 'Not a Man but a Grey-hound'.[27] A typical Kentian joke, and, as so often, featuring a dog.

The grotto at the head of the river was also Kent's work, although some have suggested that Bridgeman was as responsible as his successor for the layout of the Elysian Fields.[28] Not in doubt, however, is Kent's responsibility for the winning design of the buildings, nor indeed his part in their positioning. The whole effect is described by Young, who travelled widely round Britain in later decades of the eighteenth century:

> The grove on which the grotto looks, leads you to that part of the garden, called the Elysian-fields, which are beautiful waves of close shaven grass; breaking among woods, and scattered with single trees; bounded on one side by thick groves, and shelving on the other down to the water, which winds in a very happy manner; and commanding from several spots, various landscapes of the distant parts of the garden.[29]

Stowe is a palimpsest, an accretion of layers which makes it hard to tease out how subsequent designers adapted the work of earlier ones. Kent also followed Bridgeman to Rousham. It was, in Walpole's opinion, 'the most engaging of all Kent's works'.[30]

The joy of Rousham is that we can see Kent's work much as it would have looked almost three centuries ago. Bridgeman dealt with a wedge-shaped twenty-five-acre site running down to the River Cherwell, meandering its way south to Oxford. He put in the inevitable ha-ha, laid a bowling green in front of the house, constructed a terraced theatre from the wooded hillside, and made a square pond at the bottom of what became Kent's Venus's Vale. Pope was a regular visitor to Rousham, admiring the garden as 'the prettiest place for water-falls, jets, ponds inclosed with beautiful scenes of green and hanging wood'.[31]

Kent was commissioned in 1737 to work on both house and garden by General James Dormer, a member of Burlington's inner circle, and a veteran of Blenheim. Kent added two wings to the house, and gave Bridgeman's landscape an allegorical dimension. Kent's challenges included the placement of two statues. One, a Scheemakers statue of a horse being gored by a lion, Kent set at the end of the bowling green behind which the ground drops away. The other, a gladiator, he positioned on top of a seven-arched Praeneste Arcade, Rousham's answer to the Temple of the British Worthies, atop one of Bridgeman's concave slopes.

In the lower garden, Kent turned Bridgeman's round pool into an octagonal one, loosened the river which Bridgeman had canalised, and levelled the terraces into two smooth slopes. Across fields beyond the garden, he fashioned two eye-catchers: a Triumphal Arch and a Temple of the Mill, an existing cottage to which buttresses, quatrefoils and battlements were added.[32]

The iconography of Rousham is more metaphysical than Stowe's: broadly, the upper garden represents this life, and the lower garden the next. There are many military allusions: Minerva, for instance, the goddess of both wisdom and warfare, guards two Kent seats, representing the ideals of Dormer's life. Water cascades down through three arcades in Venus's Vale, a statue of Venus flanked by Pan and Faunus evoking the erotic aspects of love.

Kent appeared no more than once or twice a year at Rousham, leaving supervision of the garden's construction to Dormer's steward, William White. Plaintive letters from the head gardener, John MacClary, suggest that often he and the gardening team didn't know what to do next 'till Mr Kent comes down and tells me'. Even Dormer was on occasion driven to write to his cousin to say that 'I hope Ld.Burlington does not forget his word & if Kent can be persuaded to come I shall take it very kindly'.[33]

Absentee designer or not, Kent worked his sorcery at Rousham, creating a landscape which remains allusive, beautiful and puzzling, while a note to Dormer's steward, specifying flowering shrubs to be used, suggests that the designer Kent had acquired familiarity with plants.

The garden was virtually complete by 1741, after which Kent worked again at Holkham, building a Triumphal Arch. At Euston Hall in Suffolk, Kent transformed a valley with a pavilion and turned the Duke of Grafton's seat, according to Walpole, into 'one of the most admired seats in England – in my opinion, because Kent has an absolute disposition of it. Kent is now so fashionable, that, like Addison's Liberty, he can make bleak rocks and barren mountains smile'.[34]

Kent died in April 1748 at Burlington House, 'of a Mortification all over', and was buried, as he requested in his will, in the Burlington family vault at Chiswick church.[35] He left an annuity of £50 to his sister, Esther, as well as the legacy of £1,200 to Elizabeth Butler of the parish of Saint Paul Covent Garden and her two children. Other legacies were works of art to Lord Burlington, his wife and daughter, and to Henry Pelham, by then prime minister, suggesting that Vertue is right in claiming that Kent had 'amassed riches and some curious works of art'.[36]

'All gardening is landscape painting,' wrote Pope. 'You may distance things by darkening them, and by narrowing towards the end, in the same manner as they do in painting.'[37] 'Painter enough' to understand that, Kent effectively became the founder of the English landscape garden. Another friend of Kent's, Isaac Ware, wrote in his 1756 *Complete Body of Architecture* that English gardens are an improvement on 'those of our ancestors; in effect more extensive; and throughout more agreeable; everything pleasing is thrown open; everything disgustful is shut out; nor do we perceive the art, while we enjoy its effects'.[38]

CHAPTER 8

'Capability' Lancelot Brown (1716–1783)

Legend has it that 'Capability' Brown met the gout-crippled William Pitt the Elder, by then Earl of Chatham, tottering down the steps of St James's Palace. As Brown helped the earl to his carriage, Chatham said, 'Now, sir, go and adorn your country,' to which the gardener replied, 'Go you, my lord, and save it.'[1] An apocryphal story, no doubt, but it illustrates how far the Northumberland farm boy had travelled, able to spar with the great statesman on almost equal terms. Chatham wrote to a friend that the designer 'shares the private hours [of the King], dines familiarly with [the King's] neighbour of Sion, and sits down at the tables of all the house of Lords'.[2] Such was Brown's relationship with Chatham that he was even asked by the architect of Britain's triumphs in the Seven Years War to act as an intermediary with the king over American hostilities in 1777. Brown reported back to Chatham that he had been 'heard with attention' by George III and that he, Brown, 'went as far as I durst ... upon such tender ground'.[3]

The former kitchen gardener's clients included the king, six prime ministers, and much of the aristocracy. He has been associated with over 250 sites, created more than 150 ornamental lakes and planted over a million trees. His success was built on a combination of business acumen, an understanding of land management, and skill at integrating agriculture and sporting activities within a pleasing landscape. Few individuals, if any, have done more to change the landscape of England. 'I very earnestly wish I may die before you,' someone is alleged to have said to a puzzled Brown. 'I should like to see Heaven before you have improved it.'[4]

Innumerable myths swirl about the name of 'Capability' Brown, not least about how he acquired his nickname: he was said to be able to assess at a glance the 'capabilities' of any landscape for improvement. Brown's surname became a verb in his own time, with one of his clients, Lady Irwin at Temple Newsam, writing to a friend that 'Col Pitt & my husband have been Brownifying my dear gravel walk'.[5]

'Capability' Lancelot Brown by John Keyse Sherwin after Nathaniel Dance. (Yale Center for British Art)

Gardening was a constant theme in eighteenth-century literature: in his *Epistle to Lord Burlington*, Alexander Pope exhorts his aristocratic friend that the proper use of wealth was to make his mark on the land. His prescription could have been a resumé of Brown's endeavours:

> Consult the Genius of the Place in all;
> That tells the Waters or to rise, or fall,
> Or helps th'ambitious Hill the heavn' to scale,
> Or scoops in circling theatres the Vale,
> Calls in the Country, catches opening glades,
> Joins willing woods, and varies shades from shades,

> Now breaks or now directs, th'intending Lines;
> Paints as you plant, and, as you work, designs.[6]

Brown scooped out great tracts of earth to turn flat fields into rolling parkland, and used water, trees and surrounding countryside to create visual pictures. He was fêted by the Reverend William Mason in his poem, *The English Garden*, but satirised by William Cowper in 'The Garden', part three of his extended poem, *The Task* (1785).

> Lo, he comes!
> Th' omnipotent magician, Brown, appears!
> Down falls the venerable pile, th' abode
> Of our forefathers ... The lake in front becomes a lawn;
> Woods vanish, hills subside, and valleys rise:
> And streams, as if created for his use,
> Pursue the track of his directing wand.[7]

As Cowper suggests, not altogether admiringly, in Brown's hands, the English landscape garden became an even more powerful force than in those of his more volatile predecessor, William Kent. Like Kent, Brown worked for aristocrats who had been on the Grand Tour and who returned influenced by the landscapes of Claude Lorrain and Nicolas Poussin. Also, like Kent, he used those Arcadian images to fashion a particular vision of landscape, yet set within the pastoral tradition of English literature and gardening. We look now at a Brown landscape and think we see natural countryside. In fact, what we see was carefully and brilliantly manipulated by a designer of genius.

* * *

That genius was baptised Lancelot Brown in the Northumberland village of Kirkharle in August 1716, the fifth child of a yeoman farmer, William Brown, who died before Lancelot's fourth birthday. He was educated at nearby Cambo School, and apprenticed as a kitchen gardener by the local landowner, Sir William Loraine, who was remodelling his estate. In 1739 he left Northumberland and spent some time in Boston, Lincolnshire, where he met Bridget Wayet, an alderman's daughter and his future wife. Here, Brown may first have studied water management in an area cut through by drainage channels. He also worked briefly in Oxfordshire for the Grenville brothers at Wotton Underwood, where he would have heard that the Stowe head gardener, William Love, was retiring.[8]

He applied for the job, was accepted, and in February 1741 arrived at Lord Cobham's 5,000-acre estate. A leading Whig, and an imperious, unforgiving man, Cobham could be a hard master, as can be seen from the thin-lipped face staring challengingly from his portrait. Within eighteen months of Brown's arrival, a steward hanged himself, while another made off with the wages, leaving the twenty-six-year-old Brown as clerk of works responsible for Cobham's extensive development programme of both house and gardens.[9] It was the ideal opportunity for an ambitious young man, as Humphry Repton, his would-be successor, summed up in *The Art of Landscape Gardening*:

> Of this art painting and gardening are not the only foundations. The artist must possess a competent knowledge of surveying, mechanics, hydraulics, agriculture, botany, and the general principles of architecture. It can hardly be expected that a man bred and constantly living in the kitchen-garden should possess all these requisites ... It may be asked from whence Mr Brown derived his knowledge? – the answer is obvious: that being at first patronised by a few persons of rank and acknowledged good taste, he acquired by degrees the faculty of prejudging effects, partly from repeated trials and partly from the experience of those to whose conversation and intimacy his genius had introduced him.[10]

There is a hint of snobbery in the better educated Repton's description of the kitchen gardener's training, but Stowe would have been a remarkable experience for Brown. He worked alongside Kent, imbibing from him sense of the theatrical, how to place buildings and eye-catchers, and something of Kent's Gothick taste. Brown gardened within a landscape laid out by Bridgeman and amid buildings designed by Sir John Vanbrugh and James Gibbs, and was employed by Cobham, who orchestrated these talents in creating the greatest British garden of the age.

Brown was not overawed by Stowe. He designed the Grecian Valley, which acts almost as a counterpoint to Kent's Elysian Fields. It was Brown's first essay in major earth works, and already his hallmarks are apparent: a softening of the contours of the land and judicious planting of belts of trees. The only ingredient missing from the quintessential Brownian landscape is water, but an ornamental lake was originally intended before it was turned into a valley, sloping away from the Temple of Concord and Victory, inspired by the Maison Carrée in Nîmes.

Brown replaced Bridgeman's parterre with a lawn in front of the house in 1743, cut cross-views through avenues of trees, and planted thousands of trees, including beech, elm, and Scots fir. In order to plant and transplant mature specimens, he invented a tub-like machine to lever them out and convey them to their new position.[11] He also constructed his first garden building at Stowe, a fluted octagonal pillar, 104 feet high, ordered by Lady Cobham, two years before her husband's death in 1749. It may have been designed by James Gibbs, but Brown adapted the original plan because he realised that 'the Wind has a very great effect on Buildings that stand on so small a Base'.[12]

Some years after their first meeting, Brown married Bridget Wayet in November 1744. Biddy was his mainstay to whom he returned from his endless journeying up and down the country. They moved into one of the Boycott Pavilions, a pair of rusticated cubes designed by Gibbs for the new western entrance to the park and named after a vanished hamlet nearby.[13] It was an imposing but eventually rather cramped home for the Browns' growing family.

Stowe would have made Brown conscious of the contemporary political scene. The aristocracy wanted to show off, not just in front of their peers but also before the visiting public, ever more interested in travel and tourism. Brown worked on an estate with a didactic purpose: the first guides to Stowe garden, some in the form of Socratic dialogues, were published by Benton Seeley, a Buckingham bookseller, in 1744. It may well have fallen to Brown to admit visitors at the Bell Gate and show them round Stowe in the owners' absence.

Even with these other calls on his time, Brown worked within his capacity at Stowe, often being loaned out by Cobham to his lordship's neighbours and friends. It was a time of great social and political change, and of upheaval in the countryside. After the crushing of the Jacobite rebellion at Culloden in 1746, the country was at peace internally, while successes on land and at sea in the Seven Years War turned Britain into a colonial world power. The economy was booming, and the Whig oligarchy, its fortunes made through political office and colonial interests, had money to play with. Brown helped them spend it.

Between 1750 and 1810, almost four thousand enclosure acts were passed, affecting about twenty per cent of the total acreage of England and Wales.[14] Open-strip farming and rights over common land were abolished, villages were removed, and arable farming dwindled in importance. The aristocracy still farmed, but mostly cattle, often used ornamentally, while woodland became an important crop, especially as that, too, could be used ornamentally.

Brown's stints with other landowners helped him hone his expertise and make contacts with men such as Sanderson Miller, an amateur architect who owned an estate near Edge Hill in Warwickshire. After Cobham's death in 1749, Brown set out the following year to explore estates in central England. This expedition was a kind of post-graduate education for Brown, a chance to see work in progress or completed, as well as to look out, with Sanderson Miller's assistance, for future projects. As a result, Brown was commissioned to work at Warwick Castle, Charlecote in Warwickshire, and Packington in Leicestershire. Most importantly, he was introduced, probably by Miller, to George William, 6th Earl of Coventry, who commissioned Brown to redesign his estate at Croome in Worcestershire. They would remain life-long friends: it was after dinner at Coventry's London house that Brown collapsed and died in February 1783.

***

Brown designed gardens and landscapes too numerous to describe them all here. But it is worth focussing on a few and giving particular attention to Croome, which contains all the Brownian ingredients of trees, water, grass, and also architecture. Set against the backdrop of the Malvern Hills, Croome would be Brown's first complete landscape and his first major architectural project.

Coventry was twenty-eight when he inherited Croome, seven years after the death of his beloved elder brother. Both brothers were interested in architecture and garden design, so Croome was for Coventry a sacred charge to realise the vision he and his brother had shared. It would take him fifty years and cost him £400,000 (about £35 million today).[15] When Coventry died in 1809, the botanical collection at Croome was considered second only to that of Kew, with some 5,000 plant species, including introductions from James Cook's voyages to Australia and the South Seas. Like Cobham at Stowe, Coventry employed the best, Robert Adam as well as Brown, and had decided views. He rightly rejected Adam's first design for the ceiling of the Long Gallery; Adam's second design is cleaner and more elegant.

When the National Trust acquired the park in 1996, it was overgrown, much of its land used for arable farming, and its buildings and statuary were derelict and defaced. Thanks to the trust's careful restoration, it is possible now to gather a fair impression of Croome as Brown would have designed it, with the house, in the flood plain between the rivers Avon and Severn, an integral part of the picture. Brown wrapped bays and four corner turrets round the Jacobean house and built a fashionable Palladian main entrance. The medieval parish church considered too close to the house was demolished and a new one built on a rise to the north of the house. Designed in the Gothick style by Brown (with more than a hint of Kent's influence), and with interiors by Adam, it is an eye-catcher from many windows of the house. Standing beside the church today, you look over a typical Brownian landscape, encompassed by a hidden ha-ha, and with views towards the Malverns over encircling woods. Within these are more irregular shelter belts and softening clumps of trees, and half-hidden shrubberies, Brown's original plantings augmented later in the century by Coventry's newer introductions, and replanted in recent years. What looks like a tributary of the Severn threads its way through the centre of the parkland. This is in fact an ornamental lake, stretching for a mile and three-quarters and created by Brown from a boggy marsh, by damming streams and installing eighteen brick-lined culverts or drainage channels hand-dug over twelve years from the mid-1750s. Brown was often called back by Coventry to deal with leaks and seepage.

Croome is an effervescent Kentian mixture of classicism and the Gothick. As well as the church, other eye-catchers include Brown's Grotto of tufa and limestone, and his Corinthian and pedimented Island Pavilion and Rotunda. The latter is presided over by a cedar of Lebanon, one of Brown's favourite trees. Brown worked on the estate for over twenty years, getting off to a good start: in November 1752, Coventry was writing to Miller that 'Mr Brown has done very well by me, and indeed I think has studied both my Place and my Pocket, which are not always conjunctively the Objects of Prospectors'.[16] Coventry outlived Brown by many years, erecting a lakeside memorial to him in 1797. On the pedestal supporting a casket were engraved the words: 'To the Memory of Lancelot Brown, who by the powers of his inimitable and creative genius formed this garden scene out a morass.'

Croome established Brown's modus operandi, not least his probity, as witnessed in Coventry's letter to Miller. He was scrupulous in his financial dealings, not fearing to chase money he was owed, but also ready to restore overpayments. In July 1779, for instance, he returned £100 to his banker, Robert Drummond, noting in his account book that 'you added for my trouble on the Out of Doors work, two hundred pounds, which is more than I can possibly accept from you by one hundred pound'.[17]

In his *Mélanges sur l'Angleterre*, Rochefoucauld writes that Brown's eye was so quick and sure that he could plan a new landscape from an hour's ride round an estate.[18] Brown then had the site professionally surveyed. Using that survey, he drew up his plans, employing a foreman to carry out his instructions, or, in some cases, leaving the client to pick his own. Brown specified the plants, shrubs and trees, but often the client would order them direct from the nurseryman. Brown tended to use the same trusted foremen and surveyors, paying regular site visits to check that the work was being carried out to his specifications. This method was not fool-proof. 'I have so much to do that it neither answers for profit nor pleasure, for when I am galloping in one part of the world my men are making blunders and neglects which [make] it very unpleasant,' he wrote grumpily to one client.[19]

Croome gave Brown the impetus to establish his own freelance practice. The Browns moved in 1751 to a house on Hammersmith Mall, not far from Christopher Gray's nursery at Fulham and John Williamson's in Kensington Gore, from whom he ordered flowering shrubs. Through these contacts, Brown met Philip Miller of the Chelsea Physic Garden, and also Peter Collinson, the British agent of American plant collector John Bartram. Lord Bute at Luton Hoo, the Duke of Marlborough at Blenheim, the Northumberlands at Syon House and Viscount Weymouth at Longleat bought plants from Collinson, and all became clients of Brown's. American plants were the rage, and Brown planted maples, thorns, robinias, red oaks, liriodendrons and cornus along with his favoured beech, elms and cedars of Lebanon.[20]

Brown was often employed as an architect, as at Croome. In Hammersmith he became friendly with the builder Henry Holland, and the two men worked together informally. The Holland and Brown children grew up together and in 1773, Lancelot's daughter, Bridget, married Henry Holland Junior. Brown entered into a more formal partnership with the younger Holland, an architect, giving him £5,000 worth of stock as a wedding present.[21] Holland was later the pupil master of the architect and collector Sir John Soane.

Brown was less respected as an architect than as a landscape gardener in his own time, but Repton leapt to his defence:

> Mr Brown's fame as an architect seems to have been eclipsed by his celebrity as a landscape gardener, he being the only professor of the one art, while he had many jealous competitors in the other. But when I consider the number of excellent works in architecture designed and executed by him, it becomes an act of justice to his memory to record that, if he was superior to all in what related to his own particular profession, he was inferior to none in what related to the comfort, convenience, taste, and propriety of design in the several mansions and other buildings which he planned.[22]

Many of his commissions involved architectural as well as landscape design. Early work at Warwick Castle for Lord Brooke was admired in 1751 by Horace Walpole, who said of the scheme 'it is well laid out by one Brown who has set upon a few ideas of Kent and Mr Southcote'.[23] The acid-tongued Walpole admired Brown, saying in his *Modern Taste in Gardening* that 'it was fortunate for the country and Mr Kent, that he was succeeded by a very able master; and did living artists come within my plan, I should be glad to do justice to Mr Brown'.[24]

Another early commission was Petworth in Sussex, where Brown built a classical temple and a stone boathouse by the lake he created. He drew up several plans and eventually brought rough grass right up to the house with no dividing terrace, separating pleasure grounds from the park with a ha-ha. He scattered single trees and clumps of sweet chestnut, beech and elm to frame views from the house and planted flowering shrubs through his pleasure grounds. A 1753 bill from the nurseryman, John Williamson, shows that Brown had ordered eighty sweet briony, thirty honeysuckles, ten altheas (hollyhocks), eight Persian jasmines, two different types of cherry trees, eighty-five roses, maples, sumac, laburnums, lilacs and acacias.[25]

The same year that Williamson sent in this bill, Brown opened a bank account at Drummonds Bank at Charing Cross, a measure of his success at a time when holding a bank account was not routine. He was in good artistic and social company as the bank's other clients included architect James Gibbs, court painter Johann Zoffany, furniture-maker Thomas Chippendale and Captain Thomas Coram's Foundling Hospital.[26]

By the late 1750s, Brown was working on half a dozen commissions simultaneously, including for Lord Essex at Burghley, where he spent over a quarter of a century on the parkland and building works. The first contract with Lord Weymouth at Longleat was signed in 1757; by 1760, Lord Weymouth had paid Brown over £6,000 for removing Wise's parterre and making the canal into a series of lakes. Mrs Delaney, visiting Longleat in November 1760, wrote that the original gardens had been 'succeeded by a fine lawn, a serpentine river, wooded hills, gravel paths meandering round a shrubbery, all modernised by the ingenious and much sought-after Mr Brown'.[27]

***

Brown never needed to advertise: his commissions came by word of mouth, and his popularity kept him permanently on the road. So much travel took its toll. An asthmatic, he had two prolonged periods of illness when he was confined to home and looked after by Biddy, while his clients wrote badgering letters, requesting site visits. The letters also indicated the respect and affection in which this doughty man was held by his aristocratic employers. When fit, he would turn up, unannounced, to give instructions both to his foremen and, if necessary, to his clients, with whom he would often dine. 'A great Man has paid us a visit,' wrote Lady Amabel Polwarth to her sister in 1778. 'You will guess that I mean the illustrious Mr Brown.'[28]

Brown endeared himself by his scrupulous honesty, economy and organisation, and by his pleasant, respectful but robust personality. In his portraits, one sees a man with a serious, slightly quizzical expression, one eyebrow slightly raised. In some, he wears his own hair; in others, he has a neat grey wig; in both a professional man to his fingertips.

Despite ill-health, the round of work continued. In 1764, he was appointed Master Gardener at Hampton Court by George III, at £2,000 a year, paid in £500 instalments each quarter. The appointment brought with it accommodation, Wilderness House, within the grounds of the palace, to which the family moved and where Brown remained until his death. Brown laid a light hand on the palace gardens, leaving Wise's Privy Garden intact. His main contribution was the planting of the great vine in 1768, which was listed in 2005 as the world's longest grapevine.

Brown became friendly with the actor David Garrick, for whom he built a tunnel to connect his house at Hampton with his riverside garden across the road. Through him he met the evangelical writer Hannah More, to whom we are indebted for a description from Brown himself as to how he worked. 'He told me he compared his art to literary composition. "Now *there*" said he, pointing his finger, "I make a comma, and there" pointing to another spot, "where a more decided turn is proper, I make colon; at another part, where an interruption is desirable to break the view, a parenthesis; now a full stop, and then I begin another subject."'[29] Given that he wrote almost nothing about his work, such glimpses provide rare insights. As does his account book, a thick vellum-bound volume held by the Royal Horticultural Society's Linley Library. It reveals the scale and scope of Brown's work, suggesting that his fees for 1764 amounted to £6,000. He was still being paid in 1764 for work at Croome, while the 3rd Earl of Shelburne has been billed for £4,015 for work carried out between 1762 and 1766 at Bowood, where Brown created a curvaceous lake by damming two streams and removing cottages.[30]

By the early 1760s, Brown had spent time at Chatsworth, where his parkland still looks like Derbyshire scenery and perfectly sets off the formality around the house. The Marlboroughs spent over £30,000 on Brown's improvements at Blenheim, where he removed another Wise parterre and planted a lawn by the palace. More importantly, he created a majestic cascade and provided a proper setting for Vanbrugh's monumental Grand Bridge, which had previously looked over-scaled for the stream it crossed. Massive earthworks reshaped the banks of the River Glyme, a tributary of the Thames. Tree-planting completed the scene, with vistas appearing and disappearing as visitors approached the palace on horseback or by carriage. Another Brown myth: so pleased was he with the effects he had achieved at Blenheim that he is alleged to have exclaimed: 'Will the Thames ever forgive me?'[31]

Brown worked simultaneously for political opponents, such as the Whig Pitt and the Tory John Stuart, 3rd Earl of Bute. Landscape gardening was Pitt's chief interest apart from politics, and Brown worked for him at Burton Pynsent in Somerset, erecting a column to Pitt similar to Cobham's memorial at Stowe.[32]

At the same time, he was employed by Bute at Luton Hoo, the estate Bute had bought for £94,700 in 1763. The Scottish peer, who had introduced Brown to George III, was a detested politician, pilloried in the press and afraid to travel without an armed guard. An accomplished amateur botanist instrumental in founding Kew Gardens, Bute saw Luton Hoo as a haven, with its mature parkland trees immortalised by Paul Sandby. Brown stayed for two nights with Lord Bute in 1775, when they drank a bottle of Tokay each evening, 'which was rather too much for me as my cough has been very troublesome,' he wrote to Biddy.[33]

Brown's eventual bill to Bute amounted to £12,000. For that, he framed views from the Robert Adam-designed house, built a ha-ha through existing groves of trees, and dammed the River Lee in two places to create a pair of elongated lakes eventually of over fifty acres in spread, work which took over a decade. While still in progress, it was admired by the agricultural writer Arthur Young in 1770: 'We … drove along the banks of the river, which was naturally a trifling stream, but is here now making, and is made further on, the finest water I have any where seen; the plantations on the top of the hills to the right as we entered, are very beautiful … a spot wonderfully capable.'[34]

***

While working for the Earl of Northampton, Brown bought an estate from him at Fenstanton in Huntingdonshire. There is no obvious reason for this purchase, as he never lived there, although he and Biddy and other family members (including a woman, possibly his illegitimate daughter) were buried in the parish church. By the 1760s, he had two sons at Eton, where the elder one, Lance, was allegedly known as 'Capey', suggestive of the snobbery the boys may have encountered sharing schooling with the sons of their father's patrons. Lance later became an MP, while another son, Jack, went into the navy and fought in the American War of Independence. On Jack's return home as an officer, father and son argued about journey times. Brown wrote to his daughter, 'I will give up the Sea to him, but the Land he had best leave to me.'[35] One daughter, Peggy, helped her father with his correspondence. She married in Fenstanton church after his death.

The marriage in 1773 of his other daughter, Bridget, to Henry Holland heralded a new development in Brown's working pattern. Brown and Holland co-operated on Claremont, bought in 1769 by Robert, Lord Clive, from the widowed Duchess of Newcastle. Clive had accumulated a fortune as a major-general in the British East India company and spent over £30,000 on building the Palladian house, designed by Brown and built by Holland, and on Brown's alterations to pleasure grounds previously worked on by Vanbrugh, Bridgeman and Kent. Sloping lawns were separated by a ha-ha from farmland turned into parkland and offering views towards Windsor Castle and St Paul's Cathedral. Clive committed suicide in 1774 without spending a night at Claremont.

The partnership between Brown and Holland seems to have been a happy one, with Holland eulogising his father-in-law's abilities as an architect after his death:

> No man that I ever met with understood so well what was necessary for the habitation of all ranks and degrees of society; no one disposed his offices so well, set his building on such good levels, designed such good rooms, or so well provided for the approach of every part of a place he was concerned in.[36]

The last project on which Brown and Holland worked was Berrington Hall, the home of a Tory, Thomas Harley, in Herefordshire. Holland designed the house, a miniature version of Claremont, in the local red sandstone, on a spot predetermined by Brown, who landscaped the park, creating a fourteen-acre lake with a wooded island. Berringon was emphatically a park to be farmed so that the beauty of the scenery did not require otherwise unjustifiable maintenance. Today, it remains a rustic scene: sheep graze just across the ha-ha from the lawn, the lake half-hidden by trees, and breaks in the shelter belts offer glimpses of the Brecon Beacons and the Black Mountains. Berrington is also a reminder that the former kitchen gardener didn't just design parkland: he created an egg-shaped redbrick-walled kitchen garden with internal walls for glasshousing.

***

Name a stately home and Brown probably worked there: Alnwick, Harewood and Holkham are just a few not yet mentioned. But not everyone thought as well of Brown as did Pitt, Bute and son-in-law Holland. His detractors at the time and since have believed that Brown laid waste to the English landscape and felled more trees than he planted. Timothy Mowl, William Kent's biographer, has suggested that 'Capability Brown ... may have destroyed more fine Arcadian gardens than he ever laid out himself in his own distinctive style of vacant elegance'.[37] In his own time, a spat brewed up in the early 1770s with a rival, William Chambers, Princess Augusta's favourite architect. Chambers, disappointed in Brown being preferred to work on the king's Richmond Gardens, published a spiteful veiled attack on him in 1772 in his *Dissertation on Oriental Gardening*:

> In England ... a new manner is universally adopted, in which no appearance of art is tolerated, our gardens differ very little from common fields, so closely is vulgar nature copied in most of them; there is generally so little variety, and so much want of judgment, in the choice of the objects, such a poverty of imagination in the contrivance, and of art in the arrangement, that these compositions rather appear the offspring of chance than design; and a stranger is often at a loss to know whether he be walking in a common meadow, or in a pleasure ground, made and kept at a very considerable expence: he finds ... little to flatter the senses, and less to touch the passions, or gratify the understanding.[38]

A contemporary plan of Richmond and Kew suggests that the king was well advised to choose Brown, rather than Chambers. Brown knocked down Kent's odd buildings and opened up the views across the Thames towards Syon House (where he also worked) and carved what is now the Rhododendron Dell out of the Thames flood plain in 1773. The sinuous lines and broad vistas of Brown's creation are still visible today. By comparison, Chambers' plans for Augusta's Kew on the other side of Love Lane (the two halves were not united until 1802) look less free-flowing and his wooden buildings were derided by Walpole. Walpole was among those who leapt to Brown's defence, saying that Chambers' paper had been 'written in wild revenge against Brown: the only surprising consequence is, that it is laughed at, and it is not likely to be adopted ... for nothing is so tempting to fools, as advice to deprave taste'.[39]

Brown, jibed at by Chambers for having been a kitchen gardener, chose to ignore the attack, although Chambers had opened up a debate about the Picturesque which reignited twenty years later when Humphry Repton was seeking to adopt Brown's mantle. 'Taste', as referred to by Walpole, had a particular meaning in the eighteenth century, being seen as a matter of moral imperative, rather than merely aesthetic opinion. The word is used again by Thomas Whateley in his 1770 *Observations on Modern Gardening*, in which he implicitly praises Brown's achievements:

> Gardening, in the perfection to which it has been lately brought in England, is entitled to a place of considerable rank among the liberal arts. It is as superior to landskip painting, as a reality to a representation: it is an exertion of fancy; a subject for taste; and being released now from the restraints of regularity, and enlarged beyond the purposes of domestic convenience, the most beautiful, the most simple, the most noble scenes of nature are all within its province.[40]

Lancelot Brown died at the Mayfair home of his daughter, Bridget Holland, on 6 February 1783, and was buried in Fenstanton parish church. His wife was buried with him three and a half years later, only then paying her first visit to Fenstanton. Brown was not knighted, as he would have been today, nor was any national memorial raised to the man who had transformed the English landscape. His influence became international after his death: what was known as *le jardin anglais* shaped gardens in France, Russia, and America. His gardens are his memorial, along with a simple tree on Hilton Green, near Fenstanton, 'planted in memory of Lancelot "Capability" Brown 1716–83, Lord of this Manor, Who planted a million others'.

CHAPTER 9

Humphry Repton (1752–1818)

Jane Austen makes surprisingly few references to contemporary events and personalities. One exception, however, is to the landscape gardener Humphry Repton, whose fashionable expertise is noted in *Mansfield Park*, published in 1814. Mr Rushworth, luckless suitor of Miss Bertram, has been much taken with Repton's work on a visit to a friend. 'Smith's place is the admiration of all the country; and it was a mere nothing before Repton took it in hand.' We hear that 'his terms are five guineas a day', although that would be of no account to the wealthy Mr Rushworth, who determines, 'I shall have Repton.'[1] Austen's mention is barbed, of course, for she sees the goofy Rushworth as having more money than sense, and dazzled by an over-valued brand.

The sharp-tongued Austen is perhaps too harsh on Repton. By 1814, he was a sick man, with his business in recession because of war with France, concomitant taxes and agricultural depression. He saw himself as successor to William Kent and 'Capability' Brown, but he was different from both, in his style and approach. As one garden historian has written, 'if Kent had seen that all nature was a garden, Repton created a garden from that nature, and put a fence round it'.[2]

When Brown died in 1783, he had many imitators, but no single landscape designer was of sufficient stature to fill his shoes. Within five years, however, Repton, after a chequered career, decided that he would take up landscape design and aspire to Brown's pre-eminence. 'Now at the age of thirty six years I commence a new career,' wrote Repton in his memoirs, 'and after a temporary rest and half seclusion from the world, I boldly venture forth once more, and with renewed energy and hope push off my little bark into a sea unknown.'[3]

He turned himself into a suave professional, who always described himself as a 'landscape gardener'. He did more in the way of consulting and was concerned less with the contracting side than Brown. Over thirty years, he was employed by country squires, merchants and professionals

Humphry Repton with his theodolite on his business card.

as well as aristocracy.[4] Unlike Kent and Brown, and to his chagrin, he never designed for the royal family, his plans for the Prince of Wales's Brighton Pavilion being rebuffed in favour of those by John Nash.

Handing over the contractual side meant that Repton often found that his orders were not carried out or were ignored altogether, as he complained in his *Observations on the Theory and Practice of Landscape Gardening*, published in 1803. His designs, he wrote, had often been compromised by 'the death of the proprietors, the change of property, the difference of opinions ... the frequent opposition I have experienced from gardeners, bailiffs and land stewards, who either wilfully mar my plans, or ignorantly mistake my instructions'.[5]

Repton was a man of energy and with a talent, like his predecessor, for seeing the potential in any landscape. This combination made him perhaps the last figure to have such complete hegemony over English landscape design.

* * *

Humphry Repton was born in Bury St Edmund's in April 1752, the son of an excise officer, John Repton. The first of our gardeners from a middle-class professional background, he was never employed as an estate gardener or nurseryman. He received a classical education at Norwich Grammar School, where he befriended James Edward Smith, the future botanist and founder of the Linnaean Society. John Repton, who became a merchant, intended his son for the same career and sent him to Holland to learn the language of commerce. Humphry lived with the family of an international banker, Zachary Hope. In the Hopes' Rotterdam and Amsterdam homes, Repton enjoyed an affluent, sophisticated lifestyle, and was introduced to the Prince of Orange. He learnt the flute, and became interested in the theatre and literature, and in drawing and painting.[6] His memories of Dutch gardens would influence his later gardening style: recalled in his memoirs is 'a parterre ... in which the design traced on the ground was like a pattern for working muslin on embroidery'.[7]

In 1768, Repton returned to Norwich to work in a textile house, where he saw himself as a man about town. Unlike Brown, Repton wrote extensively, so we can build up a picture of him from his own account. 'In those days of my puppy-age every article of my dress was assiduously studied ... I recall to mind the white coat lined with blue satin, and trimmed with silver fringe, in which I was supposed to captivate all hearts on one occasion.'[8]

He captivated one heart at least, that of Mary Clarke, whom he married in May 1773. The couple had sixteen children, of whom seven survived infancy. Two became architects, and later assisted their father. Another son studied for the church at Magdalen College, Oxford. On his marriage, Repton was set up in business by his father, but he didn't flourish. When his parents both died in 1778, he used their legacy and what he could retrieve from his business venture to buy a seventeenth-century brick manor house, Old Hall, near Aylsham, where he settled down as a country gentleman.

For the next five years, Repton applied himself to farming, gardening, writing and sketching. He moved among the county set, given access to the library of William Wyndham, the owner of Felbrigg Hall. He learned about arboreal management from naturalist Robert Marsham, and encountered Sir Joseph Banks, director of the royal gardens at Kew.

Repton scarcely had the means to finance such a high-stepping lifestyle. He worked for Wyndham as his parliamentary agent in two elections and became Wyndham's private secretary when the latter was sent to Ireland as chief secretary to the lord lieutenant. As Wyndham resigned almost immediately, Repton's civil service career was short-lived. He wrote with good-natured elan to his wife:

> I have learned to love my own home; I have gained some knowledge of the world; some of public business, and some of hopeless expectancies; I have made some valuable acquaintances; I have formed some connections with the great; I have seen a fine country, in passing through Wales, and have made some sketches; I have lost very little money; I shall have got the brogue; and you will have got a cabinet gown. So ends my Irish expedition.[9]

Although Repton had 'lost very little money', he hadn't made any, and had to accept that his time as a country gentleman was drawing to a close.

He sold Old Hall in October 1783 and bought a cottage at Hare Street in Essex, which became his permanent home.

Repton spent the next four years or so without regular employment, although he invested both money and energy in a scheme to reform the mail coach system, dreamt up by a Bath businessman, John Palmer. The scheme's success indirectly benefited Repton when he later journeyed around the country as a landscape gardener. But in the short term, he gained nothing while Palmer was rewarded with government office and a pension.[10]

It was typical of the vicissitudes that constantly befell Repton, most borne with ironic good humour. He tried his hand at becoming an art critic and a playwright with an engaging nonchalance. Then, after a sleepless night, he came up with the idea of landscape gardening, writing within a few months that 'my ambition leads me to hope that I may stand at the head of my profession'.[11]

His words are extraordinarily confident, given that his new career was based solely on his habit of sketching landscapes, and knowledge of trees acquired from Wyndham's Norfolk friend, Marsham. But Repton's confidence was well placed, and within a few years, he established himself as a landscape gardener.

Repton was launching himself in an age of accelerating change, with Britain a very different country from that in which Brown had begun designing half a century earlier. The Industrial Revolution was under way, canals were being built and road transport was being transformed. These developments contributed to the growth of Manchester and Birmingham, and to the metamorphosis of London into a world metropolis at the centre of a world trading empire.

Parliamentary enclosures led to the disappearance of common land and even entire villages, with farm labourers moving into factory work. Land usage was changing but it continued to have a symbolic role: the first thing the successful industrialist Josiah Wedgwood did was to buy himself a country estate. As cultural geographer Stephen Daniels has written, 'landscape was ... central to the sensibility of polite society in later Georgian England; it was a cultural arena for its most pressing concerns, a field of inquiry, debate and conflict.'[12] The debate had become more nuanced than when Lord Cobham was creating a philosophical canvas or scoring party political points at Stowe against other Whig factions. There were different arguments: men who had made their fortunes in mills, factories or through overseas trade did not want the naturalism of a Brown semi-agricultural landscape, which suggested that they might need to farm their land. They wanted gardens qua gardens, and this is what Repton gave them. Setting out to emulate Brown, he eventually created a very different aesthetic, one which emphasised gardens rather than landscape, in response to his clientele's requirements. Land continued to matter, and Repton, with his drawing technique influenced by contemporary artists such as Thomas Rowlandson, William Gilpin and Thomas Gainsborough, chose an opportune moment to venture forth.

The shift in land ownership can be seen by comparing Brown's and Repton's first major clients. After working for Lord Cobham, Brown would be employed by another Whig peer, the Earl of Coventry. Repton, on the other hand, began the first of his 400 or so commissions for a wealthy merchant, Jeremiah Ives, at Catton Hall near Norwich. Brown never needed to advertise; Repton's potential clients being so much more diverse, he sent out mail shots to friends and friends of friends to rustle up business:

> H. REPTON having for many years (merely as an amusement) studied the picturesque effect resulting from the art of LAYING OUT GROUNDS, has lately been advised by many respectable friends (to whom he has occasionally given sketches for the improvement of their own places) to enlarge his plan, and pursue professionally his skill in LANDSCAPE GARDENING.[13]

Brown, even if short of work, is unlikely ever to have written in such terms. Repton wished to associate himself socially with the patrons for whom he hoped to work: the indication that he, too, was a member of the leisured classes implied that he was taking up the profession because of his talents rather than because of any pressing need for money. The former might have been true, the latter was not, as Repton was banking on making a financial success of this latest venture after several failures. He became a moderately wealthy man, educating his children, as did Brown, with his clients' sons. But he never amassed a fortune, nor did he enjoy Brown's easy familiarity with political leaders.

One imagines Brown dining with his clients, pointing out politely but firmly changes to be made to the implementation of a project, and moving quickly on. The appeal of his new profession initially for Repton was that he might, too, be wined and dined by the aristocracy and, sharing their accomplishments from his years as a country gentleman, be treated as an equal. He calculated in his *Memoirs* that out of the 365 dinners a man may eat in a year, he 'partook of 150 served on plate with every luxury, and 100 were such as no gentleman could wish better'. Hear him, too, on Harewood in Yorkshire, where he was asked to make alterations to grounds that Brown had worked on thirty years earlier: 'The magnificence of this palace is ... well known, but of its comforts as an English Home those only can speak who like myself have been permitted to share them.'[14] He was wrong if he thought himself universally welcome: the travel writer Viscount Torrington wrote how he had intended to ride out, 'but Mr Repton – the now noted landscape gardener – came in and delay'd me half an hour. He is a gentleman I have long known and of so many words that he is not easily shaken off.'[15] Other aristocrats were even more outspoken: the Duke of Bedford made it clear to Repton that he wasn't invited to Woburn as a guest, nor was he required to discuss anything other than the garden. 'Freely give me your opinion, as to what alterations or improvements suggest themselves to your judgement, leaving the execution of them to my own direction.'[16] Bedford's father, negotiator of the Treaty of Paris after the Seven Years War, would hardly have addressed Brown in such terms.

Repton may have wanted to play the courtier like, say, William Kent, and have affected in his original publicity material to be a talented amateur, but he represented the professionalisation of landscape gardening, started by Brown and continued by John Claudius Loudon in the nineteenth century. This reflected the same social upheaval which turned merchants and industrialists into landowners: with an expertise themselves, they expected it in those whom they employed. Repton recognised this in the first chapter of his *Observations on the Theory and Practice of Landscape Gardening* (1803):

> The Theory and practice of Landscape Gardening have seldom fallen under the consideration of the same author; because those who have delivered their opinions in writing on this art have had little practical experience, and few of its professors have been able to deduce their rules from theoretical principles.

It was because Repton was able to combine theory with practice that he was successful: 'I made the attempt; and with the counsels and advice of men of science, and the countenance of some of the first characters in the kingdom, a very large portion of its scenery has been committed to my care for improvement.'[17]

***

Repton may never achieved the lofty heights, commercially or socially, of his illustrious predecessor, but commissions flooded in, and he made a net profit of £411 2*s* 8*d* in 1790.[18] He soon had as much work as he could handle thanks to a facility he describes in his *Memoirs*:

> In every place I was consulted I found that I was gifted with a peculiar faculty for seeing almost immediately the way in which it might be improved. I only wanted the means of making my ideas equally visible or intelligible to others. This lead to my delivering reports in writing accompanied by maps and such sketches that at once showed the present and proposed portraits of the various scenes capable of improvement.[19]

The 'means' Repton used were his famous 'Red Books'. These books, bound either in the red morocco which gave them their name or in brown calf, were mostly about eight and a half by eleven and a half inches in size. Larger, folio versions were produced for the most prestigious of his potential commissions, such as the Prince of Wales's Brighton Pavilion, Magdalen College, Longleat, Uppark, Sheringham and Woburn; for Welbeck Abbey, he created three Red Books. His first was presented to Lady Salusbury (*sic*) for Brandsbury in Middlesex on 13 March 1789 at the cost of ten guineas; the second was a gift to the wife of Thomas Coke of Holkham and was delivered in October the same year. It has been estimated that he completed between 200 and 220 of these Red Books in the course of his career, with 123 of them now traced.[20]

The books followed a similar pattern. The inside back cover would be Repton's business card, 500 of which were first engraved by Thomas Medland in August 1788, with a further 500 ordered the following April. Repton is shown, theodolite in hand, surveying an Augustan scene, with a ruined building on a hill above a smooth surfaced lake, while men labour at moving earth on its banks. Behind Repton stands his foppish assistant, holding a tall, wand-like pole, and glancing out at the onlooker rather than concentrating on helping his master.

The Red Books featured watercolour sketches, each with a hinged overlay, to show clients the scene before and after Repton's intended improvements. The scenes were full of people to stress the human element, and were accompanied usually by a fulsome dedication and a detailed description of what Repton had in mind. These exquisite volumes were splendid advertisements for Repton's practice, and works of art in their own right. Therein lay a drawback: they were often proudly displayed by clients who had no intention of carrying out such expensive alterations. Moreover, so detailed were Repton's explanations that some clients took the work in hand themselves.

Repton established his working patterns as he felt his way into his new career, and learnt about draining, planting and earth-moving from his third commission, Brandsbury. He walked the ground to be improved, often with the client, then surveyed the site himself, after which he provided sketches of his intentions. These were sometimes based on existing estate maps and were accompanied by expansive text which referred to conversations held with the client.

If commissioned, Repton returned later to mark and stake out the work, although there were often long gaps between his visits as his practice grew. At the height of his career, Repton claimed to travel over 500 miles every month, and thought himself 'very fortunate when I was able to spend some of those days in my own home with the society of my happy family'.[21] He travelled by stagecoach, post-chaise, hackney carriage and his clients' coaches, and consulted on estates in forty-six counties, from Cornwall to Essex via the Isle of Wight, South Wales to Anglesey, Liverpool to North Yorkshire and across to north Norfolk.[22]

Jane Austen says Repton's terms were five guineas a day. In fact, he started out at three guineas a day, plus expenses, but was paid an annual salary of 100 guineas by the Dukes of Bedford and Portland on projects that lasted for several years. The outbreak of war with France in 1793 hampered Repton's career, with higher taxation hitting not only his pocket but those of his clients. The more relaxed eighteenth-century *noblesse oblige* world of the gentleman amateur was vanishing and forcing Repton to become more businesslike, never his strongest suit. But by 1807, he was laying down a clear structure of charges: ten guineas for a first visit within one stage of London; fifty guineas for up to 100 miles and seventy guineas over 140 miles.[23] Sentimentally, however, he only charged Norfolk clients twenty-five guineas for a 100-mile visit.[24]

Repton followed Kent and Brown to several estates, starting with Holkham in Norfolk, and he, too, was often involved with architectural issues. He also worked for William Pitt the Younger at his estate at Holwood in Kent. If Repton didn't become as close to the younger as Brown had been to the elder, he knew him well enough to ask him to find a position for his own son, Humphry, in the civil service when the young man gave up his first idea of landscape gardening. Harewood, Longleat, and Corsham were all Brownian landscapes to which Repton was called, and at Welbeck Abbey in Nottinghamshire he was consulted three times: in 1789 and 1793 by the Duke of Portland, and again in 1803 by his son, Lord Titchfield. Repton was more reluctant than Brown to embark on massive earthworks, but Welbeck was an exception. The house, which stood in a slight depression, was caused to stand proud by Repton's raising the bank around it to conceal the basement and making the main entrance a storey higher.

In 1790, he went to Wentworth Woodhouse, a massive three-acre palace belonging to the Whig peer Lord Fitzwilliam. We know from Repton at first-hand what he intended and why. 'When I first consulted respecting Wentworth House, the lawn behind it appeared circumscribed, and the large trees which surrounded that lawn appeared depressed by four tall obelisks: these have since been removed, the stately trees have assumed their true magnitude, and the effect of confinement is done away.' Another commission took him to Hurlingham, now an exclusive sports club on the Thames at Putney.

> The lawn in front of the house was necessarily contracted by the vicinity of the river, yet being too large to be kept under the scythe and roller, and too small to be fed by a flock of sheep, I recommended the introduction of Alderney cows only; and the effect is that of giving imaginary extent to the place, which is thus measured below a true standard; because if distance will make a large animal appear small, so the distance will be apparently extended by the smallness of the animal.[25]

This sounds a Brownian solution, and initially Repton followed in the master's footsteps, even if his style was always prettier and more structured round the house. At Wentworth Woodhouse, he planted the hill with trees and turned ponds into a lake in the Brown tradition; but he also made a terrace garden. As the peopled landscapes of his Red Books show, Repton's landscapes were sociable, with views of cottages with smoking chimneys, and he sought to integrate park and village. At Tatton, he rebuilt a line of cottages at the entrance to the park, rather than the approach being through a guarded lodge.

Repton's early reverence for Brown had repercussions for his career when an unpleasant quarrel broke out in 1794 about the Picturesque. This was presaged by Chambers' attack on Brown two decades earlier, when he wrote that 'our gardens differ very little from common fields, so closely is vulgar nature copied in most of them'.[26]

Naturalism was already under attack when Repton attempted to succeed Brown. But the tension was cranked up by an onslaught on Repton's work by two Herefordshire landowners, Sir Uvedale Price, and Richard Payne Knight, whom Repton had met fifteen years earlier at William Wyndham's in Norfolk. The debate returned to that vexed eighteenth-century question of taste: Price, Knight, and, before them, the Reverend William Gilpin, argued that Brown's naturalistic landscapes were a breach of taste. 'How flat, and insipid is often the garden scene,' Gilpin had written, 'how puerile, how absurd! The banks of the river, how smooth and parallel! The lawn and its boundaries, how unlike nature!'[27]

The publication in 1794 of Price's *Essay on the Picturesque* and Payne Knight's poem *The Landscape* took the attack on Brown to Repton, pens sharpened by the fact that Repton was carrying out commissions in the landowners' home territory of Herefordshire. They criticised Repton for schemes 'designed and executed exactly after Mr Brown's receipt, without any attention to the natural or artificial character of a place'.[28] Price and Payne Knight advocated a new aesthetic, a more rugged Picturesque style, such as that evoked by Wordsworth's *Lines written a few miles above Tintern Abbey*, published just four years later: 'Once again/Do I behold these steep and lofty cliffs/Which on a wild secluded scene impress/Thoughts of a more deep seclusion.'[29]

Political events had a role in this dispute. By the 1790s, war with revolutionary France compromised the Grand Tour, leading to the birth of outdoors home tourism with Gilpin's travels in the Wye Valley. The landscape was invested with a fresh set of political meanings, part of an evolving sense of Britishness. These Picturesque theorists rejected the self-consciousness of earlier eighteenth-century design and advocated instead the rugged, irregular and decaying, with dilapidated country villages as part of a natural wild beauty.[30]

Repton, described by Price as 'a coxcomb', was surprised by the virulence of the attack, and, being a writer, fought back in print, unlike Brown who merely ignored Chambers. He postponed the publication of his *Sketches and Hints on Landscape Gardening* in order to respond to Price and Payne Knight. When it was published the following year, Repton had added an Appendix and a lengthy letter he had sent to Price, in which he thanked Price and Knight for accounting him 'an exception to the tasteless herd of Mr Brown's followers'. He added that 'it is difficult to define GOOD TASTE (Repton's capitals) in any of the polite arts; and ... I am sorry to observe that it is seldom allowed in a rival'. He believed that '*Beauty*, and not "*picturesqueness*," is the chief object of modern improvement ... [and] ... the unprejudiced eye will discover innumerable beauties in the works of that great self-taught master (Brown)'.

Price and Payne Knight were influential commentators, with the potential to harm Repton's business, but he firmly set out his stall. His introduction echoes Thomas Whately in saying that 'Gardening, in its more confined sense of *Horticulture*, has been likewise brought to the greatest perfection in this country, I have adopted the term *Landscape Gardening*, as most proper, because the art can only be advanced and perfected by the united powers of the *landscape painter* and the *practical gardener*.'[31] *Sketches and Hints* is his manifesto, in which he makes clear that he was motivated less by theory and more by the practical and social considerations of his clients. And they were numerous: Red Books for almost sixty estates are listed here.

***

Although Repton was supported by the dying Horace Walpole, the Picturesque and indeed the *zeitgeist* caused him to adapt his style, which became more ornamental and flowery. This can be seen from his later Red Books and designs, for example for Sir William Stanley's Hooton. That included viewing balconies, a pergola overrun with climbers and a formal wall decorated with urns.[32] Merchants and lawyers, with small estates, wanted gardens in which to socialise and enjoy well-earned leisure. Repton had an acute ear, his eagerness to please an advantage. He had strong views on certain aspects, however, using rounded deciduous trees as a foil around irregularly shaped buildings, and 'spiry-topped trees' (his words) as a contrast to classical buildings. 'Trees of a conic shape,' he wrote, 'mixed with Gothic buildings displease from their affinity with the prevalent lines of the architecture.'[33]

Repton's Gardenesque style (a term coined in the 1830s by John Claudius Loudon) developed out of his growing sympathy for the Picturesque advocated by Gilpin, Price and Payne Knight. This doesn't mean he sold out: landscape historian John Dixon Hunt believes Repton was an original contributor to the development of English landscape gardening, 'in both its theory and its practice'.[34] What he produced increasingly were gardens rather than landscapes, demonstrating his expanding plant knowledge: in 1815, for example, he presented a paper to the Linnaean Society on ivy.

But his career was never plain sailing. He struck up a partnership with architect John Nash, and they worked together on Luscombe Castle in Devon and on Corsham Court in Wiltshire. But the relationship foundered when Nash failed to pay Repton his agreed percentage. Repton's one potential royal commission, Brighton Pavilion, went to Nash instead, despite the wonderfully quirky and Gardenesque plans that Repton had drawn up for the building in a particularly opulent Red Book.

Repton subsequently worked with his son, John, most notably on Woburn for the Duke of Bedford, where his proposals were carried out in full, after some sharp exchanges between duke and consultant. He and John designed and built the early Tudor-style lodge or cottage at Woburn Sands. Bedford also employed Repton to lay out Russell Square in London, where he used hedges of hornbeam and privet around the perimeter, screening a broad gravel walk. Within were lime trees over paths winding round grass and beds of flowers and shrubs.[35]

In November 1811, as he escorted two of his daughters home from a ball, their coach struck compacted snow. Repton's spine was injured: he was initially paralysed, and was confined increasingly to a wheelchair, with his heart badly affected by the shock. He retained his sense of humour, sending his daughters cartoons of himself, wheelchair-bound, but with arms and legs waving, on a seaside trip. He also began work on Sheringham Hall in Norfolk, which he regarded as his masterpiece, although it wasn't finished in his lifetime.

Unlike his royal gardener predecessors Wise, Kent and Brown, Repton was never painted in oils. We have to rely on his business card, a couple of engravings and cameos used in his work, and miniatures commissioned as frontispieces. These show him with white hair receding from a high-domed forehead, a beaky nose, a smart jacket and white stock, very much the business professional. He could be a solicitor or merchant were it not for the fact that he is painting a watercolour of trees – perhaps a sketch for one of his Red Books.

Central to his life was his roadside home at Hare Street in Essex. The house was covered with treillage, and was where 'many friendly people met ... which was greatly encreased by my proposal that about half a dozen families should join in a monthly meeting at the village Inn, in a room that was large enough to contain 20 couple of dancers, and two card tables for those who did not dance'.[36] Coming full circle, this description sounds like something straight out of Jane Austen.

On 24 March, 1818, he collapsed and died on the way to breakfast. He was buried in Aylsham church, to which his devoted wife followed him within a few months. In his *Memoirs*, Repton saw his life as a journey. There were moments of bitterness, such as when he was brushed off by the Prince of Wales to be 'superseded by one who alas is my friend no more', but he is generally sanguine, especially as he believes that 'as landscape gardener I have never been superseded by a more successful rival'. At the end, he wrote: 'My ship of life is sinking, and it is time to quit it; these pages will show how actively I have performed the voyage ... I have touched at every port, and where have we met with happiness unalloyed? or, where found a man not disappointed? Nowhere! Yet still I must repeat, that there is more of good than evil.'[37]

PART IV

THE INDUSTRIAL AGE

CHAPTER 10

John Claudius Loudon (1783–1843)

In March 1814, John Claudius Loudon, the horticultural polymath, was abandoned by his coachmen in a snowdrift between St Petersburg and Moscow. The men took the horses, promising to return with fresh ones in the morning, and assuring him he would be safe from wolves if he kept the carriage windows shut. Snow blew in through the curtains, and the wolves howled all night. Loudon doubted whether, if the men returned, they would find the carriage. But they did, and Loudon passed the rest of the journey 'without any difficulty'. 'Few men were better fitted by nature

John Claudius Loudon.

for bearing the horrors of such a night than Mr Loudon, from his natural calmness and patient endurance of difficulties,' wrote his devoted wife, Jane, in her account of his life.[1]

Loudon was not faint-hearted: he later weaned himself off addiction to laudanum, taken for excruciating rheumatic pain, and had to be forcefully prevented from returning to work the afternoon his right arm was amputated. It was typical that he saw a brief lull in the Napoleonic Wars as the moment for a European gardens tour. His eighteen-month journey, however, furnished him with an understanding of garden design across a broad sweep of European countries, informing his magisterial *Encyclopaedia of Gardening*.

Loudon was born in the eighteenth century but his work and vision anticipated the Victorian age. On his 1814 trip, Loudon experienced first-hand the effects of the twenty-year war which had blighted Repton's landscaping career. Repton's younger contemporary had already clashed with the older designer in his early writings, for Loudon had a very different sensibility, a down-to-earth approach to horticulture, which was reinforced by friendship with the utilitarian philosopher Jeremy Bentham. Loudon gardened when the Industrial Revolution was well under way, its prophets men such as the china magnate Josiah Wedgwood, the scientist Joseph Priestley, the industrialist Matthew Boulton, and the engineer James Watt. For his part, Loudon stressed the importance of a scientific, systematic approach to botany, of professional education, and of new horticultural technology.

In Loudon's books and his powerful periodical, *The Gardener's Magazine*, he wrote about design and plantsmanship, described the uses of thousands of new imported plants, and discussed vegetable and fruit growing, as well as the design and heating of greenhouses. Loudon invented the term 'Gardenesque' which defined Repton's later work and indeed the style of gardening for sixty years of the nineteenth century. The focus was no longer on setting a house in a naturalistic landscape, with agricultural land used partly decoratively. Instead, gardeners and designers were bringing gardens up to the house, and planting borders and beds, in which individual plants were shown off to their best advantage. The landscape movement was over.[2]

As the aristocracy felt the pinch after long years of war and agricultural depression, it was professional businessmen, profiting from defence contracts and trade, who had the wealth to spend on gardens. A greater range of plants than ever before was affordable, and the invention of equipment such as lawnmowers meant gardening became the pastime of a broader cross-section of British society, not just that of the privileged few. Loudon may have designed his first garden for the Earl of Mansfield at Scone Palace in 1803, but it was for the growing middle class that he wrote some four million words, across dozens of publications. An austere, somewhat humourless man, Loudon was a visionary, who, with his wife, Jane, exercised an unparalleled influence on nineteenth-century amateur gardening.

* * *

John Claudius Loudon was born in April 1782 at Cambuslang in Lanarkshire, the eldest son of William Loudon, a Lothian farmer, and his wife, Agnes. The boy demonstrated an early interest in planning walks and flowerbeds, and, when an uncle sent a jar of tamarinds from the West Indies, John was happy to exchange his share of the fruit for all the seeds.[3] William Loudon, ambitious for his son, sent him to school in Edinburgh, where the boy showed aptitude for drawing. Apprenticed to Edinburgh nurserymen, John acquired knowledge of plants, landscape gardening and the management of hothouses, while taking classes in botany and agriculture given by Dr Andrew Coventry at the University of Edinburgh.

Loudon kept a journal from his early teens, writing it for practice in French, and learning Latin, Italian and German as well. In one diary entry quoted by his wife, he mourned: 'I am now 20 years of age, and perhaps a third of my life has passed away, and yet what have I done to benefit my fellow men?'[4] That year, Loudon arrived in London, with letters of introduction from Coventry. Through him, he encountered Sir Joseph Banks, president of the Royal Society and director of Kew Gardens, and Jeremy Bentham.

By late 1803, Loudon was already writing to *The Literary Journal* with his *Hints respecting the manner of laying out the grounds of the public squares in London to the utmost picturesque advantage*. He was struck by the gloomy appearance of most London squares, planted with dark evergreens, and advocated instead deciduous trees such as planes, which would cope better with city smoke. 'It is curious to observe how exactly his suggestions have been adopted,' recalled his wife, 'as these trees are now to be found in almost every square in London.'[5] If Jane is right, then Londoners have Loudon to thank for the ubiquitous plane in their streets.

Loudon's use of the word 'picturesque' in his comments in *The Literary Journal* allied him with the Picturesque movement, headed by Uvedale Price and Richard Payne Knight, and against Repton, whose star was fading. Loudon took up cudgels the following year, answering Repton's *Observations on the Theory and Practice of Landscape Gardening* with his first published treatise, *Observations on the Formation and Management of Useful and Ornamental Plantations, on the Theory and Practice of Landscape Gardening*. This was a bold move for someone with just a nursery apprenticeship and design work on a handful of gardens to his name. A second treatise followed in 1805, *On Several Improvements Recently Made in Hot-Houses*, based on plans he had made several years earlier; that is, at the tender age of eighteen or nineteen.[6] In 1806, a two-volume treatise *On Forming, Improving and Managing Country Residences* attacked Repton's only Scottish project, Valleyfield in Fife, and endorsed Price and Payne Knight's view of what Loudon termed 'landscape husbandry'.[7]

Loudon was no ordinary young man: in 1804, while making his way as a garden designer, he exhibited three landscapes at the Royal Academy. The following year, he was elected to the Society of Arts, and in 1806 became a fellow of the Linnaean Society. His early treatises helped establish Loudon, who saw his writing as inextricably bound up with his practical experience as a garden designer.[8]

Loudon also criticised the current state of English husbandry, and introduced, with his father's help, Scottish methods on a small estate at Pinner in Middlesex. This move from central London was partly triggered by a bout of rheumatic fever in 1806 which left him with an ankylosed knee and a permanently contracted right arm.

Within a year, Loudon was invited to manage an Oxfordshire estate, where in 1809 he established an innovative agricultural college. The results of his labours at Pinner and Oxfordshire were embodied in *Designs for Laying out Farms and Farm-Buildings, in the Scotch Style*, published in 1811. A year later, his *Hints on the Formation of Gardens and Pleasure Grounds* provided patterns to be carried out by nurserymen, builders, gardeners or owners themselves on estates from one to a hundred acres.[9] Loudon continued meanwhile to design gardens in England, Wales and Ireland, amassing through this work, the sale of his agricultural college, and his writing a fortune of £15,000 before he was thirty.

With money in the bank, Loudon set off for Europe. He was impressed by Sweden, but was 'too impatient to visit the theatre of war to stay long' there, moving on instead to Germany, Latvia and Russia. In East Prussia, he found 'every where traces of war: skeletons of horses lay bleaching in the fields, the roads broken up, and the country houses in ruin'. He encountered the aftermath of Napoleon's disastrous retreat from Moscow, and in St Petersburg he was arrested as a spy 'while making a drawing of a picturesque old fort'.[10] He arrived in a Moscow still black from the fires which sent Napoleon packing.

Loudon met visiting eminent scientists in Moscow, Berlin and Potsdam, and was elected member of several learned societies. He drew 'views of nearly all the palaces and large rural residences in the countries through which he passed; and he visited all the principal gardens, frequently going two or three days' journey out of his route, if he heard of any garden that he thought worth seeing,' recorded Jane, who experienced first-hand Loudon's relentless itineraries on journeys around England and Scotland.[11] He took a dim view of Russian gardens and gardeners and considered that Gregory Potemkin's English former gardener, a disciple of 'Capability' Brown, had been corrupted. 'Even the moral sense of Englishmen, who settle in Russia, becomes in time contaminated by the baleful influence of Russian manners.'[12]

Loudon docked at Yarmouth in September 1814, intellectually enriched by his travels, if not financially by his bankers, who had speculated unsuccessfully on his behalf. His fruitless attempts to recover his losses affected his perennially precarious health. Undiminished, however, was his mental energy. He wrote papers and carried out experiments on the construction of hothouses, devising a glazing bar in wrought iron that could be made in curvilinear sections. Loudon's designs were patented by W. and D. Bailey of Holborn with whom he collaborated on building glasshouses. Loudon's name was not mentioned on the patent, and he didn't gain financially from his invention.[13]

Inspired by seeing so many different gardens on his travels in 1813/14, Loudon was obsessed with the idea of producing a gardening encyclopaedia. In 1819, he set off again, with letters of introduction from Sir Joseph Banks, to explore the gardens of France and Italy, despite looking so ill that a friend who saw him at Dover thought he should be in bed rather than embarking on a journey. 'Mr Loudon, however, was not easily deterred from any thing he had resolved upon,' stated Jane.[14] Loudon visited botanic gardens across Europe, sent orange trees from Genoa home to his Bayswater greenhouse, discovered new methods of grafting by Italian gardeners, and cossetted in a tin can a small vallisnèria plant from Venice. The plant survived a mule journey through the Simplon Pass, and stops in Switzerland and France. Loudon then left the wilting plant on the windowsill of his Paris bedroom: in the morning the can remained but the vallisnèria had vanished, stolen by sparrows, Loudon believed.

Returning home, Loudon spent three years on his *Encyclopaedia of Gardening*, which was published in 1822. Throughout, he suffered chronic pain from rheumatism in his right arm. His agony was intensified by a Brighton masseur, who, far from relieving Loudon's discomfort, broke the arm so close to the shoulder that it couldn't be set. The arm needed supporting in an iron case day and night, and, in 1825, after being broken a second time, it was amputated. As his left arm was also crippled by rheumatism, he was only able to write and draw using the third and little fingers of his left hand. He became addicted to laudanum, but after his amputation, gradually weaned himself off it by weakening his dosage day by day.

His *Encyclopaedia of Gardening* of over twelve hundred pages of small print was an immediate success. It ran through eight editions in twelve years and continued to be reprinted into the 1870s.[15] 'This book had an extraordinary sale, and fully established the literary fame of its author,' wrote Jane.[16] In his massive work, Loudon distilled the knowledge gleaned on his continental travels, providing a history of gardening styles, and also covering every aspect of practical gardening. Loudon, a one-man publishing industry, followed up the encyclopaedia's success with a stream of articles, plus further books, including *The Green-House Companion* (1824), *Encyclopaedia of Agriculture* (1825) and *Encyclopaedia of Plants* (1829). These books cemented Loudon's reputation as an authority on gardens and gardening.

The plant encyclopaedia was timely. Sir Joseph Banks, director of Kew, had seen both the decorative and the economic potential of plants, and used Kew as a home-based showcase for Britain's influence overseas. He sent out plant hunters to China, South Africa, the South Seas and Australia, while the intrepid David Douglas, an acquaintance of Loudon's, scoured North America for pines, including the Monterey pine (*Pinus radiata*) and his eponymous Douglas fir (*Pseudotsuga menziesii*).

Plant-hunting was a dangerous business: Francis Masson, a young gardener dispatched by Banks to South Africa, spent thirty-three years plant hunting for Kew, only to freeze to death in North America in 1805. Douglas's life was brought to a brutal end when he stumbled into an occupied bull pit in 1834 in Hawaii. British gardeners, advised by Loudon, profited from these daring endeavours. The development of hothouse technology, together with improved methods of transport, particularly after the invention of the Wardian case in 1841, meant that more tender plants could be grown. Loudon computed that by about 1839 over 18,000 plants were being actively cultivated in England.[17]

In 1826, he launched *The Gardener's Magazine*. Four thousand copies were sold of the first issue, which cost five shillings and had wood engravings rather than colour plates to keep the price down. Initially a quarterly, it went bi-monthly in 1827 and monthly in 1831, with its cover price reduced to one shilling and tuppence by 1834.[18] 'This work was always Mr Loudon's favourite,' wrote Jane, 'and the organ through which he communicated his own thoughts and feelings to the public.'[19] Despite competition from other magazines, including Joseph Paxton's *Horticultural Register*, the magazine remained popular and only ceased publication with Loudon's death in 1843.

Loudon laid out his magazine's mission in the first issue: 'We had two grave objects in view: to disseminate new and important information on all topics connected with horticulture, and to raise the intellect and character of those engaged in this art.'[20] He was passionate about improving the education, welfare and housing of gardeners, many of whom were woefully underpaid. In the magazine's second issue, he pointed out that an illiterate bricklayer might earn five to six shillings a day, while 'a journeyman gardener who has gone through a course of practical geometry and land surveying, has a scientific knowledge of botany, and has spent his days and nights in reading books connected to his profession, gets no more than two shillings or two and sixpence a day'.[21] His words struck home: Jane wrote that she 'never saw Mr Loudon more pleased than when a highly respected gardener once told him he was living in a new and most comfortable cottage, which his master had built for him; a noble marquess, who said he would never have thought of it, but for the observations in Mr Loudon's *Gardener's Magazine*'.[22]

The magazine included book reviews and reports on garden visits and on the activities of garden societies and of nurserymen, as well as Loudon's own campaigning articles. The pugnacious editor attacked the management of the London Horticultural Society while in the same issue exhorting gardeners to improve themselves and putting forward plans for the improvement of Kensington Gardens, plans eventually in part adopted. He advocated garden libraries and a holistic plan for the development of London with residential and commercial areas being alternated with open spaces. Alongside were articles on new garden equipment and on manure. Loudon preferred to write most of the features, although the magazine did become a forum for gardening debate. There were a few quaint contributions, such as N. M. T.'s thoughts 'On the Evils of indiscriminately watering Plants in Pots immediately after being shifted', and a Musselburgh gardener's suggestions for the 'Best Mode of Washing Water Cresses and other Salads so as to free them from the Larvae of Insects and Worms'.[23]

Loudon also edited non-gardening titles, including the *Architectural Magazine*, in which he published an essay by the fifteen-year-old John Ruskin on the colour of the Rhine. In time, he would relinquish this other work to concentrate on *The Gardener's Magazine* and his books.

Technological and political developments drove the growth in publishing: the advent of steam-driven printing presses between 1810 and 1814 help cut the cost of producing books and magazines. The Reform Parliament of 1832 reduced tax on paper and stamp duty on newspapers, leading to the growth of newspaper and periodical publishing, which benefited Loudon but also his competitors, such as Joseph Paxton.[24]

***

Loudon's workload was that of several men, and all the more unforgiving once he was no longer able to write. In Jane Wells Webb he found the perfect amanuensis, her dedication to Loudon's causes as great his. They met in 1830 when he was forty-seven and she was twenty-two, the only daughter of a Birmingham businessman. After her mother died in 1819, Jane and her father travelled in Europe before returning to the countryside near Birmingham where she kept house for her father until his death in 1824. When winding up his affairs, Jane realised she had to support herself financially. She published *The Mummy*, a futuristic novel set in the twenty-second century, demonstrating the literary talents she later used in the service of horticulture. It enjoyed some success, and a review of it in the *Literary Gazette* caught Loudon's eye. 'As among other things I had mentioned a steam-plough,' wrote Jane without a trace of irony, 'it attracted his attention.' To a mutual friend, Loudon expressed his interest in meeting the author, whom he assumed to be a man, and they were introduced at a party in February 1830. 'It may be easily supposed that he was surprised to find the author of the book a woman; but I believe that from that evening he formed an attachment to me.'[25]

Loudon and Jane were married in September 1830. 'To make ourselves useful to our fellow-creatures is the only true path to happiness,' Jane had written in *The Mummy*, an aim shared by her moral, exacting husband. She looked up to him as her 'able and never-wearied instructor', and she appreciated his encouragement to write on her own account. Although sounding patronising to twenty-first-century ears, Loudon had relatively advanced views on women, believing that female skills, such as millinery and dressmaking, equipped women as well as any man to be a landscape gardener. It might, he suggested, in 1838 in his *Suburban Gardener and Villa Companion*, lead to improvements: 'If we can succeed in rendering every lady her own landscape-gardener, which we are confident we can do, we shall have great hopes of effecting a general reform in gardening taste.'[26]

The couple became not just husband and wife but a working partnership. Being his amanuensis was an education, and Jane herself played a role in involving women in gardening. She wrote reviews for *The Gardener's Magazine* and published a book, *Gardening for Ladies*, in 1841. In it, she covered suitable dress and tools, before getting down to the nitty-gritty of sowing, watering, grafting, making hot-beds, pruning and transplanting. There is charm in Jane's book, and indeed in her account of her husband's life, which you sense was entirely lacking in Loudon himself. It was probably Jane, rather than Loudon, who was responsible for their entertaining frequently – and counting Charles Dickens, William Thackeray and later Wilkie Collins among their friends.

The house to which Loudon brought his young bride in 1830 was one of a pair of semi-detached villas, with a domed conservatory entrance. These he had designed and built himself, arising at four in the morning to supervise the builders. The 'villa residences', as Loudon called them, were in Porchester Terrace, Bayswater, a semi-rural district near the canal, a mile from Tyburn (Marble Arch). Loudon's mother and two sisters lived in no. 3, while Jane and her husband moved into no. 5, both houses and gardens being a combined stage for Loudon's vision of domestic architecture and gardening. The houses were modern and well-appointed, with indoor lavatories, and the gardens, planted systematically, were both beautiful and productive. They were showcases of Loudon's work and beliefs, containing over 2,000 plant species.

Jane's account of Loudon's life indicates that she took personal satisfaction in supporting her husband in every way she could. Tireless himself, Loudon assumed his wife was, too. In 1832, Loudon began work on his *Encyclopaedia of Cottage, Farm, and Villa Architecture*, with the assistance of several draughtsmen, but just one amanuensis: Jane. 'The labour that attended this work was immense,' she wrote, 'and for several months he and I used to sit up the greater part of every night, never having more than four hours' sleep, and drinking strong coffee to keep ourselves awake.'[27] This was as Jane was attending lectures on botany and was pregnant with, and then mother to, the Loudons' only child, Agnes, born in October 1832.

The pace was inexorable. *Cottage Architecture* was another overnight success, inspiring Loudon to embark on his *Arboretum Britannicum*, published in 1838 (the same year as the *Suburban Gardener and Villa Companion*). Loudon decided that all the illustrations should be taken from nature. He employed seven artists, spending day after day outside with them from breakfast until dinner 'without taking the slightest refreshment, and generally without even sitting down,' wrote Jane. 'After dinner he resumed the literary part of the work, and continued writing, with me as his amanuensis, till two or three o'clock in the morning.'[28]

Their literary work was interspersed with garden visits around England and Loudon's native Scotland, all of which Loudon recorded in the minutest detail and used for articles in *The Gardener's Magazine*. Jane outlines some of these journeys in her account of her husband's life, and, despite her resolutely cheerful manner, it is obvious she often found them gruelling. Latterly, their trips were made easier by the advent of the railways: by 1837, over 700 miles of track had been laid.[29] Coaches, however, were still the only way of reaching many places. The Loudons arrived on one occasion to find no accommodation, and their horse 'very much tired', like Jane herself, one imagines. Loudon had the happy thought that only a few miles away was 'a fine collection of American plants' belonging to a Mr Bell. He 'determined to call there, to ask permission to see them. We did so; and when Mr Bell heard how we were situated, he most hospitably insisted on our staying at Woodhouselee all night, though we were wholly strangers to him.'[30] Both exhaustion and embarrassment can be read into this account.

The railways that speeded their journeys were altering travel patterns as well as the landscape of England and Scotland, with Midland industrial towns mushrooming. Land ownership was changing, too, with commercial leaders, industrialists and professional men moving out into the countryside and buying aristocratic estates. Those estates which remained in the hands of aristocracy were less well maintained than in the eighteenth century. All this Loudon saw and recorded in some 400,000 words in the pages of *The Gardener's Magazine*. He took no hostages, always willing to point out any defects. Take, for example, his account of Lord Cobham's great landscape garden on a visit in the summer of 1831:

> *STOWE* ... considering it as a work of art, appears to us the most perfect of residences; nature has done little or nothing; man a great deal, and time has improved his labours. The extensive pleasure-grounds have been greatly improved since we first saw them in 1806, by the present gardener, Mr Brown, who may justly be said to have received the mantle of his great namesake and predecessor in the same garden, our common father in landscape-gardening. We were sorry to learn that these gardens are not kept up as they used to be; the number of hands being yearly lessened. In new and rare plants, trees, and shrubs, the grounds are not keeping pace with the nurseries, as the furniture of the house, especially the grates of the fireplaces, is falling behind the best fashions of the day.[31]

'The grates of the fireplaces': was no detail too insignificant for the eagle-eyed Loudon? He was equally disparaging about garden design at many 'villa residences':

> The faults of the villa residences ... are ... those of the mansion residences; and there are other faults, both in the original laying out and in the keeping and management, which are also common to both. We shall pass over the ridiculous twisting and turning of walks, without real or apparent reason, which is so frequently met with, and rather dwell on the bad shapes of improper places of groups of shrubs and flowers on lawns. In several parts of this Magazine we have laid down the fundamental principles which ought to guide the placing of groups, viz. to arrange them so as to render them cooperating parts, with those which surround them, in the formation of one whole.

This passage gives a strong flavour of Loudon's writing, with his prodigious use of the royal 'we': 'Though we are not a professional architect, yet we pretend to as thorough a knowledge of the principles of architecture, as those of landscape-gardening.'[32] He was happy to ruffle feathers, and was less than complimentary about Paxton's work at Chatsworth, his strictures perhaps fuelled by the launch of Paxton's *Horticultural Register* in competition with *The Gardener's Magazine*. On a visit in 1831, Loudon noticed that in the kitchen garden, 'the box-edgings were ragged; and, in one part, a long bed of ornamental plants was introduced, and bordered by turf serrated on the edges ... Nothing of this sort ought, in our opinion, ever to be introduced in such a kitchen-garden as that at Chatsworth; we would as soon introduce a plot of cabbages in the newly formed parterre at the house. We regret that we did not find Mr Paxton at home; and this circumstance prevents us from saying more on the subject at present.' Loudon admired the Duke of Devonshire, however, who 'has expressly ordered the waterworks to be played for every one, without exception. This is acting in the true spirit of great wealth and enlightened liberality.'[33]

Loudon was lionised at dinners and receptions held in his and his wife's honour, particularly when touring Scotland. Sometimes, even Loudon was impressed, as on a visit to Mr and Mrs Sopwith in Newcastle. Jane, with another irony by-pass, tells us that 'Mr Loudon was highly gratified with the arrangement of Mr Sopwith's library, which we found a perfect temple of order.'[34]

There was no let-up in their day-to-day production of books and articles. He produced an inexpensive edition of Repton's oeuvre, to which he added 'an Historical and Scientific Introduction, a Systematic Analysis ... and a Copious Alphabetical Index'.[35] Loudon's respect for Repton had increased since his first critical article almost forty years earlier. He approved of Repton's motto, 'Gardens are works of art, not of nature', believing that any attempt to make gardens look like unadorned nature was deceitful and in poor taste.[36] In a footnote, he takes issue with Repton's endorsement of Edmund Burke's claim in his *Essay on the Sublime* 'that a true artist should put a generous deceit on the spectator'.

Far from it, argued Loudon. 'This is unquestionably a false principle, though laid down by so great a master.'[37]

***

Loudon designed a public garden in 1835 at Gravesend in Kent, and an arboretum in Derby on which work began in 1839. He published a catalogue of its plants in 1840, the year it opened. That year, he also laid out the grounds of Castle Kennedy, near Stranraer, for the Earl of Stair.

Loudon often battled ill-health, with fevers brought on by visits, for example, to the Leeds Botanic Garden in a thunderstorm in 1841. He journeyed on to look at the Liverpool Botanic Garden, but there 'he was unable to get out of the coach, and was obliged to send me [Jane] to look at some of the plants he wished to have examined' before sailing on to Greenock that night.[38]

When Loudon's father died in 1809, Loudon designed a pyramidal monument for his grave in Pinner churchyard, an earnest of later work on cemeteries. Loudon believed that graveyards should not look like public parks, but should mix architecture and landscape in a way both solemn and uplifting. His ideas were embodied in yet another book, *On the Planting, Managing, and Laying out of Cemeteries*, published in 1843. This book, together with his designs for cemeteries in Southampton, Cambridge and at Bath Abbey (none completed in his lifetime), would influence that quintessential Victorian creation, the ornamental cemetery.

Loudon was beset by financial problems and despite suffering inflammation of the lungs he continued to work frantically, attempting to pay off debts of £1,500 incurred by the production of *Arboretum et Fruticetum Britannicum*. Against his wife's wishes, he spent a fortnight on Southampton cemetery, while correcting proofs, before moving on to Bath to inspect ground for another cemetery. Then, while visiting Mortimer Ricardo's Oxfordshire estate, he had to be wheeled around in a Bath chair. 'His body was rapidly wasting away; but his mind remained in all its vigour, and he scarcely allowed himself any rest in his eagerness to complete the works that he had in hand.'[39]

Loudon died standing in his wife's arms at Porchester Terrace, on 14 December 1843 and was buried in Kensal Green cemetery. His wife and daughter were left virtually penniless, although a public meeting was held in February 1844 to raise funds to clear Loudon's remaining debts, supported by Joseph Paxton, with whom Loudon had often been at odds. Sir Robert Peel provided Jane with an annuity.[40]

Jane Loudon was an established author by her husband's death, having produced not only *Gardening for Ladies* but also *The Ladies' Flower-Garden*, which was published in monthly parts at 2*s* 6*d* each. *The Ladies' Companion to the Flower-Garden* was published in 1841 and dedicated to the wife of the surgeon who had helped keep Loudon alive. Other books included *British Wild Flowers* and *The Amateur Gardener's Calendar*, of which William Robinson thought so well that he re-edited it in 1870.[41] In 1848, she became editor of *The Ladies' Companion: At Home and Abroad*, only to be replaced by a man two years later.

By the late 1840s, Loudon's books were no longer selling so well. To make economies, Jane let the house in Porchester Terrace and travelled abroad with Agnes, returning to find the cherished garden had become a wilderness. Agnes was a source of joy but also of pain, falling in love with a succession of unsuitable suitors. Jane died in July 1858 and was buried with Loudon at Kensal Green. Knowing she was dying, Jane destroyed all the letters between herself and her husband on their rare separations. Agnes eventually married after Jane's death but died of puerperal fever less than five years later and was buried with her parents.

Loudon's reputation might have been briefly eclipsed by that rising star Joseph Paxton, but the effect he and Jane had on gardening would live long after their deaths: the encouragement of amateur gardeners was really their major achievement.

A touching scene at Loudon's burial encapsulates the influence of this curious but remarkable man. 'When the coffin was lowered into the grave, a stranger stepped forward from the crowd and threw in a few strips of ivy. This person ... was an artificial flower maker, who felt grateful to Mr Loudon for having given him, though a stranger, tickets for admission to the Horticultural Gardens, and who, never having been able to thank Mr Loudon in person, took this means of paying a tribute to his memory.'[42]

CHAPTER 11

William Andrews Nesfield (1794–1881)

In April 1816, General Sir Gordon Drummond, Governor of Canada, sent his young aide-de-camp to draw Niagara Falls, from the American and Canadian sides. Drummond also commissioned a large-scale map of the area from the lieutenant, William Andrews Nesfield, who now realised that art rather than soldiering was his calling. He had spent two years travelling between Kingston, Montreal and Quebec, and was ready to return home.

Nesfield's awed appreciation of natural phenomena such as Niagara indicated a taste for the picturesque, helpful in his third career – that of a landscape designer. A decade in the army might seem unlikely preparation for art or landscape design, but during his training at Woolwich, he had been taught civil architecture and perspective by Thomas Paul Sandby, son of watercolourist Paul Sandby. Work as a military engineer provided him with the knowledge to plan vast earthworks for his elaborate parterre designs.

William Andrews Nesfield was Britain's most fashionable landscape designer in the mid-nineteenth century. His many commissions included Kew Gardens, Castle Howard in Yorkshire, and Witley Court in Worcestershire. He had artistic ability, a fondness for formality and control, and a romantic view of England's past which suited high Victorian taste.

His gardens personified a reaction against both the informality of Georgian gardens and what his contemporaries saw as the Georgians' lax social morals. The straitjacket that the Victorians put on their women, Nesfield put on their gardens. During a forty-year career, he was never out of work.

***

William Andrews Nesfield was born in County Durham on 19 February 1794, the eldest of the nine children of the rector of Brancepeth,

William Andrews Nesfield [preliminary pencil sketch by James Duffield Harding], *c*. 1840. (Courtesy Dr Shirley Rose Evans/Nesfield family)

Reverend William Nesfield, and his first wife, Elizabeth. His background was on the fringes of aristocracy: his mother had been left a comfortable legacy by her landowning father, and her sister, Anne, married the 3rd Marquess of Winchester, an alliance which helped William's military career. His early childhood, recalled by William's sister, Anne, was spent in a 'busy country rectory full of family and friends'.[1]

That rectory was geographically near to but also a world away from the coalmines and factories of the industrial north-east, and Nesfield's vision was shaped by the hierarchical world of rectory, church, landowner and villagers; he later claimed he learnt much of what he knew about trees from walks with his father on a country estate near Durham.[2] This experience gave him instinctive sympathy with landowners who wanted to recreate a mythical, prelapsarian English past on their estates.

After William's mother died in 1808, Reverend Nesfield married Marianne Mills, the daughter of a local colonel. The Mills connection was significant: Marianne's sister, Eliza, was the mother of architect Anthony Salvin, William's business partner, as well as his brother-in-law; William would marry his stepmother's niece.

At seven, William was sent to a prep school in Hampshire in preparation for admission to Winchester College. He was bitterly unhappy in both places, and Reverend Nesfield removed William from Winchester after a year, to the boy's relief: 'The fagging, bullying, bad food on wooden trenchers, chapel twice a day and three times on Sunday, plus going to the Cathedral twice, was not relished by me.'[3]

Instead, William was sent to Bury St Edmunds' grammar school, previously attended by Humphry Repton. He lodged with his paternal aunt, whose military son's tales of derring-do inspired the young Nesfield to opt for a career in the army rather than the church. After two terms at Trinity College, Cambridge, Nesfield spent three years at Woolwich from 1809. Quartered with three other cadets, Nesfield was a high-spirited youth who went sparrow-shooting and was caught poaching near Eltham one night. The boys escaped punishment by giving false names.[4]

Gazetted as a second lieutenant in a rifle regiment in 1812, he saw action in the attack on Bayonne in December 1813. On his return home, family connections secured him the role of ADC to the then Colonel Drummond, commander of the north-west army in Upper Canada. Nesfield witnessed the American assault on Fort Erie, which was repulsed, although at the cost of 500 British casualties.

In December 1814, the Treaty of Ghent ended the war between Britain and the United States, but Nesfield only set sail from Quebec in May 1816. Nesfield's letters to his father suggest he shared the prejudices of his class and time, writing that the Canadian settlers 'have been obliged to quit England to escape from an halter'.[5] But his return to England didn't offer rosy prospects: peacetime soldiering meant half-pay, so, in 1818, he finally resigned his commission to become a professional watercolourist.

Nesfield spent two years at Brancepeth, no longer a soldier and intent upon a financially more precarious career. His interest was captured by the restoration of Brancepeth Castle by the Russell family who had made a fortune from colliery speculation and banking. The restoration was being carried out in the fashionable medieval style, as self-made families such as the Russells sought to pull the drawbridge up behind themselves and retreat into an imagined chivalric, Camelot past. The restoration of Brancepeth Castle appealed to the romantic spirit of William Nesfield. His stepcousin Anthony Salvin was a pupil on the project, and the two young men discovered a mutual enthusiasm for historic detail, which played out in their later collaborations.[6]

Nesfield became friendly with a neighbouring Durham squire, Newbey Lowson, an acquaintance of J. W. M. Turner. Nesfield and Lowson went on a sketching tour in Switzerland in 1820, before Nesfield moved to London to share a house with Salvin in Newman Street (where, by coincidence, John Loudon had also briefly lodged before living at Pinner).

For almost thirty years, Nesfield exhibited regularly at the Society of Watercolour Painters, formed in 1804 in reaction against the Royal Academy's elitism. In the spirit of the Picturesque movement, its emphasis was on painting from nature. Nesfield took lessons on perspective and colouring from the society's president, Anthony Vandyke Copley Fielding, and spent the 1820s and early 1830s on sketching trips through England,

Wales and Scotland. His work was admired by no less an authority than John Ruskin, who wrote in *Modern Painters*:

> Stand for half an hour beside the Fall of Schaffhausen ... Probably you will not be much disposed to think of any mortal work at the time; but when you look back on what you have seen and are inclined to compare it with art, you will remember – or ought to remember – Nesfield. He is a man of extraordinary feeling, both for the colour and spirituality of a great waterfall: exquisitely delicate in the management of the changeful veil of spray or mist; just in his curves and contours; and unequalled in colour except by Turner.[7]

In July 1833, Nesfield married Emma Mills in what he described curiously as 'a canny quiet way'. Their first son, Eden, was born in 1835, with another son, Arthur Markham, following in 1841; both sons later worked with their father, Eden as an architect and Markham as a designer.

The Nesfields moved in the mid-1830s to Fortis Green in north London into one of a pair of houses designed by Anthony Salvin, who had married Nesfield's sister, Anne. Salvin, already an established revivalist architect, suggested that Nesfield should plan gardens for the Elizabethan and Jacobean houses he was designing.[8] Despite his critical success as a watercolourist, landscape design offered better prospects. Nesfield had experience as a draughtsman, surveyor, engineer and artist, while his childhood had given him understanding of estate management and of trees, even if he admitted to limited plant knowledge. As a first essay, he designed the gardens of the Fortis Green houses, laying out symmetrical scrollwork beds, surrounded by gravel and edged with box, a foretaste of work on a grander scale he would undertake at stately homes across England, Scotland and Wales.

Both Salvin and Nesfield were noticed by John Claudius Loudon, who helped launch Nesfield's reputation. Loudon featured the Fortis Green villas and gardens in an 1840 issue of *The Gardener's Magazine*, speaking of the 'happy circumstance when the architect and the landscape-gardener operate harmoniously together'. Nesfield, said Loudon, had met 'with so much success that his opinion is now sought for by gentlemen of taste in every part of the country'.[9] He added that 'Mr Nesfield perfectly understands the difference between the picturesque and the gardenesque; between fac-simile imitation of nature, and imitation on artistical principles; and between lowering and caricaturing real scenery, and elevating and ennobling it'.[10]

Nesfield flagged up Loudon's endorsement when writing to the Duke of Newcastle. 'At the time I was drawing the plans for Arboretum & French garden, Mr. Loudon happened to call – and I showed him the designs which he highly approved of – the latter was especially admired in as much as he begged for a tracing of it for his publication.'[11]

Nesfield's career took off with an early commission to work with Salvin at Methley Hall, West Yorkshire, home of John Savile, 3rd Earl of Mexborough. Mexborough in turn introduced him to other valuable clients, including the Duke of Newcastle and the Earl of Carlisle at Clumber Park in Nottinghamshire and Castle Howard in North Yorkshire respectively. Over the years, Nesfield worked for the royal family, aristocracy, industrialists, bankers and entrepreneurs. No advertisement was needed: his family connections and the aristocratic network were the source of over 200 commissions during his career.

***

Nesfield quickly developed his own garden design credo. He respected Repton, particularly his later work which put the house at the centre of the design, and his motto, 'Gardens are works of art, not of nature.'[12] He responded to William Sawrey Gilpin's view that 'composition in landscape embraced three distinct parts, the distant, the middle distant and the foreground.'[13] He appreciated woodland and informal parkland, so the picturesque is an important element in his designs. But it is kept at a distance from the house, foregrounded by formal parterres and not allowed up to the front door as it was by Brown.

Influences on Nesfield's style included the hillside gardens of Imperial Rome, and the formalism of Renaissance gardens; he absorbed the theories of the fifteenth-century Italian architect Leon Battista Alberti (1404–1472). Like him, Nesfield believed that a garden should reflect the period when the house was built and should create a unity and harmonisation of space. His formal parterres and avenues were focussed on the main windows and doors, but also took account of the landscape beyond, an artificial area leading on to views in harmony with nature.[14] His style was the antithesis of Brown's. In particular, Nesfield disliked Brown's clumps and shelter belts of trees, preferring avenues radiating from the house, and clear divisions between formal garden and parkland or countryside beyond: the countryside should not float seamlessly away on the other side of a ha-ha. Water, he believed, should be either artificial or natural, never a mixture of the two.

Nesfield often used the word 'artistical' in letters to his clients to describe the effects he wanted to achieve. So much so, in fact, that one garden historian has suggested 'that as Lancelot Brown was known by the appellant "Capability" so William Andrews Nesfield deserves the appellant "Artistical"'.[15] Look, for example, at his views on parterres:

> In my opinion ... parterres should be dealt with as artificially as art could desire, by means of grass slopes, terraces, panels, verges, sculpture, fountains, box embroidery, flowers and other exotics. The details should be worked into rich compartments, the main and flanking centres of which should be formed upon the most important windows

> or doors according to circumstances. This is called Architectural Gardening. The business then of an artist is to create an agreeable combination of the aforesaid materials in such a manner as to produce a concentration of effect upon the same principle as he would enhance the focus of a picture on canvas i.e. by keeping certain accessories subordinate; thus there would be a gradation from the highly artificial to the neutral character.[16]

Nesfield valued his background as an artist. He told Sir William Hooker, director of Kew Gardens, that landscape gardening was 'the Art of painting with Nature's materials'.[17] In 1838, he wrote to the Duke of Newcastle with his views on links between painting and nature harking back to those influential early drawings of Niagara Falls and to Ruskin's remarks:

> With reference to the cascade which I criticised at Clumber, I suggested improvements upon what was an evident failure from beginning to end – Your Grace's remark that 'there are *few* who have sufficient of the artist in them to *execute* a work of this kind,' is perfectly correct. As a painter, I have studied from Nature for the last 18 years and have drawn the character of torrents & cascades, perhaps with as much assiduity as any Artist in England ... it belongs to the Painter alone to see that put into execution which his feelings and impression received from Nature could alone have designed & carried into effect.[18]

Nesfield's was the sensibility of bygone ages. An older contemporary of the Pre-Raphaelites, he shared their romantic view of the Middle Ages, as well as his brother-in-law's taste for Gothic Revivalism. 'For many years having studied our old English architecture,' Nesfield wrote to a client, Lord North of Wroxton Abbey in Oxfordshire, 'I cannot help expressing a patriotic veneration for it ... & am therefore naturally zealous in rescuing places really worthy of restoration from their debased condition.'[19]

Nesfield shared the renewed taste for formal gardens, in reaction against a revolutionary age. The American and French Revolutions had challenged the certainties enjoyed by the early eighteenth-century Whig aristocrats. The Chartists were at their most active as Nesfield's landscaping career began. Industrialisation and urbanisation enriched his prospective clients, but also made them want gardens which emphasised power and control. The garden designs of the men who had worked for that symbol of autocratic power Louis XIV suddenly had a new appeal for the wealthy Victorians. This was a British patriotism which looked back artistically, even as Britain was forging ahead commercially.

Seventeenth-century garden designers such as André Le Nôtre had, in their turn, taken Italian classical gardens and remodelled them for the flatter landscape of northern France. These were Nesfield's influences and he was happy to admit to his clients that he was following the example of the designers he called 'the Old Masters'.[20] 'The Old Masters were so fastidious regarding the design of a Parterre,' he told one client, 'that it was as conformable to the rules of Art as the composition of a Picture on canvas.'[21] He always travelled with a well-thumbed pattern book of designs by Le Nôtre, Mollet, Boyceau and Le Brun. Speaking in 1901, William Miller, the head gardener of Coombe Abbey, Warwickshire, told a wry story about Nesfield and this pattern book:

> A friend asked him how he continued making so many fresh plans and to always have them different in design. Look here friend [Nesfield replied] producing a very large book which was designs from end to end – when I have exhausted and adapted all these to suit my purposes I should by that time be a very old man.[22]

Nesfield's achievement was his synthesis of Gothic Revivalism with Italian-French influences: he used their patterns to create intricate box embroidery layouts (or *parterres-de-broderie*), but filled this scrollwork with heraldic devices, family crests and monograms that flattered his clients. At Holkham Hall in Norfolk, where he followed Kent, Brown and Repton, he laid out a (surviving) parterre on a terrace by the hall with the Earl of Leicester's initials traced in box.

Nesfield's parterres were usually outlined in box, although sometimes with stone kerbs, more expensive initially but cheaper to maintain as they didn't require constant clipping. Much of his bedding – pelargoniums, lobelias, verbenas, petunias, calceolarias – was introduced in the 1830s and 1840s from South Africa, North America and the Himalayas. He also used, as had the Renaissance Italians, coloured gravels and minerals, including copper ore, shells, chalk, coloured marbles, quartz, glass, crushed tile, stone and slate.[23] For one of his most high-profile commissions, the Royal Horticultural Society's new garden in South Kensington (now the site of the Science Museum and Imperial College), Nesfield created a box and gravel parterre in the shape of the national emblems – rose, thistle, shamrock and leek. He used Derbyshire spar for white, pounded bricks for yellow and red, Welsh slate for blue, and coloured glass for the other colours. The *Athenaeum* reviewer wrote, 'It was of such a garden as this that Bacon must have dreamt.'[24] Many of Nesfield's parterres, in Italian style, surrounded fountains or planted tazzas, and were ornamented with urns and other statuary.

Although Nesfield came to be known as the master of the parterre, he also created lakes, planted avenues, designed arboreta, positioned new houses, lodges and gateways, and screened roads and railway lines (not a problem Brown had faced). At Crewe Hall in Staffordshire, where he worked from 1842 to 1866, he planted trees to conceal a railway embankment, created a new approach to the house, and both thinned trees to open up views and planted others.[25] He also laid out the north and east parterres, made stone balustrades and a boathouse with lion masks and sundials. The garden was commended in a 1902 issue of *Country Life* as 'a fine example of his style, which has in it much architectural character, and yet is inspired by the charms of the landscape school'. On the north parterre 'are design and colour in sharp and definite form, making a foreground beyond which the placid lake and the long belts of glorious trees seem to derive new beauties'.[26]

Between 1849 and 1864, Nesfield worked for the 7th Earl of Carlisle at Castle Howard. He visited the estate eleven times to create the Atlas Fountain and surrounding parterre, and to install waterways still in working order. Over 100 letters remain in the Castle Howard archives from Nesfield to the Earl of Carlisle and to his agent, John Henderson. These letters reveal Nesfield's methods and the difficulties in implementing his ambitious proposals. He appears to have established a warm friendship with Henderson. They swapped advice on medical matters, discussed personal concerns, batted proposals back and forth, and occasionally quarrelled. The manager of the estate's accounts was less taken with Nesfield, telling Henderson in 1850 that 'you will be heartily sick of Mr N before you get quit of him,' and then, in 1853, 'you will certainly with the aid of Nesfiddle, ruin us all as well as yourself, with all these abominations'. The 'abominations' had already cost £10,000 half way through the process, and Nesfield wrote that he was 'more anxious about my reputation in connection with C.H. than all my other places put together'. Work came to an end in 1864 with the death of Lord Carlisle, and the planted parterres (although not the fountain) were subsequently removed by Rosalind, 9th Countess of Carlisle, at the end of the century.[27]

What Nesfield described as his 'monster work' was Witley Court, home of the industrialist Lord Ward, who had a fortune derived from coal, iron, smelting works, factories and railway construction. Ward spent £250,000 on creating a classical revival palace, and Nesfield was employed for over a decade to design gardens to match. The centrepiece of the south parterre, now restored by English Heritage, was the massive baroque Perseus and Andromeda Fountain. It weighed twenty tons, and was powered by a forty horse-power steam engine, which threw the main jet 120 feet into the air.[28] The fountain's basin was 180 feet by 120 feet and the overall cost was estimated at over £20,000.[29]

Nesfield, like Brown and Repton before him, was on the road for months at a time. The journeys were often tedious and difficult, as he wrote on visiting a client in Norfolk: 'I came here this morning for the first time across a cold country in an open carriage dreadfully petrified, after w'h I had to explore & walk all day w'h has so knocked me up that I feel totally incapable of considering my own misdoings & yr ideas with any degree of unfatigued judgement.'[30]

As the go-to man, he could command fees of five guineas a day, plus travelling expenses. One client, Ralph Sneyd of Keele Hall in Staffordshire, grumbled that he had had 'Nesfield here for a very few hours, at a great many guineas an hour'.[31] Not only was Nesfield's initial consultancy expensive, his schemes were commensurately costly. His suggestions for a Le Nôtre-style parterre in front of Buckingham Palace, commissioned by Prince Albert, would have meant cutting into Green and St James's Parks, at an estimated cost of over £45,000. The plans were not accepted.[32]

Nesfield's plans were accepted, if somewhat reluctantly, by the Royal Botanic Gardens at Kew. The gardens' director, Sir William Hooker, wrote in February 1844 to Lord Lincoln, the Commissioner of Woods and Forests, that 'he [Nesfield] perhaps favours too much the formal or what he calls the "geometrical" arrangement, which to a certain extent, with so noble a piece of ground may be desirable. But I trust he has too much good sense to carry it too far'. These misgivings were reinforced when Nesfield's plans for a proposed arboretum insisted on the trees being arranged according to size rather than their botanical relationships. Nesfield was nettled by Hooker's tepid support, and proposed withdrawing, but Decimus Burton, creator with Richard Turner of the Palm House, argued for Nesfield 'upon whose judgement in these matters I place much reliance'.[33] Nesfield created the Palm House terrace with its parterres; the lake; a *patte d'oie* of vistas, leading to the Pagoda, Syon House and a cedar of Lebanon; and the Broad Walk. 'In essence Nesfield's grand concept survives,' a Kew historian has written, 'the parterre of geometrical beds ablaze with seasonal bedding above the embellished Palm House Pond, and, on the opposite, west side, the Rose Garden within its embracing semi-circular hedge.'[34] The *patte d'oie* vistas remain, although the cedar has long since been felled. The Kew design was influential, playing its part in introducing formality into the public parks being laid out at the time.

***

Later in his career, Nesfield worked with his sons. He and Markham, also a garden designer, laid out some 30,000 bedding plants in Hyde Park, the first instance of a public area being designed like a private display. William Eden, Nesfield's eldest son, an architect and sometime partner of Norman Shaw, architect of Bedford Park in Chiswick, collaborated with his father and brother on Regent's Park in the 1860s. The layout here was once again formal and geometric, but simpler than displays provided by Nesfield for private clients. The design included long, narrow beds and avenues of trees with gravelled paths, edged with panels of turf.[35]

Nesfield's final years were overshadowed by Markham's tragic death in a riding accident: he was just thirty-three and the father of five young children. Nesfield himself died seven years later at his London home in York Terrace, with Eden at his side, on 3 March 1881.

The fast-moving caravan of Victorian taste served to obscure Nesfield's legacy. The Royal Horticultural Society's garden at Kensington had initially received enthusiastic press coverage, but by 1870 few had anything good to say about his work. His very prominence as a designer opened him up to attack.[36] At Kew, some of his more tortuous parterres by the Palm House were simplified or laid to grass in the 1870s, as was the gravelled Syon vista in 1882, the year after Nesfield's death.

His obituaries were mixed. William Robinson, father of the English flower garden, took a predictably dim view of Nesfield's work.

> The gardens on each side of the Palm House at Kew afford good evidence of the utterly unsatisfactory character of [his] style of gardening, formal to weariness ... He approached landscape gardening from the artificial side – not as one loving Nature ... but rather that the geometry of a past age should form the foreground of what might be the fairest scenes in our garden land.

The Times was kinder, stressing Nesfield's undeniable influence on the gardens and parks of Victorian England: 'He was constantly consulted in the improvements and alterations of the London Parks and Kew Gardens. He planned the Horticultural Gardens at Kensington, and there are few of the large parks and gardens of this country that do not owe something to his taste and skill.'[37]

Nesfield was a Victorian archetype, who travelled with his seventeenth-century patterns books but also with a copy of Bradshaw's railway timetables, combining the old and new.[38] He was much appreciated in his time, as evidenced by an article published in 1869 in the *Gardeners' Chronicle* on Nesfield's work at Woolverstone Hall in Suffolk. The writer claimed he had never seen 'a happier combination of Box embroidery, flowering plants, gravel and Grass than in the garden at Woolverstone. It is perfect of its kind.'[39]

CHAPTER 12

Sir Joseph Paxton (1803–1865)

Charles Dickens, no slouch himself, described his friend Joseph Paxton as a man 'whose very leisure would kill a man of fashion with its hard work'.[1] An example of Paxton's industry is his own description of his arrival at Chatsworth, aged just twenty-two, to start as superintendent of the gardens:

> I left London by the Comet Coach for Chesterfield, and arrived at Chatsworth at half past four o'clock in the morning of the ninth of May 1826. As no person was to be seen at that early hour, I got over the greenhouse gate by the old covered way, explored the pleasure grounds, and looked round the outside of the house. I then went down to the kitchen gardens, scaled the outside wall and saw the whole place, set the men to work there at six o'clock; then returned to Chatsworth and got Thomas Weldon to play me the water works, and afterwards went to breakfast with poor dear Mrs Gregory and her niece. The latter fell in love with me, and I with her, and thus completed my first morning's work at Chatsworth before nine o'clock.[2]

Not a bad morning's work, especially as Paxton, in businesslike fashion, had even picked his bride, Sarah Bown, whom he married nine months later. Paxton was in a league of his own, a Titan of industry who combined a dozen roles in a lifetime. He was a landscape designer, an architect, a duke's confidential friend, counsellor and right-hand man, a botanical writer, a magazine and newspaper proprietor, an industrialist and railway magnate, a financial speculator, a politician and a visionary. Paxton was the very personification of the Victorian self-made man, who invested in and directed railway companies, engaged with the nascent leisure industry, and, like Samuel Smiles, believed in self-help, striving to improve the working and living conditions of the poor.

Joseph Paxton, *London Illustrated News*.

His achievements were all founded on his outstanding talents as a gardener and plantsman, identified by the 6th Duke of Devonshire. The friendship between duke and gardener helped reconstruct Victorian England. Paxton transformed Chatsworth into one of the most highly regarded estates in Europe, and in return the duke turned the farm labourer's son into a man of power and influence, honoured by royalty and nobility. The duke was an educated aristocrat, living, as one historian has said, 'at the fag-end of the Georgian tradition'.[3] Paxton's existence, according to his granddaughter and biographer, 'was grounded in service and affection for a master so immeasurably superior in rank and status that questions of birth ... were non-existent'. Paxton saw infinite possibilities in the plants arriving from all corners of the globe, and in the industrial developments then gathering momentum. The cultural influences he absorbed through time spent with the duke at Chatsworth, and on successive European tours, helped fashion his vision of a better world for ordinary working people. However rich and celebrated he became, he never lost touch with his rural past, surprising his daughter over a fine meal by saying vehemently, 'You never know how much nourishment there is in a turnip until you have had to live on it.'[4]

***

Joseph Paxton was born on 3 August 1803 in Milton Bryant, Bedfordshire, the seventh son and last child of William and Anne Paxton. William was probably a farm labourer, who had made a runaway marriage with the slightly more affluent Anne Rooke. William's death before Joseph was seven reduced the family to poverty. Joseph somehow learnt to read and write, probably at a free school for working-class children in Woburn. On that meagre foundation, Paxton managed to build an understanding of botany, technology and design, as well as considerable literary talents.

The school had been started by the Duke of Bedford, whose Woburn estate, designed by Humphry Repton, had become a centre of innovation and horticultural experimentation.[5] Repton had also designed nearby Battlesden Park, where Joseph was sent to live with his eldest brother, William, twenty years his senior and the estate's bailiff. Paxton's granddaughter believes that William treated his younger brother so roughly that Joseph ran away and made his way to Essex. There, a Quaker named Ford urged him to return home to his family and a job as gardener's boy at Battlesden. Joseph worked next at Woodhall, a Hertfordshire estate, run by a successful horticulturalist and fruiterer called William Griffin. The author of a treatise on pineapples, Griffin was an early subscriber to the new Horticultural Society Gardens at Chiswick, and probably contributed to Paxton's horticultural education.

In 1823, Paxton joined the Horticultural Society Gardens in London as a labourer. Still only twenty, the ambitious new recruit gave his date of birth as 1801 in the society's register, writing in a bold, well-formed hand. He was initially paid fourteen shillings a week, but within a year had been promoted to under-gardener in the arboretum at four shillings a week more.[6]

These gardens had been established in 1821 at Chiswick, and had a well-stocked library of which Paxton took full advantage. The death of Sir Joseph Banks had seen a decline in the status of Kew, so the acquisition of land gave the Horticultural Society (it wasn't until 1861 that it obtained its royal charter) the chance to be in the van of horticultural experimentation. Plants flowed into the gardens in the 1820s from China, Mexico and South America, while the society's lead plant hunter, David Douglas, was exploring America's north Pacific coast. These new, tender introductions led to the development of better greenhouses for their protection and propagation, all of which stimulated Paxton's emerging talents and interests.[7]

The thirty-three acres of land were leased from the 6th Duke of Devonshire, who owned the adjacent Chiswick House. To the gardens designed in the 1720s by William Kent for Lord Burlington, the 6th Duke had added an Italian garden, with a 300-foot-long domed conservatory, and a zoo.[8]

Born in 1790, the Bachelor Duke had a childhood overshadowed by the estrangement of his parents, the 5th Duke and his wife, the notoriously extravagant Georgiana, whose mountainous gambling debts her morose husband refused to pay. 'Hart', as he was known by the family, was brought up alongside siblings both legitimate and illegitimate, and was twenty-one when, on his father's death, he inherited estates in London, Derbyshire, Yorkshire, Sussex and Ireland. A liberal-minded man, he supported Catholic Emancipation and the abolition of slavery, abhorred the abuse of childhood labour, and valued his employees.[9] He poured money into his houses and gardens, and his extravagant tastes in collecting valuable plants and minerals as well as works of art meant that he, like the mother he resembled, was permanently in debt.[10] Although charming and hospitable, he was isolated by severe deafness, and suffered from depression and hypochondria; in middle age, he developed a religious mania.[11] Although he had mistresses, he never married, finding instead solace in strong friendships with members of his own sex.[12] For much of the bachelor duke's life, Paxton was the only constant, as the gardener's vigour and easy manner acted as an antidote to the duke's depression and loneliness. Through Paxton, the reforming peer would meet scientists, engineers, inventors, and industrial leaders, 'men for the most part from the peasantry, not even from the middle class'.[13]

Wandering through the gate which led from his estate at Chiswick House into the Horticultural Society Gardens, the duke often stopped to talk to the stocky young man in charge of new plant introductions. So impressed was the duke by the gardener's obvious intelligence that he offered Paxton the superintendence of his own gardens at Chatsworth.[14]

The duke's offer was daring, given Paxton's relative inexperience. The new gardener arrived at Chatsworth just two days before the duke sailed to attend the coronation of Tsar Nicholas I of Russia. Both house and gardens had been neglected by the 5th Duke, although Paxton's new employer had commissioned royal architect Sir Jeffry Wyatville to add an Italianate wing to the Palladian house built in 1687. Little, however, had been done in the gardens. Paxton, who needed no hand-holding, had made a noticeable difference by the duke's return from his Russian mission in December. 'I am enchanted with the progress my new gardener … Paxton, has made,' the duke wrote in his diary.[15] 'In a very short time a great change appeared in pleasure-ground and garden: vegetables, of which there had been none, fruit in perfection, and flowers. The twelve men with brooms in their hands on the lawn began to sweep, the labourers to work with activity. The kitchen-garden was so low, and exposed to floods from the river, that I supposed the first wish of the new gardener would be to remove it to some other place – but he made it answer.'[16]

Paxton's character, above all his ability to inspire his workforce, is revealed here. A young unknown man had appeared at Chatsworth, and yet the gardeners seemingly responded immediately to his orders. His openness, dedication and authority disarmed criticism, and even the duke's senior advisers, such as his lawyer, Benjamin Currey, accepted that Paxton was the conduit to their boss.[17] Also indicated is his essential frugalness: he would never spend more money than necessary, unlike his often profligate master.

Over the next thirty years, the rate of change in the Chatsworth gardens mirrored the speed of contemporary technological developments. Within a year of his arrival, Paxton was tactfully advising Wyatville on the design of the Orangery, and, in 1828, he began experimenting with greenhouse construction. By 1832, twenty-two hot houses and forcing pits had been built in the kitchen garden.[18] Loudon was surprised that Paxton should prefer wood to metal in the construction of glasshouses, but Paxton believed wood was more resistant to corrosion, easier to repair, and vastly cheaper. He experimented with Loudon's ridge and furrow design to let in more daylight.[19] He also invented the 'Paxton gutter', a wooden glazing bar with an outside channel for rain water and, inside, channels to catch condensation.[20]

Paxton's responsibilities multiplied: in 1829, put in charge of forestry, he enclosed eight acres of the park for a pinetum. In 1835, work began on the forty-acre arboretum, where 1,670 species formed the largest collection of herbaceous plants in Europe at the time.[21] Nothing daunted Paxton: he organised transport from Derby for a mature weeping ash weighing eight tons with its rootball and earth. The ash took three days to travel the twenty-eight miles to Chatsworth, accompanied by twenty men, who manoeuvred it, rootball first, through narrow toll gates, while people turned out to see the phenomenon go past. On 10 April 1830, the duke wrote in his diary: 'The tree got to the gate of the park at 11 o.c. but not to its place till 9. It is miraculous to have come safe so far. I was enchanted with it and its place in my courtyard.'[22] A decade later, he arranged for the transfer of several twelve-ton date palms to Chatsworth from Walton-on-Thames in Surrey. Eleven horses were needed to draw a special wagon, while the Walton palm house had to be demolished to get the palms out and turnpike gates removed.[23]

Another Paxton achievement was the Rock Garden, begun in 1842 and created on what Deborah, Dowager Duchess of Devonshire, has described as 'a gargantuan scale'. Again, Paxton invented a machine to move enormous rocks and winch them into place, creating a naturalistic mountainous landscape down which water tumbles from a great height. 'The spirit of some Druid seems to animate Mr Paxton in these bulky removals,' wrote the duke.[24]

The duke took a generalised interest in his gardens when Paxton first arrived. 'Not till 1832 did I take to caring for my plants in earnest,' the duke recorded, but from then on his passion for new plants was second only to Paxton's.[25] This led to the construction of more hothouses and stoves at Chatsworth and indirectly to Paxton's work on Crystal Palace.

Both duke and gardener were bitten by the fashion for growing orchids, with the acquisitive duke desperate to get his hands on a prize collection when it came up for sale. He was delighted when John Lindley, formerly secretary of the Horticultural Society Gardens and now Professor of Botany at University College London, named a genus of plants *Cavendishia*.[26]

An under-gardener, John Gibson, was sent in 1836 to India and Burma. During his year-long mission, Gibson collected over a hundred types of orchids, as well as the scarlet-flowered *Amherstia nobilis*. Paxton wrote excitedly to his wife that, on its arrival, 'the Duke ordered his breakfast to be brought to the Painted Hall, where the plant stands, and he desired me to sit down and lavish my love on the tree'.[27] Such plant-hunting treks were dangerous: two Chatsworth gardeners were drowned when their canoe hit a rock on the Columbia river, putting an end to expeditions organised by Paxton and his master.

The year that Gibson set out for India, the foundation stone was laid for Paxton's Great Stove, another improbable success for a man with no architectural or engineering training. The vast conservatory was 277 feet long, 123 feet wide and 61 feet high, and was heated by three underground boilers fuelled by coal delivered on underground trams. A carriage and pair could be driven through the conservatory, which was planted with orange trees, hibiscus, the palms from Walton-on-Thames, stephanotis, bougainvillea and many other exotics. Queen Victoria and Prince Albert visited in 1843, and the queen described the conservatory as 'the most stupendous and extraordinary creation imaginable ... This Conservatory was planned by the Duke's gardener, Mr Paxton, a very clever man ... quite a genius, for he plans out all the buildings, as well as laying out his gardens and the Horticultural garden.'[28]

Paxton staged a firework display, illuminating the waterfall, cascade and fountains and seen by 30,000 visitors in the park. The Duke of Wellington, who was in the royal party, went out early the next morning to find everything pristine: a Paxton-led team of two hundred had worked through the night to clear the debris and restore order. Astounded, Wellington told Devonshire, 'I would have liked that man of yours for one of my generals.'[29]

Paxton and his master were always ambitious. The Conservative Wall (another conservatory) was built in 1842 against a wall along a walk to the stables, and constructed with a system of flues and hot-water pipes to protect tender climbers. The central section was added in 1850 by John Robertson, draughtsman to Loudon.[30] Robertson also worked with Paxton on the rebuilding of Edensor village, an early essay in social welfare, with cottages designed in a bewildering mix of Swiss, Italian, Elizabethan and other styles.[31]

The Great Stove, always expensive to maintain and heat, was eventually demolished in 1920, ironically by Charlie Markham, Paxton's grandson.[32] Paxton's majestic Emperor Fountain, his major waterworks at Chatsworth, survives, however, still sending jets 264 feet into the air. Over 100,000 cubic feet of earth were moved to make a reservoir on the moors to feed the fountain, which was built in 1844 for a visit from Tsar Nicholas I which never materialised.

***

Paxton designed glasshouses, built fountains, laid out shrubberies, restored woodland, planted trees, tended exotic plants, and popularised the newly introduced monkey-puzzle tree, *Araucaria araucana*. He worked not only at Chatsworth, but also on the duke's other estates in Yorkshire and at Lismore in Ireland. He and Sarah had eight children, six daughters and two sons, one of whom, William, died aged five, taken ill when Paxton was away on one of his many journeys with the duke. The Paxtons' remaining son, George, became a constant worry to both parents, with Paxton mostly too busy to devote time to a troubled boy living in the shadow of a dead brother and an exceptional father. With a dowry of £5,000, Sarah had been something of a prize for the newly arrived gardener, and prize she was, tirelessly supporting him over their twenty-eight-year marriage. In her husband's frequent absences, Sarah and Paxton wrote almost daily to each other, while she handled accounts, both for Paxton and for Chatsworth, and ran the gardens staff. 'Her astonishing executive ability fitted like a glove into his brilliant and creative mind,' their granddaughter wrote. 'She was a first-rate woman of business; for years she held in her hands all the threads of the Chatsworth estate. If, nominally, he was the Agent, she in fact did the work.'[33] Later in life, though, she was often lonely, with her daughters married and Paxton spending more time in his Sydenham house than with her at Chatsworth.

Sarah shared Paxton with the duke, who always had first call on his gardener's attention, even when Paxton was building Crystal Palace for the Great Exhibition. Paxton was taken by the duke, first to Paris, and then in 1838 on a nine-month tour through Italy, Sicily, Malta, Greece and Constantinople, before returning home via Algiers, Gibraltar, Lisbon and Paris. This was Paxton's grand tour, which gave the self-educated man a rich draught of European culture, attracting him to the arts, and in particular to literature. In an article on 'Hints to Young Gardeners on Mental Improvement', he encouraged his audience to broaden their horizons. 'Literary composition is invaluable to the gardener. If it were universally practised and properly pursued, it would have an unequivocal tendency to augment his articles and refine and exalt his whole character.'[34]

He practised what he preached: in 1831, Paxton launched a monthly gardening magazine, *The Horticultural Register and General Magazine*, in competition with John Claudius Loudon's *The Gardener's Magazine*. Their relationship was always prickly thereafter, although Loudon reluctantly admitted to Paxton's genius, and Paxton supported a fund to help Jane Loudon, in straitened circumstances on Loudon's death. The duke's gardener aimed his *Horticultural Register* at the general gardener, embracing 'everything useful and valuable in horticulture, natural history and rural economy'. In his view, experimentation and developments being carried out on estates such as Chatsworth were prompting a much wider appreciation of and enthusiasm for gardening. The first issue featured articles on greenhouses, and on how to change the colour of hydrangeas and hold back the flowering of roses. One article was reprinted from *The Gardener's Magazine*, then common practice, but not likely to have endeared Paxton further to Loudon.[35]

The Horticultural Register was followed three years later by the *Magazine of Botany and Register of Flowering Plants*, illustrated with colour plates and offering detailed descriptions of plants and how to care for them. It, too, was targeted at a wide, general market.

Paxton stopped editing *The Horticultural Register* in 1835, but continued to write, producing a treatise in 1838 on the cultivation of the dahlia which was translated into several languages. He collaborated with John Lindley on other botanical works, and launched with him a new weekly paper, the *Gardeners' Chronicle*, in 1841.

In 1845, Paxton and three partners launched a national newspaper, the *Daily News*, edited by Charles Dickens at a salary of £2,000 a year. Dickens was not a natural editor; he became instead a contributor and was replaced by John Forster, a *Punch* journalist and later Dickens's biographer. Paxton soon withdrew from active involvement with the paper, unsuited for a specialism different from others he had previously tackled. His investment in the paper had been considerable, £16,500, for by the mid-1840s, Paxton was a rich man in his own right, able to afford a Georgian house with an acre and a half of land.[36]

Paxton also served on a commission which examined the management and expenditure of the royal gardens, including the neglected Royal Botanic Gardens at Kew. As a result of his report, Paxton was sounded out for the post of head gardener at Windsor at a salary of £1,000 a year. Paxton's first allegiance was to Chatsworth, and the very intimation to the duke that he might lose his right-hand man encouraged him to increase Paxton's salary by £50 to £276 a year.[37]

In 1842, a private investor asked Paxton to design an urban park in Liverpool, by then an industrialised trading city of 100,000 people, and needing public open spaces. Paxton put into practice at Prince's Park ideas for subscription gardens near cities broached in *The Horticultural Register* over a decade earlier. The acreage was divided up into allotments, with a flower garden at the centre, and houses and a carriage drive around the outside.[38] Public commissions followed, including for Birkenhead Park in 1844, with plans drawn up by John Robertson to Paxton's designs, and for a number of cemeteries.

Paxton's real wealth came from his investment in railways, expanding rapidly in the 1840s. Many lines would run through the Devonshire estates, so Paxton was drawn into a field which was already fascinating him. In 1848, Paxton was appointed a director of Midland Railway, and became friendly with George Stephenson and his son, Robert; the contractor, Thomas Brassey; the great engineer, Isambard Kingdom Brunel; and the 'Railway King', George Hudson. The Paxtons put such eye-watering sums into railways – £136,000 in two years in the early 1840s – that even the phlegmatic Paxton at times felt unnerved.[39] He invested in the construction of the East Bengal Railway and, by the end of his life had money in railways on three continents. Paxton, wrote Charles Dickens, 'has the command of every railway influence in England and abroad except for the Great Western. He is in it heart and purse.'[40]

Dealing with engineers in financing railways might seem closer in spirit to Paxton's most ambitious venture – masterminding the construction of Crystal Palace – but it was, in fact, a giant water-lily which inspired that incomparable feat of engineering. The *Victoria regia* lily had been discovered in the Amazon in 1836. Seeds were sent to Kew, but as the plant refused to flower, in 1849 Kew's director, Sir William Hooker, turned to Paxton. With customary vim, Paxton went up and down in a day by express train, arriving at Kew before six o'clock in the morning on his forty-sixth birthday to pick up a plant with four leaves no more than six inches across.[41] Once back at Chatsworth, Paxton set about mimicking Amazonian conditions in the Great Stove, and by September the leaves were three and a half feet in diameter.[42] The plant continued to outgrow successive tanks until on 2 November a bud appeared, swelling six days later into a pure white flower smelling of pineapple. The duke rushed back from Ireland, while Paxton took a flower in person to the queen at Windsor. He knew instinctively what to do: when a bud faded instantly on being cut, Paxton revived it by pouring warm water into the stalk, and then put its root in fine sand to reproduce the action of gnawing fish.

The leaves of the water lily grew to four-and-a-half feet across, large enough for Paxton's daughter, Annie, to stand on one. As the plants needed not just a bigger tank but a new building, Paxton devised the Lily House. The fruit of his greenhouse experimentation over the past twenty years, this was his final contribution to the infrastructure at Chatsworth. In a Royal Society of Arts lecture in 1850, Paxton explained that the principle for the glasshouse was derived from the leaves of the lily itself. Thick ribbing prevented the leaf from buckling, and the flat ridge-and-furrow roof of the lily house acted like the cross girders on the lily leaf.[43] The building was composed of standardised units, and Paxton employed the same principle at the Great Exhibition the following year.

The exhibition, billed as displaying 'the Works of Industry of all Nations', was the brainchild of Prince Albert, and was steered by a Royal Commission. Over 240 designs for the exhibition building were received from round the world, but none was thought suitable for a building which needed to be built quickly and then dismantled. The Royal Society of Arts had decided on its own brick and iron building when, at a railway meeting in Derby in July 1850, Paxton sketched his proposal on a piece of blotting paper. (This sketch is one of the few Paxton designs extant.) Based on his design for the Chatsworth Lily House, its virtue was that it could be made in sections to be assembled on site. He travelled down to London with Robert Stephenson, a royal commissioner and civil engineer, who looked at Paxton's plans, which he described as 'admirable'.[44]

Within a few days, Paxton fleshed out his plans, liaised with railway manufacturers Fox and Henderson and glass maker Robert Lucas Chance, and had his design accepted. Chance had perfected a cylinder process which enabled him to produce industrial quantities of sheets up to three feet long. Paxton visited Chance's factory and concluded that the sheets could be made a foot longer to suit his design. He had bought himself a Boulton & Watt steam engine back in the 1830s and had experimented with different cutters to shape and groove his sash bars, winning a Society of Arts silver medal in the process.[45] All this assisted the construction at breakneck speed of the building for which *Punch* magazine coined the soubriquet 'Crystal Palace'. At one point, three columns and two girders were being erected every sixteen minutes.[46]

Paxton was supported on the Great Exhibition by Chatsworth staff and by advice from Sir Charles Barry, architect of the Houses of Parliament, and generously from Brunel, given that Brunel's design had been dropped in favour of Paxton's blotting paper sketch. But it was Paxton's vision and determination which propelled the project forward and ensured its success, creating a building six times the size of St Paul's Cathedral in a little over six months. Paxton, as *Punch* noted, should turn his hand to speeding up Barry's construction of Parliament: 'Sir, you can do it in a morning. You have only to don your working coat, to clap on your considering cap – that pretty tasteful thing bent from a leaf of the *Victoria regia* – and the matter is done.'[47]

The opening of the Great Exhibition on 1 May 1851 was the apogee of Joseph Paxton's career. Three hundred thousand people gathered in Hyde Park to watch the arrival of the great and the good. Paxton, in full court dress, was later knighted by Queen Victoria, while the Duke of Devonshire, watching from a gallery, played second fiddle to his right-hand man. The building cost £169,998 to build, but by October, £356,000 had been taken in entry fees. The surplus was used to purchase land in South Kensington (the site of London and Wise's nursery a century-and-a-half earlier) on which were built the Victoria & Albert, National History and Science Museums. Paxton's great building had a lasting influence on the nation's cultural life.

The building was always intended to be temporary, but Paxton foresaw its future as a temple of leisure for working people. He formed a public company, raising £70,000 to buy Crystal Palace and re-erect it on a site in Sydenham. The new building, which Paxton remodelled, was even larger and took longer than anticipated to erect, especially as Paxton was determined to outdo Versailles with elaborate waterworks and Italianate terraces of planting on the south London hillside.[48] The new Crystal Palace was also opened by Queen Victoria, on

10 June 1854, and was regarded by press and public as an ever greater triumph. Despite admitting two million visitors a year, the new palace never made money, however, and was a grumbling financial concern for Paxton as his own health deteriorated. The palace eventually burnt down on 30 November 1936.

Paxton, already beset by rheumatism, was injured in a train crash in 1853. But his pace of work did not abate, as he was employed increasingly as an architect. He was commissioned by Baron Mayer Rothschild to design Mentmore in Buckinghamshire. The glass-domed house was surrounded by elaborate gardens, designed in a late eighteenth-century Reptonian fashion, suggesting that Paxton was beginning to run on an empty tank. The result was nevertheless one of fabulous luxury: Lady Eastlake suggested that 'the Medicis were never lodged so in the height of their glory'. Another Rothschild commission led to Paxton's designing a mansion and laying out lakes, terraced gardens and orchid-filled hothouses on a 9,000-acre estate at Ferrières near Paris.[49] Between 1845 and 1847, he also designed public parks, including Kelvingrove Park and Queen's Park, Glasgow; the People's Park, Halifax, and Coventry Cemetery.

It was for Coventry that Paxton became one of two MPs in 1854. He wasn't much of a debater, but took an enthusiastic role in public life, among other things petitioning Parliament to repeal taxes destroying the Coventry silk industry.[50] He sat on committees on sewage and sanitation, a growing problem in Britain's over-crowded industrial cities, and had a hand in plans, not realised in his lifetime, for Bazalgette's work on the Victoria and Albert Embankments.

An achievement of his Parliamentary years was the formation of an Army Works Corps, composed of Sydenham navvies, to support British troops during the Crimean War. Paxton designed a simple ridge tent for their use, and, as ever, this design inspired another project. He set up a business selling flat-pack hothouses, amalgamating the ridge tent design with his experience of building glasshouses. These sold well, as tender and unusual garden plants were now affordable by the mass market. Joseph Paxton contributed to putting a greenhouse in the corner of every suburban garden.

***

The week before the opening of the Sydenham palace, the Duke of Devonshire suffered a serious stroke. Ever dependent on Paxton, the duke started staying for long periods at Rockhills, Paxton's Sydenham house, forcing Paxton to vacate his own bedroom. The duke died at Chatsworth on 18 January 1858, while Paxton was at the Devonshire estate in Yorkshire. Paxton hurried back and was chief mourner at the duke's funeral at Edensor church.

Later that month, Paxton resigned all his offices at Chatsworth, although he kept his house there for his lifetime and was paid an annual salary of £500 a year for consultancy work. He continued working on many other projects for the remaining seven years of his life, and also joined the Reform Club. There, his friends included writers Charles Dickens, Wilkie Collins, and William Thackeray, and politicians Gladstone and Palmerston.[51] The railways still occupied him, as did Crystal Palace and committees on sewerage.

His sudden death at Rockhills on 8 June 1865, aged sixty-one, was attributed to heart and liver failure. No doubt underlying this was a workload which would long since have killed anyone less formidable. This driven entrepreneurial man left an estate of £180,000 (just under £9 million in today's money). Sarah received an annuity of £2,000 and ownership of their considerable property in Derbyshire. She died six years later.

The obituaries were fulsome: *The Times* called him, with justice, 'the greatest gardener of his time ... and a man of genius', while Gladstone's wife wrote to Sarah that 'Mr Gladstone valued him not only for his power of mind, but for the more quiet qualities which are more precious. And there was something about him which we do feel made him loved peculiarly.'[52]

On 15 June 1865, he was buried in Edensor churchyard near the Bachelor Duke who had helped make his fame and fortune.

PART V

THE FLOWER GARDEN

CHAPTER 13

William Robinson (1838–1935)

A tale is told about William Robinson. It goes thus: while working at Ballykilcavan in Ireland, the twenty-two-year-old Robinson rowed furiously with the head gardener. That night, a particularly cold one, he put out the fires in the greenhouses, opened all the windows and doors, and left the tender plants to perish. The next morning, he saw Dr David Moore, director of the National Botanic Garden at Glasnevin, Dublin, for whom he had previously worked. Dr Moore gave Robinson letters of introduction to Robert Marnock, curator of the Royal Botanic Society's garden in Regent's Park in London, and set Robinson on his way.

The damage caused by Robinson has probably been exaggerated; why would the director of Glasnevin promote a young man guilty of such reckless behaviour? How then has the story come to be so embellished? Was it bruited about by one of Robinson's (many) antagonists in later years as an example of his explosive temper?

The story, amplified or not, is revealing about Robinson's personality and career. He was a peppery, difficult man, inclined to get into spats with other gardeners and horticultural writers. But he had charm when he wanted to show it, making life-long friendships with, for example, Robert Marnock, his first employer at Regent's Park. And the mystery of this story is one of several ambiguities in his career. How did an unknown gardener so swiftly win a position of responsibility in London? And how could a former gardener and *Times* gardening correspondent in Paris, with no other visible means of support, return to London after a year's semi-sabbatical in France and set himself up with housekeeper and gardener in a large house in Kensington?

Mostly self-taught like Paxton, Robinson built his reputation on his vigorously expressed literary outpourings as much as on his achievements at his Sussex estate of Gravetye and the handful of gardens he helped design. But despite publishing magazines and periodicals and writing a

William Robinson in later life. (Courtesy Gravetye Manor)

score of books and hundreds of articles, Robinson remains enigmatic, with strange gaps in his curriculum vitae.

Robinson's was a rags to riches story. Gardening, as for Kent, Brown and Paxton before him, bestowed wealth and social status on a gardener's boy. Writing about the subject gave him sway over garden design and planting, not just for his contemporaries but for future generations. He broke away from the Victorian formality of Nesfield and Paxton and promoted the more naturalistic style of gardening which still remains popular. Robinson's ideas, combined with those of his friend Gertrude Jekyll, influenced Lawrence Johnston at Hidcote, Vita

Sackville-West at Sissinghurst and Christopher Lloyd at Great Dixter. As a result, Robinson's impact is still apparent in British gardens. We might not be growing hardy perennials in the relaxed informal way we do, had it not been for Robinson's two major books, *The Wild Garden* and *The English Flower Garden*.

***

William Robinson was born in Co Down on 15 July 1838. He was ten years old when his land agent father, also William, eloped with Lady St George, the wife of his employer, an event recorded in the family bible. William, the eldest of three, needed to help support his mother, Catherine, so started work at Curraghmore, home of the Marquess of Waterford. There, he carried buckets of water from the River Clodiagh, which ran through the estate, a backbreaking job which possibly fuelled his dislike of the greenhouses for which the water was intended. He then trained at Glasnevin, studying under David Moore, before joining the gardening team at Ballykilcavan. He rose to foreman but quickly became frustrated with the large but unremarkable garden, overlooked by Loudon in his account of gardens in the area.[1]

Robinson was lucky, therefore, that he must already have impressed Moore by the time he turned up at Glasnevin on that chilly January morning in 1861. Armed with Moore's letters of introduction, Robinson reached London as Nesfield was designing the new Horticultural Society garden at Kensington, a masterwork of scrolls, patterns and coloured stones. Briefly the height of fashion, Nesfield's garden represented everything Robinson came to dislike. Robinson's arrival in London also coincided with the foundation by William Morris in Bloomsbury of a design company, Morris Marshall & Faulker, ushering in the Arts and Crafts movement that underpinned Robinson's philosophy.

Robinson was fortunate that Moore recommended him to the Royal Botanic Society gardens rather than to Kew or to the Horticultural Society gardens at Kensington, both of which Robinson later blasted in his magazine, *The Garden*. The Royal Botanic Society had been set up in 1839 by the Duke of Norfolk, partly to rival the Horticultural Society. Its gardens within the Inner Circle of Regent's Park had been designed by Marnock, with the plants arranged geographically.[2] The society's gardeners' work at Regent's Park, Robinson later wrote, 'helped to keep a true spirit of landscape gardening from slumbering among us during one of the most marked periods of retrogression that it has ever lived through'.[3]

Marnock, a plantsman with a strong sense of design, set up his own landscape gardening practice in 1863. Before leaving, he promoted Robinson as overseer of the herbaceous plant collection, and encouraged him to replenish it by plant collecting around London and southern England. Marnock also arranged finance for Robinson to visit botanic gardens across the British Isles to exchange and gather live plants and seeds.

Marnock wrote of Robinson: 'I have found Mr Robinson to be a very fit person to manage the medical and herbaceous gardens, and a zealous botanist.' He recommended a wage rise from twenty-five to thirty shillings a week, at a time when gardeners at Kew were only earning twelve shillings.[4] Also through Marnock's friendship, Robinson was elected as a fellow of the Linnaean Society. Robinson's ten sponsors included James Veitch, whose Chelsea nursery Robinson had much admired, David Moore of Glasnevin, and Charles Darwin, with whose theories he would late virulently disagree.[5]

Robinson had a less happy relationship with Marnock's successor, Thomas Don, a competent administrator rather than a botanist, employed as superintendent rather than curator of the garden. Robinson's trip to most of Britain's botanic gardens, as well as several important private gardens, encouraged him to look critically at the Regent's Park design. Never emollient, he made radical suggestions which annoyed Don. Robinson's plans included the planting of a fernery, while dispensing with one of the borders and relocating its plants, and removing what he described as 'the wretched old experiment, called a greenhouse'. Robinson's round-Britain trip proved fruitful in acquiring new plants from Kew, Glasnevin, Hull, Glasgow, Belfast and Liverpool, and from private gardens, too. He extended the exchange system overseas, with plants transported in Wardian cases from botanic gardens in South Africa and Mauritius.[6]

Robinson began writing regularly for the *Gardeners' Chronicle*. As with Paxton, it was remarkable that a man with so little schooling should turn successfully to print, quickly developing the ability to write what has been described as 'forceful prose that made him nearly the equal of a Loudon'.[7] It can only be assumed that at Regent's Park he worked diligently on his own education, for his later work displays a broad sweep of literary references.

Through his tours and writing, he built up a network of plant enthusiasts and collectors in Britain, France, America and elsewhere, with whom he corresponded regularly. Robinson resigned from the Botanic Society's gardens in July 1866, explaining he wished 'to devote myself to the study of our Great Gardens and of the literature of Horticulture for a year or two'.[8]

Robinson was drawn to France, where an International Exhibition was planned from April to October 1867. His interest in France had been stimulated by reading old French gardening books in the Botanic Society's library, and to prepare himself, he employed a French émigré to teach him French. His accent allegedly became so good that he was often thought to have French ancestry, a mistake that Robinson would let pass.[9] He travelled to France in January 1867, an independent and informed horticulturalist, only six years after throwing open the greenhouse doors at Ballykilcavan. He took with him commissions from British periodicals, including *The Field*, the *Gardeners' Chronicle* and *The Times*.

The International Exhibition was held in a Paris which had become, thanks to Napoleon III and his architect, Georges Haussmann, a city of boulevards, parks, squares and elegant buildings. Robinson devoted several columns to the squares and parks of Paris, thinking them far superior to those of London. He was struck by the quality of French horticulture and systems of fruit training, and by the tasteful arrangements of plants at the exhibition. Robinson also visited the Jardin des Plantes and other gardens around Paris. He made useful friendships; for example, with the Anglophile horticulturalist Henry Vilmorin (who anglicised his name and sent his son to school in England).

This initial visit to France resulted in his first two books, *Gleanings from French Gardens* and *The Parks, Promenades and Gardens of Paris*, published in 1868 and 1869 respectively. Here, as in his regular columns from the exhibition, he annoyed British growers by his outspokenness. A review of *Gleanings* in the *Gardeners' Chronicle* admitted that Robinson was 'a diligent and accurate observer', but also that he had, 'with more boldness than judgement, set himself in opposition to the views of practical men of larger experience than his own'.[10]

In 1868, Robinson ventured abroad again to view alpine plants in France, Switzerland and Italy. He was attracted by Ruskin's idealisation of mountains, Ruskin having written that 'the best image which the world can give of Paradise is in the slope of the meadows, orchards, and cornfields on the side of a great Alp, with its purple rocks and eternal snows above'.[11] Robinson wanted to learn about these tough, low-growing, colourful plants in their natural habitat, believing them eminently suitable for English gardens. 'There is not a garden of any kind, even in the suburbs of our great cities,' he wrote, 'in which the flowers of alpine lands may not be grown and enjoyed.' He added that 'intelligent cultivation will prove as successful ... in our open gardens' with alpines 'as it has already proved with the choicest plants of steaming tropical forests in hot-houses', the latter being something he deplored.[12] Travelling with a guide, Robinson braved precipitous paths, frequent soakings, and gloomy tales of deaths caused by falling boulders and avalanches. Despite these rigours, *Alpine Flowers for English Gardens*, published by John Murray in 1870, was a joyous celebration of these alpine plants written in almost biblical prose. 'What are alpine plants?' asked Robinson.

> Above the cultivated land these flowers begin to occur on the fringes of stately woods; they are seen in multitudes in the vast and delightful pastures with which many great mountain-chains are robed, enamelling their soft verdure with innumerable dyes; and where neither grass or loose herbage can exist; where feeble world-heat is quenched by mightier powers; where mountains are crumbled into ghastly slopes of shattered rock by the contending forces of heat and cold; even there, amidst the glaciers, they brilliantly spring from Nature's ruined battle-ground, as if the mother of earth-life had sent up her sweetest and loveliest children to plead with the spirits of destruction.[13]

Robinson was not content just to promote the virtues of alpine flowers. In *Alpine Flowers*, he also took side-swipes at his perennial bug-bears such as carpet bedding, which he described uncompromisingly: 'The process which is commonly called "bedding out" presents to us simply the best possible appliance for depriving vegetation of every grace of form, beauty of colour, and vital interest. The genius of cretinism itself could hardly delight in anything more tasteless or ignoble than the absurd daubs of colour that every summer flare in the neighbourhood of most country-houses.'[14]

Under Robinson's fire was Paxton's new terraced garden around the re-erected Crystal Palace in Sydenham, which the latter conceived as being Britain's answer to Versailles. Robinson had admired much in Paris, but not Versailles, which he saw as a monument to French absolutism as the Whigs had done a century and a half earlier. Robinson, inspired by the Arts and Crafts movement's social idealism, lamented that thousands of French serfs had been forced to construct the garden. In the Great Exhibition, Robinson saw something comparable. It was Paxton's crowning moment, but for William Morris, Ruskin and Robinson, the manufacturing industry the exhibition vaunted was dehumanising. The Crystal Palace displays, they believed, were factory-made by workers torn from their rural roots and villages, where objects were crafted by hand. That ideal of craftsmanship was what the Arts and Craft movement sought to uphold, and its leading horticultural exponents were Robinson and Gertrude Jekyll. Ruskin's famous mantra was their motto: 'Nothing but Art is moral: Life without Industry is sin, and Industry without Art, brutality.'[15]

In the late nineteenth century, taste swung away from Nesfield-style gardens to the greater naturalism and focus on individual plants advocated by Robinson. For Robinson, as earlier for the Whig aristocracy, horticultural taste was not just a case of personal preference: there were moral and political implications to how plants were used. Robinson believed they should be grown in the conditions to which they were suited rather than hot-housed before being corralled into beds to provide great blasts of colour. 'We have to deal with the future,' wrote Robinson in an issue of his magazine, *The Garden*. 'The coloured gravel, terrace wall, water-squirt pattern bed properties have nearly served their turn.'[16]

Robinson would continue to fight this battle, returning to it in *The English Flower Garden* in 1883. There, he stated that 'for a true flower garden one must have freedom to select from every source of beauty among hardy things,' unlike in contemporary 'mosaic culture', where 'beautiful forms of flowers are degraded to crude colour without reference to the natural forms or beauty of the plants, clipping being freely done to get the carpets level'.[17]

***

Robinson published book after book, and contributed regularly to periodicals. In 1868, he revised and edited Jane Loudon's *Amateur Gardener's Calendar* 'to bring it down to the wants of the present day'. In his introduction, he recognised the widening interest in gardening and the importance of Loudon's book. For many, 'gardening is usually a recreation after the toils of the day, or in the evening of life, and as they are frequently without practical experience, a simple hand guide to the various everyday operations is ... a necessity to success. The *Amateur Gardener* was written to meet this want.'[18]

In 1870, Robinson published *The Wild Garden*, responsible for the lasting popularity of the wild and woodland look. Five new editions have been published in the last forty years, edited by gardening writer Robin Lane Fox and naturalist Richard Mabey, among others.[19] *The Wild Garden* displays Robinson's extensive reading, with an epigraph by Sydney Smith, and Shakespeare, Milton and Bacon cited on the first page. As in *Alpine Flowers*, he criticised the current taste for brightly coloured annual bedding which left beds bare in winter. He suggested that 'few have any conception of the great number of really pretty flowers that may be selected from wild places in various parts of the British isles, and cultivated with success in the garden'. What he proposed was 'a charming little hardy garden, or series of beds filled exclusively with the better kinds of our native plants, dotted here and there with our native shrubs'.[20]

This played well with suburban gardeners to whom Jane Loudon's *Amateur Gardener's Calendar* appealed, and *The Wild Garden* went into seven subsequent editions or reprints between 1881 and 1928. Other books appeared more or less simultaneously: *Mushroom Culture* (1870), motivated by his time in France; *A Catalogue of Hardy Perennials*, and *The Subtropical Garden*, in which he advocated mixed planting of flowers, foliage, ferns, shrubs and trees. Hardy subtropical plants favoured by Robinson included acanthus, bamboos and fennel.[21] Also in 1871, he published *Hardy Plants*, which described over 1,300 ornamental species with advice on planting, the only endeavour in half a century to match William Townsend Aiton's *Hortus Kewensis* (1810–1813).

In 1870, Robinson set sail for America on a trip shrouded in mystery. He made his way across the continent to San Francisco, it is thought in search of his long-absent father. If he had hoped that his experiences would contribute to a book, he was disappointed, writing that 'as regards horticulture [I] have found as much interest and novelty as a student of snakes could collect during a like period in the land of St. Patrick'.[22] His first impressions of American cities were similar to those of Charles Dickens. But, unlike Dickens, he warmed to the country, making useful contacts among its botanists, visiting Washington's Mount Vernon and collecting penstemon and phlox seeds. He particularly enjoyed the Sierra, drawn again, like Ruskin, to mountains. 'The autumn days I spent among these trees were among the happiest one could desire.'[23]

If Robinson did find his father, it may be that Robinson père, pricked perhaps by guilt from having abandoned his first family, or by being strong-armed by this determined, articulate man of thirty-two, volunteered enough money for Robinson to achieve his long-cherished desire of setting up a magazine.

Robinson seems certainly to have returned in funds. He was an astute businessman who ploughed the proceeds of his writing into the London property market, and never failed to spot a commercial opportunity. Setting up as a periodical publisher, he tried his hand briefly at a daily newspaper, *London*, and also, for a while, became a bookseller, using rooms at his offices in Southampton Street for a mail order business.[24]

Dark, imposing and six foot tall, Robinson was interested in women, but never married after being jilted by a young woman for an affluent tradesman. While in America, he admired the wife of botanist Asa Gray, but wrote sadly to Gray that 'nearly all the nice women I have ever seen were married, though it is very rare indeed that one of them is secured by a botanist, who, like myself, is frequently obliged to console himself with flowers of a less exalted type'.[25]

He consoled himself not only with flowers, but also with publishing. *The Garden*, his weekly magazine, launched in November 1871, featured articles on subjects as various as new parks in America, road-widening schemes in London, garden tool recommendations, and the culture of flowers, fruit and vegetables. *Gardening* (later becoming *Gardening Illustrated*) followed in 1879, designed for suburban gardeners. By the spring of 1881, *Gardening* had a weekly circulation of over 30,000 and gave Robinson a platform to attack carpet bedding, topiary, fussy gardening at Kew, the use of botanical Latin, and greenhouses. His contributors included botanising clergymen and authors, and Henry Elwes, discoverer in Turkey in 1874 of the tulip-shaped snowdrop, *Galanthus elwesii*. They often found him exacting. One of them, Canon Ellacombe, wrote to Sir Joseph Hooker, director of Kew. 'As to Mr Robinson, I give up trying to set his twist right – but I regret it because I think his paper does much good ... Like Elwes and Maw I constantly threaten that I will send him no more notes, but he will not let us alone.'[26]

Most significantly, through *The Garden* he encountered Gertrude Jekyll in 1875. She became a regular contributor, and took over briefly as editor when Robinson stepped down in 1899. Robinson also helped Jekyll with planting her garden at Munstead and attended her funeral in 1932, although aged ninety-four and in poor health himself.

More periodical launches followed, including *Farm and Home* (founded 1882), *Woods and Forests* (1883), *Cottage Gardening* (1892), and *Flora and Sylva* (1903).

Robinson's ideas on wild gardening and on mixed planting were not entirely novel, but his writing reflected a mounting reaction against Paxton and Nesfield. In 1883, Robinson reprised this theme in *The English Flower Garden*, which ran into fifteen editions and nine reprints in his lifetime.

This manual of design and horticulture included contributions from Gertrude Jekyll on colour. Robinson wanted his readers to see that 'the work of the true artist ... is always marked by respect for Nature and by keen study of her'. Gardens singled out for particular condemnation were Crystal Palace, the Royal Horticultural Society's garden at Kensington, Witley Court, Castle Howard, Mentmore, Drayton and Crewe Hall, all the work of either Paxton or Nesfield. During the previous half century, he claims 'there was hardly a country seat laid out that was not marred by the idea of a garden as a conventional and patterned thing'.[27]

Robinson had no garden of his own. This, combined with his often dyspeptic manner, exposed him to criticism as 'an eminent "arm-chair" gardener [who] in the seclusion of his study, has discovered that hardy plants are beautiful'.[28] In 1885, however, he bought Gravetye Manor, a dilapidated Elizabethan house in Sussex, with an overgrown 360-acre estate, to which he devoted the rest of his life. He planted thousands of trees and put into practice what he had been preaching about throughout his working life.

Robinson moved for the first four years into a farmhouse on the estate while the manor itself was completely remodelled in the Arts and Crafts style. The house's hillside site meant that, paradoxically, one of Robinson's first acts was to make a wide terrace retained by a sandstone wall, despite all his attacks on formality in gardens.[29] Robinson's defence was that he was going with the lie of the land, rather than following the taste for introducing terraces 'in level plains'.[30]

There was formality, too, in the layout of the terraced beds, long borders and pergolas, but the planting was a world away from the serried carpet bedding that, for example, characterised Cragside, the estate of the industrialist William Armstrong in Northumberland. The planting was mixed, with the drive lined by low native shrubs, such as heather, gorse, brambles, sloes, dogwoods and plums. In long borders, he mixed hardy subtropical plants such as yuccas with native shrubs, asters and other perennials. He had a particular fondness for roses, often underplanted with alpines. He created an alpine meadow, and in woodland around the fringe of the estate planted 5,000 hollies, 1,000 Cedars of Lebanon, and 1,000 acers and 100 liquidambar for autumn colour.[31] In his planning and design, Robinson was assisted by his former mentor, Robert Marnock, until the latter's death in 1889.

His views on gardening continued to attract controversy: in 1892, Sir Reginald Blomfield's *The Formal Garden in England* praised the history of formality in England and criticised gardeners such as Robinson for having no understanding either of design or of how a garden relates to the house. Robinson, incensed, fought back with a little book entitled *Garden Design and Architects' Gardens*. Gertrude Jekyll, a friend of both men, tried to pour oil on troubled waters, pointing out in the *Edinburgh Review* that there were rights and wrongs on both sides.[32]

***

In 1909, on his way to church, Robinson slipped on a stile, injuring his back. What might have been a minor injury proved to have a lasting effect as a result of syphilis, which had lain dormant for years. He spent twenty-five years in a wheelchair, although he continued to visit France and Switzerland, work on the garden, and invite guests who included Gertrude Jekyll, plant-hunters Augustine Henry and Reginald Farrer, Harold Peto (pioneer of Italianate gardening) and Ellen Willmott. Robinson produced an account of his work at Gravetye in 1911, *Home Landscapes*, in 1912, and two books on wood fires, another of his fixations.

From 1910, he was supported by Ernest Markham, a gardener of considerable experience who shared Robinson's passion for Gravetye and who died there in 1937, just two years after Robinson. Together, they developed a remarkable collection of clematis, one of them being named after Markham. A book, *The Virgin's Bower* (1912), resulted from this mutual enthusiasm.

A curious car with tracks instead of back wheels, bought in 1922, enabled Robinson to visit the remoter parts of his estate. He was cared for by a nurse, Mary Gilpin, who came initially for a month in 1909 and stayed until his death. As he died, the children of the village were enjoying a fireworks display he had arranged to celebrate George V's Silver Jubilee. Although unmarried, Robinson was fond of children, virtually adopting Mary's niece, Iris, for a few years when Iris's mother was unable to look after both her and an ailing husband. The child delighted Robinson, playing pat-a-cake with the elderly bachelor and growing her own little garden. It was a sadness to him when Mary insisted Iris should go off to school. His last words were said to be: 'Children are always very delightful.'[33]

Besides generous bequests to his staff, Robinson left half his estate to the Gardeners' Royal Benevolent Institution, and half to the Shipwrecked Fishermen and Mariners' Royal Benevolent Society. The house, gardens and woodlands were given to the nation for state forestry, with the firm proviso that they should never be used for teaching purposes: 'The trees, woods and landscapes shall be the only teachers.'[34] After various incarnations, the house became a hotel in the late 1950s, its garden remaining a living monument to its creator.

Ninety-five when he died, Robinson was the grand old man of gardening. He was still replanning an orchard and planting a new one, and writing letters to his many correspondents. There had been disappointments: the Royal Horticultural Society's prestigious Victoria Medal of Honour eluded him, a strange omission for a gardener of his distinction and possibly because he made too many enemies. Robinson was offered a knighthood in 1933 by Ramsey MacDonald, leader of the National Government, but the old gardener turned it down, feeling the honour had come too late.

Robinson lived through periods of great change, including a world war and several revolutions. He had his detractors, but also many admirers, including thousands of weekly subscribers. He caught the crest of the turning horticultural tide as he first sailed his boats upon its stormy waters. Through his magazines, and books such as *The Wild Garden* and *The English Flower Garden*, he captured the imagination of the gardening public and influenced many of his successors. Brent Elliott, former Royal Horticultural Society historian, believes Robinson was a populariser whose importance has been exaggerated, and that 'to a considerable degree he engineered the creation of his own myth'.[35] But this seems a harsh judgement on a gardener who, directly or indirectly, influenced gardening for 150 years, as is shown by a glance at Chelsea Flower Show gardens in the early twenty-first century.

The equally spiky Reginald Farrer's tribute is fitting. The two often squabbled (Robinson disliked Farrer's dotted used of alpines), but Farrer recognised the achievements and perplexities of the venerable gardener. 'Like all true prophets,' wrote Farrer, 'he arose magnificent, passionate, unguided and unguidable.'[36]

CHAPTER 14

Gertrude Jekyll (1843–1932)

In 1889, Harold Mangles, a rhododendron enthusiast, invited Gertrude Jekyll to tea at Littleworth Cross in Surrey. He wanted to introduce the eminent forty-five-year-old gardener to a nineteen-year-old architect working on his first independent commission. Edwin Lutyens had 'eagerly accepted the privilege', he later recalled. 'We met at a tea-table, the silver kettle and the conversation reflecting rhododendrons.' Jekyll was dressed in what Lutyens described as 'her Go-to-Meeting Frock', her hat trimmed with 'alert cock's-tail feathers, curving and ever prancing forwards', which gave her a more irreverent look than her withdrawn manner betokened. She didn't address a word to Lutyens until she was leaving. 'With one foot on the step of her pony-cart and reins in hand, she invited me to Munstead on the very next Saturday.'[1]

This unlikely couple would form one of the most celebrated partnerships in gardening history. Some of her best garden designs were collaborations with Ned Lutyens (as he was known); together, they worked on over a hundred commissions, including Jekyll's own home at Munstead Wood, where she tested planting and design ideas for fifty years.[2] Jekyll helped refine the vision of the brilliant young architect, while Lutyens developed her understanding of how architecture and gardening could enhance one another. 'The truth appears to be that for the best building and planting ... the architect and the gardener must have some knowledge of each other's business, and each must regard with feelings of kindly reverence the unknown domains of the other's higher knowledge,' Jekyll later wrote.[3]

Even without Lutyens, Jekyll would have been a major figure in gardening. During her career, she worked, her nephew believed, on around 340 garden commissions and was consulted by some fifty architects, as well as writing a dozen books and publishing over a thousand articles. Originally an artist, she was also a craftswoman, embroiderer and photographer, who turned to garden design when her eyesight worsened. Her training as a painter (and hours spent copying Turner's paintings in

Gertrude Jekyll at the Deanery, Sonning, home of Edward Hudson, founder of *Country Life*, *c.* 1901.

the National Gallery) taught her the use of colour in the garden, her legacy to future gardeners.

***

Gertrude Jekyll was born on 29 November 1843 in London's Mayfair, the second daughter and fifth child of Edward Jekyll, a former Grenadier Guards officer, collector of Etruscan vases and amateur scientist. His wife, Julia, a banker's daughter, had taken music lessons from Mendelssohn. Gertrude's brother, Herbert, wrote in a family memoir that the Jekylls 'were reputable gentlefolk, lawyers, clergymen, bankers, merchants, soldiers, sailors and servants of the Crown'. Only one achieved much distinction: Sir Joseph Jekyll, knighted by William III in 1697 and a Privy Councillor and Master of the Rolls under George I. Gertrude's grandfather, another Joseph, was an MP, a fellow of the Royal Society and the Society of Arts, and was painted by the society portraitist Sir Thomas Lawrence.[4]

The Jekylls' was a secure, happy and cultured home, in which hard work was valued, and the children were encouraged to play and sing. Gertrude's earliest memories were associated with gardens. In her 1908 book, *Children and Gardens*, she recollected grass, flowers, the pungent aroma of a dandelion sniffed during walks around Green Park and Berkeley Square.[5]

In 1848, the family moved to Bramley near Guildford in Surrey. Gertrude loved the Surrey countryside, relishing its secluded lanes with tangled tree roots, sandstone hills, and hazel- and chestnut-covered slopes. Seeing a primrose copse at Bramley fostered her delight in the beauty of nature.[6] She delighted, too, in her father's experiments with electricity, her 'small fingers ... often called in for the preparing of some of the humbler appliances', and training her for her own diligent craftswork in her adult life.[7]

She spent holidays roaming with her brothers but term-times were solitary, when the boys were at school and her sister, Caroline (Carry), six years older, was more remote. Gertrude had to amuse herself after lessons with her governesses, turning into what her father described as 'a queer child'.[8] Her education in art, music and languages seems to have been reasonably thorough, as she spoke German well. Her early love of Surrey and of its wild flowers was augmented by her exhaustive study, as a teenager and young woman, of its architecture, crafts, and working customs. She was instinctively sympathetic to the Arts and Crafts movement, a reaction against the vaunting of capitalism and manufacturing industry at the 1851 Great Exhibition. She applauded the founding of the Art Workers' Guild in 1884, sharing with William Morris an idealised view of country life and valuing what she saw as the threatened traditional crafts of her native Surrey. 'Have nothing in your houses,' said Morris, 'that you do not know to be useful, or believe to be beautiful.' Jekyll would have agreed.

Unusually for a woman of her time and class, she was set upon a career and her open-minded parents encouraged (and paid for) her to go to the South Kensington or Central School of Art in 1861. There, she studied applied and decorative arts and sketched classical statues (women were not allowed to paint live models).

As a student, Jekyll read and annotated John Ruskin's books, *Seven Lamps of Architecture* and *Stones of Venice*. After graduating, she travelled to Greece, Turkey, and Constantinople with Charles and Mary Newton. Newton, keeper of antiquities at the British Museum, had been at Oxford with Ruskin. Mary, his wife, was an artist, and, during the three-month trip, Gertrude and Mary both drew and painted assiduously.[9]

Jekyll returned home to England on Boxing Day 1863, aged twenty, committed to being an artist. For the next ten years she painted but also took up craftwork such as embroidery, marquetry and carving. She was commissioned by the Duke of Westminster to embroider panels for a new wing at Eaton Hall in Cheshire and by Lord Leighton to produce cushions and a tablecloth for his London home. She designed interiors for Jacques and Leonie Blumenthal's house at Hyde Park Gate, and for their chalet in Switzerland, where she also worked on the garden. The Blumenthals were leaders of the Arts and Crafts movement, and numbered high-flying feminists among their friends: Barbara Bodichon, a founder of Girton, Cambridge, asked Jekyll to advise on the college's interior decoration.

She enjoyed travel. In 1868, she admired the great Renaissance water gardens at Hadrian's villa and the Villa d'Este in Rome, and realised how the classical style could be transmuted into English gardens, having none of the stubborn resistance to formality which characterised William

Robinson's approach. She designed a special little pick for uprooting rocky plants, such as *Lithospermum rosmarinifolium*, crocuses, campanula and *Rosa sempervirens*, and primulas and fritillaries, which she brought back from Capri and the Pyrenees in 1883.[10]

This fulfilling, industrious time was full of new friendships. In the 1860s, Jekyll met Ruskin, William Morris, Octavia Hill, later founder of the National Trust, and the painters G. F. Watts and Hercules Brabazon, the latter influencing her ideas on colour. 'Brabazon is the only man since Turner,' said Ruskin, 'at whose feet I can sit and worship and learn about colour.'[11] The marriage in 1881 of her brother, Herbert, to Agnes Graham, an art collector's daughter, introduced Herbert and Gertrude to the world of Dante Gabriel Rossetti and Edward Burne-Jones. Gertrude's status as a craftswoman was high: a tortoiseshell casket and an iron tray were bought by what later became the Victoria and Albert Museum as a superb example of contemporary craftwork.[12]

Another artist, George Leslie, described Jekyll as

> ... a young lady of such singular and remarkable accomplishments ... Clever and witty in conversation, active and energetic in mind and body, and possessed of artistic talents of no common order ... there is hardly any useful handicraft the mysteries of which she has not mastered, carving, modelling, house-painting, carpentry, smith's work, repousée work, gilding, wood inlaying, embroidery, gardening and all manner of herb and culture ... her artistic taste is very great.[13]

Leslie implies that Jekyll was impressive by her mid-twenties. Her hair was pinned up in a tight knot, and her sharp eyes were hidden behind thick glasses. Intellectually self-confident, she would have been a daunting prospect for any young Victorian male, and indeed there never seems to have been any love interest in Jekyll's life.

As she worked at her painting and craftwork, and gardened at her parents' homes, Jekyll was almost unwittingly training herself in garden design. Studying at art school under Christopher Dresser, a pivotal designer in the Aesthetic Movement, enriched her understanding of colour, and embroidery worked its magic, too, with its rich weaving of colour, pattern and texture.[14] As garden historian Mavis Batey has written, Jekyll, 'herself a designer craftsman in the Morris mould, brought gardening into the Arts and Crafts movement'.[15]

***

In 1868, Jekyll was wrenched away from Surrey when the family moved to Wargrave Hill in Berkshire. 'June 8th,' she wrote in her diary, 'To my great grief left Bramley for Wargrave.' But, given 'ample scope' by her parents, Jekyll launched into making 'Chinese screen, pear-wood frames, imitation Rhodian pots, open-work silver pins, gold stands for china', all

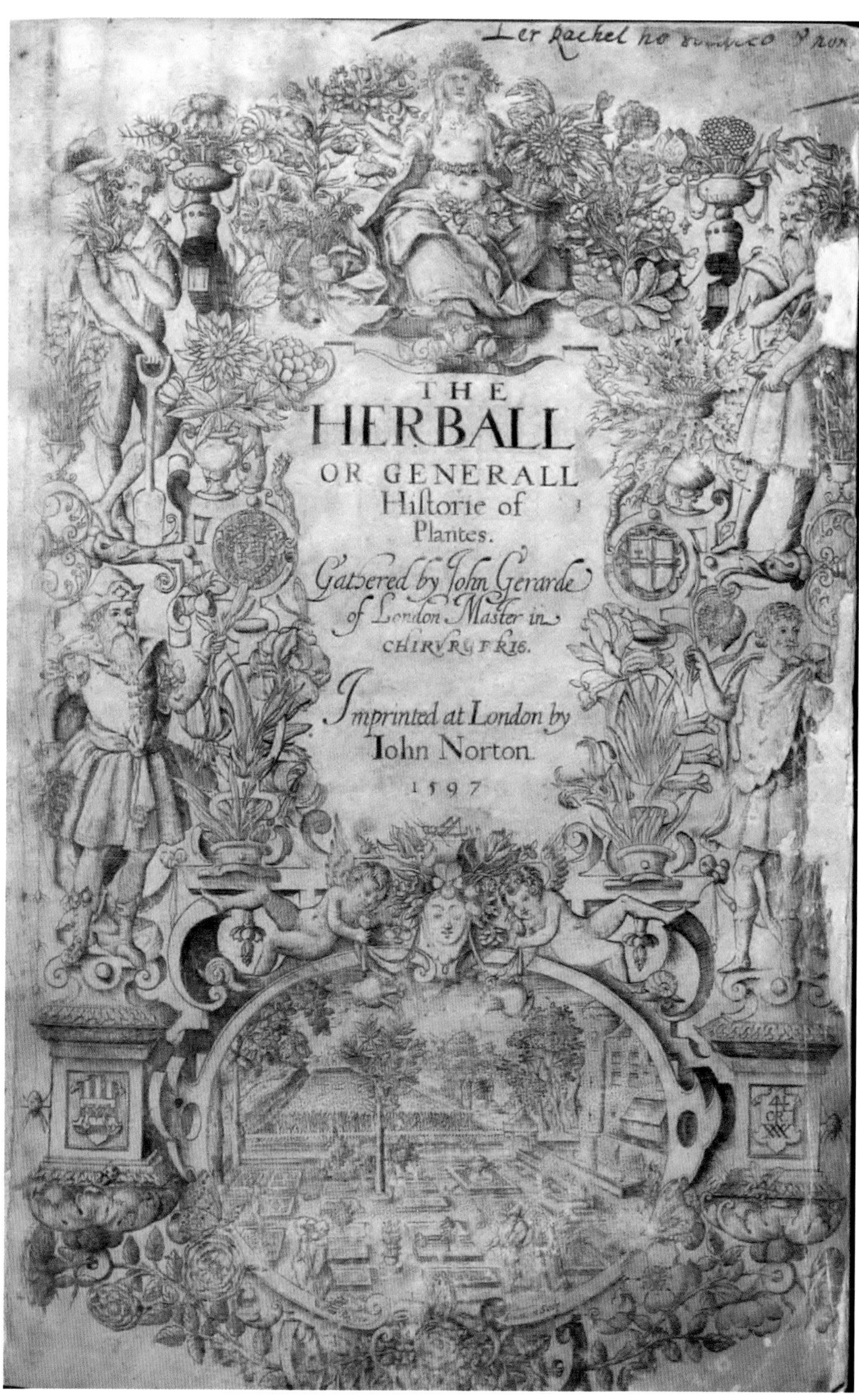

THE
HERBALL
OR GENERALL
Historie of
Plantes.
Gathered by John Gerarde
of London Master in
CHIRURGERIE.
Imprinted at London by
Iohn Norton.
1597

The title page of the original edition of Gerard's *Herball*, published by Queen Elizabeth I's printer, John Norton, in 1597.

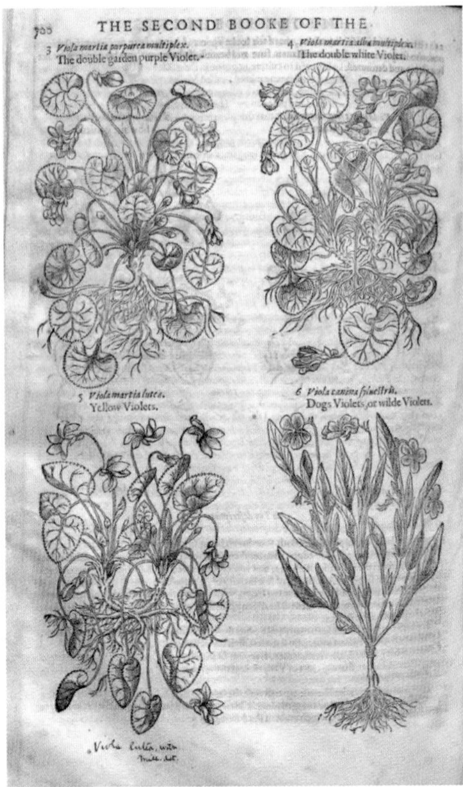

700 THE SECOND BOOKE OF THE

3 *Viola martia purpurea multiplex.*
The double garden purple Violet.

4 *Viola martia alba multiplex.*
The double white Violet.

5 *Viola martia lutea.*
Yellow Violets.

6 *Viola canina ſyluestris.*
Dogs Violets, or wilde Violets.

Gerard's *Herball* was illustrated by German woodblocks.

Left: The wild field violet.

Below left: What Gerard described as the prickly Indian fig is now called a prickly pear.

Below: Gerard was discredited by claiming to have seen the Barnakle tree with his own eyes.

HISTORIE OF PLANTS. 1329

they ſlaken the paſſages, make the conduits ſlipperie, and open them, and do alſo ſomewhat clenſe:
whereupon after the eating of the ſame, it hapneth that much grauell and ſand is conueied foorth.
Drie or barrell Figs, called in Latine *Caricæ*, are a remedie for the belly, the cough, and for old in- O
firmities of the cheſt and lungs; they ſcoure the kidneies, and clenſe foorth the ſand; they mitigate
the paine of the bladder, and cauſe women with childe to haue the eaſier deliuerance, if they fee de
thereof for certaine daies togither before the time of deliuerance.
Dioſcorides ſaith, that the white liquor of the Figtree, and iuice of the leaues, doth curdle milke P
as the rennet doth, and diſſolueth the milke that is cluttered in the ſtomacke, as doth vineger.
It bringeth downe the menſes if it be applied with the yolke of an egge, or with yellow waxe. Q

Of the prickly Indian Figtree. Chap.128.

1 *Ficus Indica.*
The Indian Fig tree.

Fructus.
The fruit.

The deſcription.

1 THis ſtrange and admirable plant called *Ficus Indica*, ſeemeth to be no other thing then a multiplication of leaues, that is, a tree made of leaues, without body or boughes: for the leafe ſet in the grounde doth in ſhort ſpace take roote, and bringeth out of it ſelfe other leaues, from which do grow others one after another, till ſuch time as they come to the height of a tree; hauing alſo in the meane ſeaſon boughes as it were comming from thoſe leaues, ſometimes more, otherwhiles fewer, as nature liſt to beſtow, adding leafe vnto leafe, whereby it occupieth a great peece of ground; theſe leaues are long, and broad, as thicke as a mans thumbe, of a deepe greene colour, ſet full of long, ſlender, ſharpe, and [illegible] prickles: on the tops of which leaues come forth long flowers, not vnlike to thoſe of the [illegible] tree, or rather the Maruell of Peru, of a yellow colour: after which commeth the [illegible], like vnto the common Fig, narrow below,

HISTORIE OF PLANTS. 1391

Of the Gooſe tree, Barnakle tree, or the tree bearing Geeſe. Chap.167.

Britannica Concha anatifera.
The breede of Barnakles.

The deſcription.

HAuing trauelled from the Graſſes growing in the bottome of the fenny waters, the woods, and mountaines, euen vnto Libanus it ſelfe; and alſo the ſea, and bowels of the ſame: we are arriued to the end of our Hiſtorie, thinking it not impertinent to the concluſion of the ſame, to end with one of the maruels of this land (we may ſay of the world.) The Hiſtorie whereof to ſet foorth according to the woorthines and raritie thereof, woulde not onely require a large and peculiar volume, but alſo a deeper ſearch into the bowels of nature, then my intended purpoſe wil ſuffer me to wade into, my inſufficiencie alſo conſidered; leauing the hiſtorie thereof rough hewen, vnto ſome excellent men, learned in the ſecrets of nature, to be both fined and refined: in the meane ſpace take it as it falleth out, the naked and bare truth, though vnpoliſhed. There are founde in the north parts of Scotland, & the Ilands adiacent, called Orchades, certaine trees, whereon doe growe certaine ſhell fiſhes, of a white colour tending to ruſſet; wherein are conteined little liuing creatures: which ſhels in time of maturitie doe open, and out of them grow thoſe little liuing things; which falling into the water, doe become foules, whom we call Barnakles, in the north of England Brant Geeſe, and in Lancaſhire tree Geeſe; but the other that do fall vpon the land, periſh and come to nothing: thus much by the writings of others, and alſo from the mouths of people of thoſe parts, which may very well accord with truth.

But what our eies haue ſeene, and hands haue touched, we ſhall declare. There is a ſmall Ilande in Lancaſhire called the Pile of Foulders, wherein are found the broken peeces of old and bruſed ſhips, ſome whereof haue beene caſt thither by ſhipwracke, and alſo the trunks or bodies with the branches of old and rotten trees, caſt vp there likewiſe: wheron is found a certaine ſpume or froth, that in time breedeth vnto certaine ſhels, in ſhape like thoſe of the muskle, but ſharper pointed, and of a whitiſh colour; wherein is conteined a thing in forme like a lace of ſilke finely wouen, as it were togither, of a whitiſh colour; one ende whereof is faſtned vnto the inſide of the ſhell, euen as the fiſh of Oiſters and Muskles are; the other ende is made faſt vnto the belly of a rude maſſe or lumpe, which in time commeth to the ſhape & forme of a Bird; when it is perfectly formed, the ſhel gapeth open, & the firſt thing that appeereth is the foreſaid lace or ſtring; next come the legs of the Birde hanging out; and as it groweth greater, it openeth the ſhell by degrees, till at length it is all come foorth, and hangeth onely by the bill; in ſhort ſpace after it commeth to full maturitie, and falleth into the ſea, where it gathereth feathers, and groweth to a foule, bigger then a Mallard, and leſſer then a Gooſe; hauing blacke legs and bill or beake, and feathers blacke and white, ſpotted in ſuch maner as is our Magge-Pie, called in ſome places a Pie-Annet, which the

Above: The Tradescants' tomb at St Mary's, Lambeth, now home of the Garden Museum. (© The Garden Museum)

Right: Henrietta Maria, 'the Rose and Lily Queen', employer of both Tradescants. A miniature by David des Granges after Anthony van Dyck, *c*. 1636. (Courtesy Yale Center for British Art)

Henry Wise, royal gardener, by Sir Godfrey Kneller. (Royal Collection Trust/© Her Majesty Queen Elizabeth II, 2018)

Above: A rare surviving formal French-style garden at Melbourne Hall, Derbyshire, originally designed by London and Wise. (© Andrea Jones/Garden Exposures Photo Library)

Right: Plan for a city garden which unfolds from the pages of Thomas Fairchild's *The City Gardener.*

Nurseryman and first hybridiser Thomas Fairchild, by an unknown artist. (© Department of Plant Sciences, University of Oxford)

Philip Miller's *Gardeners Dictionary* went into eight editions in his lifetime.

Right: The frontispiece.

Below: The title page.

Below right: The opening page of the fourth edition (1754).

THE

Gardeners Dictionary.

Containing the METHODS of CULTIVATING and IMPROVING ALL SORTS OF TREES, PLANTS, *and* FLOWERS, FOR THE *Kitchen*, *Fruit*, and *Pleasure Gardens*; AS ALSO Those which are used in MEDICINE. WITH DIRECTIONS for the Culture of VINEYARDS, and Making of WINE in *England*. In which likewise are included The PRACTICAL PARTS of HUSBANDRY.

Abridged from the last Folio Edition,
By the AUTHOR, *PHILIP MILLER*, F.R.S.
Member of the Botanic Academy at *Florence*, and Gardener to the Worshipful Company of APOTHECARIES, at their Botanic Garden, at *Chelsea*.

—— *Digna manet divini gloria ruris.* Virg. Geor.

In THREE VOLUMES.

VOL. I.

The FOURTH EDITION, Corrected and Enlarged.

LONDON:
Printed for the AUTHOR;
And Sold by JOHN and JAMES RIVINGTON, at the *Bible* and *Crown*, in *St. Paul's Church-Yard*.
M.DCC.LIV.

THE

Gardeners Dictionary.

VOL. I.

AB

ABELE Tree. *Vide* Populus.

ABIES; The Fir-tree.

The *Characters* of this Tree are;

It is ever-green; the Leaves are single, and, for the most part, produced on every Side the Branches; the Male Flowers, or Catkins, are placed at remote Distances from the Fruit on the same Tree; the Seeds are produced in Cones, which are squamose.

The Difference between these and the Pines is, the latter having two or more Leaves produced out of each Sheath or Cover.

The *Species* of this Tree, which are at present to be found in the *English* Gardens, are;

1. ABIES *taxi folio, fructu sursum spectante. Tourn.* The Silver or Yew-leav'd Fir-tree.

2. ABIES *tenuiori folio, fructu deorsum inflexo. Tourn.* The Common Fir or Pitch-tree; sometimes called, The *Norway* or Spruce Fir.

3. ABIES *minor, pectinatis foliis, Virginiana, conis parvis subrotundis. Pluk. Alm.* The *Virginian* Fir-tree, with small roundish Cones, commonly called Hemlock Fir.

4. ABIES *piceæ folio, fructu longissimo, deorsum inflexo.* The Yew-leav'd Fir-tree, with long hanging Cones, commonly called, The Long-coned *Cornish* Fir.

5. ABIES *piceæ foliis brevibus, conis minimis. Rand.* The Pitch-leav'd Fir-tree, with small Cones, commonly called, The *Newfoundland* Black Spruce Fir.

VOL. I. B 6. ABIES

A view of the Chelsea Physic Garden from the Thames, showing the original Cedars of Lebanon, *c.* 1790. (© Chelsea Physic Garden)

The statue of Sir Hans Sloane in the centre of the Chelsea Physic Garden, *c.* 1770, at the end of Miller's tenure as head gardener. (© Chelsea Physic Garden)

The clubbable Charles Bridgeman in a portrait attributed to William Hogarth, *c*. 1725–30. (© Vancouver Art Gallery, Founders' Fund)

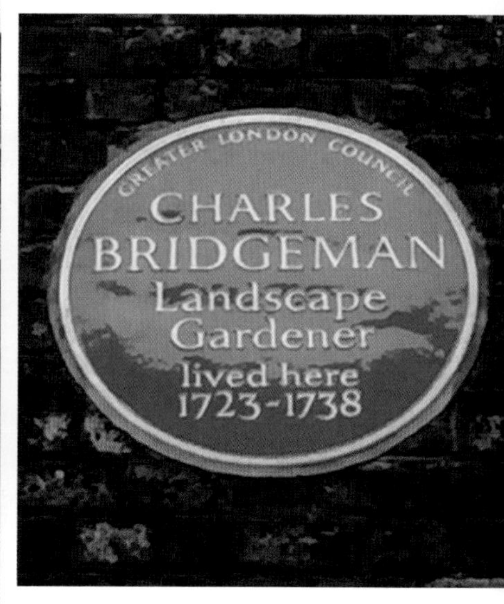

Left and above: Successful garden designer Charles Bridgeman could afford a large house in Broadwick Street, London W1, now marked by a blue plaque. (Author's collection)

Left: Richard Temple, Viscount Cobham, the creator of the landscape garden at Stowe, by Jean-Baptiste Van Loo. (Courtesy Stowe House Preservation Trust/ Hall Bequest Trust)

View from Nelson's Seat at Stowe, Buckinghamshire, in an engraving commissioned by Charles Bridgeman from Jacques Rigaud. (Courtesy Stowe House Preservation Trust/Stowe School)

A view of the Rotunda designed in 1721 by Sir John Vanbrugh and situated in a Bridgeman landscape at Stowe. Jean B. C. Chatelain, 1753. (Courtesy Yale Center for British Art)

Left: Bon viveur William Kent engraved by Alexander Bannerman after William Aikman, 1762. (Courtesy Yale Center for British Art)

Below left: The seven-arched Praeneste Arcade at Rousham, Oxfordshire, designed by Kent. (Author's collection)

Below right: Venus's Vale at Rousham. (Author's collection)

Above: Croome Park, its church and landscape were all designed by 'Capability' Brown as his first freelance commission. (© National Trust Images)

Below: Holkham Hall's parkland, in which both 'Capability' Brown and Humphry Repton had a hand. (© Holkham Estate)

Above: Holkham Hall's landscape, the work of Brown and Repton, seen in winter. (© Holkham Estate)

Left: The Marble Hall at Holkham Hall, Norfolk, one of Kent's crowning achievements. (© Holkham Estate)

Above: William Andrews Nesfield's elaborate parterre at Broughton Hall, Yorkshire. (Courtesy The Tempest family at Broughton Hall)

Right: Nesfield's 1855 plans for the Broughton parterre. (Courtesy The Tempest family at Broughton Hall)

The South Front parterre at Holkham Hall was designed by Nesfield. (© Holkham Estate)

THE GIGANTIC WATER-LILY (VICTORIA REGIA), IN FLOWER AT CHATSWORTH.

The giant waterlily leaves at Chatsworth were strong enough to bear the weight of a child. Depicted in *The Illustrated London News*, 17 November 1849.

Above: Joseph Paxton's Conservative Wall at Chatsworth, Derbyshire. (Courtesy alh1 under Creative Commons 2.0)

Right: The interior of Paxton's Crystal Palace, by John Saddler, 1851. (Courtesy Yale Center for British Art)

Below: Crystal Palace after it was rebuilt at Sydenham, by Robert Carrick. (Courtesy Yale Center for British Art)

Above and below: The planting at Gravetye Manor, now a hotel, is still maintained in Robinson's style. (© Claire Takacs)

Above, below and overleaf top: The gardens at Hestercombe, Somerset, designed and planted by the partnership of Edwin Lutyens and Gertrude Jekyll. (Courtesy Hestercombe Gardens Trust)

Below: Hidcote Manor, Gloucestershire, in the early days of Lawrence Johnston's ownership. (Courtesy Gloucestershire Archives/CCHS Jesse Taylor photographs)

The Cottage Garden at Sissinghurst in May. (© National Trust Images)

This spread: Margery Fish's cottage garden at East Lambrook Manor, Somerset. (Courtesy Mike Werkmeister)

A drawing by Russell Page of a pavilion at Battersea for the Festival of Britain in 1951. (Courtesy The Garden Museum)

Russell Page sketching. (Courtesy The Garden Museum)

The grass walk at Rosemary Verey's Barnsley House garden. (Courtesy National Garden Scheme)

Right: The famous laburnum walk at Barnsley House. (© Andrew Lawson)

Below: A view over the parterre beds to the William and Mary Barnsley House. (Courtesy National Garden Scheme)

Above: Penelope Hobhouse's garden at The Coach House, Bettiscombe, Dorset.

Below: The architectural planting at Penelope Hobhouse's present home in Somerset. (Both courtesy Penelope Hobhouse)

Three of John Brookes' projects.

Above: Part of the garden and the Clock House at Denmans, Sussex.

Right and below right: A garden in Umbria.

Below: The Zespol Palace in Poland. (All courtesy John Brookes Design)

The long border at Christopher Lloyd's Great Dixter in East Sussex. (Courtesy Anntin under Creative Commons 2.0)

A wild flower meadow at Great Dixter, originally seeded by Lloyd's mother, Daisy. (Courtesy Miles Berry under Creative Commons 2.0)

Above: The water garden and grass dams at the Beth Chatto Gardens at Elmstead Market, Essex.

Below: The drought-resistant planting of Beth Chatto's famous dry garden. (Both courtesy The Beth Chatto Gardens)

Above: Poppies and *Gladiolus byzantinus* in Beth Chatto's dry garden.

Below: Chatto's woodland garden. (Both courtesy The Beth Chatto Gardens)

Above and below: A wild flower garden, planted by Tom Stuart-Smith for a bio-dynamic wine grower, in the Duero Valley of central Spain. (Courtesy Tom Stuart-Smith)

Above: Stuart-Smith has planted the Italianate terraces at Broughton Grange, Oxfordshire, with eryngiums, alliums, grasses and pillars of yew.

Below: Low box hedging, interplanted with annuals, mimics the cell structure of leaves at Broughton. (Both © Jonathan Buckley)

listed by her nephew, Francis Jekyll. So well placed were Jekyll's terracotta 'Rhodian' pots that they remained in situ in the garden long after she and her mother returned to Surrey. The garden provided compensation and three years later Jekyll was writing in her diary, 'July 1871 – Much interested in garden plants – always collecting.' She created a garden where 'a perfect wilderness of sweets, and old-fashioned flowers bloomed ... in the greatest profusion', according to George Leslie. 'There were lavender hedges of marvellous growth, and the generous way she, with a lavender sickle of her own construction, reaped me an armful, I shall long remember.'[16]

Jekyll's first garden commission came during the Wargrave years from a Rochdale factory lad, who wanted a window-box planted up. 'So advice was sent and the box prepared,' Jekyll recalled in *Wood and Garden*. 'The size was three feet by ten inches. A little later the post brought him little plants of mossy and silvery saxifrages, and few small bulbs. Even some stones were sent for, for it was to be a rock garden ... It was delightful to have the boy's letters, full of keen interest and eager questions ... I could picture his feeling of delightful anticipation.'[17] Jekyll's pleasure in this boy's interest suggests why she later wrote to encourage the wider gardening public.

When Captain Jekyll died in March 1876, Gertrude, the unmarried daughter, continued living with her widowed mother. (Carry had married Frederick Eden in 1865, and lived in Venice, where they created an English garden on Giudecca.) Julia Jekyll and her daughter returned to Surrey, buying twenty acres between Bramley and Godalming. An architect was selected and work began on what would become Munstead House in autumn 1877, when fruit trees and many other plants were transplanted from the chalk of Berkshire to acidic Surrey sand. A year later, mother and daughter moved into their new house. 'Sept. 26th. – To Munstead for good,' wrote Jekyll prophetically in her diary. She was just under thirty-five and would spend the next fifty-four years within half a mile of that new home. 'I only hated Berkshire,' she recalled to George Leslie, 'because it was not Surrey, and chalk because it was not sand.'[18]

Jekyll was already becoming known as a gardening writer, and had advised family and friends on their gardens. In January 1875, she visited William Robinson at his office and began writing for *The Garden*, a magazine she briefly edited when Robinson retired.

Munstead House gave Jekyll virgin soil in which to develop ideas she had discussed in *The Garden*. Pope's dictum 'to consult the Genius of the place in all' had been overlooked by many Victorian garden designers, but Jekyll always considered the lie of the land, its soil and other aspects. When as an elderly garden designer she was too infirm to travel to consultations, she would request soil samples and details about the local stone and trees before starting work on a meticulous plan. Her love of Surrey scenery, and of its architecture, were embodied in the gardens she made first at Munstead House, and later across the road at her own home,

Munstead Wood. In both places, she ensured that the boundaries of the garden meshed seamlessly with the chestnuts, birch, heathers and gorse of the surrounding heathland.[19]

In *Wood and Garden*, published in 1899, she encapsulated the joy of starting work at Munstead House. A religious woman, she saw God-given nature as her instructor, as did Ruskin:

> Looking back on nearly thirty years of gardening (the earlier part of it in groping ignorance with scant means of help), I can remember no part of it that was not full of pleasure and encouragement. For the first steps into a delightful Unknown, the first successes are victories all the happier for being scarcely expected, and with the growing knowledge comes the widening outlook, and the comforting sense of an ever-increasing gain of critical appreciation ... And a garden is a grand teacher. It teaches patience and careful watchfulness; it teaches industry and thrift; above all, it teaches entire trust ... The good gardener knows with absolute certainty that if he does his part ... so surely will God give the increase.[20]

Munstead House featured a pergola, alpine garden, hardy flower garden, azalea grove, Italianate cypress-flanked walk, orchard, kitchen garden and nut walk. All these features would appear in various future garden commissions, and at Munstead Wood.[21] The herbaceous border existed before Jekyll gardened, but she perfected it through her careful understanding of individual plants and of colour. 'It is not enough to cultivate plants well; they must be used well,' she wrote in *Wood and Garden*.[22] 'Her methods were the antithesis of modern instant gardening,' wrote garden designer Penelope Hobhouse in her introduction to an anthology of Jekyll's writing. 'She liked to study a plant, relating it to its natural habit, and then using it appropriately, placing it comfortably next to plants with similar environmental needs.'[23]

Jekyll's philosophy on colour in the garden reached triumphant expression in the main border at Munstead Wood, two hundred feet long and fourteen feet wide. Like Robinson, Jekyll disliked carpet bedding, but had no fear in principle of vivid colours in the garden as long as they enhanced the plants' natural beauty. And, like another great artist, Claude Monet, Jekyll had poor sight, so her use of colour was often impressionistic. In a seminal work, *Colour Schemes for the Flower Garden*, published in 1908, she described the colour scheme for her magnificent border, which was backed by a sandstone wall.

> The planting of the border is designed to show a distinct scheme of colour arrangement. At the two ends there is a groundwork of grey and glaucous foliage – Stachys, Santolina, *Cineraria maritima*, Sea-Kale and Lyme-grass, with darker foliage, also of grey quality, of Yucca,

> *Clematis recta* and Rue. With this...there are flowers of pure blue, grey-blue, white, palest yellow and palest pink; each colour partly in distinct masses and partly inter-grouped. The colour then passes through stronger yellows to orange and red. By the time the middle space of the border is reached the colour is strong and gorgeous, but, as it is in good harmonies, it is never garish. Then the colour strength recedes in an inverse sequence through orange and deep yellow to pale yellow, white and palest pink; again with blue-grey foliage. But at this, the eastern end, instead of the pure blues, we have purples and lilacs.[24]

Although remembered most for her cottage-gardening style and her fondness for British natives, Jekyll was happy, as was Robinson, to use hardy perennials gathered from across the world when they fitted into a planting scheme. Here, for instance, she combines clematis and rue with Mediterranean plants such as santolina and cineraria, with yucca, an American/Mexican introduction, and with Middle Eastern stachys. Stachys, with its soft, grey foliage, was one of Jekyll's signature edging plants.

***

As Jekyll worked, first at Munstead House and then at Munstead Wood, she also mastered photography. Between 1885 and 1914, Jekyll took photographs of cottage gardens, trees and their roots, architectural details, crafts, and villagers in her beloved Surrey.[25] These photographs provided a framework of reference for her garden designs, especially when working with Lutyens. Jekyll always owned several cats, who often feature in her photographs. Her favourite subject was Munstead Wood, the creation and growth of which she documented on film and on the page.

In 1881, she was asked for the first time to be a judge at a Royal Horticultural Society show. By then, Jekyll had friends drawn from several different worlds. In 1880, Dean Hole, founder of the National Rose Society, and William Robinson visited Munstead House, the latter offering advice on the plantings. Sir Thomas Hanbury, creator of La Mortola, the famed garden near Ventimiglia, also came to Munstead House, as did Sir Joseph Hooker, director of Kew. Female gardening friends included the gardening writer Theresa Earle and Ellen Willmott. Willmott's garden at Warley Place in Essex was as admired as Munstead Wood, but Willmott spent so extravagantly on her three gardens in England and abroad that she was penniless in old age. The essayist and critic, Logan Pearsall Smith, brother-in-law of Bertrand Russell, zoologist Alfred Russel Wallace, and painters Henry Moon and Helen Allingham also visited Munstead.

Constant visitors began to tire Julia Jekyll, by then over seventy. When building work was threatened nearby in the early 1880s, Mrs Jekyll purchased the fifteen acres to give Gertrude her own home. Gertrude was still living with her mother when she met Edwin Lutyens in 1889, but had been working for six years on the awkward triangular-shaped site at Munstead Wood. She had laid out her herbaceous border, created shrubberies, a copse, nut walk, spring garden, and sunken rock garden, designed for different seasons of the year.

Meeting Edwin Lutyens was a watershed for Munstead Wood, providing the garden's projected house with its architect. The young man who faced Gertrude Jekyll across Harold Mangles's tea-table was on the first rung of a dazzling career, culminating in a knighthood in 1918 and his designing the Cenotaph in London and New Delhi. An army officer's son, he missed years of schooling through ill-health, wandering instead through the countryside as Jekyll had done. After art school, he worked for a year in the offices of Ernest George and Harold Peto before setting up his own practice.[26] His love of nature and his dedication to his art struck a chord with Gertrude, and when he turned up to tea at Munstead House in 1889, a friendship began which would last until Jekyll's death, with Lutyens fondly christening her 'Aunt Bumps'.

Together, they rode in Jekyll's pony-cart around Surrey, Jekyll introducing Lutyens to its architecture and countryside. The thatch, brick, tiled roofs and timber frames of Surrey houses were admired not only by Jekyll but also by other members of the Arts and Crafts movement, such as Ruskin. Before the main house at Munstead Wood, Lutyens designed a smaller building, The Hut, with a studio, bedroom and a staff bedroom. Jekyll lived there from 1895 after her brother, Herbert, inherited Munstead House on their mother's death. The main house at Munstead Wood, completed in 1897, was a brick and tiled Arts and Crafts house, with half-timbered gallery and ornate Elizabethan-style chimneys, a perfect synthesis of old and new, set in an already mature garden. Jekyll felt as though she had finally come home, as she wrote in *Home and Garden* three years later:

> My own little new-built house is so restful, so satisfying, so kindly sympathetic ... In some ways it is not exactly a new house, although no building has ever before stood upon its site. But I had been thinking about it for so many years, and the main block of it and the whole sentiment of it were so familiar to my mind's eye, that when it came to be a reality I felt as if I had already been living in it a good long time.[27]

Like William Kent two centuries earlier, Jekyll came to gardening from painting and interior design. She retained her painter's vision even after her eyesight deteriorated. In 1891, she went to Wiesbaden to consult an eminent ophthalmologist, who discouraged her from close work such as painting and embroidery in the hope of arresting further decline.[28] Jekyll's reaction was customarily robust, for, as she wrote in *Wood and Garden*, she believed that 'the will and power to observe does not depend on the possession of keen sight'.[29] From then on, she concentrated on designing, planting and writing about gardens, and she continued to be a great reader.

Lutyens' arrival was opportune. He and Jekyll shared an understanding of the importance of regional characteristics, and of uniting house and garden. In the early 1900s, they embarked on several projects in the Surrey Arts and Crafts style, such as Goddards at Abinger Common, built as a rest home for ladies of slender means, or Millmead, a speculative project suggested by Jekyll on a derelict site in Bramley village. Another early project was the Deanery at Sonning in Berkshire for Edward Hudson, founder of *Country Life*, a magazine to which Jekyll contributed for many years. The partnership's trademarks were on display at the Deanery: Lutyens's pergolas, courtyard, rills and walks, and Jekyll's softly coloured borders edged with grey foliage, rambling roses and alpines studding the walls. The duo also worked for Hudson on Lindisfarne Castle in Northumberland. Lutyens rebuilt the ruined castle, installing a gallery similar to that at Munstead Wood, while Jekyll created a walled garden on the sea marshes. The planting has been restored to Jekyll's plans, with stachys surrounding sedums in the central bed, and a glorious mix of marigolds, santolina, fuchsia, scabious, poppies and hollyhocks in other beds. Symmetrical across the diagonals, it is the mixture of the formal and informal at which Jekyll excelled. The final Lutyens/Jekyll collaboration was also for Hudson, in 1928 at Plumpton Place, a derelict moated manor in Sussex,

Other joint commissions included Marsh Court, near Stockbridge in Hampshire (1901–4), Folly Farm in Berkshire (1906, and further work in 1912), and Les Bois des Moutiers in Normandy in 1904. Their best preserved project is Hestercombe in Somerset, where Lutyens designed the formal garden in 1904 for an eighteenth-century house given a Victorian facelift. Pergolas, rills and stone steps once again featured in Lutyens's design, with brick paths cutting through lawn and between flower beds edged with bergenias, another of Jekyll's favourite plants. Hestercombe, according to architectural historian Christopher Hussey, represented 'the peak of [Lutyens's] collaboration with Miss Jekyll, and his first application of her genius to classical garden design on a grand scale'.[30]

Jekyll also collaborated with Arts and Crafts architects Robert Lorimer and Hugh Baillie-Scot, and designed gardens under her own aegis. These latter projects included, in 1908, the five-acre garden at the Manor House, Upton Grey, which had drystone terraces embossed with alpines, pergolas with roses, jasmine and Virginia creeper, herbaceous borders packed with cottage garden flowers planted in characteristic gradations of colour, and a formal rose lawn. In the late twentieth century, the garden was restored from dereliction by Rosamund Wallinger, who used copies of Jekyll's plans. Open during the summer months, it is probably now the best representative of Jekyll's gardening style.

Jekyll's garden for the Arts and Crafts inspired King Edward VII Sanatorium at Midhurst, Sussex, featured knot-like formal gardens edged with rosemary and filled with scented flowers and herbs.[31] The garden was planted up by students of the Glynde School for Lady Gardeners, of which Jekyll was a patron, as were William Robinson and Ellen Willmott.

A water garden designed for architect W. D. Caroe at Vann, Hambledon, Surrey, in 1912, still opens annually for the National Garden Scheme. For this garden, she supplied ferns, hostas, bog myrtle, fritillaries and marsh marigolds, an exceptional range of plants given they were originally grown in sandy Surrey heathland.[32]

Jekyll built up a nursery, supported by her gardeners at Munstead Wood, publishing a catalogue, and supplying plants for many of her design schemes. For Barrington Court in Somerset, for instance, she supplied £400 worth of plants. Primroses were favourites, as described in this vignette in *Wood and Garden*: 'All day for two days I sit on a low stool dividing the plants. A boy feeds me with armfuls of newly dug-up plants, two men are digging-in the cooling cow-dung at the farther end, and another man carries away the divided plants tray-by-tray and carefully replants them.' Much time was dedicated to searching for rare or new plants, and to breeding new varieties. She won an RHS Award of Merit in 1901 for 'The Sultan', one of her primrose introductions, and twenty-five of the plants she bred remain in circulation today, including *Nigella damascena* 'Miss Jekyll Blue' and *Lavandula spica* 'Munstead'.[33]

***

Jekyll moved into Munstead Wood house in October 1897, the day after receiving the Victoria Medal of Honour, inaugurated that year by the Royal Horticultural Society to mark Queen Victoria's Diamond Jubilee.

By then, Jekyll was an established gardening writer, contributing not only to Robinson's *The Garden* and *Gardening Illustrated*, and *Country Life*, but also to the *Edinburgh Review*. In the latter, Jekyll intervened in the dispute between Reginald Blomfield and William Robinson over formality and informality. Her godson, Harold Falkner, an architect who had worked in Blomfield's office, recalled that his godmother 'used to relate with great glee the fact that Robinson designed himself a garden all squares, and Reggy a garden on a cliff with not a straight line it'.

But the decisive blow in the argument was struck not on paper but on the ground by Jekyll's collaboration with Lutyens. Christopher Hussey wrote that their work at Hudson's Deanery garden, 'at once formal and irregular, virtually settled that controversy ... Miss Jekyll's naturalistic planting wedding Lutyens' geometry in a balanced union of both principles'.[34] Furthermore, says Mavis Batey, the pair 'gave the new century a new style which would reconcile architects, gardeners, craftsmen and the rival merits of formal design and natural planting'.[35]

Jekyll balanced writing and designing, becoming editor of *The Garden* on William Robinson's retirement in 1889. More conciliatory than Robinson, she proved herself a natural editor, bringing out the best in her contributors and judging accurately the magazine's tone. But she was accustomed to her own timetable at Munstead Wood and did the job for little more than a year.

Jekyll also published eleven books between her first, *Wood and Garden* in 1899, and the outbreak of war in 1914. Her subjects included lilies, roses and flower decoration in the home, as well as a nostalgic book on her home county, *Old West Surrey*. All were written in her elegant prose and without affectation. She was aware few readers would have the acres of her clients, and so offered advice and encouragement which emphasised the importance of personal commitment. 'The size of the garden has very little to do with its merit. It is merely an accident relating to the circumstances of the owner. It is the size of his heart and brain and goodwill that will make his garden either delightful or dull, as the case may be, and either leave it at the usual monotonous dead-level, or raise it, in whatever degree may be, towards that of a work of fine art.'[36]

Among her pre-war books was *Colour in the Flower Garden*, published by *Country Life* in 1908. This book influenced generations of gardeners in Britain and elsewhere. In it, she taught that 'the possession of a quantity of plants, however good the plants may be themselves and however ample their number, does not make a garden; it only makes a *collection*. Having got the plants, the great thing is to use them with careful selection and definite intention ... The duty we owe to our gardens ... is to use the plants so that they shall form beautiful pictures.'[37]

Gertrude Jekyll was seventy at the outbreak of the First World War. She counselled *Country Life* readers to plant parsnips, swede and Jerusalem artichokes to augment potatoes.[38] There were local casualties in the war, the Munstead Wood staff was depleted as the gardeners went off to fight, and nursery beds and the main flower border were turned over to potatoes. Garden commissions still came and, after the war, she advised on the planting of the war grave cemeteries, with headstones designed by Lutyens.

Jekyll found herself out of sync with the post-war world and modernism in art and literature. Although in her youth she had idealised the customs and dress of the local cottagers, she had no instinctive sympathy for working people, believing them less discerning than her own class. She admired Humphry Repton rather than Brown, for the former was 'of much better taste and education'.[39]

Even in old age, she seldom completed fewer than fifteen commissions a year. She was particularly gratified by the award of the gold Veitch Memorial Medal and the American Horticultural Society's gold medal. Visitors came to Munstead Wood from across the world, above all from America. Always a private person, she restricted visits to late afternoon to give her time for a post-prandial rest. Children and noise she disliked in equal measure. 'I am growing old and tired, and suffer from very bad and painful sight. My garden is my workshop, my private study and my place of rest. For the sake of health and reasonable enjoyment of life it is necessary to keep it quite private, and to refuse the many applications of those who offer it visits.'[40]

Gertrude's brother, Herbert, died on 29 September 1932. By 8 December, she, too, was dead. 'It was Sir Herbert's death which must have hastened her death for her last letter to me was very pathetic,' wrote Ellen Willmott, who, despite their extreme old age, travelled with William Robinson to attend Jekyll's funeral.[41] Gertrude was buried next to Herbert in Busbridge churchyard, where his wife, Agnes, would also be laid to rest. Lutyens designed their monument, engraving on Gertrude's headstone the words, 'Artist, Gardener, Craftswoman'.

After Gertrude's death, Munstead Wood passed eventually to her nephew, Francis ('Timmy') Jekyll. He lived in The Hut, wrote his aunt's biography, and looked after the nursery in an unfocussed way. By 1934, Lutyens was lamenting that the the garden had 'collapsed ... but it can't be helped. No Bumps.'[42] Most of Jekyll's possessions were dispersed in an auction in 1948, while the estate at Munstead Wood was split up, with the various buildings becoming separate homes, and a further house built on the former kitchen garden. The framework of the garden remains, however, and can still be visited during spring and summer months.

Gertrude Jekyll raised gardening to an art form. Her inheritance, through her gardens and her writing, remains with us, reinterpreted by subsequent gardeners and designers. Jekyll, like Nature, is still 'a grand teacher', whatever the size of our gardens. 'Today we can extract from her writings the essence of her art,' Hobhouse has written, 'and, forgetting the scale on which she and her contemporaries (and clients) gardened, make use of certain elements in her plant pictures that will fit smoothly into corners of the small garden, or form the basis of a whole garden scheme ... Her philosophy combines the qualities of her painter's training with a genuine and simple love of flowers and woodland.'[43]

CHAPTER 15

Lawrence Johnston (1871–1958)

On 22 October 1914, Major Lawrence Johnston of the Northumberland Hussars was so badly wounded at the first Battle of Ypres that he was laid out for burial. Fortunately, his commanding officer spotted a flicker of life in Johnston's supposed corpse and had him sent back to the field hospital. Johnston's recovery was protracted but he lived to fight again; and to complete work on his garden at Hidcote in Gloucestershire. Johnston owed the officer his life – and the time to create one of Britain's most important twentieth-century gardens.

Johnston had been at Hidcote Manor for seven years when he went to France in 1914, aged forty-three, but the garden he had begun laying out was still immature. Had he died at Ypres, his restless American mother, Gertrude Winthrop, would almost certainly have sold up in Gloucestershire and reverted to her ceaseless shuttle between New York, London and France.

Johnston's gardens at Hidcote and at Serre de la Madonne at Menton in the south of France are his monuments: he wrote no books, drew no plans, and kept no account of his design and planting work, and had a relatively low profile in the horticultural world compared with his older contemporaries William Robinson and Gertrude Jekyll. Hidcote and Serre were complementary as, between them, the plantsman Johnston was able to grow a vast array of trees, shrubs and flowers. Serre de la Madonne was bought and sold several times in the years following Johnston's death in 1958 and restored in the early twenty-first century.

At Hidcote, one comes closest to understanding Johnston's intentions. He gardened there initially in the Arts and Crafts style, but designed a garden with less stonework and timber than those of Lutyens and Jekyll. Much of the garden is set away from the house, and yet is related in style and scale to the seventeenth-century manor. It is divided not by walls but by hedges of yew, beech, holly and hornbeam into a series of hidden rooms, each devoted to particular types or colours of

Laurence Johnston and his gardeners in the early 1910s. (Courtesy of Gloucestershire Archives/CCHS Jesse Taylor Photographs)

planting; this use of space influenced many other gardeners and garden designers. Johnston sponsored and went on plant-hunting expeditions to develop his collection. Like Jekyll, Johnston matched the cool excellence of his design with richly varied planting, creating a garden which has been maintained in the same spirit by the National Trust since 1948. Harold Nicolson visited Hidcote in 1953, and compared it favourably in his diary with his and Vita Sackville-West's Sissinghurst. He wrote: 'We go over the garden ... It is still the loveliest small garden in England ... We get home at ten to 6 ... The garden [Sissinghurst] is looking well, and we prefer it to all those we have seen, with the exception of Hidcote.'[1]

***

Lawrence Johnston was born in Paris on 12 October 1871, elder son of a Baltimore banker, Elliott Johnston, and his wife, Gertrude Waterbury, daughter of another New York banker and heiress to a fortune based on rope-making. Theirs was a world of privilege: the Johnstons had family connections with two American presidents and owned homes in Paris, London and New York. They belonged to that peripatetic caste of cultured Americans who people the novels of Henry James and Edith Wharton, the latter subsequently a close friend of Lawrence's.

His childhood was unsettled: he travelled with a tutor from the age of seven, and was twelve when his parents divorced. Elliott Johnston at fifty-nine married a woman of eighteen, cutting the sons of his first marriage out of his will on his death in 1901. Gertrude also remarried; her second husband, Frank Winthrop, a Paris-based stockbroker, being described in the *Baltimore Sun* as 'a confirmed bachelor'.[2] The marriage foundered and when Winthrop died in 1898, he, too, left nothing to his wife or stepsons.

Lawrence and his younger brother, Elliott, spent time at Columbia University, Lawrence in the school of architecture and Elliott as an engineer. Lawrence didn't graduate from Columbia but instead left for England with his mother, who seems to have cleaved to her elder son even before Elliott died in California in 1912 from horrific burns sustained in a gas explosion. Johnston was enrolled in a crammer to prepare him to read history at Trinity College, Cambridge, from 1894 to 1897.

After Cambridge, Johnston studied agriculture in Northumberland, and became a British citizen in 1900. He enlisted in the Imperial Yeomanry and set sail for South Africa to serve in the Boer War to escape, at least for a while, his suffocating mother. He fought in the Transvaal and the Orange Free State, before returning in poor health to Little Shelford in 1902, where he created a rock garden at Woodville Lodge, his first essay in garden design and still extant.

His interest in gardening led to his admission in 1904 as a fellow of the Royal Horticultural Society. With access to the society's Lindley Library, he took out in 1905 books on plant breeding, wild gardens, climbing plants, and on alpines, including William Robinson's *Alpine Flowers for English Gardens*. Most significantly, he borrowed Thomas Mawson's *The Art and Craft of Garden Making* (1900), to which he would refer constantly when laying out Hidcote.[3]

He continued to serve as a lieutenant with a territorial regiment, the Northumberland Hussars, and in July 1906 commanded the escort for a visit by Edward VII and Queen Alexandra to Alnwick Castle in Northumberland.

***

In 1907, Gertrude Winthrop bought Hidcote Manor, the hamlet of Hidcote Bartrim and 280 acres for £7,500. A small and not particularly distinguished Gloucestershire farmhouse might have appeared a surprising choice as the main residence of a trans-Atlantic socialite, but the Cotswolds held attractions for cultured Americans in the early 1900s. Social life in nearby Broadway was dominated by American expatriates, among them actress Mary de Navarro, a friend of Henry James and Edith Wharton. Beyond Broadway, at Stanway House, Lord and Lady Elcho entertained the Souls, a group of artistically minded aristocrats. The Souls were patrons of Arts and Crafts designers, of architects such as Charles Ashbee, a Cambridge contemporary of Johnston's, Ernest Gimson, and Ernest and Sidney Barnsley. All had set up their businesses in the Cotswolds, employing local craft skills and the materials and styles of the region.[4] What better place, then, for an aspiring garden maker and his mother to set up an English salon?

Johnston had chosen an exposed site: Hidcote is 600 feet above sea level, and the land slopes uncomfortably away from the house to the south, up to the west, and is only level to the north. Too close to the house for comfort is a massive cedar of Lebanon. He used the cedar as his starting point, sowing a lawn around the tree and driving a corridor east-west past it through the garden. 'One of the finest things that the estate improvers have been able to do, has been to rear a noble, stately avenue,' wrote Thomas Mawson in *The Art and Craft of Garden Making*, and Johnston took this on board. Mawson's book, containing 130 plans and details of gardens designed by the author, summed up the various battles over garden design and inspired Johnston. The argument over formality and informality between Blomfield and Robinson, caused by 'the revival of interest in, and study of architecture and allied crafts ... during the last twenty or thirty years' had led, argued Mawson, to 'a greater appreciation of the English garden'. Although a devotee of the Arts and Crafts movement, Mawson was not doctrinaire: 'I have endeavoured to make it clear that whilst I consider a formal treatment the one most likely to give satisfactory result, I do not think that "the Art and Craft of Garden-Making" is advanced to a slavish adherence to style or tradition.'[5] Mawson presented Johnston with basic precepts while allowing him freedom to develop as a gardener himself, blending his borrowings from earlier designers into a style very much his own.

The early stages of the garden – the east-west corridor, the White Garden, the Old Garden, the Maple Garden, and the initial planting of the yew and tapestry hedges and of topiary – all bear Mawson's influence: 'The definite lines of the hedges and accompanying walks assist the grouping, and furnish an extended base to the architectural scheme,' Mawson had written. 'Hedges impart an idea of shelter in almost all kinds of weather, and suggest protection for flowers of half-hardy habit, and the ground thus protected is much more enjoyable than the bald, wind-swept pleasure grounds so often met with.'[6] These hedges give Hidcote its distinctive structure, protect it from winds whipping across the high Cotswold escarpment, and provide shelter for Johnston's more tender planting. They were admired by Vita Sackville-West, who liked the 'flatness' of the yew mixed with gleaming holly, and the tapestry hedges of beech, yew, box, holly and hornbeam 'like a green and black tartan'.[7] They were also imitated by his next-door neighbour, Heather Muir, at Kiftsgate Court garden.

The beds within the White and Maple Gardens (the latter then devoted to peonies) were edged with box, mirroring the hedges which frame the garden rooms, while topiary birds flanked the entrance between the White and Old Gardens and the vista beyond. Johnston also laid out the yew-enclosed Bathing Pool Garden, and the brick-pathed Fuchsia Garden. It follows the Mawson lines, and yet the flight of steps leading up from the Bathing Pool Garden, the paving of the Maple Garden, and the eventual grandeur of the two main vistas all hint at the influence of the Renaissance gardens of Italy and France which Johnston visited on youthful travels.

Across the road from the manor, Johnston planted a lime avenue, leading up to a statue of Hercules. By lowering the wall, he created the impression that the avenue opens straight off a small cobbled parterre by the house. Initial planting began of what would become the Red Borders, backed by trellising until the hedges should mature. Already Johnston was showing signs of true plantsmanship. In 1911, he was unanimously voted an Award of Merit at a Royal Horticultural Show for a strain of *Primula pulverulenta*, commended by *The Times*. 'Of the many new Chinese primroses none has spread from garden to garden so rapidly as pulverulenta, but hitherto the typical crimson flowers only were known. The Hidcote strain adds the soft pinks from primula Japonica, at the same time retaining the mealy stem and other characteristics of pulverulenta.'[8]

This short commendation is a snapshot of the Edwardian gardening world, with plants arriving in Britain from aristocratic-funded plant hunters in the Far East, such as Ernest Wilson (born in nearby Chipping Campden), Reginald Farrer, George Forrest and Frank Kingdon-Ward. In the post-war years, Johnston joined their number.

Johnston still attended the summer camps of the Northumberland Hussars, being made up to major in 1913. The outbreak of war brought mobilisation, but after his critical wounding he was repatriated to the King Edward VII Hospital in Grosvenor Gardens, near the Lindley Library. Convalescence enabled Johnston to resume his horticultural reading, with books often signed out by the Hidcote butler. Again, he read widely, tackling the two volumes of Wilson's *A Naturalist in China*, Inigo Triggs's *Garden Craft*, and *Some English Gardens* by George Elgood and Gertrude Jekyll.[9]

Further recuperation at Hidcote enabled Johnston to continue work aided by the war-time skeleton staff of old retainers and young boys. He completed the two red-brick gazebos along the east-west corridor, and planted the French-style pleached hornbeams on a raised platform beyond. At the end of this long avenue, he set a pair of wrought-iron gates, known as Heaven's Gate: as you look up the avenue, the gates appear to open on to the sky. At the gate, however, is a panoramic view towards the Malverns, Brecon Beacons, and Black Mountains.

Returning to the Western Front, Johnston was again wounded in the last British cavalry charge, convalescing afterwards in the south of France. When he was finally demobilised in April 1919, his papers gave his occupation in civil life as 'gentleman'. In the year of Johnston's demobbing, Gertrude Winthrop bought more land, enabling her son to continue his garden project.

The second phase in Johnston's design struck a different note, and was less cottagey and Arts and Crafts in style. He threw out another, wider avenue to the south, at right-angles to the pre-war axis, opening off the gazebos, and sweeping up to another pair of wrought-iron gates at the far end. Hornbeam hedging flanks this walk, with other gardens glimpsed through windows and arches. The stream, which snakes through the manor gardens, is half-hidden like a ha-ha a third of the way down, deceptively appearing further away. This long vista, connecting garden and countryside beyond, has the éclat of a Renaissance garden, and is a spectacular surprise as you walk up through the Red Borders and turn into the gazebos.

In the early 1920s, Johnston also laid out the Theatre Lawn, a vast yew-framed lawn, parallel with the Red Borders. Pictures taken in the 1920s and 1930s show Johnston and his guests playing bowls on this lawn, the green lungs of the garden.

Beside the Long Walk, he made three stream gardens. Mrs Winthrop's Mediterranean-style garden, created as a warm place for his aging mother, is still planted with the blue and yellow flowers she favoured and fringed by a lime arbour. He enlarged the bathing pool, so that it seems almost too big for its enclosure, and planted up the Pillar Garden on a series of shallow terraces, running down from the Stilt Garden. Here, in a mix of formality and informality, clipped pillars of yew are surrounded by planting which peaks in May when peonies are at their best, followed later by fuchsias and nerines.

A taste for the newly fashionable rhododendrons, introduced from China and the Himalayas, required Johnston to change the naturally alkaline soil of the Cotswolds. He imported sawdust from local sawmills to make three areas in which the rhododendrons continue to flourish.[10] On farmland to one side of the Long Walk, an area named 'Westonbirt' by Johnston was first planted in 1926, a woodland tribute to the Gloucestershire arboretum.

The result was a garden of complexity, rich in interest, and cut through by paths of grass, brick and stone. The firm architecture, formed out of living material rather than stone, was crucially designed as a backdrop to the plants, always Johnston's chief love. This balance between structure and planting, and between formality and informality, was Johnston's gift to the gardening world. It was summed up by country house expert James Lees-Milne in his diaries:

> It is not only beautiful but full of surprises. You are constantly led from one scene to another, into long vistas and little enclosures, which seem infinite. Yet the total area of this garden does not cover many acres. It is also full of rare plants brought from the most outlandish places in India and Asia. When my father and Laurie Johnston were absorbed in talk I was tremendously impressed by their profound knowledge of a subject which is closed to me, like hearing two people speak fluently a language of which I am totally ignorant.[11]

Johnston's commitment to the garden was strategic rather than manual, his staff claiming that he never actually dirtied his hands. The gardeners (and the house staff) were mostly drawn from the cottages of Hidcote Bartrim, or from Mickleton a mile away down the hill. But in 1922, Johnston hired his only professional head gardener, Frank Adams, who had worked for George V at Windsor Castle. In Johnston's winter absences in Menton, Adams worked on schemes devised together during the summer months. When Adams died in 1939, Johnston resumed the role of head gardener, depending upon a less gifted gardener, Albert Hawkins, to oversee the rest of the garden staff.[12]

***

At Serre de la Madone (the greenhouse of the Madonna) on the French Riviera, Johnston experimented with planting unsuited to the harsher Cotswold climate. By 1924, Mrs Winthrop, at nearly eighty, was spending winters in southern France, as did Johnston, his lungs weakened by his war wounds. They would travel out in style accompanied by staff: maids for Gertrude, a valet for Lawrence and possibly a butler as well. Johnston might drive out in his sporty Lancia, but the chauffeur would follow in the Bentley.[13] That year, Johnston bought his first parcel of land in the Val de Gorbio, buying more land over the next fifteen years to create the garden of Serre de la Madone. It had similar features to those at Hidcote: the Bowling Green and Plane Garden, for instance. As at Hidcote, each area was given its individual character by its planting, although Serre lacked the clean lines of Johnston's Gloucestershire garden. A friend, society garden designer Norah Lindsay, complained 'it's too tricky about with tiny paths and tiny rocks and tiny sitting places – it wants all simplifying and pushing out in all directions'.[14]

The two gardens sustained one another: the olive trees that Johnston admired in Menton were replicated in Gloucestershire by holm oaks; the sheltered, west-facing Rock Blank is a Mediterranean scree slope of pines, succulents and cistus. Tiered beds backed by the wall below the Stilt Garden are also redolent of the Alpes-Maritimes, planted with rare alpines, and covered with glass in winter.

By the time Johnston bought Serre de la Madone, his mother was suffering from dementia. Gertrude Winthrop had always exercised an adamantine grip on her money, doling out sums to her son, whom she thought extravagant. Just how distrustful she was became apparent when she died in December 1926, leaving Johnston Hidcote, but only a life-time interest on her capital. Not the capital itself, which would go to any children of Johnston's on his death – an unlikely prospect as Johnston was unmarried and fifty-five when his mother died. Gertrude had minimised death duties, left Johnston with a considerable income, but tied his hands when it came to parting with Hidcote.

Photographs of Lawrence Johnston with his mother suggest that it was never an equal relationship. In one, he stands nervously behind his seated mother, her lips set in a thin line and fierce, angry eyes glaring. Mrs Winthrop was a termagant, organising Sunday Schools for the village children and then chasing them to ensure they attended. Johnston was meeker, allowing his garden staff to take surplus produce from the garden in the 1930s after his mother's death. James Lees-Milne, recalling visits as a child with his father to Hidcote, thought Johnston 'a dull little man ... Mother-ridden. Mrs Winthrop, swathed in grey satin from neck to ankle, never let him out of her sight.'[15] 'Johnston's life,' wrote Roy Strong, 'was haunted by the spectre of his formidable mother ... We still have practically nothing to round out [his] life ... [He] never formed any partnership, either hetero- or homosexual, although one would guess that ... any outward leaning in the latter direction would have been suppressed. [He] found [his] salvation in the garden.'[16]

Johnston left few records, apart from an appointments diary and a couple of notebooks. Papers relating to the creation of Hidcote may well have been destroyed after his death by plantswoman Nancy Lindsay, daughter of Norah Lindsay, in a fit of pique against the National Trust.[17] He clearly disliked being photographed: most photographs show him standing almost in the wings, or with a hat obscuring his eyes. A smallish man, with a neat military moustache, he reserved his chief affection for dogs such as the 'three brown satin dachshunds' who developed a fondness for Norah and followed her everywhere. 'This quite upset Johnny and Fredo [his valet] who are insanely jealous and say it's the first time the dogs have taken to anyone.' Even close friends such as Norah Lindsay found him enigmatic and buttoned-up: 'Bless him he is such a busy bee, one can't rely on anything he does ... He is a sort of Rumpelstiltskin isn't he, and can't be altered in any way.'[18]

The late 1920s and early 1930s were Hidcote's heyday, when Johnston entertained guests regularly at tennis and swimming parties. Gardeners Ellen Willmott and E. A. Bowles were friends, as was the society interior designer Sibyl Colefax. Norah Lindsay, who designed gardens for the aristocracy at Blickling, Cliveden and Mottisfont Abbey, often stayed at Hidcote. Heather Muir of Kiftsgate Court was also a good friend. The Muirs bought the house in 1919, and Mrs Muir, with no horticultural training, was encouraged to garden by friendship with Johnston. They put in joint orders for peonies which would take six months to arrive from Japan.

In 1921, Johnston had joined the Garden Society, its numbers limited to fifty members of the Royal Horticultural Society. Johnston took part in members' syndicates, who, along with botanic gardens and commercial nurseries such as James Veitch & Sons and Bees, sponsored overseas plant-hunting expeditions. He himself travelled with fellow society member E. A. Bowles to the Swiss Alps in 1922. In September 1927, Johnston spent four months plant hunting in South Africa, taking with him his chauffeur, Ernest Daniels, and cook-valet, Fredo Rebuffo. Johnston kept a notebook of plants collected in South Africa, including aloe, cotyledon, cyrtanthus, felicia, hypoxis, ipomea, jasminum, kniphofia and lobelia, all at Hidcote today. In 1929, he travelled to Kenya to climb Mount Kilimanjaro, gathering seeds of impatiens, senecio and hypericum, possibly the *Hypericum* 'Hidcote', also still growing in the garden. This trip was the spur for his only recorded article, 'Some Flowering Plants of Mount Kilimanjaro', published in October 1929 in *New Flora and Silva.*[19]

Johnston sent back to Lady Londonderry at Mount Stewart a sample of *Camellia speciosa*, found growing in a temple garden in Tengyeuh during an expedition with plant-hunter George Forrest to Yunnan in 1930/1931. Always prickly, Forrest took a dislike to Johnston, writing, 'Had I raked G. B. [Great Britain] with a small tooth comb I couldn't have found a worse companion than Johnston,' who left him 'to attend to everything in the way of preparation for our journey ... There was much he could have done to lighten my labours, but he was too busy gadding around with Mrs Clerk & others all & every day, riding in the morning, tea & tennis in the afternoons & bridge at the Club in the evenings ... he changes his mind more frequently than his socks.'[20] Johnston clearly lived as he did at Hidcote, socialising with the British contingent in Rangoon and assuming that Forrest, like a paid member of his garden staff, was there to carry out the day-to-day duties. Johnston, taken ill, returned home early, while Forrest continued on, dying from a heart attack in January 1932 in China. The plants and seeds gathered from these expeditions furnished the garden rooms at Hidcote, its design virtually complete by the late 1930s. Shared with botanic gardens, such as Kew, his overseas plant acquisitions led to Johnston being awarded the gold Veitch Memorial Medal in 1947.

***

The outbreak of the Second World War found Johnston at Menton, according to Lindsay, 'quite unconscious out here of any European happenings and his little plans go on quite simply in spite of Mussolini trying to upset the whole world'.[21] When Germany invaded, Johnston was stranded at Serre de la Madone, but managed to escape to Spain with his butler, chauffeur, three parrots and two dogs in an ambulance driven by a seventeen-year-old boy. He sailed back to England and spent most of the war at Hidcote, pulling up lawns for vegetables to supply four local hospitals.

Johnston was in his seventies, concerned about rising British taxes and a declining income, when in 1943 he met James Lees-Milne. Lees-Milne recorded in his diary that 'Laurie Johnston took me aside to ask if the National Trust would take over Hidcote garden without endowment after the war, when he intended to live in the South of France for good'.[22]

The garden's lack of endowment was a stumbling block for the National Trust. By 1948, Johnston was desperate to leave, but the trust, never having previously cared for a world-class garden, was lukewarm. On a visit to Hidcote, Lees-Milne, the trust's representative, found Johnston 'incensed by a letter he had received from the trust and had now decided no longer to "give" us Hidcote'.[23] Thanks to the advocacy of Harold Nicolson and Lord Aberconway, owner of Bodnant, the Royal Horticultural Society and National Trust set up the Gardens Fund, an initiative that set the pattern for the trust's handling of historic gardens in the future. Lees-Milne painted a triste picture of Johnston signing away Hidcote in 1948:

> Laurie J. signed the deed of gift like a lamb so, since he leaves for abroad in a fortnight, the place may be said to be saved. This has been a struggle but it is accomplished. We were conducted round the gardens by the usual route. How often must the old man have done this tour? I think it was a sad occasion for him and I wondered how far he understood that he was giving away his precious treasure of a garden. 'I have another Hidcote,' he murmured.[24]

That other garden was Serre de la Madone, where he died in 1958, suffering from dementia, like his mother, and having returned just once to Hidcote in 1951. He was buried with Gertrude in the churchyard at Mickleton, his tomb engraved 'A Gifted Gardener and Horticulturalist, Deeply Loved by All his Friends'.

Over seven decades, the planting has had to be adapted, but Hidcote remains Johnston's garden in essence, and attracts almost 175,000 visitors a year. 'Perhaps Lawrence Johnston's most important contribution to modern gardening was his ability to combine plants in an unusual way,' the garden designer Russell Page wrote in the 1960s.[25] That and his numerous plant introductions, many still thriving in Hidcote's rooms and borders. *Jasminum polyanthum* and *Mahonia lomariifolia* from China, and *Lavandula angustifolia* 'Hidcote' from southern France also grow in many British gardens, a lasting memorial to Hidcote's plantsman-creator.[26]

CHAPTER 16

Vita Sackville-West (1892–1962)

Vita Sackville-West's granddaughter, Juliet Nicolson, has claimed that Vita was 'Lady Chatterley above the waist and Mellors below'.[1] Whether that's a fair summary of Vita's character, it is a useful physical description of the creator, with her husband, Harold Nicolson, of Sissinghurst garden in Kent. The familiar image is of Vita in later life, smoking a cigarette on the tower steps at Sissinghurst, wearing high, laced boots, gardener's breeches, oddly matched with a lacy blouse and strings of pearls. Her dark, heavy-lidded eyes challenge the onlooker as beside her stands her husband, the milder seeming, behatted Harold Nicolson, pipe in hand. Flanked by a German shepherd dog, the couple look comfortable together, each finding 'permanent and undiluted happiness only in the company of the other', their marriage the harbour to which 'each returned'.[2]

Vita Sackville-West was a novelist, historian, travel-writer and columnist who desired above all to be remembered as a poet. Gardening had less status in her aristocratic world than poetry, yet Vita is now renowned as a gardener. Her first long poem, *The Land*, won her the Hawthornden Prize in 1927, but *The Garden*, her response to the Second World War, was greeted coolly by the literary establishment: it was seen as passé twenty-four years after T. S. Eliot's *The Waste Land*. Vita, a confirmed traditionalist, didn't 'hold with the dunghill despair of Eliot'.[3]

When writing about the gardens of Vita Sackville-West, the deeply interwoven threads of the life of this passionate bisexual woman have to be considered. Her marriage-threatening relationship with Violet Trefusis, as well as affairs with Virginia Woolf, Alvide Lees-Milne, and others, have been covered extensively in Nigel Nicolson's *Portrait of a Marriage*, and memoirs and biographies of Vita and Harold.

An intensely private woman, Vita would not have relished this concentration on her sexuality, often at the expense of her writing and gardening. Although she opened the garden at Sissinghurst to the public, she resisted further intrusion: when asked by Nigel whether she would

Vita Sackville-West on the tower steps at Sissinghurst. (Courtesy The Garden Museum)

consider handing Sissinghurst to the National Trust, she expostulated in her diary, 'Au grand jamais, jamais. Never, never, never ... Nigel can do what he likes when I am dead, but so long as I live no Nat Trust or any other foreign body shall have my darling ... It is bad enough to have lost Knole, but they shan't take S/hurst from me.'[4]

Knole is the stately home in Sevenoaks that she failed to inherit because she was a woman. For her, losing Knole was an unparalleled tragedy, and Sissinghurst the attempt to recreate her childhood home. Although Sissinghurst belonged entirely to her (Harold never owned an inch of the estate), together they made the garden which was visited by nearly 200,000 people in 2016. The essayist and critic, Peter Quennell, having scoffed at Vita and Harold, later wrote: 'How much the garden owed to the Nicolsons, and how well it symbolized their long devotion, the alliance of a slightly feminine man and a predominantly masculine woman, I understood when I visited it after their deaths, and it was crowded, over-crowded indeed, with enthusiastic sightseers.' It was, he added, 'a place of individual beauty ... the living product of two sympathetic human minds'.[5]

Vita and Harold were, in some ways, representative of a decadent, snobbish aristocracy out of touch with their contemporary world. They thought themselves poor, but were never without a butler and other staff. Born Victorians, and brought up as Edwardians, they were at odds with modernism and social change. Yet, through their unconventionality – and near genius for gardening – they helped shape aspects of the future. 'They inherited a little,' their son Nigel wrote, 'but created more, in literature, politics, gardens and their concept of marriage.'[6]

Sissinghurst, like Hidcote, is a garden of rooms, and both Vita and Harold greatly admired Lawrence Johnston's creation. But Sissinghurst was made by a very different, restless character, who gave it perhaps a broader appeal, as their granddaughter recognised. 'Its originality, intimacy and romance have made it one of the most famous, most visited, most copied and most loved gardens in the world.'[7]

***

Vita Sackville-West was born at Knole on 9 March 1892, the only child of first cousins. Her mother, Victoria, was the illegitimate daughter of Lionel Sackville-West, the 2nd Baron Sackville, and of a celebrated Spanish gypsy dancer, Pepita, to whom Vita owed her striking Mediterranean looks. Vita's father, also Lionel, was the older Lionel's nephew and heir to the estate which had been in the Sackville family since Queen Elizabeth I presented it to Thomas Sackville. Knole, with a Great Hall built in about 1460, is a sprawling complex of stone buildings, alleged to have fifty-two staircases and 365 rooms. Set in a park of beeches, gullies and slopes, Knole is less like a house than 'a medieval village with its square turrets and its grey walls, its hundred chimneys sending blue threads up into the air', as Vita wrote in her 1930 novel, *The Edwardians*.[8]

In her late teens, Victoria acted as her father's hostess when Lord Sackville was at the British legation in Washington. A political indiscretion sent Sackville home under a cloud, but not so Victoria, who had triumphed in Washington. At Knole, she met her cousin Lionel and the pair fell in love, marrying in Knole's chapel in 1890. The marriage, which began propitiously, collapsed once the initial sexual attraction abated and the couple found themselves fundamentally unsuited. Lady Sackville ran Knole well, installing bathrooms, electricity and central heating, but Lord

Sackville looked elsewhere for comfort, eventually moving his mistress, Olive Rubens, and her compliant husband into Knole under his wife's nose. When Lady Sackville saw her husband kissing Olive under an apple tree in 1919, she moved out, leaving Vita torn between two warring, incompatible parents.

Vita alternately adored and feared her mother, and suffered from Lady Sackville's unpredictability and violent tantrums until the latter's death in 1936. '[She] loved me when I was a baby, but I don't think she loved me as a child.' Vita had more in common with her father, with whom she walked through Knole's woods and grounds, discussing Darwin.[9] She was also fond of her grandfather/great-uncle, playing draughts with him in the evening.[10]

Vita was educated at home by a rapid turnover of governesses who struggled to deal with the capricious Lady Sackville and the remote, tomboyish Vita. She saw few other children and, those she did, she terrorised and beat with nettles. She spent her days roaming Knole, absorbing its history, and nurturing an abiding love for every tapestry, painting and piece of furniture.

The gardens, too, she adored, and described bright green turf, bees buzzing in the lime trees, herbaceous borders and orchards of apple trees, with the heat 'quivering like watered gauze above the ridges of the lawn' in her history, *Knole and the Sackvilles*. She was given her own patch, but 'weeds grew too fast and flowers too slowly,' she later complained.[11] The gardeners would tidy it up when she wasn't looking, making her feel that it didn't really belong to her.

This was a cruel lesson she learned when her grandfather died in 1908. Victoria's brother, Henry, attempted to prove that Lord Sackville had actually married their mother, Pepita, meaning that he, not young Lionel, was rightful heir to Knole. The *cause célèbre* came to court, and Victoria had to proclaim her own illegitimacy and that of her siblings to ensure that Knole passed to her husband. As Pepita had already had a husband, Henry's case failed, and the new Lord Sackville returned victorious to Knole, but for the teenaged Vita the experience brought the brutal realisation that, as a girl, she would never inherit.

Vita was a surprisingly unreluctant debutante. Her suitors included Lord Lascelles (later husband of the Princess Royal), who would have set her up on an estate as grand as Knole. To her mother's consternation, she opted for a less glittering prize, Harold Nicolson, the diplomat son of diplomatic, itinerant parents, on a salary of just £250 a year. But Vita made an inspired choice, for Harold gave her the freedom to be whom she wanted. Both had affairs with members of their own sex, but, with the exception of the liaison with Violet Trefusis in 1919/1921, and her intense friendship with Virginia Woolf in the 1920s, their unconventional marriage was never really threatened. 'One of [Harold's] strengths in dealing with Vita,' according to her biographer Victoria Glendinning, 'was his steadfast refusal to lose sight of the gentle, protective woman in her that he needed so desperately and whom she never wished to deprive him of. To preserve the balance in her personality, she needed Harold's vision of her.'[12]

The marriage began conventionally enough, the only irregularity Lady Sackville's refusal to attend the wedding because one of the bridesmaids, Rosamund Grosvenor, was a recently rejected lover of Vita's. The newlyweds set sail for Constantinople, where Harold was third secretary. Vita filled their house on the shores of the Bosphorus with furniture from Knole. She appreciated their first garden, which had a pergola of grapes, a pomegranate tree and a view over the Golden Horn.[13] This was Vita's brief taste of diplomatic life: in the 1920s, when Harold was posted to Tehran and then Berlin, Vita visited, but never lived with him in either capital.

The Nicolsons returned from Constantinople for the birth of their first son, Ben, two days after the outbreak of the First World War; Nigel followed in January 1917. Harold spent the war in Whitehall, before joining the peace delegation at Versailles. The couple divided these years between weeks at their London home in Ebury Street, winter weekends at Knole, and summer weekends at Long Barn, the so-called cottage they bought for £2,500 in March 1915.[14]

Long Barn, a short walk from Knole, was a half-timbered house dating from the fourteenth, fifteenth and sixteenth centuries, and believed to have been William Caxton's birthplace. In the age of modernism, a reactionary trend was represented by people such as Nancy Lancaster and Ronald Tree at Ditchley, Norah and Harry Lindsay at Sutton Courtney and Lawrence Johnston at Hidcote. Like them, the Nicolsons, at Long Barn and then at Sissinghurst, restored ancient houses with care and sympathy and furnished them with period pieces.[15] These traditionalists seemed out of kilter with their times, and yet their restorations, designed to conserve the integrity of the original buildings, presaged future work by the National Trust.

A barn from across the road was erected in 1916 to provide another wing to what became a substantial house. The garden sloped away from a brick terrace to views over the Weald of Kent, a beautiful site on which to make a first garden; increasingly Long Barn captured Vita's imagination and time.[16]

Unlike any other gardener in this book, Vita had received no kind of training, nor had she been exposed to modern colour theories and aspects of painting as Gertrude Jekyll had been at art school. Vita was largely self-educated through the classics in the Knole library, while her fluent French came from her mother's cosmopolitan background. Throughout her life, diaries, letters, novels, history and poetry flowed ceaselessly from her pen. She approached her gardening in the same intellectual and romantic way as she did her writing, giving both her gardens spontaneity and individuality.

At Long Barn, she asked herself basic questions about what, when and where to plant, and discovered she needed damp-lovers for the lower, soggier part of the garden. She thought of planting hedges of hornbeam, beech and thorn, inspired by seeing pink and white thorn mixed in Constantinople.[17]

Lady Sackville, estranged from her husband, had a series of protectors who included Edwin Lutyens. Lutyens encouraged Lady Sackville to take fledgling gardener Vita to visit Gertrude Jekyll's Munstead Wood in August 1917. Vita recorded that Miss Jekyll 'is rather fat and rather grumbly ... and the garden was not at its best but one can see it must be lovely'.[18] Vita would share Jekyll's love of flower and of colour, but her attitude to both was very different and she didn't admire the showpiece border at Munstead Wood. Later she wrote: 'I have no great love for herbaceous borders or for the plants that usually fill them – coarse things with no delicacy or quality about them. I think the only justification for such borders is that they shall be perfectly planned, both in regard to colour and to grouping; perfectly staked; and perfectly weeded. How many people have the time or the labour?'[19] Miss Jekyll's border was 'perfectly planned', but, in wartime, she didn't have the labour to keep it 'perfectly staked and weeded'.

Jekyll did, however, influence Vita's love of roses. She covered Long Barn with them: the repeat-flowering, creamy-white, pink-tinged 'Madame Alfred Carrière' rose was used first here, and later again prolifically at Sissinghurst. Roses listed in Vita's earliest gardening notebook were all ones she would have seen at Munstead Wood.

The garden Vita created at Long Barn during the war years was, in one biographer's words, 'an English rustic version of an Italian villa garden'. Stone walls retained two south-facing terrace lawns, one edged with twenty Irish yews. Box-edged flower gardens were made outside the Nicolsons' study windows, and avenues of Lombardy poplars carried the eye from the more formal parts of the garden. What Vita called the Apple Garden recalled the orchards at Knole, and William Robinson would have admired the peppering of the walls with saxifrages, violets, violas, gentians and geums. In the outlying woodland, Vita planted medlars, hazel, dogwoods, pink and white thorn, again inspired by foreign travel.[20]

A visit from Lutyens resulted in the Dutch Garden, sketched out by Harold Nicolson in conversation with the architect. More formal than the rest of the garden, it had L-shaped beds, clipped hedging and brickwork paths. It cost £600 and was paid for by Lady Sackville, who also paid the gardener's salary.[21]

The Nicolsons shared the garden's planning, Harold providing the green framework for Vita's exuberant planting. They corresponded about it when apart. She was ambitious, writing to Harold about yew trees she was planting, 'which will look silly at first, but which when the mars [a family name for themselves] are a little grey handful of ashes will draw charabancs full of tourists from London'.[22]

The summer of 1917 'was the last of our untroubled summers', as Vita recorded.[23] In October, the Nicolsons joined a house party at Knebworth where Harold contracted a venereal disease from a fellow, male guest. This effectively ended their sexual relationship, for, by the time Harold's treatment and quarantine were over, Vita had begun a tumultuous affair with Violet Trefusis. While Harold worked at the Versailles peace conference, Violet and Vita spent months abroad, leaving Vita's two young sons shuttling between nannies and her disapproving mother. Harold was wracked by guilt, writing to Vita that 'I have exposed you to things you hate and loathe and of course you cannot help rather hating me for it.'[24]

During the affair, Violet married a war hero, Denys Trefusis, partly as a cover for her irregular romance. Vita wrote that, when she was with Violet, she felt 'like a person translated, or reborn; it was like beginning one's life again in a different capacity'. In 1920, 'the whole of that summer she was mine – a mad irresponsible summer of moonlight nights, and infinite escapades, and passionate letters, and music, and poetry.'[25]

By late summer 1921, the relationship was over, with Vita convinced that Violet was deeply manipulative and untrustworthy. Vita herself enjoyed the thrill of the chase, the beginnings of affairs and the secrecy, more than any long-term connection: that was reserved unequivocally for Harold. But, as Nigel Nicolson has written, 'she was physically attracted by women more than by men, and remained so all her life.'[26] She would have serious love affairs again, among many others with Virginia Woolf, with Hilda Matheson, director of talks at the BBC, and, on one occasion, with a man, architect Geoffrey Scott, who had a powerful intellectual influence on her.[27] Mostly, the lovers came off worse, becoming her emotional pensioners, while she returned to the haven of Harold's love and support.

Undeflected by her emotional upheavals, Vita published novels, poetry, and histories of Knole, the Sackvilles and other ancestors. By 1922, her verse had been anthologised; she had been elected to the PEN club, and both she and Harold became fellows of the Royal Society of Literature. From the late 1920s, Vita was a regular radio broadcaster and lecturer at home and abroad on literature, and later on gardening; the Nicolsons even did a double-act talk about marriage. But Vita was a popular rather than a literary success: she was never accepted by the Bloomsbury members, who were dismissive of her writing, and considered her judgements on art superficial. Clive Bell, Virginia Woolf's brother-in-law, described her as 'dear old obtuse, aristocratic, passionate, Grenadier-like Vita'.[28]

Vita was still at Long Barn when her father died aged sixty-one in January 1928. Knole and the title passed to his brother, Charles. After a dinner party at Knole, hosted by Charles's hated American wife, Anne, Vita drove away in tears, knowing her childhood home was lost to her.

On 4 March 1930, Harold recorded in his diary: 'Vita finishes her novel on the Edwardians [a popular success, published by Virginia and Leonard Woolf's Hogarth Press]. We hear that Cookes, the poultry people, have bought Westwood, the farm next to Long Barn.'[29] Long Barn's proximity to Knole was now a disadvantage, and the prospect of a poultry farm next door was the final straw.

A friend's land agent spotted a ruined castle for sale near the village of Sissinghurst, twenty miles east of Long Barn. In Henry VIII's reign, the castle had belonged to Sir John Baker, whose daughter had married Thomas Sackville in 1554, an alluring family link. It had housed French prisoners during the Seven Years War, the surviving buildings later used as the parish workhouse and then as makeshift dwellings for farm labourers. Vita 'fell flat in love with it', although Harold was less sure initially.[30] 'It is most unwise of us to get Sissinghurst,' as it would cost £30,000, for which 'we could buy a beautiful place replete with park, garage, h. and c., central heating, historical associations, and two lodges r. and l.' Then in the same diary entry, he added, 'it is most wise of us to buy Sissinghurst. Through its veins pulses the blood of the Sackville dynasty ... It is in Kent ... We like it. *They decided to buy.*'[31]

Harold had just left the Foreign Office for a job on the *Evening Standard* at £3,000 a year, which 'covers all my days with a dark cloud of shame'.[32] He relinquished a profession he loved because of Vita's detestation of diplomatic life, subsequently to involve himself, mostly unsuccessfully, in politics, including a brief flirtation with Mosley's New Party. He wrote biographies of George V and of his father, Lord Carnock, although his lasting literary achievement would be his three best-selling volumes of diaries that charted the development of Sissinghurst and painted an unrivalled portrait of British political life over three decades. They end with Vita's death in 1962, after which his health and mental faculties declined.

Sissinghurst is also his legacy. Although the garden is principally associated with Vita, Harold gave it its subtle and beautiful structure, influenced by the gardens of Persia. He planned the design, using squared paper, string, sticks and aided by a teenaged Nigel standing as a marking post.[33]

***

Before starting work on their garden, set amid fields and woods, and edged on two sides by a moat, the Nicolsons had to restore the miscellaneous collection of buildings and clear away the detritus of 'old bedsteads, ploughshares, old cabbage-stalks, old broken-down earth closets, old matted wire, and mountains of sardine tins, all muddled up in a tangle of bindweed, nettles and ground elder'.[34] The central tower was the first building made habitable, and housed Vita's writing room. The South Cottage was restored, with bedrooms and a bathroom for Harold and Vita, and a study for Harold, overlooking what would become the Cottage Garden. The Priest's House, on the far side of the garden, was where the boys, Ben and Nigel, shared a room and where the family ate. The entrance range became the 'Big Room' (or library) and servants' quarters. There was no spare room, as Vita had a horror that Sibyl Colefax might invite herself to stay. This strange, dispersed method of living suited a family whose relationships 'were created more by ... letters than by conversation, for we all wrote avidly back and forth to each other, but were reticent when we met'.[35]

Because they walked to their meals through their garden at all times of day and seasons of the year, both Vita and Harold were aware of every change or variation. Hence the post-war White Garden, a shimmering symmetrical mass of silver and white planting, a central frame canopied with the free-flowering *Rosa longicuspis*. At its best as night draws in, the garden is a perfect fusion of Harold's cooler and Vita's more romantic temperaments.

Vita liked plants for their historical and literary associations, so Sissinghurst was the perfect setting. There were ancient red-brick walls she could smother with clematis and old-fashioned roses. James Lees-Milne once asked her why she liked these roses so much, to which she replied that 'they reminded her of Tudor heraldic rose and Caroline stump-work.'[36]

The courtyard between the entrance range and Vita's tower became a green court, reminiscent of Knole's, its central path lined by four drum yews, with wall-backed beds planted in shades of purple and crimson on either side. From the top of Vita's tower the visitor today can see how Vita and Harold made sense of an unsymmetrical site, with walls and buildings at odd angles to one another. In the initial challenge to get the lines of sight right, the Nicolsons were assisted by the architect A. R. Powys, brother of the novelist John Cowper Powys. Powys suggested the ellipse at the top of the vista through the rose beds that surround the yew Rondel, the curved wall pleasingly echoing the shape of the Rondel.

Walls were restored, another was built between the courtyard and what would become the White Garden, and a pergola, known as the Erectheum, was made for summer meals in a corner by the Priest's House. A Yew Walk was planted, with a break in the hedging creating a line of sight from the entrance arch straight across the courtyard, tower, Tower Lawn and through the yew framing a statue of Dionysus on the other side of the moat beyond the orchard. Running beside the orchard is the Moat Walk, which also looks down towards Dionysus. Beside the Moat Walk is the Nuttery, beyond which, at the furthest point from the kitchen in the Priest's House, is the brick-paved herb garden: Vita was no cook. At an oblique angle to the Cottage Garden, overlooked by South Cottage, is the Lime Walk. Its planting was designed by Harold who called it 'My Life's Work'.

Tension occasionally arose between Harold and Vita, with Harold favouring a classical approach. He wrote in his diary in September 1930 that 'our general line is to keep the whole thing as green and quiet and simple as we can.'[37] Vita agreed that 'straight determined lines' were a good basis for garden design, but added that those lines should be softened by shrubs, climbers and drifts of planting. 'Too severe a formality is almost as repellent as the complete absence of it,' she said in one of her BBC gardening talks.[38]

This very tension between the classical and the romantic is what gives Sissinghurst its magic. It is a sophisticated, linear garden of strange angles, and long views, and, simultaneously, a real country garden, with a joyful confusion of plants, and with nut trees, orchards and views over the Weald of Kent. Vita planted generously, massing plants together: 'I believe in exaggeration ... in big groups, big masses: I am sure that it is more effective to plant twelve tulips together than to split them into groups of six; more effective to concentrate all the delphiniums into one bed, than to dot them about at intervals of twos and threes.'[39]

Every area has its season: Harold's Lime Walk peaks in April, the trees underplanted with forget-me-nots and euphorbia, followed by the Nuttery with a carpet of wood anemones, epimediums, woodruff and cowslips. In summer, Vita's famous White Garden is at its zenith, with roses, lilies, veronicas, gypsophila and grey-leafed plants, while the season closes with the hot-coloured planting in the Cottage Garden. 'The Sissinghurst garden enchants because it is both formal and informal,' wrote James Lees-Milne in 1949. 'The straight paths lined with yew and the pleached lime alleys lead to orchards, their fruit trees swathed in ramblers and eglantines.'[40]

Every inch a countrywoman, Vita assimilated a deep knowledge of farming and rural pursuits during her childhood at Knole. In *The Land*, she wrote:

> I sing the cycle of my country's year,
> I sing the tillage, and the reaping sing,
> Classic monotony, that modes and wars
> Leave undisturbed, for their best
> Was born immediate, of expediency.[41]

This spirit informed her gardening, for she always closely observed her plants and the conditions they required. Early plantings at Sissinghurst were of primroses and polyanthus in the Nuttery, for she had spotted that primroses flourished in their woods.[42] She enjoyed experimenting, and, intolerant of plants which did not earn their keep, would make sweeping changes. Some of her gardeners claimed they sneaked behind her, replanting stragglers she had jabbed carelessly into the soil. But she was always hands-on, her secateurs tucked into her boots or in her hand in almost every post-war photograph. 'May I assure the gentleman who writes to me (quite often) from a priory in Sussex that I am not the armchair, library fireside gardener he evidently suspects, "never having performed any single act of gardening myself,"' she wrote trenchantly in an *Observer* column, 'and that for the last forty years of my life I have broken my back, my finger-nails, and sometimes my heart, in the practical pursuit of my favourite occupation?'[43]

By the late 1930s, the garden had already achieved a considerable reputation, with requests to visit from Women's Institutes and other societies. In 1938, Sissinghurst opened for the National Garden Scheme, admitting the 'shillingses', the Nicolsons' condescending name for those who paid a shilling to look round. Eight hundred people attended their second NGS opening a year later.

During the war, when her head gardener, Jack Vass, was in the RAF, Vita managed with one gardener and a couple of Land Girls, turning over the lawns to hay. War caused Vita to return to *The Garden*, a long poem she had earlier abandoned. In it, she speaks of flowers almost as personal friends, with character traits, and 'she never lost her astonishment,' Nigel Nicolson has said, 'that something so short-lived, with no middle-age between bud and death, could put itself to so much trouble to look so beautiful.'[44] She wrote: 'I think the flowers were the lovelier/For danger.'[45]

The Garden's lukewarm reception was followed in 1946 by another blow, when fellow members of the Society of Authors did not suggest she read with other poets at the Wigmore Hall in the presence of the queen. She later wrote to her cousin, Eddy Sackville-West, that she was so hurt 'that I have never told it to anyone, not even to Harold ... I know that I am audible ... so the only inference to be drawn is that ... my poetry wasn't good enough. It had the effect on me that I have never written a line of verse since.'[46]

By contrast, her *Observer* gardening columns, which she cared less about, were acclaimed. These articles, produced weekly from 1947 until 1961, 'did more to change the face of gardening than any other writing since Robinson's *The English Flower Garden*', claimed Anne Scott-James.[47] They were read, according to Robin Lane Fox, 'not only by fanatical gardeners but by thousands of wishful thinking fellow-travellers who liked to entertain a good idea and by the many non-gardeners who liked an elegant performance'.[48] Despite gardening several acres, Vita always considered those who gardened on a smaller scale, as a recent biographer points out: '"Even the smallest garden can be prodigal within its own limitations," she trumpeted on 26 March 1950. It was a call to arms, a mission statement, an antidote to the privations and drabness of post-war Britain.'[49]

The Observer columns made both garden and creator famous. A designated post van daily delivered sackfuls of letters, all of which Vita attempted to answer. Envelopes addressed vaguely to 'The Hon. Mrs. Nicolson, A Castle, Somewhere in Kent', or to Miss V. Sackville-West, The Novelist', would find her.[50] She entered the freemasonry of gardening, sending out and receiving seeds and cuttings: her notebook lists, for instance, 'A root of comfrey Mrs. Youle, Grand Drive, Raynes Park, S.W.20', and 'To the Hon. Mrs. Fitzroy Maclean, seed of onopordum, root double blue geranium, cutting of white cistus'.[51]

The columns were written in a vigorous, conversational style, one beginning, 'I have a gardening dodge which I find very useful,' and with flashes of humour not notable in her books and letters. 'Occasionally it is borne in upon me that my taste in flowers may be peculiar. Some people, invited to admire my mountain orach, said it reminded them of nothing so much as Irish widows keening round a grave; others said it reminded them of wet umbrellas standing unfurled to drip in the porch of a seaside boarding-house.'[52]

She produced novels and biography as well as her columns in the late 1940s and the 1950s. She became a JP, regarded as too lenient by fellow members of the bench, and was made a Companion of Honour by Clement Attlee. In 1949, she joined the National Trust gardens committee, helping raise funds to preserve Hidcote, and sat on the executive of the Society for the Preservation of Rural Kent. It was an irony to her that her *Observer* columns, or 'sticklebacks' as she scornfully referred to them, brought her in 1955 the prestigious Veitch Memorial Medal, 'in recognition of her services to horticulture'.

She enjoyed the intellectual cut and thrust of the gardening world: 'If you want real highbrow talk, commend me to three experts talking about auriculas. Bloomsbury is nothing to it. I couldn't understand half they said.'[53]

***

As Vita grew older, arthritis made it difficult for her to garden, and she began to drink. 'On a few occasions the gardeners found Vita passed out in the flower beds, returning her to the cottage by wheelbarrow,' recalls her granddaughter.[54] She became even more reclusive, although was always available on open days to answer visitors' questions. She continued to write, and went on foreign cruises with Harold during her last six winters. She developed a surprising fondness for football and horse-racing on television.

Vita Sackville-West died 'without fear or self-reproach' from bowel cancer on 2 June 1962.[55] Her ashes were buried with her Sackville ancestors in the crypt beneath St Michael and All Angels, Withyham. Harold died six years later and was buried in the churchyard at Sissinghurst. At their joint memorial service at St James's Piccadilly in the summer of 1968, Cecil Day-Lewis, then poet laureate, read the poem Vita had written for Harold during the Second World War, its images drawn from the Kent countryside she loved:

> I loved you then, when love was Spring, and May.
> Eternity is here and now, I thought...
> But now when autumn yellows all the leaves,
> And twenty seasons mellow our long love,
> How rooted, how secure, how strong, how rich,
> How full the barn that holds our garnered sheaves![56]

CHAPTER 17

Margery Fish (1892–1969)

1892 was an auspicious year for British horticulture, with the birth of two of its best gardeners. Five months after Vita Sackville-West entered the world amid the splendours of Knole in Kent, another baby girl was born on 5 August in the north London suburb of Stamford Hill. The future Margery Fish was solidly middle-class, the second of the four daughters of Ernest Townshend, a City of London commercial traveller in tea, and his wife, Florence. Ernest and Florence both gardened: Margery later admitted that she could have learned much from her parents but resisted being used as a garden labourer. 'You can't really be keen on gardening until you have one of your own. Doing as you are told in other people's gardens is a bore.'[1]

Margery Fish would be forty-five before she had her own garden, but over the following thirty years, she made that garden, East Lambrook Manor in Somerset, as influential as Hidcote or Sissinghurst; in 1992, it was Grade I listed by English Heritage. She set out a blueprint for post-war gardeners with small gardens and little help. 'Many of us garden the way we do largely because of Margery Fish,' horticulturalist Graham Rice has written. 'Margery pursued her own vision of a modern, more imaginative form of cottage gardening, using the plants of the past.'[2] She popularised cottage garden plants, advocated the year-round garden and the use of ground-cover planting, and became an authority on dealing with tricky growing conditions.[3]

***

The Townshends imposing strict discipline on their four ebullient daughters, who always remained close. All academic, they attended the Friends' School in Saffron Walden, where three of them (including Margery) were successively head girls.

Education then for young women such as the Townshend sisters was principally designed to prepare them to be accomplished helpmates to

Margery Fish at East Lambrook Manor. (Courtesy The Garden Museum)

their professional husbands. Not so Margery, who wanted her own career, battling with her father to be allowed to attend secretarial college; she passed with flying colours.[4] After working for the editor of the Country Gentleman's Publishing Company, Margery began her twenty-year Fleet Street career in September 1912 as secretary to the *Daily Mail*'s advertisement manager. Her abilities were quickly recognised by the paper's owner and founder, Lord Northcliffe. The formidable self-made press baron, with political ambitions and a strong resemblance to Napoleon, was delighted to find that the French emperor's hat was too small for him.[5] His flagship *Daily Mail* (he also owned *The Times* and *The Observer* at various times), was unashamedly populist, combining news, gossip and pictures, and encouraged the aspirations of its readers, particularly women.[6]

Working for a megalomaniacal workaholic must have been some initiation for a young woman educated at a Quaker boarding school, but Margery coped. She accompanied Northcliffe as his personal assistant when he headed a three-year British war mission to the United States from 1916 and was awarded the MBE for her work. Returning to Britain, she was bored and wrote to Northcliffe in 1921. He responded immediately: 'I am sorry to hear that you are unhappy ... It is difficult to find appointments just now, but yours is an exceptional case.'[7]

With Northcliffe's help, she went back to the *Daily Mail*, becoming secretary to Walter Fish who, since 1919, had been the paper's editor and a director of Associated Newspapers. A dedicated newspaperman, he scooped Dr Crippen's arrest for the *Mail*, but his relationship with Northcliffe was so difficult that Fish began legal proceedings against his employer in 1922. These were stopped by Northcliffe's death in August, and Fish remained as editor until his retirement in January 1930.[8] He retained his directorship, and Margery, who had enjoyed working for a man many regarded as a tyrant, wrote to Fish offering to help with his secretarial work. He replied, 'I am more pleased than I can say to receive your letter. It has always been a very great pleasure to work with you.'[9]

Their association, until that point entirely professional, continued on a different footing: on 2 March 1933, the fifty-eight year old widower and the forty year old Margery were married. Her nephew, Henry Boyd-Carpenter, claimed 'she loved the company of the great and the good,' so was content to spend her early married years in London, with a busy social life and visits to theatre and opera.[10] But a holiday in Germany in 1937 led to Walter's realisation that war was imminent and the Fishes decided to leave London.

East Lambrook Manor was one of the first houses they saw but was so dilapidated that Walter refused to consider it. Margery recalled their subsequent struggles in her first book, *We Made a Garden*:

> For three months we tried to find what we wanted. We looked at cottages and villas, gaunt Victorian houses perched uneasily on hilltops, and snug little homes wedged in forgotten valleys. Some were too big and most too small, some hadn't enough garden and others too much. Some were too isolated, others so mixed up with other houses that privacy would

> have been impossible. We lost our way and had bitter arguments, but we did discover what we didn't want. I couldn't see Walter in a four-roomed cottage with a kitchen tacked on to one end and a bathroom at the other, and I had no intention of landing myself with a barn of a place that would require several servants to keep it clean.[11]

A road sign to East Lambrook took them back in November to see the house summarily dismissed in September. In that time, a developer had replaced the corrugated iron roof with tiles, cleared overgrown vegetation, and repainted inside. The fifteenth-century honey-coloured Somerset stone house had a central passage with doors at each end. 'It was late afternoon and the sun was nearly setting. Both doors were open and through them we caught a glimpse of a tree and a green background against the sunlight ... We both knew ... we had come home.'[12]

Two of her sisters had attempted previously to interest Margery in gardening – but she had preferred to play golf. The Fishes' friends, therefore, expected them to buy 'a respectable house in good repair complete with garden, all nicely laid out and ready to walk into. And when, instead, we chose a poor battered old house that had to be gutted to be livable, and a wilderness instead of a garden, they were really sorry for us. They were particularly sorry about the garden. Redoing a house could be fun, but how would two Londoners go about the job of creating a garden from a farmyard and a rubbish heap?'[13]

How indeed? 'I had come from a London flat,' she wrote, 'and although I took it as a matter of course that now we had a house in the country, I should work in the garden, I had no idea then of the fanatic I was to become.'[14]

The Fishes paid £1,000 for the house and two-acre garden, commuting for two years between London and Somerset while the house was made fit to live in. Margery's early gardening was limited to pulling up groundsel and cutting down brambles, laurels and elders in between dealing with builders. But the Fishes were 'thinking all the time what we would do with our little plot. We both knew that it had to be tackled as a whole with a definite design for the complete garden, and we were lucky in having plenty to do while our ideas smouldered and simmered.'[15]

Like the Nicolsons at Long Barn and Sissinghurst, they eschewed modernism: they chose rather to restore an old country house, retaining its spirit and creating a garden that was 'part of a single vision'.[16] Yet this apparently retrospective approach, especially in Margery's case, anticipated attitudes to gardening into the twenty-first century. 'Margery represented a more distant past transformed into the future.'[17]

Where the Fishes' path diverged from that of Sackville-West or Johnston was that they designed their garden 'with the idea that we'd have to look after it ourselves'. Although both Sissinghurst and Hidcote have something of a cottagey atmosphere, they are nevertheless grand gardens, dependent on several gardeners to maintain them. The Fishes had occasional help, but it tended to be 'brief and uncertain, and we knew we'd soon be back where so many people are today'.[18]

The garden at East Lambrook was well planned, with year-round interest, but never pristine; Margery was always happy to let plants self-seed. Despite calling one of her books *Carefree Gardening*, Margery's approach was anything but. The East Lambrook garden was high-maintenance, but maintenance at the level enthusiastic gardeners are happy to give. Vita Sackville-West in her *Observer* articles – and indeed, over a century before her, John Loudon in his books and magazines – wrote for the general gardening public, but neither owned a garden to which their readers could aspire: Vita's lay round a castle; Loudon's was a show garden. Margery Fish, however, had created her garden with her bare hands and was able to empathise with the readers of her books and articles.

> However imperfect the result there is a certain satisfaction in making a garden like no one else's, and in knowing that you yourself are responsible for every stone and every flower in the place. It is pleasant to know each one of your plants intimately because you have chosen and planted every one of them. In the course of time they become real friends, conjuring up pleasant associations of the people who gave them and the gardens they came from.[19]

In 1956, Margery published her first book, *We Made a Garden*. This delightful account, originally entitled 'Gardening with Walter', is composed of themed chapters on subjects such as 'planting', 'hedges', 'clothing the walls' and 'watering'. Margery had written freelance articles during her years in Fleet Street, schooled by Northcliffe never to use two words when one will do. Concisely, *We Made a Garden* traced how the Fishes created order from the chaos that surrounded East Lambrook Manor. It also shed light on the couple's marriage: Margery, it emerged, managed her husband with skill, no doubt as she had Northcliffe when his personal assistant.

Walter had previously gardened in Sydenham where he had lived with his first wife. He taught Margery 'that the aim of all gardeners should be a garden that is always presentable', and, as Harold taught Vita, 'that you mustn't rely on your flowers to make your garden attractive. A good bone structure must come first.'[20]

Margery discovered Walter was something of a martinet. One of his previous gardeners had been particularly fond of chrysanthemums, at the expense, Walter believed, of other jobs. 'Remonstrances had no effect so one day Walter took a knife and slashed off all those pampered darlings at ground level. It was by remembering this episode that I learnt to have a sense of proportion and fairness in my gardening, and not devote too much time to the things I like best at the expense of the rest of the garden.' Walter was a stickler: 'It was no good for me to tell Walter that I had to sandwich my gardening between housekeeping, household jobs and a certain amount of social life. In his opinion there was no excuse for not getting things done at the right time.'[21]

Their shared aim was to create a garden that 'was as modest and unpretentious as the house, a cottage garden in fact, with crooked paths and unexpected corners'. What they made was not a garden of rooms as such, but of distinct areas, each leading to the next. The long, low L-shaped house had a garden divided by walls, with patches of grass, and little in the way of planting apart from some bright pink 'Dorothy Perkins' roses. The Fishes began by dismantling the walls and piling up the stones for future use, and then cleared an area they called the barton as a drive-in between outbuildings and an orchard that they had bought from a chicken farmer. Shades of Long Barn, and shades of Sissinghurst, too, for they had to remove 'old beds, rusty oil stoves, ancient corsets, pots, pans, tins and china, bottles and glass jars, and some big lumps of stone which may at one time have been used for crushing grain'.[22]

Walls between barton and orchard were made into a rock garden, others clad with roses. Low walls erected elsewhere were planted by Margery with scrambling plants, tucked into crevices and along their tops, and she would climb up on stones, sometimes in evening dress, to water them. 'Watering was another garden job on which Walter had very strong views.' He was 'thorough in the extreme ... I can see him now on a hot summer day in an old panama hat and short sleeved shirt, with a tussore waistcoat which he wore for gardening and summer golf (to hide his braces, he always said he hadn't the figure for a belt!). He would stand all day directing the life-giving water to the thirsting plants, with brief intervals for meals.'[23]

Early on, they planted a *Lonicera nitida* hedge to hide the back door and kitchen from the garden, a decision that Margery came to laugh at. 'In those days it was unthinkable that ladies and gentlemen enjoying themselves in the garden should be disturbed by the sight of tradesmen delivering food at the back door ... No one must see the maid washing up, but it never occurred to us, the architect or the builder, how dull it was for the poor girl to be shut off like that. When the war came and I spent hours at the sink I ... had clear glass put in that window.'[24]

They improved the texture of their clay soil with bonfire ash, and used a mixture of sand and peat when planting. Margery made mistakes, described with colourful imagery. 'My planting was so insecure that the plants lurched about in the bed and were blown this way and that by the wind. Like a woman holding on to her hat they were too busy trying to keep a foothold in the earth to give a thought to anything else.' Walter was impatient with unhappy looking plants, pulling them up and leaving them 'laid out like a lot of dead rats'.[25]

Walter insisted on wide lawns, generous paths, level and good-sized beds, rather than a succession of smaller ones. 'Walter taught me ... to avoid unnecessary distraction. One must have something to separate flower beds from paths but one should not draw attention to the border and so detract from the flowers themselves ... He also taught me the value of massed effects, so instead of an odd delphinium dotted here and there, as I would have planted them, he insisted they were planted in groups of five or six.'[26]

They had their disagreements. Walter loved big blowsy dahlias, delphiniums and lupins, while Margery preferred smaller, shyer plants in pastel shades, 'for with them it is possible to have a riot without disagreement'.[27] Walter wanted to hang roses on pillars over Margery's terraced beds, and would accept that only one clematis, the blue *jackmanii*, was worth growing. Walter's taste, a hangover from the Victorian era, persisted into the 1950s and 1960s, when perfect blooms of dahlias and chrysanthemums would be displayed in serried rows at late-summer flower shows. Margery's fondness for traditional cottage garden flowers was, in fact, the more radical. Walter emphasised the importance of the garden looking at its best in high summer, with plants such as dahlias which needed lifting and over-wintering. Margery, by contrast, believed a garden should be of interest year-round, planted with treasures happy in the soil conditions and not needing constant attention.

Exasperated affection echoes through *We Made a Garden*, yet the book was in effect a love letter to her deceased husband. His death from a heart attack on 21 December 1947 was a shock for his much younger wife. 'I found it hard to believe,' she wrote in notes for a biography she didn't complete, 'that the scattering of a few ashes in a windswept crematorium garden in Weymouth one wintry morning could be the end of such an outstanding figure. He was so different from the ordinary run of people that I could not believe that anything so ordinary as death could happen to him.'[28]

To distract herself, she set off in 1948 to visit her mother's American family. This and two subsequent visits over the next three years affected how she gardened. She appreciated American plants such as the Virginian cowslip which she introduced in her own garden. On the first trip, her cousin, Bruce Buttfield, and the landscape designer Lanning Roper, organised garden tours for her around New Jersey and Pennsylvania. Margery particularly admired Beatrix Farrand's design of Dumbarton Oaks, and Farrand's use of ground-cover planting, promoting it in Britain.[29]

In her introduction to *We Made a Garden*, Margery writes that she had to simplify the garden 'even more' after Walter's death, 'as the garden can only have the odd hours that are left over in a busy life'.[30] But these years were Margery's most productive, during which she gave the garden at East Lambrook Manor rather more than 'odd hours'. It became her main focus, the subject of her books and articles. Writing in 1980, National Trust gardens adviser John Sales claimed that 'in the development of gardening in the second half of the twentieth century no garden has yet had greater effect'.[31]

Margery kept Walter's dahlias in his memory, but was glad when the collection gradually died away, leaving her space to experiment with other plants. She had read Robinson and Jekyll, and Margery shared the latter's love of cottage garden plants. 'White love-in-the-mist was one of the plants that Gertrude Jekyll loved to see in the garden, and it is as beautiful as her other favourites.'[32]

Margery's garden, however, with its little areas of sun, shade, marsh, stream and orchard, was unsuited to Jekyll-style herbaceous borders.[33] 'My idea of a natural border is one where all the plants grow happily together, often intermingling with each other. There is nothing forced or artificial about it, in fact it is just as nature would have planted it.'[34] She preferred a subtle blend of colour in her planting, resisting 'great roaring splashes of hot, hard yellow' in favour of shades of pale lemon. She was in sympathy with, and indeed led, 'the changing taste of many gardeners. Instead of planning our gardens for a riot of colour we seek satisfaction in textures, neutral shades and green in every tone.'[35]

She planted shady corners with hellebores, snowdrops and primroses, savouring their quiet contributions when little else is in flower. 'The beautiful silver and white garden at Sissinghurst is a delight,' she wrote, but for the most part disliked the idea of colour or planting segregation, recognising it was impractical for smaller gardens. Apart from anything else, 'I like every part of the garden to be interesting at every time of year.'[36]

This was very much in the spirit of William Robinson, who abhorred the idea of massed plants overwintered in hothouses for one season outside. It was Margery's acid test for other people's gardens, and she was often quoted as saying, 'If I ever hear of a good garden I visit it in winter and if I like it return in the summer.'[37]

Ground-cover plants such as epimediums were a feature, as was creeping thyme, running through crevices in paving, or carpets of creeping chamomile. She was the wry master of observation and practicality, asking 'I often wonder if the "seat" in Miss V. Sackville-West's herb garden at Sissinghurst Castle is meant to be sat on? It is an old stone seat without a seat, for the horizontal part is filled with earth and thickly carpeted with *Mentha requienii*. This little plant emits the most delicious scent of mint if one touches it. That growing on the seat is at hand level and invites a passing brush if one has not the temerity to sit on what is, after all, a planted flower bed.'[38]

Gardening on a site composed of clay soil, marsh, stony terraces, a ditch, orchards and a nuttery meant that Margery was able to write authoritatively on a variety of conditions. She saved many rare cottage garden plants from extinction by caring for cuttings from friends and local villagers. 'I feel very humble,' she wrote, 'when I think of the plants that are given to me so generously from the smallest gardens, sometimes pieces of the only plant they have.' And she added that 'nowhere in the world is there anything quite like the English cottage garden. In every village and hamlet in the land there were these little gardens, always gay and never garish, and so obviously loved ... I am afraid the cottages and their little gardens may disappear completely as the years go by and we shall have to remember them by the flowers ... Great efforts are being made to preserve our old buildings, and we must also cherish the simple flowers that brightened our cottage gardens for so many years.'[39]

Margery, in looking to the future, was constantly aware of the past, quoting, for example, the seventeenth-century botanist, John Parkinson, on crown imperials (*Fritillaria imperialis*): 'There were evidently many more varieties in his day as he says "whereof some are white, others blush, some purple, others red or yellow, some spotted, others without spots, some standing upright, others hanging or turning downwards".' She also quoted John Gerard, who mentioned auriculas, a favourite plant of hers, in his 1597 *Herball*: 'He calls them mountain cowslips and from his descriptions it is obvious that the one he is referring to is the yellow alpine auricula.'[40]

***

She wrote extensively about the plants she loved: daisies, astrantias, auriculas, pinks, primroses, heucheras, hellebores, and, in particular, geraniums. 'If in doubt,' she always said, 'plant a geranium.' Starting a nursery in the late 1950s was an obvious development, so she could supply plants to the many gardeners who were by then imitating her style.[41] Her own cultivars, many still listed and with the Award of Garden Merit in the RHS Plant Finder, include *Artemisia absinthium* 'Lambrook Silver', *Astrantia major* 'Margery Fish', *Euphorbia wulfenii* 'Lambrook Gold', *Penstemon* 'Margery Fish', and *Santolina* 'Lambrook Silver'. A database of every plant she mentioned in her books and articles was compiled by East Lambrook nursery in 1990, running to 6,500 names, including more than 200 snowdrop varieties.[42]

Margery's eight books about gardening included *An All the Year Garden* (1958), *Cottage Garden Flowers* (1961) and *Ground Cover Plants* (1964). She contributed to the *Oxford Book of Garden Flowers* and, along with Christopher Lloyd and others, to *The Shell Book of Gardens*. She wrote for *The Field*, *Amateur Gardening*, *Punch*, *Popular Gardening* and the *Journal* of the Royal Horticultural Society, as well as broadcasting regularly on the BBC Home Service. In 1963, the RHS awarded her a silver Veitch Memorial Medal for both her garden and her writing.

Into her seventies, Margery remained an impressive figure, unstooped, with a pleasant round face, grey hair scooped into a bun at her neck, and sensible shoes. She worked an eighteen-hour day, writing early and late, and gardening in between, supported by some help with the garden, nursery and secretarial work. She died, aged seventy-six, on 24 March 1969, leaving the garden to her nephew, Henry Boyd-Carpenter. A London solicitor, he was unable to take over, so in 1971 his parents, Margery's sister, Nina, and her husband, Francis, retired to East Lambrook Manor. They discovered that the garden was 'a complicated and finely balanced organism that was anything but labour-saving'.[43] When Nina died in 1984, the garden was in less good heart, and Henry decided to sell. Since then, East Lambrook Manor has passed through three owners, all dedicated to continuing Margery's life work. No garden stands still, but a visitor today will find a garden which has evolved, yet keeps alive the vision of its creator. The nursery, too, continues to attract cottage plant lovers from far and wide.

Margery Fish inspired gardeners through her own passion and enthusiasm, which bubbles up in all her books – even when she writes about weeding. 'One of my sister providentially came for a holiday and helped me clear the weeds from the bank. We had a magnificent time [and] both agreed there is no sport in the world that compares with clearing the ground of bindweed. It is far more exciting than golf or fishing.'[44] Elsewhere she admits that 'there is never enough time to do all one wants in a garden,' but also 'that is just what gardening is, going on and on. My philistine of a husband often told with amusement how a cousin when asked when he expected to finish his garden replied "Never, I hope". And that, I think, applies to all true gardeners.'[45]

PART VI

CLASSICAL AND MODERN

CHAPTER 18

Russell Page (1906–1985)

As Margery Fish beavered away at East Lambrook Manor, exploring new ways of using traditional cottage garden plants, another gardener, fourteen years her junior, was also taking his inspiration from the past to make gardening anew. Very different in style, Russell Page and Margery Fish between them represent two major aspects of British gardening through the twentieth century and into the twenty-first. Page has been described as 'the undisputed world master of garden design from the 1950s until his death in 1985'. Yet, he always called himself a gardener rather than a designer, and, whenever possible, planted every plant himself.[1] Fish was a gifted amateur, whereas Page helped establish garden design as a profession. Both loved plants, but while the bones of Fish's garden were often blurred by the ebullience of her planting, Page's gardens had a cool, geometric simplicity enhanced by his skilful restraint with plants. Fish created just one garden; Page never had a garden of his own after he was eighteen, but designed over 500 in Britain, France, Switzerland, Belgium, Italy, Egypt, Persia (as it then was) and the United States. His client list included American and European socialites, 'Lady Bird' Johnson, the impresario Sidney Bernstein and the Duke of Windsor, who described Page as 'a remarkably talented landscape architect and plantsman'.[2]

The influences on his work included Persian, Mogul, Chinese, Japanese and Italian gardens, but, as an Englishman who lived much of his life in France, he drew most deeply on English and French gardening traditions.[3] His hallmarks were symmetry and structure; proportion and harmony; scale and unity. 'His gardens are self-disciplined and correct – understated, unfussy and invariably inspiring,' one garden historian has written. 'Grand but simple, they appeal to the philosopher in each of us.'[4]

Cigarette in hand, Page was a familiar, patrician figure at Chelsea Flower Shows in the 1960s and 1970s: tall, bald, with large deep-set eyes, a wary expression and more than a passing resemblance to Picasso. Many

Russell Page. (Courtesy The Garden Museum)

of his gardens had already disappeared by his death, while others were under threat.[5] Always enigmatic, Page claimed self-deprecatingly, 'I am the most famous garden designer you have never heard of.'[6]

A profound influence on gardeners in Britain was his seminal book, *The Education of a Gardener*. First published in 1962, it was Rosemary Verey's textbook as she laid out Barnsley House garden in Gloucestershire. A cross between an artistic credo and a gardening autobiography, *The Education of a Gardener* is a witty, intelligent account of a lifetime spent gardening. Page emerges as a moody, restless individual, constantly worrying away about how to achieve balance between planting and structure, and between gardens and their surrounding landscapes, whether urban or rural. Although he writes about many grand gardens, every page contains lessons about the use of plants invaluable even for those with small city patches. It is one of the great books in the British gardening canon, even if the sharp-tongued Christopher Lloyd described it as 'an education in arrogance, not gardening'.[7]

***

The second of the three children of a Lincoln solicitor, Montague Russell Page was born at Woodhall Spa, Lincoln on 1 November 1906, the first of our gardeners to be born in the twentieth century. In 1921, the family moved to Wragby, eleven miles east of Lincoln, where they converted farm buildings into a country cottage. Page inherited his love of plants from his mother, who visited flower shows, local nurseries and gardens, tracking down plants for the garden she created at Wragby.[8] Page seems always to have been a loner, meandering about the countryside which he found 'a comfortable [world] since nature was predictable unlike the other world of peoples, opinions and events which can still confuse me'.[9]

Page began, he said, 'to understand something about plants by handling them'. Aged fourteen and bored by the equestrian competitions at a local agricultural show, he visited the flower tent. 'There in an atmosphere hot and heavy with the smell of trampled grass, people, animals and flowers, my attention was caught by a tiny plant of *Campanula pulla* with three deep purple bells, huge in comparison with its frail leaves and the minute pot in which it grew. It was mine for a shilling and it opened a new world for me.' Having no idea what to do with it, he began his gardening education by borrowing books by Reginald Farrer and Gertrude Jekyll from the local library.[10]

From then on, his pocket money was spent on plants, and he began plant hunting in the Lincolnshire countryside and further afield. Like Jekyll and Fish, he discovered quickly that the plants he couldn't find in his parents' friends' gardens 'seemed to grow only in cottage gardens in hamlets lost among the fields and woods. I gradually came to know the cottagers and their gardens for miles around, for these country folk had a knack with plants.' His passion was for rock plants, and, aged seventeen, he was paid to make his first rock garden: 'My keep and a new tennis racket were sumptuous extra rewards for all that I was learning about colour, scale and texture, and about plants and their likes and dislikes.'[11]

Before he was eighteen, he made several other rock gardens, one of which was in Devon, where T. E. Lawrence would drop in on Sunday afternoons from his station with the RAF at Plymouth. Page visited the rock garden at Abbotswood, Stow-on-the-Wold, and was by taken by its owner, Mark Fenwick, to Hidcote, then 'reaching full maturity'. Struck by the juxtaposition of peonies, campanulas and *Alchemilla mollis* with old-fashioned roses, Page recognised that it was Johnston's skill at blending plants in radically new ways that made him such an important influence on other gardeners. He also spent time in France, 'fascinated by this contact with a definite and stylised culture new to me and clearer and sharper than the English tradition which has absorbed and modified and welded together influences from so many different countries – Italy, France and Holland for design, and the whole temperate world for plants'.[12]

Educated at Charterhouse in Surrey, Page was consoled only by parcels of flowers sent by his mother from her garden, and a visit to Gertrude Jekyll at nearby Munstead Wood. 'A sympathetic art-master' interested him 'in the depiction of objects in space and so in painters and sculptors and their problems'. He took the Leach Prize for Art, and 'incapable of making any use of a formal education I saw no future except to study painting and drawing'.[13] Three years followed studying under Professor

Henry Tonks at the Slade School of Art in London, before he encouraged his father to give him a small allowance so he could continue his studies in Paris.

There, he met André de Vilmorin, whose family had been seedsmen and horticulturalists for two centuries (William Robinson had been befriended by an earlier Vilmorin). De Vilmorin made Page realise that gardening rather than painting was his metier, although he always approached garden design with a painter's eye: 'I used to be taught in art-school, "Know what it is you want to say and then try and express it as simply as you can" –So with a garden.'[14]

Through contacts with gardeners and designers, Page developed his knowledge of French seventeenth- and eighteenth-century gardens. He designed a garden at the Chateau Forêt de Senart, where the fine library of gardening books absorbed him one summer. 'I made it a habit to draw summary sketches of all sorts of objects as I came across them – the moulding of a pool-edge, a cornice, the panelling of a door or a detail of trellis work ... to train my eye and mind to look and register more carefully.'[15]

France taught Page about structure and logic in garden design. 'The clarity of French planning,' he wrote, 'was always helpful to me as discipline for my rather shapeless jungle of a mind, apt to become over-furnished with purely horticultural images and associations.'[16] The French, cerebral approach combined with an instinctive English love of growing plants shaped Page's highly individual and precise style.

Page returned to London in 1933. He worked as a salesman in a department store (it wasn't his forte) and then as an architectural draughtsman, before meeting Henry Bath, heir to Longleat in Wiltshire, 'young, gay, brimming with ideas, and devoted to the property of which he was already in charge'.[17] Page joined the roll-call of eminent garden designers – George London, 'Capability' Brown and Humphry Repton – to have passed through Longleat. Page set about the project in what would become his accustomed fashion: walking the estate for weeks, and staking out the land for himself. Page's work at Longleat was to continue on and off for the rest of his life.

The estate had been neglected, with Brown's trees, planted almost two hundred years earlier, nearing their end, and with areas of detested Victorianisation. For Page, this early commission was a chance to show what he had learned from the past, while creating a new, contemporary look. 'In England in the early part of the eighteenth century,' he wrote, 'Brown, Kent and Bridgeman with the enthusiastic help of a group of wealthy amateurs set a standard for the siting and choice of trees for park planting in temperate climates which has never since been excelled.'[18] Page revised the planting of the deer park, replaced Victorian flower beds with lawns, straightened the approach from the South Lodge, installed two symmetrical pools by the drive and planted ornamental and flowering trees along the curving approach from the Westminster gate.[19] Dying trees were axed and new ones planted, Page characteristically limiting his choice to limes and beech, to create an elegant, coherent design.

Work on the parkland led to another, rather different commission on the estate: the reorganisation of a Cheddar Gorge cave, which involved building a restaurant and museum and handling the flow of traffic and people. As this was an architectural problem as much as one of garden design, Page turned to Geoffrey Jellicoe, a founder of the Institute of Landscape Architects. In 1935, they formed a partnership which harnessed their diverse skills.

Between 1936 and 1939, Page lectured in landscape architecture at the University of Reading and contributed articles to *Landscape and Gardening*. He and Jellicoe collaborated on a development plan for the Cotswold village of Broadway, which challenged Page to apply what he had learned about planting and planning to larger compositions. In Windsor Great Park, the partnership worked for the Duke of York, the future George VI, on Royal Lodge, a Gothic *cottage orné* built by George IV. In Page's words, Jellicoe and he '"de-Victorianised" it by ... making a formal approach to the house', and by replacing 'a grassy bank with a wide, paved terrace facing across a sloping lawn to a wood planted with the rhododendron species which were a special hobby of both the Duke and his brother, then King'.[20]

At an eighteenth-century house at Ditchley in Oxfordshire, Jellicoe and Page designed a sympathetic Georgian grass terrace, hornbeam walls, a sunken garden, and pools with fountains. This 'magnificent essay in the grand manner' was for interior designer Nancy Lancaster and her second husband, Ronald Tree.[21] The Trees employed a French interior designer, Stephane Boudin, director of the respected Parisian firm of Maison Jansen. Page and Boudin struck up a friendship at Ditchley, reinforced when Page suggested Boudin as interior designer for a project in St John's Wood. 'The particular spark which started our long collaboration was a detail in this small London garden,' he recalled revealingly in *The Education of a Gardener*:

> I had just planted a long bed with orange-scarlet, crimson, vermilion, salmon and magenta geraniums spiced with enough white to make these clashing reds vibrate together. This combination caught Boudin's eye and may have been what decided him to call me over to France soon after to design gardens to complement the interiors he was designing for houses all over France. I was accustomed to the delaying, gentle, half-spoken, tentative British way of getting things done. Boudin's approach to his clients and their problems was a revelation to me and one which happened to suit my temperament. I began to learn from him how to be clear, rapid and competent when faced with a client, how to seize on the special qualities or limitations of a site, use them and turn them to advantage; and how, too, to use words to build up a picture and create the atmosphere and impetus which will give a project a flying start.[22]

The outbreak of war led to the dissolution of Jellicoe's and Page's practice, while all Page's plans, photographs and collection of eighteenth-century garden books were destroyed in the Blitz. Page had a distinguished war, working for the Foreign Office's political warfare department, and then in America with US government agencies on setting up foreign-language broadcasting services. He spent time in Cairo and the Balkans, before being sent, with the rank of Lieutenant-Colonel, to Ceylon (now Sri Lanka).

War gave him time to do little more than study a handful of gardens in Cairo and Ceylon, and to learn how to discriminate 'between a good and an indifferent mango'. The conflict, however, 'interrupted a certain complacency induced by a success which, modest enough, held too superficial a glitter'. His extensive travels gave him more than just a European perspective, and taught him, he said, 'the pleasures of silence'.[23]

Demobbed, Page returned to London, 'without money or occupation'. He met the Austrian Expressionist painter, Oskar Kokoschka, with whom he studied painting for several months. He found this 'illuminating and cathartic ... I knew again that there is a continuing reality behind the appearances and problems of everyday.' Having been 'a small cog in a large machine', Page struggled to adjust to post-war life. He became a disciple of the mystic philosopher, George Gurdjieff, whose niece, Lida, he married in Paris in 1947. Gurdjieff taught that most humans do not possess a unified mind-emotion-body consciousness and therefore live in a state of hypnotic 'waking sleep', but that it is possible to transcend to a higher state of consciousness and achieve full human potential. Page was also attracted by the work of Idries Shah, a Sufi thinker, who suggested that inner peace was attainable by non-Muslims. This search for a spiritual dimension beyond the everyday was reflected both in his designing and how he wrote about it. For him, no project was a question of a quick fix: he always worked towards a deeper understanding of its implications. 'Garden-making, like gardening itself, concerns the relationship of the human being to his natural surroundings,' he wrote. 'I always try to discover in what consists the significance of the site, and then base my garden theme on that.'[24]

In Paris, he re-encountered Stephane Boudin and André de Vilmorin. Designing with them led to Page setting up an office in Paris, where he remained for the next sixteen years. Almost at once he had as much work as he could handle, with commissions in Italy, Normandy, Switzerland, and Egypt, for King Leopold of Belgium at Waterloo, and for the Duchess of Talleyrand at the Pavillon Colombe, Edith Wharton's pre-war French garden. He worked for the Duke of Windsor at his converted mill at Gif-sur-Vyette, where he made a rock garden on a steep slope, planted flower borders designed to flower for months, and used the stone from an old quarry on the site for paving.

Many of his commissions were on the French Riviera, where people now used their houses in high summer rather than in winter as they had done previously. Houses and gardens had to be designed for open-air, summer living, with planting that flourished from early spring to September. 'This makes gardening an exercise in prolongation,' Page wrote. He would start in spring with *Jasminum primulinum*, followed by flowering peach trees in March, and mimosa in the acid soil around Cannes. Roses and geraniums provided colour from April to June, then plumbago and agapanthus in July, and lagerstroemia, a flowering shrub for August and September.[25]

As swimming pools were required by every Riviera garden, Page pioneered their design. He had already designed one for the princesses at Royal Lodge before the war, and had definite opinions on how they should be incorporated within a garden. 'A swimming pool is most satisfactory when treated as part of the general composition but isolated as a separate compartment,' he wrote. 'Where it is close to the house it is best concealed, or partly concealed, by wall or hedge. A deserted swimming pool, seen from the house in winter, is far from enticing.' But he didn't necessarily believe that a pool should be exiled to the further reaches of a garden. In one hilltop garden, where he 'wanted to make a pool more or less on a level with the house and not too far from it', he installed one next to a guest cottage, making changing rooms on the ground floor, and protecting the pool from wind by high walls continued out from the main house itself.[26]

Water, not just in swimming pools, but in rills, pools, or canals, was an essential element in every Page garden, a hangover from his childhood. 'In a flat countryside I like to use water as a mirror laid on the ground to give depth and interest by reflecting trees and sky. I have learned much about the possibilities of still water in the flat lands of East Anglia, where I was born, and in Flanders where a tree or a church miles away towers against the full inverted hemisphere of the sky.' But, 'water is only one factor, to be looked at just as impartially as the others,' and the sky was just as important, which needed to be framed. 'I learned this lesson from the unknown, probably Christian Syrian architect who built the thirteenth-century mosque of Sultan Hassan in Cairo, a miraculous and bold prayer in stone whose whole meaning culminates in the square of sky caught and held between the towering walls of the central court.'[27]

For a designer who claimed himself unable to make use of formal education, he was remarkably scholarly. As he designed, he was ever conscious of tree planting in the English landscape garden, of the richness of English flower gardens, of the formality and rigorous geometry of André Le Nôtre, the use of water in Persian gardens, and of the terracing within Italian Renaissance gardens. Page distilled this rich, intoxicating mix into gardens which were classically simple, modern and understated. Less for Page was always more, and the motif running through both his work and his discussion of it in *The Education of a Gardener* was always simplification. He had an encyclopaedic knowledge of plants, but would, within an individual garden, restrict himself to a limited palette suited to that site. 'I try to select one or two varieties [of flowering trees] for my main planting, use them boldly, and support them if necessary with small groups of other varieties in the same category.'[28]

He planted trees in the Brownian manner, and laid out symmetrical beds as Le Nôtre might have done, but then filled them with planting colour à la Gertrude Jekyll. He liked, in eighteenth-century fashion, to relate a garden to a house, whatever the difficulties of the location. A classic example is Villa Silvio Pellico, in the Po valley, designed for the Agnelli family. Page transformed a sloping, ugly site by devising 'a simple series of horizontal levels bordered by hornbeam hedges', with water used 'lavishly on each different level to make a connected series of simple stone-edged pools reflecting the sky'.[29]

Page never forgot he had clients: 'A wise garden-designer will study his site in silence and consider carefully his clients, their taste, their wishes, their way of life, their likes and dislikes, and absorb all of these as factors as least as important as the ground that lies in front of him.' He preferred a problem site to a blank canvas, relishing the intellectual challenge of sorting it out. On one occasion, his deliberations proved too prolonged: 'For three years I continued making sketch plans until I was told, "Something must be done – what would you do if it was your garden?"'[30] You can almost hear the irritation in the client's voice.

But Page mostly had good relations with clients, often working with them for many years, as with Lord Bath at Longleat. He expected to see architectural plans and to be given a precise budget for any project he was considering. Although he could charge large fees, he was never much interested in money, Persian carpets being his only luxury. He operated with no more than a secretary and help from an occasional assistant.[31]

* * *

Although much of his 1950s work was for French, Italian and Swiss clients, Page also designed for the British composer Sir William Walton and his wife, Susanna, advising them on the positioning of their cliff-backed new house, La Mortola, on Ischia in the Bay of Naples. Again, it was a long process: he worked first for the Waltons in the 1950s, returning twenty years later to make new plantings. 'In those days Ischia had little water but the soil in the gulley was good, so I designed a simple framework for a garden in which plants, Mediterranean, Californian, South African and Australian might be expected to flourish in near xerophytic "maquis" conditions.'[32]

Page was called home in 1950 to design the gardens at Battersea Park for the Festival of Britain in 1951, for which he was awarded an OBE. The idea was to create something like the Tivoli gardens in Copenhagen, with restaurants, theatres, a boating lake, cafés and an amusement park in a garden setting. He worked for eighteen months in harmonious collaboration with James Gardener, former designer for the jewellers,

Cartier, snatching cups of coffee and 'a dubious sandwich' in an attic office. It was an ephemeral project for Page, who couldn't approach it in his customary, deliberate way. 'For an exhibition one has to work with one's palette prepared ahead, like a painter boldly massing colour.'[33] Colour was indeed his watchword, his bright, modern approach designed to cheer visitors after six years of war. He planted 20,000 yellow tulips and blocks of bright pink and crimson floribunda roses.

Other exhibition work followed: in 1958, he won a gold medal at the Chelsea Flower Show for a French-style garden with symmetrical, box-edged beds, gridiron-trained apple and pear trees against a wall, and step-over apples at their base. The following spring, he designed the Vilmorin exhibit for the French Floralies, an international flower show in Paris. The prize-winning exhibit, composed of a curving pool and trees, flowers and rocks, moved visitors to tears.[34]

Constant travelling took its toll on Page, as he wrote in *The Education of a Gardener*: 'These years were rather like a club-sandwich with, as intermediate slices of bread, nights spent in the train. The layers between were gardening in Paris, in the South of France, or maybe in Italy, in Switzerland or in Belgium ... It was quite usual for me to spend four successive nights in a sleeping-car, rushing from one job in hand to another in a different country and a quite different climate.'[35]

After the birth of his only son, David, in 1948, Page's first marriage ended in divorce in 1954, when he married Vera Daumal, widow of the avant garde poet, René Daumal. Vera's death in Switzerland in April 1962 precipitated Page's return to Britain in the year he published *The Education of a Gardener*. 'To garden here is a source of refreshment,' he wrote.[36] 'Gardens here are a part of life, as in no other country.'[37] He was newly inspired by the more forgiving climate and the rich British range of plants. Structure remained, however, key to a successful design in Page's view, as in the cottage-style Culpeper Garden he created in 1980 at Leeds Castle where he had worked for Lady Baillie before the war. Asymmetric box-edged beds contained a fragrant abundance of lupins, roses, poppies, geraniums, delphiniums and bergamot, a modern take on a sixteenth-century English knot garden.

Among other British commissions, he designed Lady Caroline Somerset's garden at The Cottage, Badminton, using yew pyramids to mark the entrance to a series of green rooms with French-style treillage. At Coppings Farm in Kent, for Lord and Lady Bernstein, he planted pleached linden trees as a tunnel between a fence and a hornbeam hedge. He had always had a special interest in old-fashioned roses, often using 'Blanc Double de Courbert' as a hedge. At Owley in Kent, he made island beds of roses, mixed with flowering shrubs, to give a feeling of space and the impression of remoteness from the house.[38]

Page found it difficult to roost in one place, needing 'the challenge of new landscapes and other geographies – the stimulus of movement and effort and adaptation'.[39] He continued to design gardens in Mallorca,

Italy and the United States, all from his small flat in Cadogan Square, chosen for its view of a flowering cherry tree. His last major project, in 1981, was for the PepsiCo headquarters at Purchase in upstate New York, where he turned the 144-acre site into a landscaped park and sculpture garden. He laid a path of golden gravel, snaking through the park to link the sculptures, and, as natural sculptures, planted sugar maples and other parkland trees. Water, again, was a major feature, with a big lake, and geometric water-lily pools flanked by perennial borders. At one end was a pavilion inspired by a Humphry Repton design, Page's final nod to the masters who had so much influenced him.

Russell Page died in London on 4 January 1985, and was buried, at his request, in an unmarked grave on the Badminton estate, close to friends who had supported him in his final years.

CHAPTER 19

Rosemary Verey (1918–2001)

At Rosemary Verey's memorial service in Cirencester parish church in July 2001, her nephew, Paul Sandilands, recalled that in the 1930s Rosemary water-skied on the Thames through London. The large congregation tittered, finding it hard to imagine the *grande dame* of late twentieth-century English gardening on water skis. She was more accustomed to be seen in a cardigan, tweed skirt and pie-crust collared shirt, with a string of pearls and sensible shoes, crisply greeting visitors to her garden at Barnsley House in Gloucestershire. But Rosemary Verey was always a spirited woman, an inveterate party-goer, more interested in tennis and hunting than in gardening when she first visited Barnsley House in August 1939.[1] Indeed, only after a serious riding accident in her thirties did Rosemary's husband, David, begin urging her to garden. This self-taught amateur was sixty before she published a book, subsequently becoming known internationally as a plantswoman, garden designer, lecturer and writer.

She made waves, not just on the Thames but across both British and American gardening: in the States, her particular brand of English romanticism found great favour, as did her lady of the manor demeanour. As a designer and lecturer, she was feted across America, where sales of her eighteen books outstripped those in Britain. At Barnsley House, four miles from Cirencester, she wove together several elements of English gardening into a harmonious whole. Her style was not cutting edge, but it satisfied a taste for traditionalism, at home and abroad, after a period when private garden design had been somewhat stagnant. Post-war, there had been emphasis on easy-care, utilitarian gardening, but Verey showed what could be achieved through ingenuity, plantsmanship and hard work. She was a woman for her time: she started publishing just as Margaret Thatcher came to power, increasing home ownership and, for Verey's potential clients, wealth to be spent on houses and gardens. An advocate of box, she profited from the success of her first book,

Rosemary Verey in her laburnum walk at Barnsley House. (© Andrew Lawson)

The Englishwoman's Garden, and reintroduced 'formal gardening and green patterns for clients who were less bothered about "saving labour" and minimising expense'.[2]

Thatcherism also brought an upsurge in nostalgia, reflected by the group of gardening practitioners to which Verey belonged. Others included the Marchioness of Salisbury and Sir Roy Strong, whose designs recalled seventeenth-century English parterres as well as the Edwardian Arts and

Crafts style.[3] Their work was to the taste of the Prince of Wales, and all three advised on his garden at Highgrove, a few miles from Rosemary Verey's Gloucestershire home.

Her strong historic sense was a defining feature. 'I was influenced by gardens such as Kiftsgate, Sezincote and Broughton Castle,' she said, 'but even more by seventeenth- and eighteenth-century practical books, and by Gertrude Jekyll and Russell Page. For making one really look and think, there is nothing better than Page's *Education of a Gardener.* That was my bible when laying out Barnsley.'[4] Page became a friend, and from him she learned about structure, how to deal with space, the need for simplicity, and, most importantly, 'how to use my eyes and imagination'.[5] The Barnsley garden featured other stimuli, too, and Verey was generous in her attributions, listing several gardeners in *Rosemary Verey's Making of a Garden*. Among them were the queen's fashion designer Hardy Amies, who 'taught me that the eye of the perfectionist is all-important'. From designer David Hicks, she understood 'the importance of using different mowing heights and of linking each space to create a natural flow'. Christopher Lloyd, she pointed out, 'must be the number one influence on the late twentieth-century generation of gardeners – a brilliant plantsman, full of imaginative ideas ... Every time I think of him ... [I] remember that gardening must be fun.'[6] 'It is not a sin in any way to copy what other people have done,' she said, 'because you do it in your own way.'[7]

This tapestry of influences was what made Barnsley so significant, reviving an interest during the 1980s and 1990s in high-maintenance, elaborate gardening. Her style appealed to those for whom the point of having a garden was to garden.

***

Rosemary Isobel Baird Sandilands was born in Chatham, Kent, on 21 December 1918, the youngest of the four children of Prescott Sandilands, a Royal Marines officer, and of his wife, Gladys, a former actress. Her early childhood was peripatetic until, on her father's retirement, the family settled in Northamptonshire. She took to country life, becoming an accomplished horsewoman.

At school in Folkestone, she was 'trained not to waste good time. There was this amazing feeling of discipline and we didn't fight it. It was part of life.' Always competitive, she enjoyed games, 'even ping-pong', and, aged sixteen, won a county singles tournament.[8] She excelled at maths, a subject to which she would ascribe her interest in patterns in garden design, and studied economics and social history at University College, London, tutored by the future Labour leader, Hugh Gaitskell.

It was still unusual for women to go to university in the 1930s, and Rosemary was expected by her parents to combine her studies with a season as a debutante, a good training for juggling different jobs later in life. During that season, she re-encountered an Etonian friend of her brother's,

David Verey, who, after reading architecture at Trinity College, Cambridge, had enlisted in the Royal Fusiliers. War precipitated their engagement and marriage in October 1939 before Rosemary took her degree. 'I gave up college to become a full time wife. You had to make a decision because of the War ... You thought the end of the world might come.'[9]

The newlyweds honeymooned at Barnsley House, the 1697 Cotswold stone manor house which David's parents, Cecil and Linda Verey, had bought when Cecil retired from the church. David was away for three years with the Special Operations Executive, while Rosemary rented a cottage in Fairford with her two young sons. 'The three years I spent there were all-important in my gardening life. On Saturdays I was helped by Charlie Wall, a head gardener at nearby Quenington, from whom I learned how to sow seeds, grow vegetables, divide perennials and take chrysanthemum cuttings.'[10].

After the war, David became an architectural historian of distinction. Two daughters were born post-war, and the family moved to Ablington, not far from Barnsley, where although 'horses claimed more of my attention than gardening ... I learned a bit about the soil, the importance of using plenty of organic material. In winter, I read avidly about vegetable growing and herbaceous borders; in spring and summer I then tried to implement this knowledge.'[11]

In 1951, Cecil Verey made over Barnsley House to David, he and his wife settling into the adjacent Close, a converted stable block to which Rosemary moved in turn in 1988, when she gave Barnsley to her eldest son, Charles. At Fairford and Ablington, Rosemary had acquired some basic understanding of gardening, although had 'little idea about colour, form or design'.[12] Her immediate act at Barnsley was to grass over her mother-in-law's herbaceous borders for children's games, and to move an existing yew hedge to hide a newly built swimming pool. It wasn't until her daughters went off to boarding school that 'everything pointed in the direction of gardening. David encouraged me, and it followed a natural course. I had been reading a lot and then I became interested in designing.'[13]

Barnsley was not a blank canvas, but Verey worked her magic there over nearly fifty years, constantly refreshing the garden, and making it a byword for horticultural excellence. A perfectionist – and a shameless self-publicist – Verey propelled herself on to the world gardening stage, becoming a household name by the late 1980s.

David Verey's role in establishing the garden at Barnsley House has been rather less heralded than Harold Nicolson's at Sissinghurst, although Verey, like Nicolson, provided the framework for his wife's superb plantsmanship. Initially, with Rosemary apparently reluctant to make a start, David called on Percy Cane, an Arts and Crafts garden designer. David knew his wife: Cane's arrival was a red rag, spurring Rosemary to take ownership of the garden, which she would not relinquish even after handing on Barnsley to her son three decades later.

There was no master plan for the garden, which evolved over the years within the protecting stone walls built on three sides of the garden in about 1770. The Vereys worked with existing features, including a Gothic summer house, a castellated veranda from 1830, yew hedging and eight Irish yews, planted in 1946, guarding a path across the garden. The house was crucial: 'Gertrude Jekyll wrote that a garden should curtsey to the house,' she quoted. 'For Barnsley House, in its handsome William and Mary style, I have attempted to create a garden with strong bones, vistas, garden buildings, pleached walks, a wilderness and a potager, all to reflect the period.'[14]

Verey admired Hidcote, but decided that 'while each part of our garden must have its own theme and character, the garden as a whole would not benefit from being divided into such clearly defined "rooms"'. Instead, she relied on flowering shrubs and herbaceous borders for screening and delineation.[15] Within the relatively small compass of four acres, she created many different areas, each of which could be re-imagined in their own gardens by visitors or readers of her books.

Although Percy Cane was summarily dismissed, the Vereys took on board from him the importance of long vistas. A signal event was the arrival in 1962 of a Tuscan temple, transported from Fairford Park where David had been working for the owners. 'David got some local toughs to move it, brick by brick,' Rosemary explained. 'It was built at the same period as the garden walls so fitted in perfectly. It then became of paramount importance to make a straight, unimpeded vista from the temple.'[16] It took the Vereys eight years, from 1964 to 1972, to get the vista right, removing a rose border and David's mother's gooseberry bushes and asparagus beds to do so. The vista runs across an ornamental pool, through a pair of wrought iron gates to a statue of a hunting lady by sculptor Simon Verity across the lawn at the far end of the garden.

Alongside this vista ran an avenue of limes (*Tilia platyphyllos* 'Rubra'), clipped in the French style, and supposedly parallel with the walls. But due to the walls' unevenness, the lime walk looked out of kilter, a problem Rosemary tried to remedy by widening the path on both sides. The solution was finally offered by Nicholas Ridley, grandson of Sir Edwin Lutyens and the local MP, who suggested deceiving the eye by planting a parallel row of limes to one side.[17]

The lime walk vista was extended by Rosemary's much photographed laburnum walk. Supported by simple metal arches, and underplanted with alliums, the walk appears infinitely long in pictures. Visitors during Rosemary's lifetime were often surprised to find that there were only five *Laburnum* x *watereri* 'Vossii' on each side, with another five framing wisterias. This vista ended with a frog fountain, another Verity work.

The terrace in front of the house was widened, influenced by Page's *Education of a Gardener.* With a mathematician's love of pattern and precision, Verey quickly discovered she enjoyed drawing up plans, beginning with four parterre beds framing the lawn and leading off the expanded terrace. These beds all bear the Verey brand: intricate, many-layered planting, combining unusual herbaceous perennials with flowering shrubs, in pastel shades.[18] The tallest plants are not necessarily at the back: the plants are layered towards a high point in the centre, to give depth. Among the shrubs is shell-pink *Lavatera* 'Barnsley', propagated by Rosemary from cuttings snipped from a Gloucestershire roadside.[19]

Within this parterre is a herb garden, an example of Rosemary's willingness to adapt. Tired of walking to the far end of the garden to pick herbs, she adapted the bed nearest the kitchen in 1976 to make the herb garden. This long, narrow bed, with diamonds of low box hedging infilled with herbs, was partly inspired by *The Country Farm*, a book of 1616, Gervase Markham's translation of a French treatise, *La Maison Rustique*.

When Barnsley House was built during the reign of William and Mary, formal gardens were the fashion. It was natural, therefore, that Rosemary would decide to make a knot garden, running off a castellated veranda on one side of the house. Markham's book again provided inspiration, as did Stephen Blake's 1664 *The Compleat Gardeners Practice*. Each bed was five yards square, with interlacing threads of the knots created from two varieties of dwarf box, *Buxus sempervirens* 'Suffruticosa' and *B. s.* 'Aureomarginata', and germander (*Teucrium* x *lucidrys*). Rather than using the coloured earths suggested by Markham, Rosemary filled the knots with gravel, planting tiered 'Golden King' hollies at each corner of the double knot. Ten years after making the knot garden, Rosemary saw one in California where the threads had been clipped to look as though they flowed over and under one another. 'I had never seen this done in England, so on coming home we got busy with clippers ... The patterns were immediately given new life and a rhythm of which I feel sure the Elizabethans were aware.'[20]

The potager she created in 1979, as one commentator has written, 'played a pivotal role in making vegetable gardens chic'.[21] Two books by William Lawson, a seventeenth-century horticulturalist and clergyman from Yorkshire, prompted the potager in which vegetables, fruit and ornamental flowers were grown together in formal profusion.[22] This miniature version of the potager at Villandry in France was set apart from the main garden across a lane, surrounded by waist-high Cotswold stone walls, with a homemade trellis screen giving protection from wind. The beds were edged with box, parsley, alpine strawberries or lavender, and apples were trained into goblets in the centre of each of the four squares.

Structure mattered as much in the potager as in the main garden, especially during winter, as she explained in her still popular book, *The Garden in Winter*:

> I began to realize that the structure of my garden is even more important in winter than in other seasons because the bones become apparent and the eye is not distracted by beguiling planting. So the framework of my garden had to be set in winter. Paths, walks, hedges, allées, vistas, all would determine its form. I also had to realize that

> winter's beauty – clear and spare – is quite different from the freshness of spring blossom, the lushness of summer flowers or the richness of autumn leaves.[23]

Rosemary first began writing about her garden in the 1960s for *The Countryman*, a Gloucestershire-based magazine, and then between 1979 and 1987, she wrote monthly for *Country Life*, contributions which became *A Countrywoman's Notes* (1991). In 1980, she published her first book, *The Englishwoman's Garden*, with Alvilde Lees-Milne, a former lover of Vita Sackville-West's. It distilled what would endear Rosemary to the Americans over the next two decades, with its distinctive brand of Englishness, offering a window into thirty-six exquisite country gardens. The book also gave Rosemary the opportunity to network, a skill at which she excelled. Each Englishwoman was invited to write an essay about her garden, and all were quaintly described by their husband's name: Penelope Hobhouse was Mrs Paul Hobhouse; Beth Chatto Mrs Andrew Chatto. This success, reprinted eight times within the next four years, was followed by *The Englishman's Garden* (1982) and then as Verey's fame spread across the Atlantic, *The American Woman's Garden* (1984).

'I never think of myself as a writer,' Verey claimed. 'Even at school, I had one friend who was very good at writing; she wrote my essays for me and I did her maths.'[24] Yet, over the years, Rosemary Verey often wrote two books a year, her subjects including *The Scented Garden* (1981), *Classic Garden Design* (1988), *The Flower Arranger's Garden* (1989), and *Rosemary Verey's Good Planting Plans* (1993). All were beautifully produced, as suitable for the coffee table as for the potting shed, and many were illustrated by photographer friends of Rosemary's, Jerry Harpur and Andrew Lawson.

These books boosted Rosemary Verey's standing in America, which she visited first with David in 1978. Both were invited to talk to the North Carolina Fine Arts Society, but it was historian David who had top billing.[25] Their second visit followed the publication of *The Englishwoman's Garden*, by which time Rosemary was the star turn. After David's death in 1984, Rosemary visited America several times a year, lecturing, promoting her books, and designing gardens. In spring 1994, she and Christopher Lloyd made a formidable partnership on a lecture tour of America, while, later the same year, she was back in the States to be awarded an honorary doctorate from the University of South Carolina.[26] Other visits to the States and to Sweden and Denmark intervened.

It was a gruelling programme for a woman of seventy-five, but then Rosemary enjoyed a party: her eightieth birthday was celebrated with a black-tie dinner at Tate Britain, with Rosemary wearing a colourful dress designed by her friend, Oscar de la Renta. Much of this prodigious socialising and travel was done to finance Barnsley, David having died leaving their financial affairs in a muddle.

Back at Barnsley, her evenings were often lonely, and, drinking more than she should, she could become curt and short-tempered. Verey was exacting to work for, her staff expected to propagate plants precisely according to her methods, and hang their tools against outlined shapes on a pegboard. She walked round the garden each morning with the gardeners, 'slowly, rather than pressing on', expecting perfection to be delivered for the 30,000 visitors who came from as far afield as Japan and Australia.[27]

***

The garden at Barnsley first opened for a day for the National Gardens Scheme in 1970, and then more frequently as the years went by. Rosemary's skill as a plantswoman was highlighted, and her nursery of unusual plants she had propagated herself became a draw. 'I love propagating,' she once said. 'I cannot understand people who are very fond of gardening not propagating more. They should take cuttings, experiment.'[28]

Opening the garden led to her career as a garden designer. 'Visitors asked advice in planning their borders, so I would make a rough sketch on any odd piece of paper, using the plants we had for sale. Then came the question, "Will you come to our garden to give us some help?" It was all good fun and I discovered so much – especially about practical gardening; more than I would have learned by going to a gardening school, for every site has its own character.'[29] Like Jekyll and Page before her, Verey understood the importance of responding to the individual site and to the owners' requirements. She liked taking photographs, so she could provide her clients with a 'before and after' plan in the manner of Humphry Repton.

She needed help with technical details from professional contractors, although was happy to lay out plants on site herself. 'I have a vivid memory of Russell Page working on a large bank in the Pepsi-Cola garden in Upper New York State,' she wrote. 'He had hundreds of plants in containers, and I watched him placing them with the utmost precision. He was planning on the ground rather than on paper, creating drifts and shapes, giving each plant its correct space. It is a lesson I have never forgotten.'[30]

Her client list was international: she designed summer borders for the Marquess of Bath at Longleat, following in the footsteps of other great British gardeners; a potager for the Marquess of Bute at Mount Stuart on the Isle of Bute; a raised flower bed for Princess Michael of Kent nearby in Gloucestershire; a garden for King Hussein at Ascot; and a drought-tolerant knot garden for the Garden Club of Jacksonville, Florida. She was even commissioned to design an English garden for the Hanku department store in Osaka, Japan.

For the Prince of Wales at Highgrove, she designed cottage-garden style spring borders, helped the prince appoint a head gardener, and laid out a thyme walk redolent of the Mediterranean.[31]

Another high-profile client was Sir Elton John at Woodside, near Windsor. There, Verey designed a white garden, planted for interest throughout the seasons, and elsewhere a rainbow border, dominated by red, yellow and orange flowers, not her usual colour palette. The white garden was changed without warning or consultation by the volatile pop star who replaced it with an Italian garden. She rallied from this slight, attending Elton's fancy-dress fiftieth birthday ball dressed as a flower border.[32]

Even while Rosemary Verey's career was in full flow, taste was shifting, most significantly towards emphasis on ecology in gardening, and towards New Wave planting, arriving in Britain in the 1990s from Germany and the Netherlands. This more naturalistic look based its effects on grasses and perennials planted in swathes through prairie-style beds. Verey designed a small town show garden for the *Evening Standard* at the 1992 Chelsea Flower Show, a quintessence of her style, with a small Gothic summerhouse, lawn encircled by perennials, roses, fruit and vegetables, espaliered apples, and red brick and stone paths. It was charming, but already out of date, garnering for its designer no more than a disappointing silver medal.

Verey resisted the idea that she was old hat: in 1994, she attended a symposium on New Wave planting at Kew, and announced at the end that 'I don't know what all the fuss is about. Why that's what I've been doing all along.' Other delegates were surprised, but her friend and designer, Tim Rees, took her to mean that within formal constraints she gave her plants freedom, allowing them to self-seed and leaving seed heads for wildlife and for winter interest.[33]

Although she made it less explicit than did Beth Chatto, she was also concerned to choose the right plant for the right place. 'People buy plants from me because all our plants are potted up into natural compost,' she explained. 'When plants in peat-based compost are put in the ground, they suddenly find themselves surrounded by something they hadn't known and their roots stay in a tight little bunch.'[34]

Despite changing fashions among the gardening cognoscenti, Verey's style continued to please, both in the States and in Britain. Recognition for her achievements came, too, in the late 1990s, with the award of an OBE in 1995, and, in 1999, the much coveted RHS Victoria Medal of Honour.

Rosemary Verey died on 31 May 2001, just two months after a final design visit to Kentucky. She was buried with her husband, David, in the churchyard at Barnsley, and was celebrated in a memorial service in the cathedral-like parish church in Cirencester. Several of her friends spoke: the eminent photographer, Andrew Lawson; the sculptor, Simon Verity, who had done so much to enhance the garden at Barnsley, and Sir Roy Strong, whom she had introduced to Prince Charles at Highgrove.

Ten years after her death, the garden designer and writer Mary Keen wrote a characteristically acerbic re-appraisal of Rosemary Verey's work. Keen suggested that Verey punched above her weight thanks to her gifts as a self-publicist. That steely determination certainly helped her become as well-known as almost any late twentieth-century garden designer. But there was substance to this fame as well, as even Keen had to acknowledge: 'Her plantsmanship and sense of history were what made her name.'[35]

More generous than Keen, Penelope Hobhouse has applauded Verey's achievement: 'Rosemary was an incredible influence on middle-class gardening, bringing people back to realise that those old designs were really excellent and controlled.'[36]

CHAPTER 20

Penelope Hobhouse (1929–)

As Penelope Chichester-Clark left Cambridge University with an economics degree, she visited the appointments board. The response was not encouraging. She was told that no one really wanted to employ economists, so she wouldn't be able to work in the City, nor in a bank. She could perhaps become a journalist, or, better still, join the police. 'I blinked because I was terrified,' she recalled. 'I saw myself doing two years in dark alleys on the beat.' Later, she wondered whether she hadn't made a mistake: 'That would have been a career – I would have become a chief constable.'[1]

The police force's loss was horticulture's gain because, as Penelope Hobhouse, she became one of Britain's leading garden designers in the late twentieth century. Her transformative work at Hadspen, her husband's family home in Somerset, and her subsequent restoration of Tintinhull House as National Trust tenant, together with her numerous books, projected her on to the international gardening stage. She has designed gardens in Scotland, England, France, Greece, Germany, Italy and Switzerland, and right the way across America. She has always taken a scholarly, historical approach to garden design, writing extensively and rigorously about it, and looking at other people's gardens with a discerning eye, as in *In Search of Paradise* (2006). When she gave up designing gardens in America, she devoted herself to becoming an authority on the gardens of Islam.

Her trajectory to horticultural stardom was similar to that of Rosemary Verey: both were countrywomen who, as wives and mothers, initially forsook outside employment, only later teaching themselves about gardening and design. Hobhouse, ten years Verey's junior, began publishing earlier, and won the RHS Victoria Medal of Honour in 1996, three years before Verey, whom she nevertheless regarded as her mentor. Verey tutored Hobhouse on lecturing in the States: 'Rosemary helped me to cope with America where I was rather at sea,' Hobhouse has said. 'She told me that as you step off the

Penelope Hobhouse at Bettiscombe. (Courtesy Penelope Hobhouse)

plane, you must remember that you've come as a star – and don't behave as if you weren't one. If you did that in England, nobody would speak to you, but it taught me to have more self-confidence and to realise that Americans always want you to be a success.'[2]

Self-publicity came more naturally to Verey than to Hobhouse, who looks like everyone's image of a Cambridge don, with her iron-grey hair, often secured by a Kirby-grip, and no nonsense clothes. Hobhouse professes herself surprised that she has come to be regarded as a significant voice in garden design. 'You don't get over being self-taught,' she has claimed.[3]

Hobhouse, like Verey, was a gifted plantswoman, and even more of a designer, who, as such, helped ordinary gardeners understand the importance of good structure. 'Mrs Hobhouse is a sort of fixture in the minds of gardeners who love rooms and bones – the paths and walls and satisfying verticals that form the skeleton of a garden,' one reviewer has written.[4] With her emphasis on hard work and thorough preparation, she remains very much 'part of a seamless continuum running through the twentieth century,' according to fellow designer Andrew Wilson.[5]

Both Verey and Hobhouse have cited Russell Page's influence: his classical style, and emphasis on consulting Pope's 'genius of the place', marked Hobhouse's gardens in particular. Plants in any Hobhouse garden are pre-eminent, but each is expected to contribute to the whole picture: 'Every plant, of whatever shape or size, should be chosen not only for its individual merits but for its power to enhance the charms of neighbouring plants by contrast or combination in foliage or in flower colour.'[6] Hobhouse sees plants as requiring as much attention as people, and, in her eighties, fancifully bemoaned her loss of memory for that reason. 'It's not such a problem with people because you can apologise, and say, "I know you and I love you, but I just can't remember who you are," but you can't explain that to a plant you can't recall.'[7]

***

Penelope Chichester-Clark was born a month after the Wall Street Crash on 20 November 1929 into a political family, whose home was an eighteenth-century mansion, Moyola Park, near Castledawson in Northern Ireland. Her father, James Lenox-Conyngham Chichester-Clark, was a Northern Irish MP, as was her brother, Robin; her other brother, James (Lord Moyola), was prime minister of Northern Ireland from 1969 to 1971. Her uncle, a don at Magdalene College, Cambridge, became her guardian after her father's death when she was three, and later urged her to apply to Cambridge, despite her 'hopeless' wartime schooling.[8]

Landscapes rather than gardens influenced Hobhouse in her childhood and adolescence, her mother only gardening for flower-arranging. Holidays were spent in Donegal, or in the west of Ireland, an experience which 'made me into a designer in the end: it's that wonderful explosion of excitement when you see a landscape that you really like'.[9]

Like Verey, Hobhouse read economics, in her case at Girton College, Cambridge. Although not leading to a job, the subject did, she has suggested, make her 'precise and determined to get things done properly', a useful skill for her subsequent career as a garden designer.[10] While at Cambridge, she met John Raven, father of gardener and nurserywoman Sarah Raven, who is Hobhouse's god-daughter. Raven, a classics don at King's College, was also an accomplished botanist who took parties of students on wild flower walks. Hobhouse wasn't then much interested in plants, but she enjoyed the occasions, and turned to Raven when she eventually began planting her first garden.[11]

Employment in a Bond Street porcelain company was cut short by marriage to Paul Hobhouse, whom she had met at Cambridge. Penelope knew she had made a mistake by the end of their honeymoon, although the couple remained together for thirty years and had three children. Their first home was in Scotland where Paul worked for an English farming company, and then, in the late 1950s, Paul and Penelope moved to Shatwell Farm on the Hobhouses' family estate of Hadspen, near Castle Cary in Somerset.

Arriving at Shatwell, Penelope took a party of American visitors to Tintinhull House, near Yeovil, a garden which she subsequently ran. It had been created in the 1930s and 1940s by Phyllis Reiss, a friend and former neighbour of Lawrence Johnston's in Gloucestershire, and the loveliness of the garden astounded Hobhouse. 'I suddenly realised that gardening was about beauty and not just about cutting the nettles down.'[12]

It was the beginning of Hobhouse's gardening apprenticeship. Almost immediately, she sent John Raven a list of yellow and white plants she wanted to grow. By post, he supervised the cottage garden she created, often 'wonderfully tactful, suggesting that I might want to change my mind about this and that'.[13] Over the next nine years, Hobhouse immersed herself in the garden, learning the basic skills of gardening and plantsmanship.

In 1967, Paul and Penelope took on Hadspen House on the death of Paul's parents, Paul's elder brother having been disinherited. Despite being answerable to the estate's trustees, Penelope had a pretty free hand in restoring the once fine, eight-acre garden. It had been made in the early years of the century by Paul's grandmother, who used many new plant introductions from the Far East. Since the Second World War, the garden had been neglected with Paul's parents, like Paul himself, locked in an unhappy marriage. 'They had two gardeners, who did nothing really except grow cabbages and sometimes cut the lawn,' according to Penelope. 'So every flowerbed and shrubbery was full of bindweed and ground elder.'[14]

Penelope was undaunted, admitting that it was for the garden that she remained with Paul for another twelve years. Applying herself to learning about garden history, she joined the Garden History Society, and became a council member. She quickly appreciated that the skills required to make a good garden included 'the eye of the landscape painter with regard to composition, something of the science of the architect in the use of forms, and sufficient botanical and horticultural knowledge to ensure the growth and cultivation of the chosen plants from their early life in the garden to their maturity'.[15]

Bearing these in mind, Hobhouse worked outwards from Hadspen House, beginning by attempting to eradicate the weeds. 'Luckily, I was married to a farmer, so he knew about weedkillers, and I could get as much manure as I needed from the farm.'[16] It was a lesson in gardening on the grand scale, and in expectation management: when Paul's grandmother created the garden, she had had six gardeners, whereas Penelope had just one. Penelope planted trees and shrubs for architectural effect and avoided using too many annuals and herbaceous perennials that would require dividing and pampering. On a sheltered, south-facing slope, Hobhouse experimented with tender shrubs and evergreens from the southern hemisphere, useful experience when she began designing in America. Texture, foliage and the play of light on individual leaves became as interesting to her as flowers.[17]

She was helped by other local gardeners, including Margery Fish despite the difference in their gardening styles. At Knightshayes Court in Devon, the Heathcote Amorys had created a modern-style, hillside woodland, with winding island beds and borders following the contours of the shady slope. Loaded down with plants after her visits, Hobhouse found the Heathcote Amorys' approach appealed to her, writing that 'the plantsman's knowledge has here been combined with all the skills of the planner.'[18]

Her first book, *The Country Gardener*, published in 1976, described her work at Hadspen. The opening chapter, 'The Ideal Garden', revealed her historical sense, as she wrote knowledgeably about gardeners and gardening styles of the past. She was in tune with the eighteenth-century view that a garden 'should lead the observer to the enjoyment of the aesthetic sentiments of regularity and order, proportion, colour and utility, and, furthermore, be capable of arousing feelings of grandeur, gaiety, sadness, wildness, domesticity, surprise and secrecy'. For Hobhouse, 'additional pleasure' in gardening and designing came 'from the nostalgia of the past which can be conjured up by some aspect of a garden'. She paid tribute to Gertrude Jekyll, whose books she had read as she taught herself to garden: 'In her sense of colour harmonies and the use of foliage plants Miss Jekyll paved the way for modern types of mixed border gardening, but the success of her plant associations depended on a structural framework.' This was a theme to which she would return time and time again, as when discussing the importance of Hidcote and Sissinghurst 'where formality has been maintained by the rigid lines of the enclosures, but the planting arrangements ... emphasize the modern idea that each plant has its own shape and its own contribution to make to the whole scheme'. She also acknowledged William Robinson as an apostle 'of a more natural form of gardening'.[19]

Garden historian though she was, Hobhouse was also a highly practical, hands-on gardener, and in *The Country Gardener*, she combined historical research with down-to-earth advice. Four pages of her second chapter were devoted to soil and weed control before Hobhouse started on planning, and the following chapters emphasised the importance of ground-cover planting, trees and shrubs, and roses used as shrubs.

The timing of *The Country Gardener* was perfect. Wider home ownership and consequent interest in both interior and exterior design created a receptive market for lavishly produced coffee-table books in the 1980s and 1990s. The field was led by the independent publisher Frances Lincoln: many of Hobhouse's and Verey's books were published by Lincoln in a large, glossy format, and combined inspirational photography with pages of hard-headed instruction for real gardeners. Both reproduction values and the quality of garden photography were improving throughout this time. Now a crowded profession, garden photography was in its infancy when Hobhouse began writing books in the 1970s. One of its pioneers was Andrew Lawson, himself an artist who understood intuitively the connection between gardening and painting. He and fellow photographer Jerry Harpur contributed to popularising the work of gardeners such as Hobhouse and Verey, and to the widespread interest in gardening.

Landscape painting was an inspiration for Hobhouse when she was designing. 'Whether a great landscape or a smaller space you need to look at pictures and learn how they work, because that is what you are creating.'[20] Like Jekyll, she was interested in the theories on colour relationships of the early nineteenth-century French chemist, Michel Eugène Chevreul, who had been influential on Impressionists such as Monet. 'Monet's garden became an obsession,' Hobhouse wrote in *Colour in the Garden* (1985). 'He chose his plants and colours in order later to paint them, and made the garden itself, as much as the paintings of it, become a work of art.'[21]

Hobhouse created a work of art at Hadspen, and, in the process kick-started her writing career. While still at Hadspen, she had a stroke of what she has called 'extraordinary luck' when her mother gave her the money to buy a farmhouse near Lucca in Tuscany. From there, Hobhouse explored Italian Renaissance gardens, such as Villa Reale di Marlia and Villa Torrigiani. 'That really affected my design. The firmness of that Italian look – steps and right angles, trees, light and shade. The gardens gave me a historical reference point.' She also admired Harold Peto's garden, and the water parterre at Villa Gamberaia on the outskirts of Florence. 'Villa Gamberaria didn't teach you about Renaissance gardens, but it did teach you about beauty, and prepared me to design.[22]

***

When her youngest son was twenty-one, Penelope finally left Paul Hobhouse and Hadspen. It was a vertiginous step, but by then she had met, through the Garden History Society, her second husband, John Malins, professor of medicine at Birmingham University. She had also established her reputation in the gardening world, so when she applied to John Sales, head of gardens at the National Trust, he immediately offered her the tenancy of Tintinhull House. The garden which had originally inspired her passion for gardening would help mature her designing approach. This style, she wrote, 'influences all my gardening efforts. It is tempting to call it the "Tintinhull" style, because I learned it, in large part, from Tintinhull.'[23]

With Malins's support, Hobhouse felt able to tackle a second major garden restoration. They arrived at the end of 1979 and Hobhouse left in 1993, a year after Malins' death. During that period, the couple transformed a rundown patch into one of the National Trust's most admired gardens, the subject of Hobhouse's book, *On Gardening* (1994). At just under an acre, Tintinhull was much smaller than Hadspen, and was divided into several rooms, one of them, like Hidcote, dominated by a towering cedar of Lebanon. The simple rectangular garden had a formal, grid-like layout, with the main axis, a stone path lined with box domes, running east to west from the seventeenth-century mellow Somerset stone manor house. The rooms included green courts, a fountain garden, pool garden and kitchen garden, separated from one another by yew hedging.

The whole garden needed replanting when Hobhouse arrived. 'I had to learn a new way of gardening, because at Hadspen I had just thought in terms of trees and shrubs. I didn't let on that I knew nothing about perennials, but John did, and I learned from reading books and looking at other people's gardens.'[24]

Every border had to be stripped and covered with plastic for months to suppress weeds before being replanted. Hobhouse developed her ideas on colour, and on foliage and textural contrasts, and studied a whole new palette of plants. She resisted the National Trust's attempt to restrict her to those plants which the garden's original creator, Phyllis Reiss, had used. Mrs Reiss had been forced by lack of money and availability of plants during the war to be overly repetitive. 'I was sure she would have liked the new varieties of euphorbias and salvias, and eventually pulled rank by saying that I was the only person who actually knew Mrs Reiss. I'd only met her twice, in fact, but from that point I was given a free hand.'[25]

Such was Hobhouse's success that 20,000 visitors came each year to Tintinhull by the time she left. Less happy to lay on a show than Rosemary Verey, Hobhouse often felt over-exposed, with potential visitors knocking on the door even when the garden was shut: 'If they found you in the garden, whatever you were doing, they would demand that you come with them to another part of the garden to identify things, as if it were a right, instead of a kindness.' She also objected to people asking for Latin names and then having nothing to write them on. 'Out would come the back of a chequebook, and I felt like saying, "do buy a notebook next time."'[26]

During these engine room years of Hobhouse's career, she wrote book after book, lectured and designed gardens in America, and tried to keep abreast of the work at Tintinhull. Her interest in Gertrude Jekyll's use of colour led first to her anthologising Jekyll's writings (1983) and then to *Colour in Your Garden* (1985) in which she expanded on her theories on colour and applied them practically, providing readers with long planting lists. The latter led to her being invited to lecture in America and to design gardens in Maine, Texas, Michigan, California and elsewhere in the States. Through a friend, she was asked to design the Rothschilds' garden near Paris and the garden of German fashion designer Jil Sanders, giving her an impressive CV for American clients. The biggest test when designing in America was radically different conditions. 'By lecturing across the States, one learned a huge amount about the various climates.

If I was lucky when asked to design a garden in Maine, I might have been there the year before and have my notebook full of plant names.'[27]

She set up an office, and employed people to work up her drawings into finished plans for clients attracted by the simple, bold lines of her designs. 'I could walk into a space, and know what I wanted to do from that moment. I knew where I needed the trees; where I wanted water. I imagine that sense came from looking at landscapes.'[28] Among her many projects in the States was the Bass garden in Maine, a garden in Detroit, and a herb garden at New York Botanical Garden.

Like Robinson and Jekyll before her, Hobhouse wrote for magazines: when *Country Homes & Interiors* launched in 1986, she became gardens columnist, giving the magazine an authoritative voice in the gardening world. In the early 1990s, she and Anna Pavord helped to launch the glossy monthly, *Gardens Illustrated*, appointing its first editor, Rosie Atkins, later to be curator of the Chelsea Physic Garden.

***

In 1991, both John Malins and Penelope Hobhouse felt that the workload at Tintinhull was becoming too much. They bought a converted coach house at Bettiscombe, near Bridport in Dorset, but John died in 1992 and Penelope moved there alone the following year. Her new challenge was a small walled garden on two levels, with the house standing in the middle. At the front, looking out over the Dorset countryside, a lawn was bordered by hornbeam hedged compartments in which she grew vegetables, while within the enclosed courtyard at the back she laid a simple gravelled path through parallel beds of planting. Her style had moved on from the patterned, colourful borders which had made her name a decade earlier, to a more restrained, grey-green Mediterranean style that suited the seaside location of her new home. She planted broad-leafed, evergreen shrubs, emphasising foliage shape and texture, with spikes of colour from blue and purple salvias she propagated herself.

Hobhouse continued to publish books, *On Gardening* in 1994, based on her work at Tintinhull, and, the same year, *Plants in Garden History*, a majestic work of scholarship. The latter, which took three years to research, united her twin passions. It 'very nearly killed me. You read twelve books for every paragraph.'[29]

Through sheer exhaustion, she gave up designing and lecturing in America, but inspired by her research for *Plants in Garden History*, she decided to visit Iran. 'I had previously never been anywhere except Granada, so I wrote the chapter on Islam out of books.' On her first trip with a Cambridge alumni group, she looked at mosques, buildings, mountains, and desert, and acquired an understanding of how and why Persian gardens were so designed. Over the next eight years, she led tours to Iran, becoming in the process a recognised world expert on Persian and Mughal gardens. In 2003, she published *Gardens of Persia*, which chronicled their evolution and explored their undervalued influence across Europe and Asia: 'I fell in love with Babur, the sixteenth-century Mughal ruler who took formal gardening to India.'[30]

The effect of her immersion in Persian gardens is evident in her garden at Walmer Castle in Kent, designed in honour of the Queen Mother's ninety-fifth birthday. Opened in 1997, the garden has an Islamic-style arched pavilion, reflected in a rectangular pool of still water, which is flanked by flat-topped yew pyramids, and borders of sculptural plants, including cardoons, agapanthus, *Verbena bonariensis* and alliums.

Other important projects came to Hobhouse in the 1990s: she took part in a major garden restoration at Aberglasney, Carmarthenshire, where she designed a walled flower garden. She was also commissioned to design a garden (now called the Cottage Garden) at the Royal Horticultural Society garden at Wisley, which was completed and opened in 2000. Hobhouse created a formal layout with three horizontal areas on different levels and enclosed the garden within hornbeam hedges. Wisterias arch over pergolas through the garden, which is also planted with beds of billowing herbaceous planting, crab apples and flowering cherries. The Wisley garden was a return to her earlier, Tintinhull style, and she herself described it as 'basically Robinsonian'.[31]

Penelope Hobhouse received the RHS Victoria Medal in 1996, and an MBE in the 2014 Birthday Honours for services to British gardening. Now in her late eighties, she is slowing down, although she continues to design for friends, and remains involved in the gardening world: for several years, she judged the Garden Media Guild annual awards (formerly the Garden Writers Guild). She is also updating *The Story of Gardening*, originally published in 2002.

She sees great changes in garden design, fearing that the ecology is being emphasised at the expense of design. 'If we're not careful, designers will become scientists rather than having an eye for beauty.' But she is equally dismissive of gardens that do not take soil and climate into account: she is infuriated by a local Somerset garden where 300 tons of soil in a spring-riddled terrain were removed and replaced by 300 tons of infertile soil to provide the right conditions for prairie-style planting. 'I feel very strongly that it is immoral to do that because it's not what gardening is about. People will visit thinking that they are going to learn about gardening, but they won't.'[32]

Hobhouse lives back near Hadspen, although the family estate has been sold by her elder son. In her courtyard garden in front of a converted barn, she grubbed up an existing lawn (even before completing on the purchase), and laid a central stone path. This is set between borders of grey-green architectural plants, such as euphorbia, hoheria and stachys, and grasses, including *Molinia caerulea* 'Transparent', with dark salvias in over-sized pots; the framework is provided by low box hedging and mopheads of phillyrea, offset by the head-high planting. Both classic and modern, the garden holds plants and structure in a delicate, synergetic balance, its effects achieved mainly through foliage shape, colour and texture. Flower colour, once so important to her at Hadspen and at Tintinhull, now, she says, 'bores me to tears'.[33]

Contemporary in style, her latest garden shows Hobhouse's ability to adapt, to respond to the needs of a particular place, and to be in step with current gardening trends. It proves, if proof were needed, Hobhouse's importance as a garden designer.

CHAPTER 21

John Brookes (1933–2018)

While Rosemary Verey and Penelope Hobhouse were bringing up their families, their younger contemporary, John Brookes, was already making his way in the gardening world. Many leading British gardeners over the last century have been inspired amateurs, but Brookes was a trained horticulturalist who realised that design was his primary interest. He always regarded himself as a landscape designer rather than as a gardener: his famous garden at Denmans in West Sussex, was, he said, his hobby, run in parallel to his career as a designer, writer and teacher of landscape design.

Brookes helped to move British garden design in another direction from that taken by Page, Verey and Hobhouse. Each of these four designers responded differently to the social and artistic currents in the second half of the twentieth century. Page saw landscape in painterly, figurative terms, with his designs also answering a mid-century, southern European taste for outside living. The more traditional Verey's English romanticism of pastel-coloured borders, statuary and potagers worked for the unexpectedly nostalgic 1980s and 1990s. Hobhouse's elegant, structured style was shaped by Page, by landscapes she had admired as a child, by Italianate design, and by the gardens of Islam. And Brookes, influenced by abstract painters such as Piet Mondrian and Mark Rothko, effectively introduced modernism into British gardens from America in the 1960s.[1]

In his ground-breaking book, *Room Outside: A New Approach to Garden Design*, first published in 1969, Brookes wrote that 'a garden is fundamentally *a place for use by people* [his italics]. It is not a static picture created in plants – the reason so many of our gardens fail is that we tend to follow a plan, in a nurseryman's catalogue or garden layout sheet, which perpetuates this picture-book ideal. Plants provide the props, colour and texture, but the garden is the stage, and its design should be determined by the uses it is intended to fulfil.' Brookes saw the garden as 'not merely a collection of plants but a usable extension of the home into the outdoor world'.[2]

John Brookes and pug. (Courtesy John Brookes Design)

Brookes designed over 1,000 gardens, in every continent, many for the fabulously wealthy. But *Room Outside* set a new agenda for gardeners with limited space. Jenny Uglow says in her *A Little History of British Gardening*, that 'just opening this book, with its wide margins, square Sixties type and bold diagrams and stark pictures, is like breathing in that era.'[3] Brookes was working in Swinging Sixties London, both reacting to and leading social trends. 'In the war, nobody talked about gardens at all, but, at the end of that, we were beginning to go abroad a bit, and discover different foods, the sun, and sitting outside. There was a huge social change: the working class moved into the middle class, there were endless new houses and small gardens, and, as a result, the nursery trade expanded.'[4]

Bunny Guinness, a gold medal winning Chelsea garden designer like Brookes, claimed he 'did for garden design what Elizabeth David did for food ... David introduced us to garlic, Mediterranean cooking and pasta, John opened our eyes to the possibility of great looking, functional spaces outside.'[5]

***

John Andrew Brookes was born in Durham on 11 October 1933, the second son of Percy Brookes, the county surveyor, and his wife, Margaret. He grew up in the countryside on the city's outskirts and was educated at Durham School, where he showed little aptitude for academic subjects and sport. But he won a prize for art, played violin in the school orchestra and enjoyed school camping trips.[6]

His parents 'gardened for food during the war, and I guess I pottered a bit then,' he recalled. A more important inspiration was his maternal aunt, musician and painter Eve Strandring, who lived in the Chilterns. 'We used to walk for miles in the woods. One walk in particular sticks in my mind – looking across a valley at Shardeloes, at the top of a hill with a lake at the bottom. It was pure eighteenth century, and that's where I got a twinkling of what it was about. My aunt was a painter and I began to look at things through her eyes.'[7]

Brookes's aunt introduced him not only to the elegant proportions of designed eighteenth-century landscape, but also to the sleek lines of modernist architecture, which together helped form his design style. High and Over, at Amersham, a white concrete house with chrome double front doors and glassed-in spiral staircase, caught Brookes's attention. Now Grade II listed, the house was designed in 1929 by Amyas Connell, a New Zealand-born architect influenced by Le Corbusier.

Brookes wanted to be a farmer, but as his father couldn't afford to buy him a farm, he instead studied horticulture at the county agricultural school after his two years' National Service in the Royal Artillery. This was followed by a three-year apprenticeship with Nottingham's parks departments. 'It was literally doing the flowers in the council houses, bedding out traffic islands – all very practical stuff.'[8]

The last six months were spent in the parks' design office, working with a Dutch landscape architect. Encouraged by him, Brookes sent off drawings to Brenda Colvin, co-founder in 1929 of the Institute of Landscape Architects (ILA, later the Landscape Institute). Among Colvin's gardens was a listed landscape at Aberystwyth University. To Brookes's delighted surprise, Colvin employed him as her assistant, working in the London office she shared with Sylvia Crowe. Crowe was president of the ILA from 1957 to 1959 and was involved in landscape planning for new towns, roads, forestry and power stations. With her, Brookes worked on housing projects in Harlow and Basildon, Trawsfynydd nuclear power station, and the courtyard at Imperial College, London, while taking a diploma in landscape design at University College, London.[9]

In his twenties, Brookes found himself in a powerhouse of design. He became a probationary member of the ILA, and helped select designs at Chelsea Flower Shows for the Institute in the late 1950s and early 1960s. By then, Brookes had read Thomas Church's *Gardens are for People* (1955), and been struck by his revolutionary approach of putting people before plants. In his own design work, Brookes was also inspired by the abstract gardens of the Brazilian landscape architect, Roberto Burle Marx, and by painting. In his lunch hours, he would go to exhibitions and art galleries. 'As you got into landscape, shape and pattern began to have a relevance to abstract concepts.'[10]

Brookes credited Crowe with teaching him about ground shaping and modelling, and also with making him realise he didn't want to work in offices designing power stations and new towns. Crowe and Colvin had taught him to draw proper plans, a skill he developed further when he went, at the suggestion of a friend, landscape architect Geoffrey Jellicoe, to *Architectural Design*. At the monthly magazine, he polished up architects' drawings for publication and had a regular column. The job involved exhibition work and exposed him to international developments in art, architecture and landscape. 'We used to work from eleven o'clock through to seven or eight, and architects would come in at six o'clock for a drink. I did a bit of writing, page layouts and captions. It was a lifestyle I liked.'[11]

His time at *Architectural Design* united the three threads of his future career: writing, teaching and garden design. One afternoon a week, he taught landscape design at the Royal Botanic Gardens, Kew, eventually running a six-week course there. His students came from around the world and included the international designer and Chelsea gold medal winner, Cleve West. 'You could tell you were sowing a seed – and getting people away from just gardening.' Teaching also made him focus on how and why he worked as he did: 'Having to verbalise what I did made the teaching experience for me – having to put my money where my mouth was.'[12]

Simultaneously, Brookes built up his private practice, notably designing in 1961 a courtyard garden enclosed on three sides by glass walls for architect Michael Manser, a pioneer of the modern movement. The garden was laid out geometrically, alternating brick with grass and planting. Brookes used what became his trademark grid system, which related the proportions of the house to the outside space. This high-profile commission helped establish Brookes's reputation as a Modernist, and he and Manser worked together on six further house and garden projects.[13]

A silver medal winning garden for the ILA at the 1962 Chelsea Flower Show raised Brookes's profile, especially as it was the first Chelsea show garden by a designer rather than by a nursery: over the next few decades, Chelsea's show gardens became dominated by designers. As in Manser's garden, its effects were derived from the contrast of different materials and foliage planting. It displayed Brookes's wares to a wider market, demonstrating his interest in functionality and his wish to create a simple outdoor space that linked house and garden.[14]

Many early commissions were for small town gardens in fashionable areas of London, his clients including Annabel Birley (later Sir James Goldsmith's wife). His practice grew organically, for 'often people with small town gardens have country houses.'[15] Indeed, Annabel Birley recommended Brookes to her brother, the Marquis of Londonderry, who gave Brookes his first opportunity to work on an historic landscape at the nineteenth-century Wynyard Park in his home county of Durham (1964).[16] Commissions in the late 1960s included his celebrated modernist garden for the offices of Penguin Books at Harmondsworth. Brookes chose an abstract theme, reminiscent of a Piet Mondrian painting, with water, paving, planting, grass and white chippings alternated geometrically. Such was the garden's success that it was included by Geoffrey Jellicoe in his book of forty two modern gardens, along with gardens by icons of design Church, Burle Marx, Colvin, Crowe and Russell Page. To be in such company was a significant accolade for Brookes early in his career.

***

Later in the 1960s, he wrote for *Ideal Home*, *House Beautiful* and *Good Housekeeping*. Answering readers' planning queries and drawing up designs for their gardens brought Brookes a regular income and extended his influence on ordinary gardens. He drew more than 500 plans for both town and country gardens for *Good Housekeeping*, enabling him, on paper at least, to experiment with a variety of shapes, materials, garden features, and methods of presentation.[17]

This work provided material for his most persuasive book, *Room Outside*, designed to open the eyes of contemporary gardeners to the possibilities of even the smallest space. The book started with a chapter displaying Brookes's knowledge of garden history from Ancient Egypt to contemporary America, Japan and Scandinavia. It was a succinct, if somewhat partial summary and, often waspish in tone, revealed Brookes's agenda. About the eighteenth century, for instance, he wrote that 'the scale of the settings designed by Kent and Brown was not related to the individual and left no place for him, though there was a place for his deer, his strange sheep or highland cattle, as amusing decorations in an otherwise sublimely pastoral (some would say sublimely boring) landscape.' Repton fared no better in Brookes's hands: he 'was faced with the dictums of the eighteenth century, the demands of the nineteenth, and the need to find a way of combining the two. Since he was not, however, a horticulturalist, he probably found the increasing range of plant material on the market an embarrassment.'[18]

There spoke the horticulturalist turned designer, a master of both fields. This training underpins every page of this most practical guide to garden planning. His second chapter, 'What do you want?' asks the question, 'what has all this history got to do with me and my plot?' His first conclusion is that gardens should be designed with the style of the house in mind. 'If these old gardens had not worked, there would not still be so many of them in an excellent state of preservation today.' And, more importantly, his second conclusion is that every garden should be designed to suit its owners' requirements. These, as much as the architecture, are the starting point of any design. The principal question is 'What are your other activities besides the enjoyment of your garden? How much time can you afford, or do you want to spend in it?'[19]

Further questions are posed about size and age of the family. Even pets are considered, before Brookes starts on the nitty-gritty of laying out a garden. He covers soil and existing features, architectural styles, drainage, walls and fencing and hard landscaping, before turning to planting, maintenance and garden furniture. All in black and white, it is, as Uglow suggested, redolent of its time. One of Brookes's design heroes was Terence Conran: this book was the practical manual for the Habitat shopper, and could only have been written and published in this style in the late 1960s. As a follow-up, Brookes contributed in 1974 a twenty-six page chapter on designing and furnishing a garden to Conran's *The House Book*.

By the time Brookes published *Room Outside*, he had already designed 250 real gardens, both in Britain and in America. The questions he invited his readers to ask were those which he set his clients on every commission he ever undertook. Although seen as a modernist, Brookes always disliked being pigeon-holed, as he said: 'I wouldn't define my landscape style. I like to think I style to where I am and for whom I'm working. Each place is so very, very different. And that to my mind is the crux and interest of it all – how you realise a particular style you're working in and get into the local vernacular.'[20]

This adaptability enabled him to work across the world, with designs which included a modern garden with an infinity pool in Argentina; landscaping at St. Peter's College, Oxford; a play area in Milton Keynes; a lakeside garden of lawns and stone in Patagonia; a planterly garden with box hedging at a Gothic-style Wimbledon house where the Williams sisters have stayed for the championships; an exhibition garden in the style of Malevich in Russia; and a project two hours north of St Petersburg, on which he worked in the Thomas Church style for several years. He delighted in every aspect of working in different countries, relishing the variations in food, culture and daily life.

'Landscapes, whether they are in South America or Germany, are all different,' Brookes said. 'And it's not just to do with plants – it's to do with the lifestyles, styles of architecture, and the available materials. It's a much bigger concept than what plants you stick in. Working in Russia was very insightful, dealing with the weather and the short season. How hot it is in summer and how unbelievably cold in winter. It limits your plant range.'[21]

He always sought above all to understand the people for whom he designed, primarily by looking round their houses. He said, 'Quite often, you will walk into a garden and there is no sign of what they like – whereas if you get inside, you see their artwork, their furniture, the way they have designed the house. Presumably, they've done it to fit their taste and style. Is it trad? Is it modern? Is it awful?'[22]

Room Outside was the first of John Brookes' books, his last being a biographical retrospective of his career, *A Landscape Legacy* (2018), which he presciently called 'his last will and testament': he died before its publication. In between, he produced some two dozen books, often as many as three a year on subjects including *Living in the Garden* (1970), *Gardens for Small Spaces* (1970), *A Place in the Country* (1984), *John Brookes' Garden Design Book* (1991) and *John Brookes' Garden Design Course* (2007). All of them became glossier as the years passed and publishing values increased.

In each book, John talked to his readers, as if involving them in conversation. In *A Place in the Country*, he returned partly to his childhood love of countryside, and used the book as a platform to encourage gardeners and garden designers to respond to local architecture and landscape, and to use local resources. 'Over the last fifty years or so we have had a standardization of the materials available for gardens, and a standardization, if not a paucity, of ideas on how to use them,' he complained. 'It must be wrong that the average garden near Edinburgh looks much like one in Wales, the West Country or the south-east, and that all are based on a pre-war ideal of the Surrey country garden.' This scarcely veiled attack on dogged, latter-day disciples of Gertrude Jekyll was followed by an attack on garden centre chains which had displaced traditional nurserymen.[24]

The immediacy of his writing explains his success as a teacher. After Kew, he taught at the Institute of Park Administration near Reading and at Regent Street Polytechnic in central London. He also taught at the Inchbald School of Design, established by Jacqueline Duncan in 1960 as the first interior design school in Europe. In 1972, she widened the school's brief to include garden design and Brookes became a director, establishing a popular and well regarded course.[25]

His growing status led the *Financial Times* to commission gardens from him for the Chelsea Flower Show. In three successive years from 1971, he designed Town, Surburban and Country Gardens, each garnering a gold medal. Following this, he collaborated with gardening writers Robin Lane Fox and Arthur Hellyer on *The Financial Times Book of Garden Design* (1975). He also designed three Chelsea show gardens for the Inchbald (1975–1977), winning one gold and two silver medals.

Then, in 1978, having already designed over 550 gardens and landscapes, he took the bold decision to set up a branch of the Inchbald

School in Tehran. As Penelope Hobhouse would do two decades later, Brookes wanted to learn more about Islamic gardens, interested in their formality and religious significance. He also travelled to northern India to see how the style had been reinterpreted there.

When Brookes arrived in Tehran, Persia/Iran was teetering on the brink of revolution. 'It was odd but very interesting – a huge experience and wonderful,' he recalled. 'I arrived just at the end of the Shah and parties. It slowly became more difficult with the Ayatollah, but when you travelled outside Teheran, the country outside was lovely, exciting and as it had always been.'[26]

During the 1970s, Brookes had left London, running his design practice first from Oxfordshire, near the home of his brother, Michael, and Michael's wife, and then from near Newton Abbot in Devon. He returned from Tehran, however, without a job and to a basement flat in Shepherd's Bush, a shock after the beauty of Iran. He began looking for an escape from London and found it in Denmans, a four-acre garden at Fontwell in West Sussex.

House and garden belonged to Joyce Robinson, whose husband had bought the land in 1946 adjacent to their strawberry farm. After her husband's death, Mrs Robinson, a considerable plantswoman, began creating a decorative garden, which she first opened for the National Gardens Scheme in 1967. Influenced by Sir Frederick Stern, who gardened on chalk nearby at Highdown, she pioneered gravel gardening, making the dry gravel stream which winds its way through the garden to a pool added by Brookes; the dry bed is filled with self-seeded verbascum, sedums and *Alchemilla mollis*.[27] He had visited Denmans in the 1970s with a group of students and had admired the unashamed modernity of its informality, serpentine beds and interlocking spaces, and curving lawns which seemed to him to embody Church's philosophy.[28]

Ten years later, Denmans was the perfect solution. Brookes needed a job and somewhere to set up his own design school, while Mrs Robinson was suffering from rheumatism, able only to get about the garden in a buggy, and her gardener was threatening to retire. She liked the thought of the garden continuing under Brookes's guiding hand, and of having students around. Brookes sold his Shepherd's Bush flat and moved into a caravan while he converted the barn into the Clock House where he would live and teach his students. Mrs Robinson was initially reluctant to relinquish control of the garden she had created. 'Joyce and I danced around each other for ten years, because it took that long for me to feel the garden was mine. But in the main we got on very well – she was a direct-speaking lady so you knew where you were.'[29]

With a designer's eye, Brookes knocked the plantswoman's garden into shape. The garden's structure is quiet but insistent. The lawns, beds and gravel paths swirl round one another, offering a kaleidoscope of views to fields, copses and Fontwell racecourse next door. Grass paths mown once a week run through areas of longer grass, planted with bulbs in spring, and cut fortnightly in summer to give a two-tiered definition. Effects are created by architectural plants, including cardoons, spiky phormiums and *Stachys byzantina*. Evergreen shrubs hold winter winds at bay while strong shapes and interest are provided by trees such as the Indian bean tree (*Catalpa bignonioides*), the paperback maple (*Acer griseum*), groves of white-stemmed birches and a towering swamp cypress (*Taxodium distichum*). Line, texture and shapes were always more important to Brookes than colour, which came as a bonus.[30]

Here, Brookes set up his design school, training people who subsequently worked for him, such as Peter Gillespie, his assistant and fellow designer for over fifteen years. 'I always enjoyed looking after students – like chickens – particularly when I had them here in my own home.'[31] The school and the garden were quite separate entities in Brookes's mind, despite the fact that Denmans, open daily for over quarter of a century, made him better known to the general public than all his design commissions.

* * *

Over a career spanning almost sixty years, Brookes achieved considerable recognition, being made an MBE in 2004 for services to horticulture in the UK and overseas. Still a man of uncompromising opinions in his mid-eighties, he was excited by little in contemporary garden design, deploring in particular students' over-dependency on their computers. His critics complained he failed to move with the times, never learning to design on screen, and not developing his design style.

Brookes continued to design gardens until his death in March 2018, although doing so, he said, 'more gently'. Nevertheless, in 2017, he visited Russia twice, and oversaw commissions in Wiltshire and Scotland. He was still capable of imaginative flights. For a courtyard garden within the factory of tea and coffee makers Taylors of Harrogate, he designed a tea plantation of *Camellia sinensis*. At Itchenor, he was asked to design a garden for a New England-style house, with views to one side over the estuary. To draw the eye back to the garden and away from the view, Brookes reinterpreted a classic rill, running it from the central block of the house, across the lawn, with a zigzag in the middle like a thunderbolt.

Gillespie, Brookes's right-hand man, has paid tribute to Brookes's ability 'to look at a site, get to its heart, simplify it, and create a design which melds the clients' requirements with the architecture and the wider landscape'.[32] For Brookes himself, it was all quite simple: 'A good design is rather like a well-cut suit – it has to be right. No matter how many decorations you add to it, if the basic cut does not look right then nothing will rectify it.'[33]

PART VII

THE LATER PLANTSMEN

CHAPTER 22

Christopher Lloyd (1921–2006)

In 1993, Christopher Lloyd and his head gardener, Fergus Garrett, grubbed up the roses and instead planted exotics in the walled garden which Edwin Lutyens had designed at Great Dixter for Lloyd's father and mother. It caused a public outcry: gardeners, rose growers, garden historians, Dixter visitors and indeed the general public threw up their hands in horror at this seeming act of desecration within an historic garden. It was all a storm in a teacup, of course. The roses had been in the ground almost a century, the soil was spent and in need of a change. But the rose episode turned Lloyd into a legend, as his biographer,

Christopher Lloyd with Fergus Garrett. (© Jonathan Buckley)

Stephen Anderton, has written: 'People *outside* the garden world knew about this delightfully wicked old man who had dared to take on the establishment and remove something so immutably English as a rose garden; it was as if Henry VIII had replaced the heraldic Tudor rose with a chincherinchee.'[1]

Christopher Lloyd (or Christo as he was called by family and friends) was delighted by the uproar. He was happy to posture as the *enfant terrible* of British gardening, content to mix colours in a way which some might see as an absence of taste, and to castigate the uninformed. But he was also a reflective man, who instructed generations of amateurs on practical gardening through his many books and decades of articles for *Country Life*. *The Well-Tempered Garden* has been essential reading for serious gardeners since it was first published in 1970. He turned the home where he was born, Great Dixter near Rye in East Sussex, into a place of pilgrimage for gardeners and non-gardeners alike. He built on the work begun by his architect father, Nathaniel, and his gardening mother, Daisy, and made Great Dixter a byword for inspired plantsmanship. He truly cared for his plants, and in so doing fashioned an elaborate, attention-demanding planting style. 'He had the eye of a practised naturalist, alert to capsid bugs on the young shoots of a fatsia, and no less to reasons why some, but not all, shrubby hebes have a hardy strain in the breeding,' as Robin Lane Fox wrote in a tribute to Lloyd.[2]

On a personal level, he collected a large coterie of friends, many much younger than him, from the fields of music, art and writing as well as botany and gardening. He entertained them in his idiosyncratic way, often organising trips and picnics for guests to nearby Glyndebourne, and cooking for them with produce gathered from his garden.

His reputation spread to the United States and Australia, thanks again to his writing, and to his celebrated lecture tours, on which he was accompanied by his friend and fellow plant lover, Beth Chatto, as well as by Penelope Hobhouse and Rosemary Verey. Since his death in 2006, his right-hand man, Fergus Garrett, has continued to change and provoke as they did in Lloyd's lifetime. Great Dixter never stands still. 'Great Dixter was, and continues to be, rather like some vast extended family, with everyone drawn together by mutual interest and a love for the place,' wrote Rosemary Alexander, founder of the English Gardening School, in her preface to *Dear Christo*, a scrapbook of memories by his friends, acquaintances and professional contacts.[3]

***

Christopher Lloyd was born at Great Dixter on 3 March 1921, the youngest of six children. His father, Nathaniel was a printer turned self-trained architect and architectural historian, who wrote a book on English brickwork: he photographed the brickwork at Sissinghurst before Vita Sackville-West first saw the castle. Nathaniel's wife, Daisy, a solicitor's daughter some thirteen years his junior, was descended from Oliver Cromwell, something she felt keenly. She believed in plain living and high thinking, affecting a belted, grey Puritan dress as her evening gown, and, after a visit to Austria in 1936, always wearing a dirndl skirt.[4]

The Lloyds bought the fifteenth-century timber-framed manor house in 1910 and employed Edwin Lutyens. He opened up the Great Hall and added a new wing in the same vernacular. Integrated into these two wings was a hall house, dating from 1500, which Lutyens dismantled and brought beam by beam from nearby Benenden. There was no garden, apart from two orchards, and farm buildings from different periods. Lutyens worked these buildings into his Arts and Crafts framework, designing the walled areas around the house, and the layout of the hedging, while Nathaniel oversaw the planting of the yew and box hedging and the topiary. He also made the Sunk Garden two years after Christopher's birth.[5]

Both Christopher's parents were gardeners, opening Dixter initially for the National Gardens Scheme in 1929. Christopher showed a taste for gardening from early childhood, being photographed as a tot standing next to a huge lily in a pot. 'There was no one defining moment when I knew I was going to be a gardener,' he said. 'It didn't creep on me gradually. I just can't remember when I wasn't interested in gardening and flowers.'[6]

Daisy Lloyd, a follower of William Robinson's *The English Flower Garden*, planted the orchards and Upper Moat as meadow gardens. Known by all as 'The Management', she exercised a controlling influence over her youngest child, living with him at Dixter until her death in 1972 at the age of ninety-one. Christopher was then fifty-one. 'When you have two strong-willed people working in the same garden,' Christopher wrote after she died, 'there are sure to be many clashes ... But, as we loved each other, our shared pleasures in the garden were by far the strongest element in this partnership.'[7]

Christopher was twelve when his father died in 1933. A few months later, he started at Rugby School, where, separated from his mother, he was cheered by a Spanish chestnut tree outside his dormitory window. Like Russell Page at Charterhouse, Lloyd also received weekly packages of fresh flowers from his mother's garden. He benefited from the support of the school's director of music, Kenneth Stubbs, who encouraged the piano-playing Christopher to take up the oboe. Stubbs, too, was interested in gardening and his young pupil helped him plant up the walled plot behind his Victorian house.[8]

Christopher wanted to become an architect like his father, but after a year in Paris, in October 1939 he went up to King's College, Cambridge, to read modern languages. A shy, solitary undergraduate, he nevertheless relished the architecture, attended concerts, plays and films, and hired a piano to practise on in his room. In the vacations, he returned to Great Dixter to garden with his mother.[9]

He studied for just two years at Cambridge, before being called up into the ranks of the Royal Artillery. He spent most of the next five years in this country, able to get home frequently to Dixter: he only went abroad, to East Africa, as the war was ending. Mordant, almost daily letters to his mother honed his writing skills. He hated army life, as witness a letter of November 1941: 'I did not put my name down for any game, and those who do not play, have to spectate. That is to say it is preferred that one should watch extremely inferior soccer for 1½ hours than that one should take a nice brisk walk, which was what I wanted.'[10]

Lance Bombardier Lloyd was demobbed in 1946 to a Dixter laid low by six years of war. Needing to rebuild the garden, he took a BSc in decorative horticulture at Wye College, part of the University of London. 'University and the army gave me time to think about what I wanted to do.'[11] After completing his degree, he stayed on at Wye as an assistant lecturer, which 'gave me just the scientific and practical training I needed to make me feel at home in my subject'.[12]

Lloyd had found his vocation. From then on, he divided his time between gardening, writing and teaching. As well as lecturing, he encouraged aspiring gardeners at Dixter: Fergus Garrett is just the most eminent of those who have profited from working with Lloyd. At thirty-one, Lloyd had his first article published: on *Lobelia cardinalis* in *Gardening Illustrated*.[13] This was followed in 1957 by a book, *The Mixed Border*. It was the beginning of a writing career spanning half a century.

During his seven years at Wye, Lloyd spent a day or two a week in the garden at Dixter, leaving instructions for his mother in his absence.[14] After four years' teaching at Wye, he decided in 1954 to run Dixter as a business, starting a nursery for clematis and other cherished plants. His brother, Quentin, who lived across the road with his wife at Little Dixter, looked after the estate, and together the brothers built up the visiting side, incrementally opening both garden and parts of the house to the public. For Lloyd, it was a delicate balancing act: 'An old house like this is very expensive and not easy to keep going. It's a responsibility as well as a privilege, but, luckily enough, my subject enabled me to work from home. It's like having your hobby as a profession.'[15]

Lloyd never actually laid out a garden from scratch, for, at Dixter, 'the gardens were so well designed that I haven't needed to make major alterations to them.'[16] The garden to which he turned his full attention in 1954 still had the framework conceived by Lutyens and Nathaniel Lloyd, and some of Daisy's original plantings. Christopher himself was always a plantsman rather than a designer: in fact, his biographer claimed: 'Christo ... forever confused spatial design with planting design.'[17]

This is not to minimise Lloyd's achievement at Dixter: indeed, taking on such a weighty heritage could have been a straitjacket. But Lloyd never allowed himself to be circumscribed, declaring he was 'a forward-looking, not a backward-looking, gardener'.[18] The fine old house, its walls, hedging and topiary gave the plant-loving Lloyd the freedom to experiment and to allow his imagination to run wild. What he achieved at Dixter was wizardry: he transformed an already lovely place into somewhere even more magical, where he constantly discovered and relished new plants and planting combinations.

The setting helped. Great Dixter stands ten miles from the sea in the high weald, on a south-facing slope which runs down to the valley of the Rother. Protected from prevailing winds by hedging and shelter belts of trees planted over the last century or so, the garden has a rich, well-worked Wadhurst clay soil and a mild climate supporting a wide variety of planting. The manor house is anchored roughly in the centre of the garden. This is, as Lloyd said, 'a satisfyingly intimate arrangement. If you want to dash out to pick some *Iris stylosa* buds or some sprigs of witch hazel or a bunch of lilies-of-the-valley or a last-minute lettuce or bowl of raspberries, you can choose a door of exit so that nothing is too far from your starting point.'[19]

The various areas are linked by Lutyens' flagstone paths, rather than being discrete rooms on the Hidcote and Sissinghurst lines: on the whole, Dixter has a greater feeling of openness. There are gardens enclosed by hard landscaping, such as the Sunk and Barn gardens, and what was once Lutyens' Rose Garden; and others hedged in by castellated yew, like the High Garden, where both flowers and vegetables are grown, and the formal Topiary Lawn, with clipped chess pieces of yew on an apron of well-mown grass. Then, by contrast, are the orchards and Meadow Garden, where grass paths are cut through longer grass filled first with spring bulbs such as small narcissi and then with wild flowers. Established by Daisy Lloyd, these meadows anticipated by almost eighty years what became high fashion in the early twenty-first century.

Lloyd understood plants individually, but also focussed on the way they work together within a planting scheme. 'It is best to anticipate how the plant is going to develop and what its needs will be and that requires experience, but experience is soon acquired. Once is enough. We need never be ashamed of a disaster so long as it is not repeated,' he wrote unforgivingly.[20]

Within the firm historic structure Lloyd created contrasts of pace, and quirky surprises: in the rectangular Wall Garden, a mass of aeoniums set against silver-leafed plants, Lloyd laid a pebble mosaic of two of his adored dachshunds, Dahlia and Canna. The garden has always been dynamic, Lloyd believing that annuals, perennials, shrubs and climbers should not be fiercely segregated as they once were in so many gardens; he used them together to give his planting depth and vitality.

Each day began with Lloyd touring the garden, usually with a dachshund in tow. Robin Lane Fox, an exacting and observant gardener himself, recalled one such tour:

> In summer at Dixter mornings started early, with a pre-breakfast survey of the garden before 7a.m. On my visit, we stopped beneath

> a magnificent clematis, *flammula* I think, and Christopher told me with typical mischief that Graham Thomas had dismissed it as a second-rate variety. It looked stunning, and from the surrounding greenery Fergus emerged, weeding skilfully. We talked amiably but, as we turned to go, Christopher remarked that the tips of the left-hand edge of this enormous wall-plant were showing the first signs of wilt and should be sprayed in the next few hours. I had never even noticed them. He exemplified the view that you get as much out of gardening as you put into it.[21]

Lloyd's gardening was cumulative: he didn't rashly change the planting, but gradually improved it, enlarging, for instance, the majestic Long Border which, at 110 yards long and mostly fifteen feet deep, is a glory of the garden. He altered planting not just annually, but seasonally, planting bulbs for spring, with bedding plants changed twice, even three times a year to give a long period of interest. 'You must resign yourself to the necessity of big upheavals and rearrangements from time to time, right through the years,' he wrote in *The Well-Tempered Garden*. 'It is obvious that close planting gives a furnished look to a border almost immediately; equally obvious that it is wasteful and expensive.'[22]

Lloyd broke boundaries, blurring the lines between so-called garden plants and wild flowers; mixing colours that shocked more conservative gardeners, and encouraging people to get rid of ground-cover planting. He replaced the roses in Lutyens's Rose Garden with late-summer sub-tropical plants that had brilliant colours and extravagant foliage. Large-flowered dahlias at head-height were planted among agaves, cannas, bananas, ginger lilies, daturas and cotyledon, with graceful accents of *Verbena bonariensis*. 'A delightful little kaleidoscope,' was Beth Chatto's judgement.[23] 'Every gardener should be experimenting and be on the frontiers of what they know about,' Lloyd believed. 'They should be trying to grow plants which perhaps they shouldn't, and in different ways from what they have always done. Gardeners shouldn't just settle down to something they know to be successful, but should be adventurous.'[24]

He had strong likes, among them conifers, cacti and alpines, and equally strong dislikes, such as bergenias. These he castigated in *The Well-Tempered Garden*, to Chatto's annoyance: his strictures got off to a rocky start what became a fond, if occasionally thorny, friendship. Although some might question his definition of taste, he, like other gardeners before him, took it as having almost moral connotations: 'I just don't happen to believe that "it's all a matter of taste" excuses or justifies every indiscriminate use of colour in gardening. I believe there are absolute standards of what goes and what doesn't in matters of taste.'[25]

Colour is the feature with which Lloyd was most associated, because of his work in the Exotic Garden, the rich hues of the Long Border, and the plant associations in pots grouped around the front door of the house and elsewhere. But other issues were equally important to Lloyd: 'The placing of plants in relation to their neighbours is so important and so fascinating, colour being only one aspect to consider,' he wrote to Beth Chatto. 'Heights, shapes and textures, as well as season of comeliness, are all factors to be considered. Up to a point, it comes instinctively, but thought is more dependable than instinct, while experience (or discovery, when they are new) of your plants' preferences is most important of all.'[26]

Forward-looking though Lloyd might have been in his planting combinations and ideas, he created a garden which has always required an Edwardian-sized staff to undertake the multitude of daily tasks throughout the year. Daisy Lloyd had six gardeners, and there have seldom been fewer than five full-time workers, plus volunteers, in Lloyd's time, and since his death. Thousands of tulips are planted, for example, every autumn, and then lifted in late spring/early summer after flowering, their bulbs cleaned, and stored for replanting the next autumn. Propagation of annuals, biennials, perennials, climbers and shrubs is always in train, as the extensive chapter, 'To Make More and Still More', made clear in *The Well-Tempered Garden*'.[27] 'I have never made any bones about the fact that this is a high-maintenance garden because I think that is the most exciting sort of gardening,' he once said.[28] Garden design historian Tim Richardson believes that 'Dixter is gardened at a connoisseurial level that is probably unmatched worldwide, the result of a continuous programme of aesthetic appraisal and alteration'.[29]

***

Lloyd's first book, *The Mixed Border*, encouraged gardeners to mix shrubs with perennials within herbaceous borders, revealing in print, as well as in his garden, his dislike of pigeon-holing plants. Six years later, in 1963, he was invited to contribute weekly to *Country Life*, becoming as much an institution for that magazine's readers as Vita Sackville-West had been for those of *The Observer*. He was given no specific brief, so he chose topics as they presented themselves to him, month by month, at Dixter. He wrote with wit and authority, often referring to readers' letters, and remonstrating with them like a cherished, sometimes cantankerous uncle. The columns weave neatly back and forth, as in one, for instance, where he elegantly justifies his interest in ferns:

> Once you develop an interest in hardy ferns they almost become an obsession. I try to resist that; after all, it can't be healthy to be obsessed. You're no longer master of your passions, and anyway other plants tend to become unfairly excluded. But ferns, it seems to me, can find places in so many parts of the garden without excluding anything. They are

> of those ingredients, like bulbs, that add an extra dimension, an added richness, a deeper texture, setting off or alternating with other plants in or out of their season.[30]

His tone is often pugnacious. Another column opens: 'When I was on my knees weeding, during our open hours, I heard a disgruntled male voice addressing me obliquely through his companions: "If the plants were labelled we should know what we were looking at." "If I was writing labels, I shouldn't be here weeding," I replied. Silence.'[31]

During the forty years Lloyd wrote for *Country Life*, he published over twenty books, including *Clematis* (1965), *The Adventurous Gardener* (1983), *The Year at Great Dixter* (1987), *In My Garden* (1993), a compilation of his *Country Life* features, and *Colour for Adventurous Gardeners* (2001).

His gardening classic, *The Well-Tempered Garden*, was published first in 1970 and has been revised and updated several times since then. It was a personal manifesto. 'There is room for many approaches to gardening,' he wrote, 'and they give us the satisfaction of expressing ourselves. Ours, in its humble way, is an art as well as a craft. At the same time it keeps us in touch with the earth, the seasons, and with that complex of interrelated forces both animate and inanimate which we call nature. It is a humanizing occupation.'[32]

Although unillustrated, it is a colourful, evocative book, its pictures provided by the detail, vibrancy and humour of Lloyd's writing. Beth Chatto paid it tribute, saying 'I was entertained, amused, informed again and again of things I had forgotten, or things I had never known, tipped head-over-heels by controversial ideas, led on by an opinionated style of writing – which far from being off-putting, became addictive.'[33] Opinionated, certainly; the attack of his *Country Life* pieces is ever-present. He advises, in the case of doubt, on deferring moving shrubs or splitting up herbaceous plants until the spring. 'That is my official pronouncement. Don't expect me to follow it myself, because I'm also a great believer in doing a job when I want to do it, and to hell with the consequences.' Elsewhere, there is the professional nurseryman's contempt for those less scrupulous than himself: 'There will always remain the irresistible temptation to trade on the folly of the masses.'[34]

After his mother's death, Lloyd became an accomplished cook and *Gardener Cook* (1997), with photographs of Dixter's garden and its produce, was the result. 'I haven't always been interested in cooking, but when the cooks fall away from your life, you have to take it up,' he said. A cook in the Jane Grigson mould (heavy on butter and cream), he enjoyed using what he grew. 'I have never really thought of vegetable and flower gardening as separate issues. They are all part of gardening.'[35]

Some of his later books perhaps lack the freshness and immediacy of the earlier ones, as Lloyd began recycling ideas, driven by the need to maintain both house and garden at Dixter. Garden designer Penelope

Hobhouse learned much from Lloyd's earlier books, but felt 'the sad thing in the end was that he sat indoors writing books to pay for the garden.'[36]

An exception to this unhappy trend is a book inspired by friendship: *Dear Friend & Gardener* (1998), an engaging exchange of letters between Lloyd and Beth Chatto. They discuss gardening, but also other issues, such as Lloyd's dog, Canna, who 'has just been sick in the darkest recesses of the room'. A letter from Chatto to Lloyd records an autumn visit from Fergus and Lloyd to her garden at Elmstead Market. 'I much enjoyed having you and Fergus share the garden with me ... I loved the way you both lingered over almost every plant.'[37]

Fergus Garrett was almost always at Lloyd's side, 'a freshly renewed joy' each morning, in Lloyd's words.[38] Garrett had previously worked for Chatto in Essex, and on gardens in France and Switzerland, before Lloyd appointed him as head gardener in 1993. From the outset, Lloyd found in Garrett someone to whom he could entrust his garden and his home. 'Christo was an old man with a young heart and head,' Garrett has said. 'He was like a father to me and my wife – a magical man who left a big hole.'[39]

Lloyd filled his house with younger people as he aged. 'I much enjoyed the company of your young friends, feeling part of an extended family,' wrote Chatto to Lloyd. 'You might have become a crusty old bachelor rattling around in your medieval halls like a pill in a box, but you are such a wonderfully generous host to many of us who look upon Dixter both as an inspiration and retreat from our own worlds.'[40]

'Christo loved youth,' wrote Rory Dusoir, a gardener at Great Dixter from 2000 to 2003. 'He enjoyed passing on the benefit of his experience to young and enquiring minds.'[41] Lloyd's predilection for young men is discussed by his biographer, Stephen Anderton, who concludes that none of his relationships was ever consummated, with the possible exception of that with the American landscape designer, Lanning Roper.[42] Anderton's biography, although authorised, ruffled the feathers of Lloyd's friends who felt that Anderton had dwelt at unnecessary length on an area of Lloyd's life that he had resolutely kept private.

***

Lloyd's achievements were recognised in 1979 by the Royal Horticultural Society's award of the Victoria Medal of Honour; by an honorary doctorate from the Open University in 1996; and by an OBE in 2000 for his services to horticulture.

With Garrett at his side, his final years were mostly happy, only marred by the vandalising of the topiary birds which had graced the hedges since Nathaniel Lloyd's time. Lloyd lived for all of his eighty-five years in the house where he was born, and was allowed by his siblings to take control of that home and garden from a relatively early age. That, however, was both a privilege and a responsibility, and the cost of Dixter and its future were constant worries. This was mainly why he kept on writing, his columns continuing to go out weekly to *Country Life,* always on time, and requiring little editing. Then, in September 2005, it was suggested in an email by the then editor, Clive Aslet, that Lloyd might like to reduce his contributions to twice monthly for a while before stopping altogether. Angrily, Lloyd resigned, receiving acknowledgement by email, but no celebratory send-off. As Lloyd's biographer says, 'it was a sorry ending to such an extraordinary career.'[43]

Four months later, on 27 January 2006, Lloyd died in hospital after a stroke. His legacy has been preserved by Garrett, as chief executive of the Great Dixter Charitable Trust. The greatest complication after Lloyd's death was that Lloyd only owned forty per cent of the estate; the other sixty per cent belonged to his niece, Olivia Eller. With a £3.79 million Heritage Lottery Fund grant and money from the Monument Trust and other private bodies, the Dixter trust secured Olivia's share. Horticultural students are still trained and live in the house at Great Dixter, while Garrett has continued and advanced Lloyd's work. 'We are always looking at the garden with fresh eyes, as Christo did, to make sure it remains his wonderfully charming place. If you lose that character, you lose everything,' he has said. 'We often talked about the future and our responsibility to pass on our plant knowledge. Christo always said: "Think about the plants and the people who love plants, and everything will fall into place."'[44]

CHAPTER 23

Beth Chatto (1923–2018)

In the early 1990s, as Christopher Lloyd was replacing his historic rose garden with thirsty exotics, his friend and fellow plant-lover, Beth Chatto, was using the serpentine curves of a hosepipe to map out beds for her new gravel garden at Elmstead Market in Essex. Her plan was less iconoclastic than Lloyd's, given that she was not replacing a Lutyens-designed garden. Instead, she was digging up a car park on the driest and most exposed part of her garden to demonstrate a type of gardening which perfectly expressed contemporary concerns with water conservation and climate change. 'My thinking on the subject is based on the assumption that water is our most precious commodity,' she wrote later to Lloyd, 'and modern demands for water are often in excess of actual need. Combine this with the likelihood of hotter and drier summers to come, then surely we must be prepared to reconsider some of our gardening practices.'[1]

Beth Chatto, vigorous promoter of choosing plants adapted to local conditions, took several months to prepare the soil before planting the gravel garden. The plants, from round the world, were all chosen for their drought-tolerance, and included some not hardy enough for East Anglian winters in the past. Bergenias, grasses, graceful *Verbena bonariensis*, grey-leafed Mediterranean santolina and lavender, antipodean eucalyptus, American agaves, sedums and verbascums were planted among whispering grasses in a free-flowing style more dependent on leaf and seedhead shape than on flower colour. The result was a garden which made an already renowned plantswoman even more famous: the public flocked in their thousands to view her experiment.

The gravel garden was the latest of the gardens that Chatto had created over more than thirty years in an inhospitable hollow of gravel, clay, silt and sand. Gardening in such a place enforced Chatto's respect for soil variations, and scrupulously she used only plants which would grow naturally in the wild in such conditions – a radical notion when she started her garden in 1960.

Beth Chatto. (Courtesy The Beth Chatto Gardens)

She was always more interested in the shape of her plants, and how they worked with others in a bed, rather than with hard landscaping and garden design. Garden design historian Tim Richardson has suggested that this leaning means that Chatto has 'somehow been left out of the grand narrative of gardening in the twentieth century'.[2] It is true she designed no other gardens than her own, and virtually no plans exist even for that. Beatles' lead guitarist George Harrison asked Chatto for plant suggestions in 1981 and encouraged her to become his gardener and design consultant. (She refused, saying that she didn't think her husband, Andrew, would like it.) She was also invited to France to advise on Baron Rothschild's garden, but otherwise she focussed on her own garden and nursery at Elmstead Market.

Indeed, Chatto's work seems very much part of the continuing story of British gardening. Her garden, her Unusual Plants nursery, her Chelsea Flower Show stands, and her books introduced gardeners to unfamiliar plants and encouraged them not to fight nature but to work with it, to help maintain the delicate natural balance in our environment. She pioneered a new attitude to gardening, now taken almost for granted. As her official biographer has written, Chatto 'has been one of the most influential in shifting the mindset away from the serried ranks of scarlet geraniums and hybrid tea roses stiff as flagpoles to the natural country look which so many gardeners now strive for'.[3]

***

Beth Chatto's story is, like Christopher Lloyd's, effectively the tale of one garden. She, too, was deeply rooted, spending her entire life in Essex. She and her twin brother, Seley, were born on 27 June 1923 in the village of Good Easter, near Chelmsford in Essex, to William Little, a police constable, and his wife, Bessie. When the twins were two, the family moved to Great Chesterford, near Saffron Walden, where a younger brother, David, was born. Both William and Bessie Little were keen gardeners and accustomed their daughter to the practical side of gardening. 'It was enough to get the feel of it – to get your hands dirty and the pleasure of it.'[4]

Beth attended Colchester County High School for Girls before teacher training at Hockerill College, Bishop's Stortford. While at Hockerill, she met Andrew Chatto, a scion of the publishing house, Chatto & Windus. They quickly discovered a shared passion for plants, fostered in Andrew's case in California, where the Chattos lived in his childhood for his American mother's health. 'Although Andrew was only ten years old, he was enchanted by seeing ceanothus and poppies growing in the wild,' according to Beth. 'He was told that they were native to California, as brambles and elderflowers are in England.' Andrew developed a life-long interest in the origins and natural associations of garden plants, in retirement reading widely in French, German and Russian botanical literature.[5]

Finishing his education in England, he trained, as had Christopher Lloyd, at Wye College in Kent, having decided on fruit farming rather than a sedentary publishing job in London. It was naturally therefore to Andrew Chatto, thirteen years her senior, that the young Beth Little turned when working on her final student project on the plant life of the salt marshes in Essex. 'With [his] highly informed help … I started an interest which has lasted all my life, and directly influenced my gardening. By studying the marshes in detail I learnt how marvellously plants adapt themselves to their environment, and also how that environment can change in a matter of a few yards, and that each differing section has a slightly modified plant community.'[6]

The couple married in 1943, and Beth taught for two years, before leaving to support her husband and Land Girls on the family farm. As was then the custom, Beth and Andrew moved in with his mother, who died within a year of the marriage.[7] They remained, however, for eighteen years at Braiswick, a suburb west of Colchester, during which time two daughters were born (Diana, 1946, and Mary, 1948), and Beth began gardening. The Chattos' holidays were spent in the Mediterranean, the Dolomites and the Alps, exploring the indigenous flora and building up Beth's plant knowledge.[8]

Beth constantly credited Andrew with giving her confidence as both gardener and writer, although the marriage was not to be without its difficulties. 'She was so lovely because she always said it was her husband,' Penelope Hobhouse has said. 'She started every sentence by quoting Andrew.'[9] Two other people, however, also profoundly affected Beth Chatto's career.

The artist Sir Cedric Morris lived an hour's drive away at Benton End, Hadleigh. Morris bred (and painted) irises in the late 1940s and early 1950s, forming a rare collection now held by Sarah Cook, former head gardener at Sissinghurst. Irises were Morris's chief love, but he also grew species plants, such as alliums and fritillaries, then less available than mass-produced cultivars. 'They were considered "wild", and had unfamiliar Latin names – but times and fashions change, and today such plants are esteemed world-wide.'[10] Morris, in Chatto's words, 'was part of a small, charmed circle of people, including Vita Sackville-West, who grew species plants'.[11]

The prevailing fashion was for highly-bred delphiniums and lupins, with gardeners ignoring their planting conditions rather than going with them. At Benton End, plants were grown in soil to which they were best suited. Beth had been apprehensive before meeting Morris, and was initially 'overwhelmed by the wealth of plants I did not know but which I knew I must grow and treasure'.[12] With Morris's support, 'I taught myself to propagate plants from the precious screws of paper full of seed, berries or cuttings I have been given by Cedric as well as generous earthy bundles of roots, tubers and bulbs.'[13]

Pamela Underwood, a local nurserywoman and neighbour of the Chattos, was another major figure in Beth's career. In the archive of diaries, letters and notes donated by Chatto to the Garden Museum in July 2017 is a review of one of her first flower arranging demonstrations in 1955. Flower clubs had started up across England in the early 1950s to brighten the lives of women tied down by family cares. The Colchester Flower Club was the second of these clubs, set up by Underwood. According to Beth, 'she soon roped me in. She saw me growing unusual things and decided to take me out of the kitchen.'[14]

Chatto, having read books on Japanese flower arranging, was impressed with the Japanese view that plants should be arranged to reflect the triangle of heaven, earth and man, with tall verticals surrounded by lower plants; it was a pattern she also adopted when planting in the garden. Armed with plants she had grown herself, she was sent off by Underwood to open a new flower club as its first speaker and demonstrator. Chatto spent the next few years travelling round the country, lecturing, demonstrating and showing plants from her garden. Her arrangements of alliums, poppies and seedheads seemed revolutionary. 'Audiences were intrigued that

I used green flowers and created wonderful shapes – so different from just buying roses, lilies and gladioli from the shops.'[15] She was always alert and seeking to extend her range: lodged with her papers in the Garden Museum is a sketch of a flower arrangement she admired in her bedroom while staying with Christopher Lloyd at Great Dixter.

Chatto continued to demonstrate flower arranging for many years with plants she had grown or propagated herself: in 1973, for instance, she gave forty-six demonstrations between March and October, from Lincolnshire to Chingford and Felixstowe, then across the country to Bath, all the time keeping a note of the plants shown and sold.[16]

***

In 1960, Beth persuaded Andrew that they should build a house on wasteland backing on to his fruit farm near Elmstead Market on the other side of Colchester. It was a brave decision, for the five acres to be shaped into formal gardens were on several different levels, with a spring-fed boggy hollow, its slopes filled with deposits of gravel, clay, silt and sand from the melting glacier of the Ice Age. Around the margins was dry shade beneath ancient hedgerows and 300-year-old oaks. But Chatto was excited by the terrain and the opportunity to grow an enormous variety of plants. 'It sounds mad to want to make a garden here,' she once said, 'especially in a place which has the lowest rainfall in the country, but I was absolutely driven to do it.'[17]

An architect was commissioned to design White Barn, a modern, split-level house, with long windows, more or less at the garden's centre. The Chattos began improving the soil, and bringing over plants, many given her by Cedric Morris. 'Because these plants, mostly species as opposed to cultivars, were adapted to thrive in problem areas, much of the garden originated from Cedric. It is a tribute to him.'[18]

The gravel was tackled first, fed with vegetable waste to improve the depleted soil. Then, over several years, four large ponds, each slightly lower than the other, were created, separated by dams. The grass is emerald and the vegetation lush throughout the year, beginning with thick white spears of *Lysichiton americanus*, candelabra primulas, then huge parasols of gunnera in summer, with winter colour provided by the dogwood stems. Chatto was pleased with the contrast: 'To sit on one of the grass-covered dams, surrounded by almost tropical-looking plants, and listening to the splash of water as it falls from one level to another is an unexpected luxury in the heart of dry Essex farmland.'[19]

On arid stony terraces around the house, Chatto created the Mediterranean and scree gardens, while beneath the ancient oaks which fringed the garden, she planted a shady walk with species plants from temperate woodland areas around the world. After the drought of 1976, surplus clay from an adjacent farm's reservoir was laid over an area of waste, with holes filled with gritty compost for new trees and shrubs. What is now called the Reservoir Garden consists of large, informal, well-mulched borders with broad paths of mown grass weaving between them.

The hurricane of October 1987 'twisted trees out of the ground like corkscrews, whipping off heads and limbs indiscriminately'. In its wake, Chatto decided to make a new woodland garden, 'where, beneath green-lichened tree trunks, shade-loving plants would carpet the floor and groups of shrubs would create microclimates and backgrounds for herbaceous plants and bulbs that provide a long season of interest'.[20]

Then, in the 1990s, she created the gravel garden which mimics a dried-up river bed. It was ploughed and composted, but has no irrigation system, yet drought-loving plants from the Mediterranean and other temperate climes thrive where once weeds curled up and died.

Beth Chatto turned a hostile tract of land into a garden of great beauty fitting seamlessly into the surrounding countryside. Chatto's mantra, 'the right plant for the right place', is still given expression in every bed and every corner; its influence is also felt in gardens across Britain. Leaves, textures and shapes are as important as flower colour, and extend the garden's season of interest. Plants are in carefully planned groups, rather than 'dotted like pins in a pincushion', with the occasional bold plant as an accent.[21] Garden historian Jane Brown has written that 'in a compact area she runs the gamut from wet to dry (and through shade and sun), from lush ferns, ornamental rhubarbs, bog arums and hostas to her Mediterranean planting of euphorbias, ballota, Jerusalem sage, santolina, salvias and alliums. In one afternoon it is rather like having seven-league-boots.'[22]

Andrew Chatto was always more of a scholar than a businessmen, and, facing competition from cheaper imports, sold his fruit farm in 1967. He retired, already suffering from emphysema caused by smoking. Partly prompted by needing material for flower demonstrations, Beth then started her own nursery, Unusual Plants. New stock was propagated by seeds and cuttings from the plants in her garden. An evocative and frequently updated catalogue (*The Beth Chatto Handbook*) was published, revealing Beth's ability to paint plant portraits. Take, for example, *Doronicum pardalianches* or 'The Great Leopard's Bane':

> Although its tuberous roots are somewhat invasive I admire this plant's ability to thrive in thin woodland, even in grass. It will look well in a border and is easily restrained. In my wood garden the effect of a glade of yellow daisies on branching stems is a delight when they fill the space taken earlier by snowdrops and daffodils.[23]

Any gardener would thrill to that description.

The business flourished, both on the ground and through mail order, and now, after Chatto's death, still helps support the cost of maintaining the garden. By the early 2000s, over twenty people were employed by the nursery in winter, with double that number in summer. In a letter to Christopher Lloyd, Chatto described painstaking preparation work in February:

> My three propagating girls were left to spring-clean their areas, painting the walls, organizing better shelving for all their record books, reference books and the tools of their trade ... The stock control girls in the adjoining room have been cleaning pots all winter, waiting for the new packing season to begin. Each day they load trolleys with trays of potted plants taken from outside and push them along gangways of the propagating house to be certain of having thawed pots for the next day ... The central benches are full with trays of root-cuttings, an on-going job for the propagating team throughout the winter.[24]

Chatto staged her first stand at a Royal Horticultural Show in January 1975. She showed hellebores, London Pride, saxifrage and tellima, all regarded as weeds by one dyspeptic judge. He was talked down, however, and Chatto was awarded a silver medal, following that up with a silver-gilt at the autumn show.

The Chelsea Flower Show was the next step. At the time, great colourful cultivars – forced for the show – were displayed with military precision and no attempt at naturalism. Chatto was the first to bury her plants in earth, showing them apparently growing naturally in separate areas of damp and dry. 'I did not aim for a showy display of unseasonal plants in flower but tended to concentrate on the effect of contrasting shapes, sizes and designs of leaves.'[25] With this radical departure, Chatto altered how many nurseries exhibited at Chelsea – and won ten consecutive gold medals in the process. She paved the way for plantswomen such as Carol Klein, Rosy Hardy and Jekka McVicar. Their loose association planting remains popular three decades after Beth Chatto broke the mould, yet still co-exists happily with showy displays of single species, such as lilies, dahlias, roses and sweet peas.

Her stands at Chelsea brought her personal fame, and encouraged the R.H.S. to invite her onto its council. On the surface a modest and unassuming woman, more concerned with her garden, her nursery and caring for her sick husband, she turned down the honour. Her refusal was unprecedented. 'I was grateful ... but not so starry-eyed that I could accept something that I knew I couldn't cope with ... I wasn't aware it was like refusing the Queen!'[26]

Chatto needed time for writing; at the urging of Graham Stuart Thomas, she published her first book, *The Dry Garden*, in 1978. She opened: 'It is not always obvious, especially to new gardeners, that some plants do not take kindly to being pushed into the nearest empty space.'[27] It was natural that the teacher turned gardener should seek to educate others, and she started as she meant to go on: writing only from her own experience, using her own garden as the basis for everything, and taking her time over each book. *The Damp Garden* followed next in 1982, and other titles over the next twenty years or so included *Beth Chatto's Garden Notebook* (1988), *The Green Tapestry* (1990), *Beth Chatto's Gravel Garden* (2000) and *Beth Chatto's Woodland Garden* (2002; republished in 2017 as *Beth Chatto's Shade Garden*).

Chatto was less prolific than Rosemary Verey and Christopher Lloyd, hampered partly by never learning to type. But she wrote with ease and elegance, as when describing her garden in August:

> Dramatic foliage is provided by the great phormiums, or New Zealand flax, which can be plain, purple, or variegated, while a towering grass, *Miscanthus sacchariflorus*, [catches] the light like a waterfall ... Adding lightness to these architectural giants are such plants as Mr Bowles's golden sedge (a form of *Carex stricta*) – a lovely grass-like plant, like a bright gold sunburst overhanging the water's edge.[28]

Chatto was as meticulous in her books as she was in her garden and nursery. Garden writer and editor Erica Hunningher remembered 'pointing out a rare inconsistency in one of her plant descriptions when I was editing *Woodland Garden* and how she took me by the hand as we practically ran to the appropriate spot. "We must look again," she said. In her book, nothing is left to chance.'[29]

In the late 1990s, Chatto and Christopher Lloyd were commissioned by Frances Lincoln to write letters over two calendar years specifically for publication. The exchange, published as *Dear Friend & Gardener* (1998), is somewhat arch in tone with both correspondents constantly aware of the public looking over their shoulders. The letters reveal affection and exasperation as they spar over the merits of organic gardening (Chatto mostly pro; Lloyd less concerned) and other ecological issues. 'Sorry I have spent over-long on drought and irrigation, but for me, it is a philosophy of gardening rather than a matter of morals or principles, and so may well run like a thread through our chain of letters.' Lloyd testily replies, 'I confess to being unattracted to the concept of gardening with a moral implication. It puts a dampener on going all out to garden full-bloodedly in whatever way appeals to you most.' A constant refrain is Chatto's anguish over her lack of rainfall. 'Visitors arrive to tell us they have driven through torrential rain only a few miles away – ugh!'[30]

Chatto was in demand as a lecturer, both in this country and overseas: starting in 1983, she travelled to New York, then to British Columbia, Canada, and the north-west states of America, and to Holland, Germany and Paris. In 1989, she and Lloyd embarked on a tour of New Zealand, Australia and Canada, a trip she recalled with dry humour:

> Perhaps my funniest memory was sitting in the first class captain's lounge waiting for Christo to join me at the airport, where we were to travel to Australia, the beginning of a world tour of lectures ... Christo

> arrived, bustling in, clutching his ancient overnight bag, the cracked black leather peeling like fish scales. From it he extracted a brown paper parcel and offered me sandwiches, his own homemade bread and sweet ham. Nothing went to waste at Dixter! It was the beginning of a unique adventure.[31]

Chatto made contacts and set up plant exchanges with gardeners worldwide, and her style is particularly admired in Japan. She surprised herself on early trips by the 'rich collection of herbaceous plants ... to be found in European nurseries. In our insular way we tend to think they are mostly a British invention but immediately I stepped into the nursery at Laufen, I felt at home ... welcomed by many familiar plants and excited by many more...You might think I had enough plants to care for, but I can't help feeling like a child in a sweetshop when faced with the temptation of new plants.'[32]

A recurring theme of *Dear Friend & Gardener* was her anxiety over Andrew. The marriage was not always easy: Andrew was a reclusive character who withdrew not only from the more public aspects of Beth's life, but at times from Beth herself. Beth, a passionate woman beneath her apparently calm exterior, felt his physical withdrawal keenly. She suffered bouts of depression, and had a stormy, twenty-year affair with a neighbouring farmer, Hans Pluygers. Beth never considered leaving Andrew, however, as she valued the intellectual companionship they shared.[33] She always saw the garden as a joint enterprise, as gardening novelist Penelope Lively recognised. 'Marital gardening in this instance seems to have been an altogether ... harmonious affair. Beth Chatto thanks her husband warmly – "whose life-long hobby has been to study the natural homes of our garden plants" ... Casting a beady eye over ... various gardening partnerships I can see that they work best where roles are tacitly defined – Andrew Chatto providing the scholarly ballast for a garden ... Harold Nicolson taking over the initial layout.'[34]

Andrew's health declined throughout the 1990s, and when he died in 1999 it was in Beth's arms, after fifty-six years of marriage, which had weathered the storms. Beth was grateful to have her garden to sustain her. 'I would be lonely down here if I didn't have the business,' she said a few years later. 'The garden is almost like a village.'[35]

***

Beth Chatto was an unlikely person to have been so much in the limelight, for she was naturally diffident. Petite, dark and with a shy smile, her relaxed, friendly manner endeared her to generations of visitors to the Beth Chatto Gardens. But the garden continued to be 'my private garden which I love to share with like-minded gardeners'.[36] She had an underlying steeliness and exacted the highest standards from those who worked for her. It was always clear that Beth was the head gardener.[37]

She was much honoured, being awarded the Victoria and Lawrence Memorial Medals by the Royal Horticultural Society in 1988, an honorary doctorate from Essex University, and an OBE in the 2002 Queen's Birthday Honours. Despite these accolades, Chatto never rested on her laurels, claiming in an interview towards the end of her life that 'I am having a new learning experience after forty-five years: how to renew and refresh the garden. It never finishes. A garden is like a quilt, it wears out in places and needs patching.'[38]

Although wheelchair bound for some years, she continued to oversee the gardens, and work closely with her team right up until her death. It remains a family-run business, managed by Julia Boulton, daughter of Beth's daughter, Diana, with a team of fifty volunteers plus the permanent staff. The Beth Chatto Education Trust has been set up at the gardens to teach young people about nature and gardening. When she died, aged 94, in May 2018, Beth was much mourned by the gardening world. 'Beth Chatto was not a designer or a trained horticulturalist, but rather a connoisseur of plants in a rarefied English tradition,' wrote her obituarist in *The Times*. 'She was also a populist: a natural teacher and communicator, with a strong desire to share her knowledge.'[39]

Ideas about communities of plants, as evidenced in the work of designer Dan Pearson, or the appeal of the new perennials approach of Dutch-born designer Piet Oudolf, are now an accepted part of contemporary gardening. But these younger gardeners owe the quietly trail-blazing Beth Chatto a huge debt. This has been acknowledged by Penelope Hobhouse, who has recalled the effect of seeing Chatto's first stand at the Chelsea Flower Show in 1976:

> I was a beginner-gardener, mad about plants, plant names and the whole idea of aesthetic colour arrangements. But Beth's stand blew away all my preconceived notions ... Beth had made plant requirements – wet or dry, acid or alkaline, well-drained or swampy conditions – much more important than the superficial flower colour schemes about which I had dreamed. Her stand was extraordinary and exciting. It marked, for me, a turning point, as her teaching, her books and her own garden have done for many others ... Thanks to pioneers such as Beth, we study plant needs and the conditions of their native habitat before we try to arrange them.[40]

CHAPTER 24

Tom Stuart-Smith (1960–)

From the early 1990s, Tom Stuart-Smith was a major figure at the Chelsea Flower Show. Over the course of the next two decades, he designed eight gold medal winning show gardens, three of them also garnering the coveted 'Best in Show' award. And, if he wasn't creating a garden, he could be seen with the judges, clipboard in hand, assessing the merits of that year's designs. At six foot five and with a mane of thick brown hair, Stuart-Smith was instantly recognisable across the showground.

We cannot yet assess how history will treat Stuart-Smith's work. Our other gardeners, three of them still alive as this book goes to press, already have their places firmly established in the centuries-long tradition of British gardening. Other contenders jostle Stuart-Smith for a place in this book, designers, who, like him have international reputations, and are Chelsea gold medal winners. Christopher Bradley-Hole is one, whose cool, elegant gardens focus on geometry and proportion. Another is Dan Pearson, a television idol for many gardening enthusiasts, and a naturalistic plantsman in the Beth Chatto mould. A third is Cleve West, trained by John Brookes at Kew, and another multiple Chelsea gold medal winner, who designs gardens with a strong structure supported by superb plantsmanship.

Even in this starry company, Tom Stuart-Smith stands out, his gifts acknowledged by his Chelsea peers. In 2011, aged fifty-one, he was the subject of a retrospective exhibition at the Garden Museum in London, the first about a living British designer. He unites many themes discussed in this book. As garden design historian Tim Richardson puts it, Stuart-Smith 'successfully straddles the divide between "high design" and traditional horticulture. His approach to planting synthesises the naturalistic style which appeared in the mid-nineties (all those grasses and "drifts") with a British tradition of intensely decorative colour-themed borders.'[1]

Tom Stuart-Smith and 'Rabbit'. (Courtesy Tom Stuart-Smith/Eva Vermandel)

Stuart-Smith's commissions range from small private gardens to large gardens and public parks: he worked on restoring Victorian terraces at Trentham in Staffordshire; designed the gardens round the new glasshouse at RHS Garden Wisley, and has now been appointed to create the master plan for the society's fifth, 156-acre garden at Worsley New Hall in Salford. This will include the restoration of an eleven-acre walled kitchen garden.

His ability to conceive of gardens on an impressive scale, relate them to their surroundings, and still pay attention to the minutiae of the planting has made him one of Britain's most successful contemporary landscape designers.

***

It helps to have gardening parents. Tom Stuart-Smith was born on St Valentine's Day, 1960, the fourth of six children of a lawyer, Sir Murray Stuart-Smith and his wife, Joan. Tom and his siblings grew up on a Hertfordshire estate, Serge Hill, bought by Joan's father in 1927. Joan, a dab hand at propagating, encouraged her children by handing out trays of plants for them to plant where they fancied.[2] 'We were all made to garden – there wasn't much option. We had to pick tomatoes, disbud chrysanthemums and look after the strawberries,' Tom remembers.[3] 'It was an intensely fortunate, bucolic childhood, and for long summer months blissfully isolated from the outside world.'[4] Tom started gardening seriously in his teens, spending his money on plants and overhauling areas of his parents' garden. In the woods, armed with an axe and billhook, he chopped down sycamores and replanted them with native saplings of the oak and beech. Equally interested in plants and design, he did not, however, imagine gardening could be his career.

From Radley, he won an exhibition to read zoology at Corpus Christi College, Cambridge, but was initially disillusioned, getting a Third and having his exhibition taken away at the end of the first year. 'I thought it would be romantic and heroic, about the zoology of Humboldt and Darwin, rather than about statistics and counting flies.' Although Stuart-Smith realised he would never make a scientist, the course began to assume relevance for him. 'I have always had an interest in phylogeny, evolution and development, and in the origins of why we do what we do. I am interested in deconstruction. I don't just want to look at a garden and think I like that – I have to go back to why a garden is pleasing and why I'm having that reaction to it.'[5]

After leaving Cambridge, he met the landscape architect and town planner, Geoffrey Jellicoe, by then in his eighties, and the seventy-year-old American-born garden designer, Lanning Roper. Stuart-Smith was encouraged by the pristine enthusiasm of the two elderly designers, and by a job offer from Roper. That opportunity, however, was snatched away by Roper's illness and death from cancer six months later. Instead, Stuart-Smith studied landscape design at Manchester University. During the two-year course, he learned to draw and wrote a thesis on Richard Payne Knight. Payne Knight was a theorist of the Picturesque movement, which reacted against 'Capability' Brown in the late eighteenth century. Payne Knight's work appealed to the young Stuart-Smith. 'I loved this colourful, bombastic character who had had enough of all these bland green spaces, and wanted roughness, activity.'[6]

Early stimuli for Stuart-Smith were the design and planting of Hidcote and Sissinghurst; the plantsmanship of Beth Chatto; and the heroic English landscapes of Vanbrugh's and Nesfield's Castle Howard and of William Kent's Rousham. But, finding little to inspire him in contemporary British landscaping, he looked abroad. Like Penelope Hobhouse, he learned from Italian and French gardens, citing the Mannerist Villa Lante near Viterbo as a particular eye-opener. Even more important to him was the Amstel

Park in Amsterdam, made at the end of the Second World War, just using native Dutch plants. 'It's astonishingly beautiful and about what you can do a small range of materials, with light and shade, and water.'[7]

For Stuart-Smith, starting out in the early 1980s, there were few similar projects in Britain. He was offered a job on one at Warrington New Town, but he decided to work for the landscape architect, Hal Moggridge. It was a steep learning curve, as aged just twenty-five, he was left to run a project for Moggridge at the headquarters of Blue Circle Cement. He then had a period with Michael Brown, according to Stuart-Smith, the best of the three designers he has worked for. 'He was a very highly principled man, a socialist and he worked on some of the best community projects of the late seventies and eighties. But I got my timing wrong: I joined him in the mid-1980s by which time Maggie had done her stuff, the GLC was dead, and there was no money for that kind of work.'[8]

***

Stuart-Smith spent two years designing car parks for Sainsbury's, then began working from the home he shared with his wife, Sue (a psychiatrist), and their small daughter, the first of their three children. Their house, The Barn, was opposite his parents' house in Hertfordshire, and was converted from farm buildings. 'The house we live in emerged from the place and the people who live here,' Stuart-Smith wrote in *The Barn Garden*,' his account of his garden's creation. 'First in the seventeenth century when all the materials for its construction would have come from less than a mile away; timber from the surrounding woods or from previous buildings, flints, cobbles and lime from the fields. Then three hundred years later the process was repeated.'[9] That sense of continuity, and awareness of local vernacular and environment, underlies much of Stuart-Smith's work.

More land bought from a local farmer gave Stuart-Smith two acres in which to create a formal garden at The Barn, with a further five acres of wildflower meadows and woodland. The garden was planned in stages, with staggered yew hedging, like stage flats, planted to form open-ended compartments. 'The hedges became our defining framework. To some extent this was a hangover from the Arts and Crafts gardens like Hidcote and Sissinghurst that I had visited with mother in my teens. I absorbed unquestioningly their language of sombre yew, shining beech and trim little box. I thought this is how gardens were made. But I also saw the structure of our plot as being a condensation of the surrounding pattern of Hertfordshire landscape into which our own patch was to be sown, like a bright square on a quilt.'[10]

The planting is mainly herbaceous, with shrubs such as viburnum, Portuguese laurel, eucryphias and osmanthus to give privacy from a flanking lane. He has used plants here as they grow naturally, as he does in other gardens he designs. He wouldn't, for instance, plant clump-forming *Geranium psilostemon* in drifts as he would grasses or tall echinaceas.

Stuart-Smith took on an eighteen-month project in Sussex for Penelope Hobhouse while she was away designing gardens in the United States. She oversaw the project, but Stuart-Smith drew up the planting plans and worked with Jim Russell, creator of the rose garden and arboretum at Castle Howard. Still in his twenties, Stuart-Smith struggled to cope with the demands of clients infuriated by the failure of ceanothus to grow between November and March.

Realising he still needed guidance, he went to work for landscape architect Elizabeth Banks, later president of the Royal Horticultural Society (2010-2013). Banks gave Stuart-Smith an ideal launching pad. He worked on the RHS Garden Rosemoor in Devon, at the British Embassy in Paris, and for Paul Getty, acquiring a prestigious address book in the process. Collaborations with Banks on gardens for the Telegraph newspaper in 1991 and 1992 introduced him to the Chelsea Flower Show, but it was his own first gold medal winning garden for Chanel and Lagerfield in 1998 which, he has said, 'thrust him surprised out into the arena'.[11] 'Le Bosquet de Chanel' was elegance personified: a hedged Baroque garden with an elaborate parterre, a seat based on a William Kent design, and a simple planting of Coco Chanel's favourite white camellias.

This was the first of his eight Chelsea gold medal winners, his next being a garden in 2000 for Laurent-Perrier and the Garden History Society. 'Homage to Le Nôtre' marked the 300th anniversary of the death of Louis XIV's gardener, and featured a parterre based on an original design by a pupil of Le Nôtre, flanked by box-edged beds of colourful bulbs and wildflowers. This harked back to an early eighteenth-century English style as well as referencing current interest in meadow planting.

After two historical gardens, Stuart-Smith feared being type-cast. His subsequent gardens were more progressive, influenced by concerns with naturalistic planting and the effect of the New Perennial movement. The idea of planting perennials and grasses in interweaving drifts had arrived in this country from the Netherlands and Germany in the 1990s and made a significant impact on Stuart-Smith. The planting in his 2003 Laurent-Perrier garden took its inspiration from an English woodland in spring beneath a canopy of flowering *Cornus kousa*, combining grace and romanticism.[12]

His 2006 garden for The Daily Telegraph was a study in romantic modernism. 'We did something that was completely contemporary but also complicated, diverse – and romantic.'[13] Rusted steel walls and grouped multi-stemmed viburnums framed rust-coloured corten steel tanks, and rich planting of dark blue salvias, bronze irises and grasses. The garden had an after-life at the Stuart-Smiths' own home. Their original courtyard garden, made almost twenty years earlier, could have been planted by Gertrude Jekyll, with red-brick paths, and roses within box hedging. By 2006, the planting was overgrown, the hedges the victim of box blight. Sue suggested replacing it with the Chelsea show garden structures and planting for an unmistakably modern look. The rusted corten steel tanks pick up the colour of the roof tiles, while the planting is a subtle blend of grasses, transparent shrubs, such as *Genista aetnensis*, and accents of rusty colour from irises and astrantias.

A sure foundation laid by a decade with Elizabeth Banks, together with the acclaim brought him by Chelsea, emboldened Tom Stuart-Smith to set up in London, sharing offices, although not practice, with fellow garden designer Todd Longstaffe-Gowan.

Stuart-Smith is a cerebral garden-maker who thinks constantly about why he is doing what he is doing, and who draws his inspiration not just from design, but also from music and from literature. A Beethoven enthusiast, he gives his work at times a symphonic quality: he reprises themes across his gardens, repeating key plants and creating crescendos and diminutions. A lover of literature, he has assimilated a sense of narrative structure, and sees garden spaces in those terms: like a writer, he has to decide how much to tell the onlooker and how much to leave to the imagination.

This is evident in one of his most celebrated, and indeed one of his own favourite projects: the garden at Broughton Grange in Oxfordshire, made for Stephen Hester, head of the Royal Bank of Scotland after the financial crash of 2008. Although it is a private house, the garden opens on occasions so the public can view Stuart-Smith's ingenious contemporary interpretation of a walled garden. His design unites elements of Renaissance Italian gardens with modern prairie planting. From a rough sloping field, he created a series of terraces, with a rill dropping down between the first and the second. On the top terrace, drifts of perennials encircle narrow yew pillars, creating a year-round contrast of shape and texture. Stone steps cross the pool on the second terrace, in which clipped bushes are reflected. On the third and bottom terrace is a parterre, planted with tulips in spring, the design of the low box hedging replicating the cell structure of beech, oak and ash leaves.

Top and bottom terraces are lined on one side by beech tunnels which frame the view beyond, as in an Italian Renaissance garden. On the opposite side, three squares of pleached limes link the three terraces. The planting throughout is dense and complicated: Russell Page meets the New Perennial school.

Mount St John in Yorkshire also displays both Stuart-Smith's romantic imagination and his attention to detail. Again, the garden is terraced, with two distinct areas partitioned by yew hedging. Within retaining walls and terraces of buffed sandstone are large zones of planting, with the seedheads of *Phlomis russeliana* (Russian sage) eye-catchers in winter, as at Broughton. Box balls are dotted about through the swathes of planting, their rounded shapes connecting the garden with the undulations of the landscape beyond. Thirty-two thousand perennials were planted in themed, reprised patterns through the vast beds in April 2006. 'The bigger the space, the simpler the effect should be,' Stuart-Smith has been quoted as saying. 'The bigger the effect, the more often it has to be repeated.'[14]

Stuart-Smith's public projects have included the landscape setting for the Bicentenary Glasshouse at the RHS Garden Wisley in 2007. The five-acre amphitheatre encircles lake and glasshouse, and is planted with bands of perennials, including echinaceas, heleniums, achilleas, salvias and grasses. The patterning of the planting scheme becomes more interwoven and complex as it moves towards the west and an area of prairie vegetation, designed and seeded by James Hitchmough, Professor of Landscape and Architecture at Sheffield University. Hitchmough's prairie style is very different from Stuart-Smith's but both enjoyed this collaboration. 'I love working with James, with me providing the context in which his planting works. Having the contrast of his work against something more structured, as at Wisley, can be very effective.'[15]

Hitchmough and his Sheffield colleague, Nigel Dunnett, Professor of Planting Design, Urban Horticulture and Vegetation Technology, were principal design consultants on the Olympic Park in 2012. Sustainability and ecology were key, the relaxed, informal planting the embodiment of cutting-edge horticulture. Dunnett was a designer, too, at Trentham Gardens in Staffordshire, devising woodland planting which blends species and cultivars to create a powerfully naturalistic effect and a long season of interest.[16] Stuart-Smith also worked on Trentham, one of his favourite projects, which has grown 'into something bigger and better than I could have imagined'.[17]

Trentham was a massive undertaking, which also involved the Dutch doyen of New Perennial planting, Piet Oudolf. The original house at Trentham was built in the sixteenth century, with a mile-long lake added in the 1700s by 'Capability' Brown. A century later, Sir Charles Barry, architect of the Houses of Parliament, laid out a titanic Italianate parterre for the Duke of Sutherland. Thereafter, Trentham's history was chequered: the Sutherland family were driven out by the smoke and fumes of nearby Stoke-on-Trent, the house was demolished in 1912 and the estate became an amusement park. By the time a property company bought Trentham in 1995, what were once pencil yews had become baggy monsters, obscuring the view from the parterre to Brown's lake. Most of the garden was derelict. Stuart-Smith was called in to produce a master plan, but it took almost a decade and a public enquiry before planting began.

The eventual result, however, has been an extraordinary success, with Stuart-Smith's contemporary reimagination of Charles Barry's parterre showing him at the top of his game. He retained the structure of Barry's garden in the ten-acre Lower Flower Garden, but doubled the area of planting, using low-maintenance perennials, such as veronicastrums, eupatoriums, and rudbeckias instead of Victorian bedding plants. Tall grasses winding through it invoke the course of the river Trent.

The formality of the layout is dramatically juxtaposed with 'something unpredictable and almost chaotic'.[18]

The yews have been clipped back into exclamation marks among the great drifts of plants, with themes subtly repeated across the huge parterre. Over 70,000 plants, comprised of some 200 species, went into the parterre beds, which are framed by Oudolf's late-summer perennial borders.

Broughton and Trentham display Stuart-Smith's reinterpretation of historic garden design in a contemporary, ecological and sustainable way which speaks to garden visitors. 'One of the functions of public spaces is about engendering a sense of attachment and belonging. The more detail and texture one has in a design, the more capacity it has to attach people and enrich the environment.' He has recently worked on some 160-yard Jekyll borders. 'I haven't replanted her scheme but I have retained some of that Arts and Crafts spirit, using delphiniums, for example. I like these little fragments of memory in a place.'[19]

Influences on Stuart-Smith come not only from garden design. At the Hepworth Wakefield gallery in Yorkshire, his design has been affected as much by African kuba textiles as by gardens. 'It's a question of looking at contemporary place-making, and seeing how the space should be interpreted. I am thinking about exploration, prospect, refuge, things unfolding.'[20] Although there are Stuart-Smith hallmarks, he has proved himself remarkably versatile, creating, in contrast to Broughton and Trentham, a simple garden of tree ferns, ferns and grasses for the dark well of the Keeper's House at the Royal Academy in London, and a minimalist 'Garden of Illusion', with a cast of an *Ilex crenata*, optic fibres, dark serpentine waters and a black granite floor for The Connaught Hotel in London.

He is currently working on a garden in Spain for a bio-dynamic wine grower. Patience is essential, as thousands of tiny shrubs have been planted out and wildflower seed sown in virtually no soil. Half of them died, and the other half grew less than an inch, but, over time, the tougher plants will adapt to the inhospitable conditions.

Stamina will also be needed for the long haul of the RHS Garden Bridgewater. In November 2015, Stuart-Smith was appointed to draw up a master plan for this fifth RHS garden, just outside Greater Salford, Manchester – reputedly the largest gardening project in Europe. 'Multifaceted restoration like this will need a sensitive landscape architect and Tom Stuart-Smith is an inspired choice,' former *Gardeners' World* presenter Nigel Colborn has written. 'Though able to connect with the zeitgeist of current design, he is mature enough to recognise value in earlier traditions.'[21]

This historic awareness and sense of place, combined with an understanding of contemporary concerns and those of his clients, and his analytical approach, have made Stuart-Smith such a presence in early twenty-first century garden design. Design will continue to be pluralistic, Stuart-Smith suggests, within the context of certain inexorable forces: more ecological awareness, lower maintenance, lower overall cost, greater sustainability. He believes it would be a tragedy if, for example, the Arts and Crafts style completely died out, while recognising few people can now afford such labour-intensive gardens. 'It's going to be much more about making a house feel really embedded in its context.'[22]

***

Fashions in gardening come and go, although a love of nature and the desire to enhance and improve our own settings, are surely eternal. Gardening remains as much a political statement as it was in the eighteenth century, when royalty used Kew Gardens to score political points. The new Hive at Kew Gardens, highlighting the importance of bees to our ecosystem, is imparting as much of a message to garden visitors as did William Kent's buildings for Queen Caroline.

How we treat the land in which we live says something crucial about us and our concerns: whether we garden organically or use pesticides is a live political issue. Garden design at the Chelsea Flower Show over the last twenty years has sought to teach lessons about sustainability and respect for the planet. Tom Stuart-Smith, veteran of a dozen Chelseas, appreciates how contemporary political concerns play out in gardening and landscaping. He has confidence that, in the future, individual gardeners may look at the bigger picture: 'With a bit of luck, people will become better gardeners because they will learn more about the process of husbandry. They will think more about how they look after a place, rather than how to look after a given set of plants. People will understand more about the importance of cutting their meadow in July to let the wildflowers get ahead of the grass, rather than spraying roses with different fungicides on alternate weeks. Gardening will become much more holistic.'[23]

Notes

Greenhouse design for RHS, 1818, by Loudon.

PART 1 – THE EARLY PLANTSMEN

Chapter 1 – John Gerard

1. Quoted by Blanche Henrey, *British Botanical Literature Before 1800: Vol. I: The Sixteenth and Seventeenth Centuries History and Bibliography* (London: Oxford University Press, 1975), p.53
2. Robert H. Jeffers, *The Friends of John Gerard (1545-1612): Surgeon and Botanist* (Falls Village, Connecticut: Herb Grower Press, 1967), p.30
3. Jennifer Potter, *Strange Blooms: The Curious Lives and Adventures of the John Tradescants* (London: Atlantic Books, 2006; paperback edition, 2007), pp.96-97
4. Jeffers, op.cit, p.22

5. John Gerard, *The Herball, or General Historie of Plantes* (London: John Norton, 1597), p.1330
6. Jeffers, op.cit, p.10
7. Gerard, op.cit, p.1230
8. Jeffers, op.cit, p.32
9. Gerard, op.cit, pp.1223,1181
10. Anna Pavord, *The Naming of Names: The Search for Order in the World of Plants* (London: Bloomsbury, 2005), p.331; Jeffers, op.cit, p.25
    * Probably what is now called *Teucrium polium*
11. Gerard, op.cit, p. 529
12. Pavord, op.cit, p.334
13. Gerard, op.cit, Introduction (pages unnumbered)
14. www.rcpe.ac.uk/heritage/william-turner. Accessed, 28.3.17
15. Benjamin D. Jackson (ed.), John Gerard, *A catalogue of plants cultivated in the garden of John Gerard, in the years 1596–1599* (London: privately printed, 1876), p.xii
16. Jackson, ibid, p.25
17. Gerard, op.cit, Dedication to William Cecil, second page (pages unnumbered)
18. Quoted by Potter, op.cit, pp.15-16
19. Gerard, op.cit, Commendations (pages unnumbered)
20. Jeffers, op.cit, p.41
21. Gerard, op.cit, p.472; Jackson, *A catalogue*, p.27
22. Alicia Amherst, *A History of Gardening in England* (London: Bernard Quaritch, 1895), p.165
23. Jackson, op.cit, p.xv
24. Gerard, op.cit, To the courteous and well-willing readers (pages unnumbered)
25. ibid, p.1391
26. Agnes R. Arber, *Herbal: Their Origin and Evolution: A Chapter in the History of Botany 1470-1670*, 3rd edition, with an introduction and annotations by William T. Stearn (Cambridge: Cambridge University Press, 1986), p.130
27. Charles E. Raven, *English Naturalists from Neckham to Ray: A Study in the Making of the Modern World* (Cambridge: Cambridge University Press, 1947), p.204
28. Prudence Leith-Ross, *The John Tradescant: Gardeners to the Rose and Lily Queen* (London: Peter Owen, 1984), p.14
29. Jeffers, op.cit, pp.49, 64
30. Gerard, op.cit, p.707
31. F. D. & J. F. M. Hoeniger, *The Growth of Natural History in Stuart England from Gerard to the Royal Society* (Charlottesville: University Press of Virginia: 1969), pp.10-11
32. Gerard, op.cit, pp.1185,701
33. H. Wallis Kew and H. E. Powell, *Thomas Johnson:Botanist and Royalist* (London: Longmans, Green & Co, 1932), pp.50,52
34. Jackson, op.cit, pp.xiv-xv
35. Gerard, op.cit, Commendations (pages unnumbered)

Chapter 2 – The Tradescants

1. Prudence Leith-Ross, *The John Tradescants: Gardeners to the Rose and Lily Queen* (London: Peter Owen, 1984), pp.105,15
2. ibid, p.13
3. Jennifer Potter, *Strange Blooms: The Curious Lives and Adventures of the John Tradescants* (London: Atlantic Books, 2006; paperback edition, 2007), p.1
4. Leith-Ross, op.cit, pp.26-7
5. Dr J. Hamel (translated by Studdy Leigh, John), *England and Russia: the Voyages of John Tradescant the Elder, Sir Hugh Willoughby, Richard Chancellor, Nelson, and Others to the White Sea etc* (London: Richard Bentley, 1854), p.266
6. Leith-Ross, ibid, pp.29-39
7. Potter, op.cit, p.44
8. ibid, p.160
9. ibid, p.220
10. Barry Juniper & Hanneke Grootenboer, *The Tradescants' Orchard: The Mystery of a Seventeenth-Century Painted Fruit Book* (Oxford: Bodleian Library, 2013)
11. Potter, op.cit, p.87
12. Hamel, op.cit, p.259
13. Leith-Ross, op.cit, p.61
14. Hamel, op.cit, p.271
15. ibid, pp.281-2
16. Mea Allan, *The Tradescants: Their Plants, Garden and Museum 1570-1662* (London: Michael Joseph, 1964), p.96
17. Potter, ibid, pp.142-6; Allan, op.cit, p.101
18. Leith-Ross, op.cit, pp.74-75
19. Philippa Gregory, *Earthly Joys* (London: HarperCollins, 1998)
20. Leith-Ross, op.cit, p.78
21. Potter, op.cit, p.180
22. Leith-Ross, op.cit, p.84
23. H. Wallis Kew & H. E. Powell, *Thomas Johnson: Botanist and Royalist* (London: Longmans, Green & Co, 1932), p.37
24. Leith-Ross, op.cit, p.101
25. Leith-Ross, op.cit, p.103; Potter, op.cit, pp.289, 297
26. Jenny Uglow, *A Little History of British Gardening* (London: Chatto & Windus, 2004; new edition with added material, 2017), p.78
27. *Musaeum Tradescantianum*, in Leith-Ross, op.cit, pp.213, 234, 245, 246

PART II – A GROWING CONCERN

Chapter 3 – George London and Henry Wise

1. David Green, *Gardener to Queen Anne: Henry Wise (1653-1738) and the Formal Garden* (London: Oxford University Press, 1956), p.7
2. Charles Quest-Ritson, *The English Garden: A Social History* (London: Viking, 2001), p.84
3. John Miller, *The Stuarts* (London: Hambledon Continuum, 2004; paperback edition, 2006), p.188
4. Ann Somerset, *Queen Anne: The Politics of Passion* (London: HarperPress, 2012), pp.100-101
5. Green, op.cit, p.6

6. John Harvey, *Early Nurserymen* (London: Phillimore, 1974), pp.54-55
7. John Harris, 'London, George (**d.** 1714)', rev. *Oxford Dictionary of National Biography*, Oxford University Press, 2004 [http://www.oxforddnb.com.ezproxy2.londonlibrary.co.uk/view/article/37686, accessed 26 April 2017]
8. Green, op.cit, p.11
9. Quest-Ritson, *The English Garden*, p.84
10. Green, op.cit, p.43
11. George W. Johnson, *A History of English Gardening* (London: Baldwin & Craddock, & Longman & Co, 1829), p.123
12. Green, op.cit, p.24
13. ibid, pp.73,74
14. ibid, p.54
15. David Jacques, 'The History of the Privy Garden', in (ed.) Simon Thurley, *The King's Privy Garden at Hampton Court* (London: Apollo Magazine, 1995), p.32
16. Mavis Batey and Jan Woudstra, *The Story of the Privy Garden at Hampton Court* (London: Barn Elms, 1995), pp.12,24
17. Joseph Addison, *Selections from The Tatler and The Spectator of Steele and Addison* (1709-1712), (ed.) Angus Ross (London: Penguin, 1982), p.380
18. Green, op.cit, pp.33-34
19. ibid, p.126
20. George London and Henry Wise, *The Retir'd Gard'ner* (translated from the French), (London: Jacob Tonson, 1706), preface
21. ibid, preface
22. Green, op.cit, pp.99,108,109
23. ibid, p.120
24. Batty Langley, *New Principles of Gardening* (London: A. Bettesworth & J. Battey, 1728), p.xi
25. Michael Leapmann, *The Ingenious Mr Fairchild: The Story of the Father of the Modern Flower Garden* (London: Headline, 2000), p.55

Chapter 4 – Thomas Fairchild

1. Andrea Wulf, *The Brother Gardeners: Botany, Empire and the Birth of an Obsession* (London: Heinemann, 2008; paperback, London: Windmill Books, 2009), p.15
2. Michael Leapman, *The Ingenious Mr Fairchild: The Story of the Father of the Modern Flower Garden* (London: Headline, 2000), pp.190-191
3. ibid, pp.40-41
4. Thomas Fairchild, *The City Gardener* (London: T Woodward, 1722), p.5
5. Leapman, op.cit, p.42
6. ibid, p.88
7. John Harvey, *Early Nurserymen* (London: Phillimore, 1974), p.77
8. Leapman, op.cit, p.50
9. John Cowell, *The Curious and Profitable Gardener* (London: Weaver Bickerton and Richard Montagu, 1730), Chapter 1
10. ibid, p.34
11. Wulf, op.cit, p.10

12. Richard Bradley, *A Philosophical Account of the Works of Nature* (London: W. Mears, 1721), p.185
13. ibid, p.191
14. Leapman, op.cit, p.140; Harvey, op.cit, p.151; Wulf, op.cit, p.27
15. Leapman, op.cit, p.142
16. ibid, pp.144,190
17. Kathleen Clark, 'What the nurserymen did for us: the roles and influence of the nursery trade on the landscapes and gardens of the eighteenth century', *Garden History*, 40:1 (Summer 2012), p.18
18. Wulf, op.cit, pp.20-21
19. Harvey, op.cit, pp.150,158
20. Clark, 'op.cit,' pp.20-21; Leapman, op.cit, p.124
21. Fairchild, op.cit, p.6
22. ibid, pp.5-6
23. ibid, pp.8,7
24. ibid, p.15
25. ibid, p.12
26. ibid, pp.16,17-18,32
27. ibid, p.29
28. ibid, p.11

Chapter 5 – Philip Miller

1. Sue Minter, *The Apothecaries' Garden: A History of the Chelsea Physic Garden* (Stroud, Gloucestershire: Sutton Publishing, 2000; paperback, Stroud, Gloucestershire: The History Press, 2003), p.19
2. Andrea Wulf, *The Brother Gardeners: Botany, Empire and the Birth of an Obsession* (London: Heinemann, 2008; London: Windmill Books paperback, 2009), p.115
3. John Rogers, *The Vegetable Cultivator* (London: 1839), pp.338-9
4. ibid, p.340
5. Hazel Le Rougetel, *The Chelsea Gardener: Philip Miller 1691-1771* (London: Natural History Museum Publications, 1990), pp.29-30
6. ibid, p.24
7. John Evelyn, *The Diary of John Evelyn* (selected from 1959 Oxford University Press edition, ed. E. S. de Beer; London: Everyman's Library, 2006), p.737
8. Minter, op.cit, pp.6-7
9. Le Rougetel, op.cit, p.22
10. ibid, p.24
11. Minter, op.cit, p.16
12. Le Rougetel, op.cit, p.34
13. ibid, p.27
14. ibid, p.38
15. Rogers, op.cit, p.337
16. Le Rougetel, op.cit, p.53
17. ibid, p.41
18. ibid, p.38
19. Matthew Biggs, *RHS Lessons from Great Gardeners: Forty Gardening Icons and What They Teach Us* (London: Mitchell Beazley, 2015), pp.26-27
20. Jenny Uglow, *A Little History of British Gardening* (London: Chatto & Windus, new edition with added material, 2017), p.147

21. Le Rougetel, op.cit, p.69
22. Wulf, op.cit, p.21
    * The Wardian case was invented in the 1830s by Dr Nathaniel Ward. These glass boxes protected plants from sea winds and temperature variations, while condensation within kept the plants moist.
23. Andrea Wulf, *The Founding Gardeners: How the Revolutionary Generation Created an American Eden* (London: William Heinemann, 2011), p.22
24. Uglow, op.cit, pp.146-147
25. Le Rougetel, op.cit, p.60
26. ibid, p.66
27. ibid, p.48
28. ibid, pp.58-60
29. Wulf, *Brother Gardeners*, p.122
30. Le Rougetel, op.cit, p.82
31. Wulf, *Brother Gardeners*, p.122
32. ibid, p.45
33. Le Rougetel, op.cit, p.93
34. Philip Miller, *The Gardeners Dictionary; Directing what works are necessary to be performed every month in the kitchen, fruit and pleasure gardens, as also in the conservatory and nursery, Eighth edition* (London: Rivington, 1768), p.1
35. ibid, p.1
36. Le Rougetel, op.cit, p.91
37. ibid, p.66
38. Wulf, *Brother Gardeners*, p.35
39. Wulf, *Founding Gardeners*, p.22
40. Uglow, op.cit, p.149
41. Wulf, *Brother Gardeners*, p.60
42. Miller, op.cit, p.1
43. Le Rougetel, op.cit, p.154
44. ibid, pp.154-161
45. Rogers, op.cit, pp.342,343

PART III – THE GREAT DESIGNERS

Chapter 6 – Charles Bridgeman

1. Jeffrey Howarth, *Lodge Park* (London: National Trust guide, 2002), p.26
2. Horace Walpole, *The History of the Modern Taste in Gardening* (ed.) John Dixon Hunt (New York: Ursus Press, 1995), pp.41-42
3. Peter Willis, *Charles Bridgeman and the English Landscape Garden* (London: A. Zwemmer, 1977), pp.26-29
4. Ray Desmond, *Kew: The History of the Royal Botanic Gardens* (London: The Harvill Press with the Royal Botanic Gardens, Kew, 1995), p.6
5. Willis, op.cit, p.70
6. ibid, pp.75, 80-82
7. ibid, p.69
8. ibid, pp.37-40
9. ibid, p.154
10. Desmond, op.cit, p.15
11. John, Lord Hervey, *Some Materials towards Memoirs of the Reign of King George II*, 3 Vols (ed.) Romney Sedgwick (London: King's Printers, 1931),

Vol.II, p.501; Vanessa Berridge, *The Princess's Garden: Royal Intrigue and the Untold Story of Kew* (Stroud, Gloucestershire: Amberley, 2015), p.21

12. Desmond, op.cit, p.11
13. Walpole, op.cit, p.42
14. Roy Strong, *Royal Gardens* (London: BBC Books/Conran Octopus, 1992), pp.40-41
15. Willis, op.cit, p.7
16. ibid, pp.129-130
17. Walpole, op.cit, p.42
18. Tim Richardson, *The Arcadian Friends: Inventing the English Landscape Garden* (London: Bantam Press, 2007; paperback, 2008), p.86
19. Anita Goodwin, *Claremont Landscape Garden* (Swindon, Wiltshire: National Trust guide, 2012), pp.6,9
20. Sophie Chessum, Kevin Rogers and Christopher Rowell, *Claremont* (London: National Trust guide, 2000), p.7
21. Willis, op.cit, p.49; Chessum, op.cit, p.21
22. Chessum, op.cit, p.21
23. Thomas Whately, *Observations on Modern Gardening* (Introduction and commentary by Michael Symes), (Woodbridge, Suffolk: The Boydell Press, 2016), p.63
24. Timothy Mowl, *William Kent: Architect, Designer, Opportunist* (London: Jonathan Cape, 2006; Pimlico paperback, 2007), p.177
25. Michael Bevington, 'Viscount Cobham' in Michael Bevington, with George Clarke, Jonathan Marsden and Tim Knox, *Stowe: The People and the Place* (London: National Trust, 2011), p.27
26. John Martin Robinson, *Temples of Delight: Stowe Landscape Gardens* (London: National Trust, 1990; 2nd edition, 1994, 2002), pp.82,12,28
27. ibid, p.64
28. Willis, op.cit, p.108
29. Robinson, op.cit, p.69-69
30. Willis, op.cit, p.108
31. ibid, pp.115,161-167
32. ibid, pp.115-116,168,43
33. Peter Willis, 'Charles Bridgeman: The royal gardens' in Peter Willis (ed), *Furor Hortensis: Essays on the history of the English Landscape Garden in memory of H F Clark* (Edinburgh: Elysium Press, 1974), p.46
34. Penelope Hobhouse, 'From Geometry to Nature', *The Spectator*, 2 February 2002, p.40
35. Willis, 'Charles Bridgeman', p.55; Walpole, op.cit, p.42
36. Richardson, op.cit, p.84
37. Alexander Pope, *Epistle to Richard Boyle, Earl of Burlington*, ll.69-70 from *The Poems of Alexander Pope* (ed.) John Butt (London: Methuen, 1963), p.590

Chapter 7 – William Kent

1. Horace Walpole, *The History of the Modern Taste in Gardening* (ed.) John Dixon Hunt (New York: Ursus Press, 1995), pp.43
2. Tim Richardson, *The Arcadian Friends: Inventing the English Landscape Garden* (London: Bantam Press, 2007; paperback, 2008), p.289
3. Lord John Hervey, *Some Materials towards Memoirs of the Reign of King George II*, 3 Vols (ed.) Romney Sedgwick (London: King's Printers, 1931), Vol.2, p.581

4. Margaret Jourdain, *The Work of William Kent: Artist, Painter, Designer and Landscape Gardener* (London: Country Life, 1948), pp.30, 35
5. Timothy Mowl, *William Kent: Architect, Designer, Opportunist* (London: Jonathan Cape, 2006; Pimlico paperback, 2007), p.109
6. Christopher Hussey, 'The Aesthetic Background to the Art of William Kent', (introduction) in Jourdain, *William Kent*, p.22
7. Mowl, op.cit, pp.4-5
8. John Dixon Hunt, *William Kent Landscape Garden Designer: An Assessment and Catalogue of his Designs* (London: A. Zwemmer, 1987), p.11
9. Mowl, op.cit, p.33
10. Jourdain, op.cit, p.27
11. James Lees-Milne, *Earls of Creation: Five Great Patrons of Eighteenth-Century Art* (London: Classic Penguin, 2001), p.106
12. H. F. Clark, *The English Landscape Garden* (Gloucester: Alan Sutton, 1980), p.22
13. Humphry Repton to Uvedale Price, 1794, in Dana Arnold, *Rural Urbanism: London Landscapes in the Early Nineteenth Century* (Manchester: Manchester University Press, 2005), p.156
14. Mowl, op.cit, p.62
15. Lucy Worsley, *Courtiers: The Secret History of Kensington Palace* (London: Faber & Faber, 2010), pp.75-80
16. Jourdain, op.cit, p.35
17. ibid, p.35
18. ibid, p.35
19. Walpole, op.cit, p.44
20. Richardson, op.cit, p.273
21. Walpole, op.cit, pp.49, 44
22. Sophie Chessum, Rogers, Kevin, and Rowell, Christopher, *Claremont* (London: National Trust guide, 2000), pp.16-17
23. Mowl, op.cit, p.128
24. Walpole, op.cit, p.47
25. Letter from Sir Thomas Robinson, Historic Manuscripts Commission, *Carlisle*, pp.143-144, quoted by Tom Williamson, *Polite Landscape: Gardens & Society in Eighteenth-Century England* (Stroud: Alan Sutton, 1995), p.59
26. Arthur Young, *The Farmer's Tour through the East of England* (London, 1771), p.32
27. Oliver Garnett, *Stowe* (Swindon, Wiltshire: National Trust guide, 2011), p.23
28. George Clarke, 'William Kent: Heresy in Stowe's Elysium', in (ed) Peter Willis, *Furor Hortensis: Essays on the history of the English Landscape Garden in memory of H. F. Clark* (Edinburgh: Elysium Press, 1974), p.51
29. Young, op.cit, pp.39-40
30. Walpole, op.cit, pp.47-48
31. Kenneth Woodbridge, 'William Kent's Gardening: The Rousham Letters', *Apollo*, C: 152 (New Series), (October 1974), p.282
32. Mowl, op.cit, p.240
33. Woodbridge, 'op.cit, pp.288, 284
34. Mowl, op.cit, p.234
35. ibid, p.245
36. Jourdain, op.cit, p.40
37. Miles Hadfield, Robert Harling, & Leonie Highton, *British Gardeners: A Biographical Dictionary* (London: A. Zwemmer, 1980), p.168
38. Woodbridge, 'op.cit, p.291

Chapter 8 – 'Capability' Lancelot Brown

1. Edward Hyams, *Capability Brown and Humphry Repton* (London: J. M. Dent, 1971), p.92
2. Jane Brown, *The Omnipotent Magician: Lancelot 'Capability Brown 1716-1783* (London: Chatto & Windus, 2011), p.262
3. Sarah Rutherford, *Capability Brown and His Landscape Gardens* (London: National Trust, 2016), p.60
4. Jenny Uglow, *A Little History of British Gardening* (London: Chatto & Windus, 2004; new edition with added material, 2017), p.160
5. Brown, op.cit, pp.192-193
6. Alexander Pope, *Epistle IV. To Richard Boyle, Earl of Burlington,* Alexander Pope, *The Poems of Alexander Pope* (ed.) John Butt (London: Methuen, 1963), p.590
7. William Cowper, *The Task*, Book III, 'The Garden' (1785), William Cowper, *Poems* (London: J. M. Dent, 1931), p.362
8. Brown, op.cit, pp.37-38
9. George Clarke, 'William Kent: Heresey in Stowe's Elysium' in (ed.) Peter Willis, *Furor Hortensis: Essays on the history of the English Landscape Garden in memory of H. F. Clark* (Edinburgh: Elysium Press, 1974), p.53
10. Hyams, op.cit, p.46
11. Dorothy Stroud, *Capability Brown* (London: Faber & Faber, 1975), p.52
12. A letter from Lancelot Brown to George Bowes, 1750, in Brown, op.cit, p.58
13. John Martin Robertson, *Temples of Delight: Stowe Landscape Gardens* (London: National Trust, 1990; 2nd edition, 1994, 2002), pp.76-77
14. Paul Langford, *A Polite and Commercial People: England 1727-1783* (Oxford: Clarendon Press, 1989), p.435
15. Matt Shinn, *Croome* (Swindon, Wilts: National Trust guide, 2016), p.6
16. Stroud, op.cit, p.58
17. Brown, op.cit, p.266
18. Hyams, op.cit, p.18
19. Brown, op.cit, p.186
20. ibid, pp.79-81
21. ibid, p.234
22. Stroud, op.cit, pp.66-67
23. Brown, op.cit, p.69
24. Horace Walpole, *The History of the Modern Taste in Gardening* (ed.) John Dixon Hunt (New York: Ursus Press, 1995), p.57
25. Stroud, op.cit, pp.68-69
26. Brown, op.cit, p.97
27. Stroud, op.cit, p.86
28. Brown, op.cit, p.261
29. ibid, p.298
30. ibid, pp.159-161
31. ibid, p.150
32. Michael Symes, 'William Pitt the Elder: The Gran Mayo of Landscape Gardening, *Garden History*, 24:1 (Summer 1996), p.127
33. Brown, op.cit, p.249
34. Arthur Young, *A Six Months Tour through the North of England containing an Account of the Present State of Agriculture, Manufactures and Population in Several Counties of this Kingdom* (London, 1770), pp.13-14

35. Brown, op.cit, p.282
36. Sophie Chessum, Kevin Rogers and Christopher Rowell *Claremont* (London: National Trust guide, 2000), pp.42,39
37. Timothy Mowl, *William Kent: Architect, Designer, Opportunist* (London: Jonathan Cape, 2006; Pimlico paperback, 2007), p.175
38. William Chambers, *A Dissertation on Oriental Gardening* (London: 1773; 2nd edition), pp.v-vi
39. Thomas Hinde, *Capability Brown: The Story of a Master Gardener* (London: Hutchinson, 1986), p.152
40. Thomas Whately, *Observations on Modern Gardening* (Introduction and commentary) Michael Symes (Woodbridge, Suffolk: The Boydell Press, 2016), p.31

Chapter 9 – Humphry Repton

1. Jane Austen, *Mansfield Park* (1814; London: Hamish Hamilton, 1949), pp.55,53,55
2. Twigs Way, *A Passion for Gardening: How the British Became a Nation of Gardeners* (London: Prion, 2015), p.19
3. Humphry Repton, *Memoirs* (eds.) Ann Gore & George Carter (Norwich, Norfolk: Michael Russell, 2005), p.25
4. Stephen Daniels, *Humphry Repton: Landscape Gardening and the Geography of Georgian England* (New Haven & London: Yale University Press, 1999), p.1
5. Daniels, op.cit, p.14
6. Edward Hyams, *Capability Brown and Humphry Repton* (London: J. M. Dent, 1971), p.116
7. Kedrun Laurie, 'Humphry Repton', in George Carter, Patrick Goode and Kedrun Laurie, *Humphry Repton: Landscape Gardener 1752-1818* (Norwich: Sainsbury Centre for Visual Arts, 1982), p.6
8. Dorothy Stroud, *Humphry Repton* (London: Country Life, 1962), p.21
9. Hyams, op.cit, p.122
10. Daniels, op.cit, pp.32-33
11. Hyams, op.cit, p.125
12. Daniels, op.cit, p.2
13. Laura Mayer, *Humphrey Repton* (Oxford: Shire Publications, 2014), p.10
14. Repton, *Memoirs*, pp.77,78
15. Hyams, op.cit, p.152
16. Mayer, op.cit, p.26
17. Humphry Repton, *Observations on the Theory and Practice of Landscape Gardening* (1803) in John Claudius Loudon, *The Landscape Gardening and Landscape Architecture of the Late Humphry Repton, Esq* (London: Forgotten Books, 2015), p.132
18. Carter, Goode and Laurie, op.cit, p.18
19. Repton, *Memoirs*, pp.25-26
20. Mayer, op.cit, p.20
21. Repton, *Memoirs*, p.77
22. Daniels, op.cit, pp.34-35
23. ibid, p.37
24. Carter, Goode and Laurie, op.cit, p.19

25. Repton, *Theory and Practice*, pp.134,135-136
26. William Chambers, *A Dissertation on Oriental Gardening* (London: 1773; 2nd edition), p,vi
27. Mayer, op.cit, p.28
28. ibid, p.30
29. William Wordsworth, *Lines written a few miles above Tintern Abbey* in Wordsworth & Coleridge, *Lyrical Ballads 1798* (ed.) W. J. B. Owen (London: Oxford University Press, 2nd edition, 1975), p.112
30. Stephen Copley and Peter Garside (eds.), 'Introduction' in *The Politics of the Picturesque: Literature, landscape and aesthetics since 1770* (Cambridge: Cambridge University Press, 1994), p.3
31. Repton, *Sketches and Hints on Landscape Gardening* in Loudon, *Landscape Gardening*, pp.104,105,29
32. Mayer, op.cit, p.48
33. Dorothy Stroud, 'Humphry Repton: A forgotten landscape at Wembley Park' in Peter Willis (ed.), *Furor Hortensis: Essays on the history of the English Landscape Garden in memory of H. F. Clark* (Edinburgh: Elysium Press, 1974), p.73
34. John Dixon Hunt, *Gardens and the Picturesque: Studies in the History of Landscape Architecture* (Cambridge, Massachusetts: The MIT Press, 1992), p.151
35. Stroud, op.cit, p.137
36. Laurie in Carter, Goode and Laurie, op.cit, p.22
37. Repton, *Memoirs*, p.156

PART IV – THE INDUSTRIAL AGE

Chapter 10 – John Claudius Loudon

1. Jane Loudon, 'A short account of the life and writings of John Claudius Loudon' in John Gloag, *Mr. Loudon's England* (Newcastle: Oriel Press, 1970), pp.194-195
2. John Sales, 'Preface', in John Claudius Loudon, *In Search of English Gardens: The Travels of John Claudius Loudon and his Wife Jane* (London: Century, 1990), p.5
3. Loudon, 'A short account', p.182
4. Quoted by Dr David Marsh, 'John Claudius Loudon and the rise of the amateur gardener' [http://www.feltonparkgreenhouse.org/history/john-claudius-loudon-an-appreciation, accessed 20 July 2017]
5. Loudon, 'A short account', pp.185-186
6. Marsh, op.cit
7. Stephen Daniels, *Humphry Repton: Landscape Gardening and the Geography of Georgian England* (New Haven & London: Yale University Press, 1999), pp.143-144
8. James Steven Curl, 'John Claudius Loudon', *Oxford Art Online* (updated and revised 21 July 2004 [http://www.oxfordartonline.com:80/subscriber/article/grove/art/T052089, accessed 18 July 2017]
9. Daniels, op.cit, p.145
10. Loudon, 'A short account', pp.193,194

11. ibid, p.195
12. Quoted by Geoffrey Taylor, *Some Nineteenth Century Gardeners* (London: Skeffington, 1951), p.23
13. Brent Elliott, 'Loudon, John Claudius (1783-1843): landscape gardener and horticultural writer', *Oxford Dictionary of National Biography* (Oxford: Oxford University Press, 2004; online edn, May 2010) [http://www.oxforddnb.com.ezproxy.londonlibrary.co.uk/view/article/17031, accessed 17 July 2017]
14. Loudon, 'A short account', p.197
15. Taylor, op.cit, p.24
16. Loudon, 'A short account', p.201
17. Kate Colquhoun, *A Thing in Disguise: The Visionary Life of Joseph Paxton* (London: Fourth Estate, 2003; paperback, HarperPerennial, 2004), p.26
18. Elliott, op.cit
19. Loudon, 'A short account', p.202
20. Mark Laird, 'John Claudius Loudon (1783-1843) and the field's identity', *Studies in the History of Gardens and Designed Landscapes*, 34:3 (2014), p.250
21. Colquhoun, op.cit, p.24
22. Priscilla Boniface, 'Introduction' to Loudon, *In Search of English Gardens*, pp.13-14
23. Laird, op.cit, pp.250-251
24. ibid, p.251
25. Loudon, 'A short account', p.205
26. Bea Howe, *Lady with Green Fingers: The Life of Jane Loudon* (London: Country Life, 1961), pp.36,54,55
27. Loudon, 'A short account', p.207
28. ibid, p.208
29. Colquhoun, op.cit, p.82
30. Loudon, 'A short account', p.206
31. Loudon, *In Search of English Gardens*, p.57
32. ibid, p.74
33. ibid, pp.73-73
34. Loudon, 'A short account', p.211
35. John Claudius Loudon, *The Landscape Gardening and Landscape Architecture of the Late Humphry Repton, Esq, Being His Entire Works on These Subject, a New Edition, with an Historical and Scientific Introduction, a Systematic Analysis, a Biographical Notice, Notices, and a Copious Alphabetical Index* (London: Forgotten Books, 2015), p.iii
36. Brent Elliott, 'Nesfield in his Victorian Context', in (ed) Christopher Ridgway, *William Andrews Nesfield: Victorian Landscape Architect – Papers from the Bicentenary Conference, The King's Manor, York, 1994* (York: Institute of Advanced Architectural Studies, University of York, 1996), p.9
37. Loudon, *Landscape Gardening*, p.77
38. Loudon, 'A short account', p.210
39. ibid, p.214
40. Elliott, 'Loudon, John Claudius'
41. Howe, op.cit, p.96
42. Loudon, 'A short account', p.216

Chapter 11 – William Nesfield

1. Shirley Rose Evans, *Masters of their Craft: The Art, Architecture and Garden Design of the Nesfields* (Cambridge: Lutterworth Press, 2014), p.4
2. ibid, p.3
3. Shirley Rose Evans, 'William Andrews Nesfield: An Introduction to his Life and Work', in Christopher Ridgway (ed.), *William Andrews Nesfield: Victorian Landscape Architect – Papers from the Bicentenary Conference, The King's Manor, York, 1994* (York: Institute of Advanced Architectural Studies, University of York, 1996), p.3
4. Evans, 'William Andrews Nesfield', p.4
5. Evans, *Masters of their Craft*, p.18
6. ibid, pp.19-22
7. A friend of the Royal Watercolour Society, 'A view of the works of William Andrews Nesfield', in M. J. Tooley (ed.), *William Andrews Nesfield 1794-1881: Essays to Mark the Bicentenary of his Birth* (Witton-le-Wear, Co Durham: Michaelmas Books, 1994), p.8
8. Evans, *Masters of their Craft*, p.38
9. Brent Elliott, 'Master of the Geometric Art', *The Garden Journal of the Royal Horticultural Society*, 106 (1981), p.488
10. Brent Elliott, 'Nesfield in his Victorian Context', in *William Andrews Nesfield*, p.9
11. Evans, *Masters of the Craft*, p.65
12. Elliott, 'Nesfield in his Victorian Context', p.9
13. Evans, *Masters of their Craft*, p.52
14. ibid, p.55
15. Michael Tooley, 'William Andrews Nesfield: Artistical Landscape Gardener', in Michael J. Tooley (ed.), *William Andrews Nesfield 1794-1881: Essays to Mark the Bicentenary of His Birth* (Witton-le-Wear, Co Durham: Michaelmas Books, 1994), p.23
16. Shirley Rose Evans, *Nesfield's Monster Work: The Gardens of Witley Court* (Worcester: Peter Huxtable Designs, 1994), p.13
17. Evans, 'William Andrews Nesfield', p.7
18. Tooley, 'William Andrews Nesfield', p.23
19. Evans, *Masters of their Craft*, p.57
20. Evans, 'William Andrews Nesfield', p.6
21. Christopher Ridgway, 'William Andrews Nesfield: Between Uvedale Price and Isambard Kingdom Brunel,' *Journal of Garden History*, 13:1/2 (Spring/Summer 1993), p.77
22. Christopher Ridgway, 'Stoke Edith: An Historical Case-Study', in *William Andrews Nesfield*, p.18
23. Evans, *Nesfield's Monster Work*, p.14
24. Elliott, 'Master of the Geometric Art', p.491
25. Evans, 'William Andrews Nesfield', p.7
26. M. J. Tooley, *William Andrews Nesfield – Bicentenary Exhibition* (Witton-le-Wear, Co Durham: Michaelmas Books, 1994), p.8
27. Christopher Ridgway, 'Design and Restoration at Castle Howard', in Ridgway (ed.), *William Andrews Nesfield*, pp.39-47
28. Shirley Rose Evans, 'Master Designer', *The Antique Collector*, 63:9 (October 1992), p.54

29. Mark Brown, 'The Gardens and Fountains of Witley Court', in Ridgway (ed.), *William Andrews Nesfield*, p.26
30. Evans, *Masters of their Craft*, p.80
31. ibid, p.79
32. Tooley, *William Andrews Nesfield*, p.12
33. Ray Desmond, *Kew: The History of the Royal Botanic Gardens* (London: The Harvill Press with the Royal Botanic Gardens, Kew, 1995), p.174
34. Allen Paterson, *The Gardens at Kew* (London: Frances Lincoln, 2008), pp.104-105
35. Evans, *Masters of their Craft*, pp.150,151
36. Elliott, 'Nesfield in his Victorian Context', p.13; Brent Elliott, *Victorian Gardens* (London: B T Batsford, 1990), p.166
37. Obituaries quoted by Tooley, 'William Andrews Nesfield', p.22
38. Ridgway, 'William Andrews Nesfield', p.86
39. Evans, *Masters of their Craft*, p.153

Chapter 12 – Sir Joseph Paxton

1. Kate Colquhoun, *A Thing in Disguise: The Visionary Life of Joseph Paxton* (London: Fourth Estate, 2003; HarperPerennial paperback, 2004), p.181
2. ibid, p.31
3. Mark Girouard, 'Genius of Sir Joseph Paxton', *Country Life*, 138, Part 2 (9 December 1965), p.1606
4. Violet R. Markham, *Paxton and the Bachelor Duke* (London: Hodder & Stoughton, 1935), pp.4-5
5. Colquhoun, op.cit, p.12
6. ibid, p.26
7. ibid, p.25
8. ibid, p.22
9. Tudor Edwards, 'Sir Joseph Paxton: the versatile gardener', *History Today*, 15:12 (December 1965), p.856
10. Amanda Foreman, *Georgiana, Duchess of Devonshire* (London: HarperCollins, 1998; paperback edition, 1999), p.400
11. The Duchess of Devonshire, *The Garden at Chatsworth* (London: Frances Lincoln, 1999), p.38
12. Foreman, op.cit, p.400
13. James Lees-Milne, *The Bachelor Duke: A Life of William Spencer Cavendish 6th Duke of Devonshire 1790-1858* (London: John Murray, 1991), p.2
14. Markham, op.cit, p.21
15. ibid, p.36
16. Devonshire, op.cit, p.49
17. John Anthony, *An Illustrated Life of Sir Joseph Paxton 1803-1865* (Princes Risborough, Buckinghamshire: Shire Publications, 1992), p.16
18. Devonshire, op.cit, pp.39,58
19. John Kenworthy-Browne and Lin Barton; bibliography updated by Lin Barton, 'Paxton, Sir Joseph', *Oxford Art Online* (2007-2017; bibliography updated 22 September 2015) [http://www.oxfordartonline.com.ezproxy2.londonlibrary.co.uk/subscriber/article/grove/art/T065884]
20. Anthony, op.cit, p.12

21. Devonshire, op.cit, p 55; Colquhoun, op.cit, p.61
22. Devonshire, op.cit, pp.55,58
23. John McKean, *Crystal Palace, Joseph Paxton and Charles Fox* (London: Phaidon, 1994), p.14; Anthony, op.cit, p.8
24. Devonshire, op.cit, p.491
25. ibid, pp.74-75
26. Colquhoun, op.cit, p.64
27. ibid, p.78
28. Devonshire, op.cit, p.69
29. ibid, pp.69.71
30. ibid, p.71
31. Anthony, op.cit, p.8
32. Devonshire, op.cit, p.96
33. Markham, op.cit, pp.31-32
34. ibid, p.7
35. Colquhoun, op.cit, pp.48-49
36. ibid, pp.139-142,137
37. ibid, pp.84-86
38. ibid, p.116
39. ibid, p.130
40. Edwards, op.cit, p.859
41. Colquhoun op.cit, p.157
42. Anthony, op.cit, p.14
43. Colquhoun, op.cit, pp.158-160
44. Anthony, op.cit, pp.24,26
45. John McKean, *Crystal Palace*, p.15
46. Anthony, op.cit, p.27
47. Edwards, op.cit, p.860
48. Anthony, op.cit, pp.31-32
49. Edwards, op.cit, p.862
50. Colquhoun, op.cit, p.247
51. ibid, p.242
52. ibid, p.252

PART V – THE FLOWER GARDEN

Chapter 13 – William Robinson

1. Mea Allan, *William Robinson 1838-1935: Father of the English Flower Garden* (London: Faber & Faber, 1982), pp.19,20
2. Richard Bisgrove, *William Robinson: The Wild Gardener* (London: Frances Lincoln, 2008), pp.27-28
3. Allan, op.cit, p.120
4. ibid, p.28
5. Geoffrey Taylor, *Some Nineteenth Century Gardeners* (London: Skeffington, 1951), p.70; Bisgrove, *William Robinson*, p.32
6. Allan, op.cit, pp.40-41,43
7. Miles Hadfield, *A History of British Gardening* (London: Spring Books, 1969), p.360
8. Bisgrove, *William Robinson*, p.32

9. Bisgrove, *William Robinson*, p.32; Taylor, op.cit, p.71
10. Bisgrove, *William Robinson*, p.54
11. Allan, op.cit, p.80
12. William Robinson, *Alpine Flowers for English Gardens* (London: John Murray, 2nd17 edition, 1875), pp.xv,x
13. ibid, p.x
14. ibid, p.xiii
15. Sally Festing, *Gertrude Jekyll* (London: Viking, 1991; Penguin paperback, 1993), p.40
16. Brent Elliott, *Victorian Gardens* (London: B. T. Batsford, 1990), p.166
17. William Robinson, *The English Flower Garden* (London: Bloomsbury Gardening Classics, 1996; paperback edition, 1998), pp.3,20
18. Bea Howe, *Lady with Green Fingers: The Life of Jane Loudon* (London: Country Life, 1961), p.13
19. Richard Bisgrove, 'The Wild Garden, 1870, by William Robinson and Charles Nelson; The Wild Garden, 1894, by William Robinson and Rick Darke', *Garden History*, 39:1 (Summer 2011), p.129
20. William Robinson, *The Wild Garden* (London: John Murray, 1870), p.158
21. Bisgrove, *William Robinson*, p.83
22. ibid, pp.85,87
23. Allan, op.cit, p.102
24. ibid, p.129
25. ibid, p.100
26. Bisgrove, *William Robinson*, pp.91-92,240
27. Robinson, *The English Flower Garden*, pp.20,22
28. Elliott, op.cit, p.161
29. Bisgrove, *William Robinson*, p.143
30. Robinson, *The English Flower Garden*, p.23
31. Allan, op.cit, pp.164,165
32. Bisgrove, *William Robinson*, pp.173-174
33. Taylor, op.cit, p.87
34. Bisgrove, *William Robinson*, p.239
35. Allan, op.cit, p.226
36. Bisgrove, *William Robinson*, p.247

Chapter 14 – Gertrude Jekyll

1. Sir Edwin Lutyens, 'Foreword', in Francis Jekyll, *Gertrude Jekyll: A Memoir* (London: Jonathan Cape, 1934), p.7
2. Judith B. Tankard, 'Gertrude Jekyll's Vision of Garden and Wood', in Judith B. Tankard and Michael R. Van Valkenburgh (eds.), *Gertrude Jekyll: A Vision of Garden and Wood* (London: John Murray, 1989), p.3
3. Betty Massingham, *A Century of Gardeners* (London: Faber & Faber), p.122
4. Jekyll, *Gertrude Jekyll*, pp.20-21
5. ibid, pp.22-23
6. Sally Festing, *Gertrude Jekyll* (London: Viking, 1991; Penguin paperback, 1993), pp.13-14

7. Jekyll, *Gertrude Jekyll*, p.26
8. Twigs Way, *Gertrude Jekyll* (Oxford: Shire Publications, 2016), p.5
9. Festing, op.cit, p.39
10. Way, op.cit, p.12
11. Jane Brown, *Miss Gertrude Jekyll 1843-1932 Gardener* (London: Architectural Association, 1981), p.3
12. Way, op.cit, p.13
13. Jekyll, *Gertrude Jekyll*, pp.83-4
14. Joan Edwards, 'Gertrude Jekyll: prelude and fugue', in Michael Tooley and Primrose Arnander (eds.), *Gertrude Jekyll: Essays on the Life of a Working Amateur* (Witton-le-Wear, Co. Durham: Michaelmas Books, 1995), pp.56,44
15. Mavis Batey, 'Gertrude Jekyll and the Arts and Crafts Movement', in Tooley and Arnander, *Gertrude Jekyll*, p.64
16. Jekyll, *Gertrude Jekyll*, pp.82,83,84
17. ibid, p.114
18. Way, op.cit, p.11
19. Festing, op.cit, p.105
20. Gertrude Jekyll, 'A Gardening Credo', in Gertrude Jekyll, *On Gardening* (London: Studio Vista, 1966), p.25
21. Festing, op.cit, p.104; Way, op.cit, pp.12-13
22. Quoted as the epigraph to Jekyll, *On Gardening*
23. Penelope Hobhouse, 'Introduction', in Penelope Hobhouse (ed.), *Gertrude Jekyll on Gardening: An Anthology* (London: William Collins, 1983; Papermac paperback, 1985), p.14
24. Gertrude Jekyll, *Colour Schemes for the Flower Garden* (Introduced and revised by Graham Stuart Thomas), (London: Country Life, 1908; this edition, London: Penguin Books, 1983), p.54
25. Tankard, 'Gertrude Jekyll's vision', p.4
26. Way, op.cit, p.15
27. Judith B. Tankard, 'The Seasons of Munstead Wood 1888-1914', in Tankard and Van Valkenburgh, *Gertrude Jekyll: A Vision*, p.29
28. Jekyll, *Gertrude Jekyll*, p.118
29. Festing, op.cit, p.130
30. Massingham, op.cit, p.117
31. Festing, op.cit, p.205
32. Way, op.cit, p.30
33. ibid, p.35,37-38
34. Massingham, op.cit, p.120
35. Batey, 'Gertrude Jekyll', p.65
36. Jekyll, 'Design and Ornament', in Jekyll, *On Gardening*, p.79
37. Jekyll, *Colour Schemes*, pp.xiii-xiv
38. Festing, op.cit, p.261
39. ibid, p.173
40. Jekyll, *Colour Schemes*, p.xv
41. Festing, op.cit, p.300
42. ibid, p.306
43. Hobhouse, 'Introduction', in Hobhouse (ed.), *Gertrude Jekyll*, pp.14-15

Chapter 15 – Lawrence Johnston

1. Harold Nicolson, *Diaries and Letters 1945-1962*, (ed.) Nigel Nicolson (London: Collins, 1968), p.245
2. Graham S. Pearson, *Lawrence Johnston: The Creator of Hidcote* (Hidcote Bartrim, Chipping Campden: Hidcote Books, 2013), p.32
3. ibid, p.54
4. Ethne Clarke, *Hidcote: The Making of a Garden* (London and New York: W. W. Norton, 2009), pp.44-46
5. Thomas H. Mawson, *The Art and Craft of Garden Making* (London: B. T. Batsford, 2nd edition, 1901), pp.2,5,xii
6. ibid, p.117
7. Jane Brown, *Vita's Other World: A Gardening Biography of Vita Sackville-West* (London: Viking, 1985; London: Penguin paperback, 1987), p.162
8. Pearson, op.cit, p.89
9. ibid, pp.100-101
10. Anna Pavord, *Hidcote Manor Garden, Gloucestershire* (London: National Trust, 1993), p.18
11. James Lees-Milne, *Diaries, 1942-1954* (abridged and introduced by Michael Bloch), (London: John Murray, 2006; paperback, 2007), p.95
12. Clarke, op.cit, pp.40,115
13. ibid, p.74
14. Allyson Hayward, *Norah Lindsay: The Life and Art of a Garden Designer* (London: Frances Lincoln, 2007), p.190
15. Clarke, op.cit, p.116
16. Roy Strong, 'Foreword', in Clarke, op.cit, p.15
17. Lees-Milne, *Diaries*, footnote, p.358
18. Hayward, op.cit, p.190-191,192-193
19. Pearson, op.cit, pp.172,175
20. ibid, p.25
21. Hayward, op.cit, p.192
22. Pearson, op.cit, p.226
23. Lees-Milne, op.cit, p.349
24. ibid, p.358
25. Russell Page, *The Education of a Gardener* (London: William Collins, 1962; London: The Harvill Press paperback, 1995), p.19
26. Clarke, op.cit, p.172

Chapter 16 – Vita Sackville-West

1. Juliet Nicolson, *Woman's Hour* interview, 2016
2. Nigel Nicolson, *Portrait of a Marriage* (London: Weidenfeld & Nicolson, 1973), p.3
3. Victoria Glendinning, *Vita: The Life of V. Sackville-West* (London: Weidenfeld & Nicolson, 1983), p.168
4. Jane Brown, *Vita's Other World: A Gardening Biography of V. Sackville-West* (London: Viking, 1985; London: Penguin paperback, 1987), p.214
5. ibid, p.13
6. Nigel Nicolson, *Long Life: Memoirs* (London: Weidenfeld & Nicolson, 1997), p.6

7. Juliet Nicolson, *A House Full of Daughters* (London: Chatto & Windus, 2016), p.131
8. V. Sackville-West, *The Edwardians* (London: Penguin Books, 1935), p.187
9. Glendinning, op.cit, pp.14-15
10. Brown, op.cit, p.20
11. ibid, pp.28,35-36
12. Glendinning, op.cit, p.93
13. Brown, op.cit, p.57
14. ibid, p.64,61
15. Robert Becker, *Nancy Lancaster: Her Life, Her World, Her Art* (New York: Albert A. Knopf, 1996), pp.196,198
16. Brown, op.cit, p.62
17. ibid, p.64
18. ibid, p.66
19. V. Sackville-West, *The Illustrated Garden Book* (A new anthology by Robin Lane Fox), (London: Michael Joseph, 1986), p.149
20. Brown, op.cit, p.67
21. Brown, op.cit, p.72; Glendinning, op.cit, p.147
22. Glendinning, op.cit, p.147
23. V. Sackville-West, 'Part One' in Nicolson, *Portrait of a Marriage*, p.45
24. Glendinning, op.cit, p.87
25. V. Sackville-West, 'Part Three' in Nicolson, *Portrait of a Marriage*, p.109
26. Nicolson, *Portrait of a Marriage*, p.139
27. Brown, op.cit, pp.46-47
28. Glendinning, op.cit, p.142
29. Harold Nicolson, *Diaries and Letters, 1930-39* (ed.) Nigel Nicolson, (London: Collins, 1966), p.42
30. Glendinning, op.cit, p.223
31. Nicolson, *Diaries and Letters, 1930-39*, pp.47-48
32. ibid, *1930-39*, p.57
33. Anne Scott-James, *Sissinghurst: The Making of Garden* (London: Michael Joseph, 1975), p.45
34. Brown, op.cit, p.111
35. Nicolson, *Long Life*, pp.12,2
36. James Lees-Milne, *Diaries, 1942-1954* (abridged and introduced by Michael Bloch), (London: John Murray, 2006; paperback, 2007), pp.404-405
37. Nicolson, *Diaries and Letters, 1930-39*, p.56
38. Glendinning, op.cit, p.266
39. ibid, p.292
40. Lees-Milne, *Diaries*, p.405
41. V. Sackville-West, *The Land* in *The Land & The Garden* (new edition, with an introduction by Nigel Nicolson), (Exeter, Devon: Webb & Bower in association with Michael Joseph, 1989), p.15
42. Scott-James, op.cit, p.78
43. V. Sackville-West, *The Illustrated Garden Book* (A new anthology by Robin Lane Fox), (London: Michael Joseph, 1986), p.57
44. Nigel Nicolson, 'Introduction' in *The Land & The Garden*, p.11
45. Sackville-West, *The Garden*, p.153
46. Glendinning, op.cit, p.342

47. Scott-James, op.cit, p.108
48. Robin Lane Fox, 'Introduction' in *The Illustrated Garden Book*, pp.9-10
49. Matthew Dennison, *Behind the Mask: The Life of Vita Sackville-West* (London: William Collins, 2014; paperback edition, 2015), p.280
50. Brown, op.cit, p.198
51. Scott-James, op.cit, p.107
52. Sackville-West, *The Illustrated Garden Book*, pp.91,136
53. Glendinning, op.cit p.293
54. Nicolson, *A House Full of Daughters*, p.133
55. Harold Nicolson, *Diaries and Letters, 1945-1962* (ed.) Nigel Nicolson (London: Collins, 1968), p.415
56. Nicolson, *Long Life*, p.17

Chapter 17 – Margery Fish

1. Quoted by Susan Chivers and Suzanne Woloszynska, *The Cottage Garden: Margery Fish at East Lambrook Manor* (London: Michael Joseph, 1990), p.3
2. Graham Rice, 'Foreword', in Margery Fish, *Cottage Garden Flowers* (London: W. H. & L. Collingridge, 1961; new edition, London: Batsford, 2016), p.5
3. Chivers and Woloszynska, op.cit, p.52
4. Horwood, Catherine, 'Fish, Margery (1892–1969)', *Oxford Dictionary of National Biography*, Oxford University Press, Oct 2008 [http://www.oxforddnb.com.ezproxy2.londonlibrary.co.uk/view/article/48830, accessed 29 Aug 2017]
5. Alfred M. Gollin, *The Observer and J. L. Garvin 1908-1914: A Study in a Great Editorship* (London: Oxford University Press, 1960), pp.1-2; Simon Jenkins, *Newspapers: The Power and the Money* (London: Faber & Faber, 1979), p.21
6. Jenkins, op.cit, p.20
7. Chivers and Woloszynska, op.cit, p.6
8. Horwood, op.cit
9. Chivers and Woloszynska, op.cit, p.6
10. ibid, p.7
11. Margery Fish, *We Made a Garden* (London: W. H. & L. Collingridge, 1956; new edition, London: Batsford, 2016), p.9
12. Fish, *We Made a Garden*, p.10
13. ibid, p.7
14. Fish, *Cottage Garden Flowers* (London: W. H. & L. Collingridge, 1961; new edition, London: Batsford, 2016), p.88
15. Fish, *We Made a Garden*, p.11
16. Chivers and Woloszynska, *The Cottage Garden*, p.10
17. Rice, 'Foreword', in Fish, *Cottage Garden Flowers*, p.5
18. Fish, *We Made a Garden*, p.7
19. ibid, p.7
20. ibid, pp.7,8
21. ibid, p.39
22. ibid, pp.7,13
23. ibid, p.50
24. ibid, pp.30,31
25. ibid, p.41

26. ibid, pp.40,41
27. ibid, p.95
28. Chivers and Woloszynska, op.cit, p.48
29. ibid, pp.48,49
30. Fish, *We Made a Garden*, p.7
31. Chivers and Woloszynska, op.cit, p.ix
32. Fish, *Cottage Garden Flowers*, p.74
33. Timothy Clark, *Margery Fish: Country Gardening* (Woodbridge, Suffolk: Garden Art Press, revised edition, 2001), p.8
34. Margery Fish, *Carefree Gardening*, (London: W. H. & L. Collingridge, 1961; paperback edition, London: Faber & Faber, 1989), p.13
35. Fish, *Cottage Garden Flowers*, pp.44,8
36. Fish, *We Made a Garden*, p.88
37. Clark, op.cit, p.13
38. Fish, *Cottage Garden Flowers*, p.15
39. ibid, pp.30-3,6
40. ibid, pp.9,47
41. Clark, *Margery Fish*, p.10
42. Horwood, op.cit
43. Chivers and Woloszynska, op.cit, p.103
44. Fish, *We Made a Garden*, p.65
45. Fish, *Cottage Garden Flowers*, p.55; Fish, *We Made a Garden*, p.98

PART VI – CLASSICAL AND MODERN

Chapter 18 – Russell Page

1. Christopher Woodward, 'Chelsea Flower Show – tribute to garden designer Russell Page, *Financial Times*, 15 May 2015
2. Charles Quest-Ritson, *The English Garden Abroad* (London: Viking, 1992; Penguin paperback, 1996), p.209
3. ibid, p.211
4. Charles Quest-Ritson, 'Great British Garden-makers: Russell Page', *Country Life*, 8 January 2011 [http://www.countrylife.co.uk/gardens/great-british-garden-makers-russell-page-19453, accessed 5 October 2017]
5. Marina Schinz and Gabrielle van Zuylen, *The Gardens of Russell Page* (New York: Stewart, Tabori & Chang, 1991), p.8
6. Woodward, op.cit
7. Robin Lane Fox, 'Christopher Lloyd', in *Thoughtful Gardening: Great Plants, Great Gardens, Great Gardeners* (London: Particular Books, 2010; Penguin paperback, 2013), p.57
8. Schinz and van Zuylen, op.cit, pp.18,20
9. Nikola Fox, *Russell Page 1906-1985: The Conservation of his Mixed Borders* (Unpublished thesis for Post-Graduate Diploma in Garden Conservation, The Conservation of Historic Landscapes, Parks and Gardens, 1995), p.4
10. Russell Page, *The Education of a Gardener* (London: William Collins, 1962; paperback, London: The Harvill Press, 1995), p.14
11. ibid, pp.15,16
12. ibid, pp.18,19,21

13. Schinz and van Zuylen, op.cit, p.16
14. Page, op.cit, p.100
15. ibid, p.24
16. ibid, p.21
17. ibid, p.25
18. ibid, pp.165-166
19. Quest-Ritson, 'Great British Garden-makers'
20. Page, op.cit, pp.33-34
21. ibid, p.30
22. ibid, p.35
23. ibid, pp.38,36,39
24. ibid, pp.39,40,45,97
25. ibid, p.296
26. ibid, pp.239,300
27. ibid, pp.224,227,104
28. ibid, p.156
29. ibid, p.291
30. ibid, pp.252,260
31. Woodward, op.cit
32. Schinz and van Zuylen, op.cit, p.196
33. Page, op.cit, p.329
34. Schinz and van Zuylen, op.cit, p.113
35. Page, op.cit, p.283
36. Fox, op.cit, p.5
37. Schinz and van Zuylen, op.cit, p.123
38. ibid, p.125
39. Quoted from Page's unpublished papers by Fox, op.cit, p.5

Chapter 19 – Rosemary Verey

1. Rosemary Verey, *Rosemary Verey's Making of a Garden* (London: Frances Lincoln, 1995), p.7
2. Robin Lane Fox, 'Box of tricks for killer pest', *Financial Times*, 2/3 December 2017, p.14
3. Tim Richardson, *The New English Garden* (London: Frances Lincoln, 2013), pp.158-159
4. Rosemary Verey, interview with the author, 5 April 1994
5. Barbara Paul Robinson, *Rosemary Verey: The Life & Lessons of a Legendary Gardener* (Boston: David R. Godine, 2012), p.53
6. Verey, *Making of a Garden*, p.15
7. Verey, author interview, April 1994
8. Robinson, op.cit, p.5
9. ibid, pp.14-15
10. Verey, *Making of a Garden*, p.8
11. ibid, p.8
12. ibid, p.9
13. Verey, author interview, April 1994
14. Verey, *Making of a Garden*, p.20
15. Rosemary Verey, *Rosemary Verey's Garden Plans* (London: Frances Lincoln, 1993), p.10

16. Verey, author interview, April 1994
17. Verey, *Making of a Garden*, p.21
18. Heidi Howcroft, *First Ladies of Gardening: Pioneers, Designers and Dreamers* (London: Frances Lincoln, 2015), p.62
19. Robinson, op.cit, pp.82-83
20. Verey, *Making of a Garden*, p.47
21. Howcroft, op.cit, p.68
22. Verey, *Making of a Garden*, pp.145ff
23. Rosemary Verey, *The Garden in Winter* (London: Frances Lincoln, 1988), p.7
24. Verey, author interview, April 1994
25. Robinson, *Rosemary Verey*, pp.58-59
26. Verey, author interview, April 1994
27. Verey, author interview, April 1994; Robinson, *Rosemary Verey*, p.ix
28. Verey, author interview, April 1994
29. Verey, *Garden Plans*, p.6
30. ibid, p.6
31. Robinson, op.cit, pp.124-127,182
32. Verey, *Garden Plans*, pp.26-49; Robinson, op.cit, p.144
33. Robinson, op.cit, pp.177-178
34. Verey, author interview, April 1994
35. Keen, Mary, 'The life and legacy of Mrs Verey', *Daily Telegraph*, 19 January 2011 [http://www.telegraph.co.uk/gardening/8264833/The-life-and-legacy-of-Mrs-Verey.html, accessed 17 October 2017]
36. Penelope Hobhouse, interview with the author, 25 October 2017

Chapter 20 – Penelope Hobhouse

1. Penelope Hobhouse, interview with the author, 25 October 2017
2. ibid
3. ibid
4. Anne Raver, 'Cuttings; Gardening is so much more than, well, plants,' *New York Times*, 22 January 1995
5. Andrew Wilson, *Influential Gardeners: The Designers Who Shaped 20th-Century Garden Style* (London: Mitchell Beazley, 2002), p.28
6. Penelope Hobhouse, *The Country Gardener* (London: Frances Lincoln, 1989), p.13
7. Hobhouse, author interview, October 2017
8. ibid
9. ibid.
10. Penelope Hobhouse, interview with the author, 5 September 1994
11. Hobhouse, author interview, October 2017
12. ibid
13. ibid
14. ibid
15. Hobhouse, *The Country Gardener*, p.13
16. Hobhouse, author interview, October 2017
17. Hobhouse, *The Country Gardener*, p.8
18. ibid, pp.16-17
19. Hobhouse, *The Country Gardener*, pp.13,16,17

20. Matthew Biggs, *RHS Lessons from Great Gardeners: Forty Gardening Icons and What They Teach Us* (London: Mitchell Beazley, 2015), p.181
21. Penelope Hobhouse, *Colour in Your Garden* (London: Frances Lincoln, 1985), p.16
22. Hobhouse, author interview, October 2017
23. Penelope Hobhouse, *On Gardening* (London: Frances Lincoln, 1994), p.8
24. Hobhouse, author interview, September 1994
25. Hobhouse, author interview, October 2017
26. Hobhouse, author interview, September 1994
27. Hobhouse, author interview, October 2017
28. ibid
29. Hobhouse, author interview, September 1994
30. Hobhouse, author interview, October 2017
31. Biggs, op.cit, p.185
32. Hobhouse, author interview, October 2017
33. ibid, 2017

Chapter 21 – John Brookes

1. Stephen Anderton, *Lives of the Great Gardeners* (London: Thames & Hudson, 2016), p.194
2. John Brookes, *The Room Outside: A New Approach to Garden Design* (London: Thames & Hudson, 1969), pp.5,2
3. Jenny Uglow, *A Little History of British Gardening* (London: Chatto & Windus, 2004; new edition with added material, 2017), p.271
4. John Brookes, interview with the author, 1 November 2017
5. Bunny Guinness, 'Happy Birthday John Brookes, the king of garden design', Daily Telegraph, 30 October 2013 [http://www.telegraph.co.uk/gardening/10409075/Happy-birthday-John-Brookes-the-king-of-garden-design.html, accessed 6 November 2017]
6. Barbara Simms, *John Brookes: Garden and Landscape Designer* (London: Conran Octopus, 2007), p.10
7. Brookes, author interview, November 2017
8. ibid
9. Simms, op.cit, p.16
10. Brookes, author interview, November 2017
11. ibid
12. ibid
13. Simms, op.cit, p.19
14. ibid, p.19
15. Brookes, author interview, November 2017
16. Simms, *John Brookes*, pp.21-22
17. ibid, p.24
18. Brookes, *The Room Outside*, pp.13,15
19. ibid, p.21
20. Brookes, author interview, November 2017
21. ibid
22. ibid
23. ibid
24. John Brookes, *A Place in the Country* (London: Thames & Hudson, 1984), p.7

25. Simms, op.cit, p.30-31
26. Brookes, author interview, November 2017
27. Vanessa Berridge, '1960-79: Years of Transition' in George Plumptre (ed.), *The Gardens of England: Treasures of the National Gardens Scheme* (London and New York: Merrell Publishers, 2013), p.112
28. Andrew Wilson, *Influential Gardeners: The Designers Who Shaped 20th-Century Garden Style* (London: Mitchell Beazley, 2002), p.176
29. John Brookes, interview with the author, 16 August 2012
30. ibid
31. Brookes, author interview, November 2017
32. Peter Gillespie, interview with the author, November 2017
33. Guinness, op.cit

PART VII – THE LATER PLANTSMEN

Chapter 22 – Christopher Lloyd

1. Stephen Anderton, *Christopher Lloyd: His Life at Great Dixter* (London: Chatto & Windus, 2010; Pimlico paperback, 2011), pp.182-183
2. Robin Lane Fox, 'Christopher Lloyd', in *Thoughtful Gardening: Great Plants, Great Gardens, Great Gardeners* (London: Particular Books, 2010; Penguin paperback, 2013), p.60
3. Rosemary Alexander, 'Preface' in Fergus Garrett and Rosemary (preface), *Dear Christo: Memories of Christopher Lloyd at Great Dixter* (London and Portland: Timber Press, 2010), p.9
4. Christopher Lloyd, *The Year at Great Dixter* (Harmsworth, Middlesex: Viking Press, 1987), p.12
5. ibid, pp.8-10
6. Christopher Lloyd, interview with the author, 24 January 1997
7. Lloyd, *The Year at Great Dixter*, p.13
8. Anderton, *Christopher Lloyd*, p.43
9. ibid, pp.66,70
10. ibid, p.75
11. Lloyd, author interview, January 1997
12. Lloyd, *The Year at Great Dixter*, p.16
13. ibid, p.7
14. ibid, p.16
15. Lloyd, author interview, January 1997
16. Lloyd, *The Year at Great Dixter*, p.17
17. Anderton, op.cit, p. 182
18. Lloyd, author interview, January 1997
19. Lloyd, *The Year at Great Dixter*, p.10
20. Christopher Lloyd, *In My Garden* (London: Bloomsbury, 1993), p.65
21. Lane Fox, 'Christopher Lloyd', p.60
22. Christopher Lloyd, *The Well-Tempered Garden: A New Edition of the Gardening Classic* (London: Cassell & Co, 2001; Weidenfeld & Nicolson paperback, 2003), p.6
23. Anderton, op.cit, p.183
24. Lloyd, author interview, January 1997
25. Anderton, op.cit, p.154

26. Christopher Lloyd, Beth Chatto and Christopher Lloyd, *Dear Friend & Gardener: Letters on Life and Gardening* (London: Frances Lincoln, 1998), p.93
27. Lloyd, *The Well-Tempered Garden*, pp.32-73
28. Lloyd, author interview, January 1997
29. Tim Richardson, *The New English Garden* (London: Frances Lincoln, 2013), p.90
30. Lloyd, *In My Garden*, pp.11-12
31. ibid, p.145
32. Lloyd, *The Well-Tempered Garden*, p.v
33. Beth Chatto, 'Foreword', in Chatto and Lloyd, *Dear Friend*, p.5
34. Lloyd, *The Well-Tempered Garden*, pp.9,67
35. Lloyd, author interview, January 1997
36. Penelope Hobhouse, interview with the author, 25 October 2017
37. Lloyd/Chatto, *Dear Friend*, pp.75,108
38. ibid, p.65
39. Fergus Garrett, interview with the author, 24 July 2009
40. Chatto, *Dear Friend*, p.30
41. Rory Dusoir, *Dear Christo*, p.39
42. Anderton, op.cit, p.122
43. ibid, p.217
44. Garrett, author interview, July 2009

Chapter 23 – Beth Chatto

1. Beth Chatto and Christopher Lloyd, *Dear Friend & Gardener: Letters on Life and Gardening* (London: Frances Lincoln, 1998), p.12
2. Tim Richardson and Catherine Horwood in discussion, 'Lives and Legacies: Beth Chatto', at The Garden Museum, 14 November 2017
3. Catherine Horwood, *Gardening Women: Their Stories from 1600 to the Present* (London: Virago, 2010), pp.68-69
4. Beth Chatto, interview with the author, 6 May 2005
5. ibid
6. Beth Chatto, *The Damp Garden* (London, 1982: J.M.Dent; Orion paperback, 1998; reissued, 2012), p.xii
7. Catherine Horwood, *Beth Chatto: A life with plants* (London: Pimpernel Press, 2019), p.34
8. Andrew Wilson, *Influential Gardeners: The Designers Who Shaped 20th-Century Garden Style* (London: Mitchell Beazley, 2002), p.45
9. Penelope Hobhouse, interview with the author, 25 November 2017
10. Beth Chatto, *Celebrating Fifty Years: The Beth Chatto Gardens 1960-2010* (Elmstead Market, Essex: The Beth Chatto Gardens Limited, 2010), p.8
11. Chatto, author interview, May 2005
12. Chatto, *Celebrating Fifty Years*, p.8
13. Diana Ross, 'Beth Chatto, Nursery Woman', *Garden Museum Journal*, 21 (Winter 2008), p.8
14. Chatto, author interview, May 2005
15. ibid
16. Catherine Horwood, 'Lives and Legacies', November 2017
17. Chatto, author interview, May 2005

18. Chatto, *Celebrating Fifty Years*, p.8
19. ibid, p.35
20. Beth Chatto, *Beth Chatto's Shade Garden: Shade-Loving Plants for Year-Round Interest* (London: Pimpernel Press, 2017), p.15
21. Beth Chatto, *The Beth Chatto Handbook: A descriptive catalogue of unusual plants* (Elmstead Market, Essex: The Beth Chatto Gardens Limited, undated), p.4
22. Jane Brown, *The Pursuit of Paradise: A Social History of Gardens and Gardening* (London: HarperCollins, 1999; paperback, 2000), p.302
23. Chatto, *The Beth Chatto Handbook*, p.62
24. Chatto, *Dear Friend*, pp.27-28
25. Chatto, *Celebrating Fifty Years*, p.39
26. Ross, 'Beth Chatto', p.13
27. Beth Chatto, *The Dry Garden* (London: J.M.Dent, 1978; Orion, revised paperback, 1998), p.1
28. Beth Chatto, 'August', in Deborah Kellaway (ed.), *The Illustrated Virago Book of Women Gardeners* (London: Virago, 1995), p.76
29. Erica Hunningher, 'Thoughts from Gardening Friends', *Garden Museum Journal*, 21 (Winter 2008), p.38
30. Chatto, *Dear Friend*, pp.13,15,40
31. Beth Chatto, 'Foreword', in Fergus Garrett and Rosemary Alexander, (preface), *Dear Christo: Memories of Christopher Lloyd at Great Dixter* (London and Portland: Timber Press, 2010), p.7
32. Chatto, *Dear Friend*, pp.55,61
33. Horwood, *Beth Chatto*, pp.74-75, *passim*
34. Penelope Lively, *Life in the Garden* (London: Fig Tree, 2017), p.75
35. Chatto, author interview, May 2005
36. Chatto, *Dear Friend*, p.12
37. Horwood, *Beth Chatto*, p.174
38. Ross, 'Beth Chatto', p.6
39. Unsigned obituary, *The Times*, 18 May 2019, p.53
40. Penelope Hobhouse, 'Thoughts from Gardening Friends', p.36

Chapter 24 – Tom Stuart-Smith

1. Tim Richardson, 'Tom Stuart-Smith: see the exhibition, read the book, visit the garden', *Daily Telegraph*, 23 May 2011 [http://www.telegraph.co.uk/gardening/8525860/Tom-Stuart-Smith-see-the-exhibition-read-the-book-visit-the-garden.html, accessed 16 October 2017]
2. Tania Compton, 'Sibling Harmony', *House & Garden* (June 2014), p.122
3. Tom Stuart-Smith, interview with the author, 24 November 2017
4. Tom and Sue Stuart-Smith, *The Barn Garden: Making a Place* (Abbots Langley, Herts: Serge Hill Books, 2011), p.9
5. Stuart-Smith, author interview, November 2017
6. ibid
7. ibid
8. ibid
9. Stuart-Smith, *The Barn Garden*, p.10
10. Ibid, p.13
11. Stuart-Smith, author interview, November 2017

12. Tom Stuart-Smith website; [http://www.tomstuartsmith.co.uk/projects/show-gardens/chelsea-1998, 2000, 2003, 2006, accessed 27 November 2017]
13. Stuart-Smith, author interview, November 2017
14. Tim Richardson, *The New English Garden* (London: Frances Lincoln, 2013), p.28
15. Stuart-Smith, author interview, November 2017
16. Noel Kingsbury, 'Trentham stands triumphant', *The Garden*, 142:10 (October 2017), p.36
17. Stuart-Smith, author interview, November 2017
18. Tom Stuart-Smith, 'Trentham's Italian Renaissance', *Daily Telegraph*, 26 October 2007 [http://www.telegraph.co.uk/gardening/gardenstovisit/3345229/Trenthams-Italian-renaissance.html, accessed 28 November 2017]. Quoted by Kingsbury, 'Trentham stands triumphant', p.34
19. Stuart-Smith, author interview, November 2017
20. ibid
21. Nigel Colborn, 'A new RHS garden at Bridgewater', *The Garden*, 142:9 (September 2017), p.50
22. Stuart-Smith, author interview, November 2017
23. ibid

Bibliography

PRIMARY SOURCES

Addison, Joseph, *Selections from The Tatler and The Spectator of Steele and Addison* (1709-1712), (ed.) Angus Ross (London: Penguin, 1982)

Bradley, Richard, *A Philosophical Account of the Works of Nature* (London: W. Mears, 1721)

Brookes, John, *Room Outside: A New Approach to Garden Design* (London: Thames & Hudson, 1969)

Brookes, John, *A Place in the Country* (London: Thames & Hudson, 1984)

Chambers, William, *A Dissertation on Oriental Gardening* (London: 1773; 2nd edition)

Chatto, Beth, *The Beth Chatto Handbook: A descriptive catalogue of unusual plants* (Elmstead Market, Essex: The Beth Chatto Gardens Limited, undated)

Chatto, Beth, *The Damp Garden* (London, 1982: J. M Dent; Orion Books paperback, 1998; reissued, 2012)

Chatto, Beth, *The Dry Garden* (London: J. M. Dent, 1978; Orion, revised paperback, 1998

Chatto, Beth and Lloyd, Christopher, *Dear Friend & Gardener: Letters on Life and Gardening* (London: Frances Lincoln, 1998)

Chatto, Beth, *Celebrating Fifty Years: The Beth Chatto Gardens 1960-2010* (Elmstead Market, Essex: The Beth Chatto Gardens Limited, 2010)

Chatto, Beth, *Beth Chatto's Shade Garden: Shade-Loving Plants for Year-Round Interest* (London: Pimpernel Press, 2017)

Cowell, John, *The Curious and Profitable Gardener* (London: Weaver Bickerton and Richard Montagu, 1730)

Cowper, William, *Poems* (London: J. M. Dent, 1931)

Evelyn, John, *The Diary of John Evelyn* (selected from 1959 Oxford University Press edition, ed. E. S. de Beer; London: Everyman's Library, 2006)

Fairchild, Thomas, *The City Gardener* (London: T. Woodward, 1722)

Fish, Margery, *We Made a Garden* (London: W. H. & L. Collingridge, 1956; new edition, London: Batsford, 2016)

Fish, Margery, *Cottage Garden Flowers* (London: W. H. & L. Collingridge, 1961; new edition, London: Batsford, 2016)

Fish, Margery, *Carefree Gardening* (London: W. H. & L. Collingridge, 1961; paperback edition, London: Faber & Faber, 1989)

Gerard, John, *A catalogue of plants cultivated in the garden of John Gerard, in the years 1596–1599* (ed.) Benjamin Daydon Jackson (London: privately printed, 1876)

Gerard, John, *The Herball, or General Historie of Plantes* (London: John Norton, 1597)

Gerard, John, *The Herball, or General Historie of Plantes*, enlarged and amended by Thomas Johnson (London: Adam Islip, Joice Norton and Richard Whitakers, 1633)

Hervey, John, Lord, *Some Materials towards Memoirs of the Reign of King George II*, 3 Vols (ed.) Romney Sedgwick (London: King's Printers, 1931)

Hobhouse, Penelope (ed.), *Gertrude Jekyll on Gardening: An Anthology* (London: William Collins, 1983; Papermac paperback, 1985)

Hobhouse, Penelope, *Colour in Your Garden* (London: Frances Lincoln, 1985)

Hobhouse, Penelope, *A Book of Gardening: Ideas, Methods, Design* (London: Pavilion Books, 1986)

Hobhouse, Penelope, *The Country Gardener* (London: Frances Lincoln, 1989)

Hobhouse, Penelope, *On Gardening* (London: Frances Lincoln, 1994)

James, John, *The Theory and Practice of Gardening* (London: George James, 1712; Farnborough: Gregg, 1969)

Jekyll, Gertrude, *On Gardening* (London: Studio Vista, 1966)

Jekyll, Gertrude, *Colour Schemes for the Flower Garden* (Introduced and revised by Graham Stuart Thomas), (London: Country Life, 1908; London: Penguin Books, 1983)

Langley, Batty, *New Principles of Gardening* (London: A. Bettesworth & J. Battey, 1728)

Lees-Milne, Alvilde, and Verey, Rosemary, *The Englishwoman's Garden* (London: Chatto & Windus, 1980)

Lees-Milne, James, *Diaries, 1942-1954* (abridged and introduced by Michael Bloch), (London: John Murray, 2006; paperback, 2007)

Lloyd, Christopher, *The Year at Great Dixter* (Harmsworth, Middlesex: Viking Press, 1987)

Lloyd, Christopher, *In My Garden* (London: Bloomsbury, 1993)

Lloyd, Christopher, *Other People's Gardens* (London: Viking, 1995)

Lloyd, Christopher, *Gardener Cook* (London: Frances Lincoln, 1997)

Lloyd, Christopher, *The Well-Tempered Garden: A New Edition of the Gardening Classic* (London: Cassell & Co, 2001; Weidenfeld & Nicolson paperback, 2003)

London, George, & Wise, Henry, *The Retir'd Gard'ner* (translated from the French), (London: Jacob Tonson, 1706)

Loudon, John Claudius, *In Search of English Gardens: The Travels of John Claudius Loudon and his Wife Jane* (London: Century, 1990)

Loudon, John Claudius, *The Landscape Gardening and Landscape Architecture of the Late Humphry Repton, Esq, Being His Entire Works on These Subject, a New Edition, with an Historical and Scientific Introduction, a Systematic Analysis, a Biographical Notice, Notices, and a Copious Alphabetical Index* (London: Forgotten Books, 2015)

Mawson, Thomas H., *The Art and Craft of Garden Making* (London: B. T. Batsford, 2nd edition, 1901)

Miller, Philip, *The Gardeners Dictionary; Directing what works are necessary to be performed every month in the kitchen, fruit and pleasure gardens, as also in the conservatory and nursery, Eighth edition* (London: Rivington, 1768)

Nicolson, Harold, Nicolson, *Diaries and Letters, 1930-1939* (ed.) Nigel Nicolson (London: Collins, 1966)

Nicolson, Harold, Nicolson, *Diaries and Letters, 1939-45* (ed.) Nigel Nicolson (London: Collins, 1967)

Nicolson, Harold, *Diaries and Letters, 1945-1962* (ed.) Nigel Nicolson (London: Collins, 1968)

Page, Russell, *The Education of a Gardener* (London: William Collins, 1962; London: The Harvill Press paperback, 1995)

Pope, Alexander, *The Poems of Alexander Pope* (ed.) John Butt (London: Methuen, 1963)

Sackville-West, V., *The Edwardians* (London: Penguin Books, 1935)

Sackville-West, V., *In Your Garden* (London: Michael Joseph, 1951; Marlborough, Wiltshire: Oxenwood Press, 1996)

Sackville-West, V., *In Your Garden Again* (London: Michael Joseph, 1953; Marlborough, Wiltshire: Oxenwood Press, 1998)

Sackville-West, V., *The Illustrated Garden Book* (A new anthology by Robin Lane Fox), (London: Michael Joseph, 1986)

Sackville-West, V., *The Land & The Garden* (new edition, with an introduction by Nigel Nicolson), (Exeter, Devon: Webb & Bower in association with Michael Joseph, 1989)

Scott-James, Anne, *Sissinghurst: The Making of Garden* (London: Michael Joseph, 1975)

Smith, Alan G. R. (ed.), *The Anonymous Life of William Cecil, Lord Burghley* (Lewiston/Queenstown/Lampeter: Edwin Mellen Press, 1990)

Stuart-Smith, Tom and Sue, *The Barn Garden: Making a Place* (Abbots Langley, Herts: Serge Hill Books, 2011)

Repton, Humphry, *Observations on the Theory and Practice of Landscape Gardening* (London: T. Bensley, 1805)

Repton, Humphry, *Memoirs* (eds.) Ann Gore & George Carter (Norwich, Norfolk: Michael Russell, 2005)

Robinson, William, *The Wild Garden* (London: John Murray, 1870)

Robinson, William, *Alpine Flowers for English Gardens* (London: John Murray, 2nd edition, 1875)

Robinson, William, *The English Flower Garden* (London: Bloomsbury Gardening Classics, 1996; paperback edition, 1998)

Rogers, John, *The Vegetable Cultivator: containing a plain and accurate description of all the different species and varieties of culinary vegetables ... also, some recollections of the life of Philip Miller* (London: Longman, Orme, Brown, Green & Longmans, 1839)

Verey, Rosemary, *The Garden in Winter* (London: Frances Lincoln, 1988)

Verey, Rosemary, *A Countrywoman's Notes* (London: Frances Lincoln, 1991; Frances Lincoln Miniature Edition, 1993)

Verey, Rosemary, *Rosemary Verey's Garden Plans* (London: Frances Lincoln, 1993)

Verey, Rosemary, *Rosemary Verey's Making of a Garden* (London: Frances Lincoln, 1995)

Walpole, Horace, *The History of the Modern Taste in Gardening* (ed.) John Dixon Hunt (New York: Ursus Press, 1995)

Whately, Thomas, *Observations on Modern Gardening* (Introduction and commentary by Michael Symes), (Woodbridge, Suffolk: The Boydell Press, 2016)

Wood, Martin (ed.) *Gertrude Jekyll: The Unknown Gertrude Jekyll* (London: Frances Lincoln, 2006)

Wordsworth, William, *Lines written a few miles above Tintern Abbey* in Wordsworth & Coleridge, *Lyrical Ballads 1798* (ed.) W. J. B. Owen (London: Oxford University Press, 2nd edition, 1975)

Young, Arthur, *A Six Months Tour through the North of England containing an Account of the Present State of Agriculture, Manufactures and Population in Several Counties of this Kingdom* (London, 1770)

Young, Arthur, *The Farmer's Tour through the East of England*, 4 vols (London, 1771)

SECONDARY SOURCES

Allan, Mea, *The Tradescants: Their Plants, Gardens and Museum 1570-1662* (London: Michael Joseph, 1964)

Allan, Mea, *William Robinson 1838-1935: Father of the English Flower Garden* (London: Faber & Faber, 1982)

Amherst, Alicia, *A History of Gardening in England* (London: Bernard Quaritch, 1895)

Anderton, Stephen, *Christopher Lloyd: His Life at Great Dixter* (London: Chatto & Windus, 2010; Pimlico paperback, 2011)

Anderton, Stephen, *Lives of the Great Gardeners* (London: Thames & Hudson, 2016)

Anthony, John, *An Illustrated Life of Sir Joseph Paxton 1803-1865* (Princes Risborough, Buckinghamshire: Shire Publications, 1992)

Arber, Agnes R., *Herbals, Their Origin and Evolution: a Chapter in the History of Botany 1470-1670*, 3rd Edition, with an introduction and annotations by William T. Stearn (Cambridge: Cambridge University Press, 1986)

Arnold, Dana, *Rural Urbanism: London Landscapes in the Early Nineteenth Century* (Manchester: Manchester University Press, 2005)

Barlow Rogers, Elizabeth, *Writing the Garden: A Literary Conversation across Two Centuries* (London: Allison & Busby, 2014)

Batey, Mavis, & Woudstra, Jan, *The Story of the Privy Garden at Hampton Court* (London: Barn Elms, 1995)

Becker, Robert, *Nancy Lancaster: Her Life, Her World, Her Art* (New York: Albert A. Knopf, 1996)

Berridge, Vanessa, *The Princess's Garden: Royal Intrigue and the Untold Story of Kew* (Stroud, Gloucestershire: Amberley, 2015)

Bevington, Michael, with Clarke, George, Marsden, Jonathan and Knox, Tim, *Stowe: The People and the Place* (London: National Trust, 2011)

Biggs, Matthew, *RHS Lessons from Great Gardeners: Forty Gardening Icons and What They Teach Us* (London: Mitchell Beazley, 2015)

Bisgrove, Richard, *The Gardens of Gertrude Jekyll* (London: Frances Lincoln, 1992)

Bisgrove, Richard, *William Robinson: The Wild Gardener* (London: Frances Lincoln, 2008)

Bisgrove, Richard, 'The Wild Garden, 1870, by William Robinson and Charles Nelson; The Wild Garden, 1894, by William Robinson and Rick Darke', *Garden History*, 39:1 (Summer 2011), pp.129-130

Blomfield, Reginald, *The Formal Garden in England* (London: Macmillan, 1901)

Borman, Tracy, *King's Mistress, Queen's Servant: The Life and Times of Henrietta Howard* (London: Jonathan Cape, 2007; Vintage paperback, 2010)

Brett-James, Norman C, *The Life of Peter Collinson FRS, FRA* (London: E G Dunstan & Co, 1925

Brown, Jane, *Miss Gertrude Jekyll 1843-1932 Gardener* (London: Architectural Association, 1981)

Brown, Jane, *Vita's Other World: A Gardening Biography of V. Sackville-West* (London: Viking, 1985; London: Penguin paperback, 1987)

Brown, Jane, *The English Garden in Our Time: From Gertrude Jekyll to Geoffrey Jellicoe* (Woodbridge, Suffolk: Antique Collectors' Club, 1986)

Brown, Jane, *The Pursuit of Paradise: A Social History of Gardens and Gardening* (London: HarperCollins, 1999; paperback edition, 2000)

Brown, Jane, *The Omnipotent Magician: Lancelot 'Capability' Brown 1716-1783* (London: Chatto & Windus, 2011)

Campbell-Culver, Maggie, *The Origin of plants: The people and plants that have shaped Britain's garden history since the year 1000* (London: Headline, 2001; Eden Project Books paperback, 2004)

Carter, George, Goode, Patrick and Laurie, Kedrun, *Humphry Repton: Landscape Gardener 1752-1818* (Norwich: Sainsbury Centre for Visual Arts, 1982)

Chessum, Sophie, Rogers, Kevin, and Rowell, Christopher, *Claremont* (London: National Trust guide, 2000)

Chivers, Susan, and Woloszynska, Suzanne, *The Cottage Garden: Margery Fish at East Lambrook Manor* (London: Michael Joseph, 1990)

Clark, Kathleen, 'What the nurserymen did for us: the roles and influence of the nursery trade on the landscapes and gardens of the eighteenth century', *Garden History*, 40:1 (Summer 2012), pp.17-33

Clark, H. F., *The English Landscape Garden* (Gloucester: Alan Sutton, 1980)

Clark, Timothy, *Margery Fish: Country Gardening* (Woodbridge, Suffolk: Garden Art Press, revised edition, 2001)

Clarke, Ethne, *Hidcote: The Making of a Garden* (London and New York: W. W. Norton, 2009)

Cloutman, Paul, *Royal Botanic Gardens Kew: Souvenir Guide* (Kew: The Royal Botanic Gardens, Kew, 2004; revised edition)

Colborn, Nigel, 'A new RHS garden at Bridgewater', *The Garden*, 142:9 (September 2017), pp.48-52

Colquhoun, Kate, *A Thing in Disguise: The Visionary Life of Joseph Paxton* (London: Fourth Estate, 2003; HarperPerennial paperback, 2004)

Compton, Tania, 'Sibling Harmony', *House & Garden* (June 2014), pp.118-125

Copley, Stephen and Garside, Peter (eds.) *The Politics of the Picturesque: Literature, landscape and aesthetics since 1770* (Cambridge: Cambridge University Press, 1994)

Daniels, Stephen, *Humphry Repton: Landscape Gardening and the Geography of Georgian England* (New Haven & London: Yale University Press, 1999)

Dennison, Matthew, *Behind the Mask: The Life of Vita Sackville-West* (London: William Collins, 2014; paperback edition, 2015)

Desmond, Ray, *Kew: The History of the Royal Botanic Gardens* (London: The Harvill Press with the Royal Botanic Gardens, Kew, 1995)

Devonshire, The Duchess of, *The Garden at Chatsworth* (London: Frances Lincoln, 1999)

Dixon Hunt, John, *William Kent Landscape Garden Designer: An Assessment and Catalogue of his Designs* (London: A. Zwemmer, 1987)

Dixon Hunt, John, *Gardens and the Picturesque: Studies in the History of Landscape Architecture* (Cambridge, Massachusetts: The MIT Press, 1992)

Drewitt, F Dawtrey, *The Romance of the Apothecaries' Garden at Chelsea* (London: Chapman & Dodd, 1922)

Duff, Andrew, 'A Design for Life', *The English Garden*, 240 (Spring 2017), p.10

Edwards, Tudor, 'Sir Joseph Paxton: the versatile gardener', *History Today*, 15:12 (December 1965), pp.855-864

Elliott, Brent, 'A Master of the Geometric Art', *The Garden Journal of the Royal Horticultural Society*, 106 (1981), pp.488-491

Elliott, Brent, *Victorian Gardens* (London: B. T. Batsford, 1990)

Evans, Shirley Rose, 'Master Designer', *The Antique Collector*, 63:9 (October 1992), pp.52-55

Evans, Shirley Rose, *Nesfield's Monster Work: The Gardens of Witley Court* (Worcester: Peter Huxtable Designs, 1994)

Evans, Shirley Rose, *Masters of their Craft: The Art, Architecture and Garden Design of the Nesfields* (Cambridge: Lutterworth Press, 2014)

Fearnley-Whittingstall, *The Garden: An English Love Affair* (London: Weidenfeld & Nicolson, 2002)

Festing, Sally, *Gertrude Jekyll* (London: Viking, 1991; Penguin paperback, 1993)

Field, Ophelia, *The Kit-Kat Club: Friends who Imagined a Nation* (London: Harper Press, 2008)

Foreman, Amanda, *Georgiana, Duchess of Devonshire* (London: HarperCollins, 1998; paperback edition, 1999)

Fry, Carolyn, *The World of Kew* (London: BBC Books, 2006)

Gammack, Helene, *Hidcote* (Swindon, Wiltshire: National Trust guide, 2017)

Garnett, Oliver, *Stowe* (Swindon, Wiltshire: National Trust guide, 2011)

Garrett, Fergus, and Alexander, Rosemary (preface), *Dear Christo: Memories of Christopher Lloyd at Great Dixter* (London and Portland: Timber Press, 2010)

Girouard, Mark, 'Genius of Sir Joseph Paxton', *Country Life*, 138, Part 2 (9 December 1965), pp.1606-1608

Glendinning, Victoria, *Vita: The Life of V. Sackville-West* (London: Weidenfeld & Nicolson, 1983)

Gloag, John, *Mr. Loudon's England* (Newcastle: Oriel Press, 1970)

Gollin, Alfred M., *The Observer and J. L. Garvin 1908-1914: A Study in a Great Editorship* (London: Oxford University Press, 1960)

Goodwin, Anita, *Claremont Landscape Garden* (Swindon, Wiltshire: National Trust guide, 2012)

Green, David, *Gardener to Queen Anne: Henry Wise (1653-1738) and the Formal Garden* (London: Oxford University Press, 1956)

Gunther, Robert T., *Early British Botanists and their Gardens, based on the unpublished writings of Goodyer, Tradescants and others* (Oxford: Oxford University Press, 1922)

Hadfield, Miles, *A History of British Gardening* (London: Spring Books, 1969)

Hadfield, Miles, *Pioneers in Gardening* (London: 1955; paperback edition, London: Bloomsbury, 1998)

Hadfield, Miles, Harling, Robert, & Highton, Leonie, *British Gardeners: A Biographical Dictionary* (London: A. Zwemmer, 1980)

Hamel, Dr J. (translated by Studdy Leigh, John), *England and Russia: the Voyages of John Tradescant the Elder, Sir Hugh Willoughby, Richard Chancellor, Nelson, and Others to the White Sea etc* (London: Richard Bentley, 1854)

Harvey, John, *Early Nurserymen* (London & Chichester: Phillimore & Co, 1974)

Hayward, Allyson, *Norah Lindsay: The Life and Art of a Garden Designer* (London: Frances Lincoln, 2007)

Henderson, Paula, 'A Shared Passion: the Cecils and their Gardens', in (ed.) Pauline Croft, *Patronage, Culture and Power: The Early Cecils* (New Haven & London: Yale University Press, 2002)

Henrey, Blanche, *British Botanical Literature Before 1800: Vol. I: The Sixteenth and Seventeenth Centuries History and Bibliography* (London: Oxford University Press, 1975)

Hinde, Thomas, *Capability Brown: The Story of a Master Gardener* (London: Hutchinson, 1986)

Hobhouse, Penelope, 'From Geometry to Nature', *The Spectator*, 2 February 2002, p.40

Hoeniger, F. D., & Hoeniger, J. F. M., *The Growth of Natural History in Stuart England from Gerard to the Royal Society* (Charlottesville: University Press of Virginia: 1969)

Horwood, Catherine, *Gardening Women: Their Stories from 1600 to the Present* (London: Virago, 2010)

Horwood, Catherine, *Beth Chatto: A life with plants* (London: Pimpernel Press, 2019)

Howarth, Jeffrey, *Lodge Park* (London: National Trust guide, 2002)

Howcroft, Heidi, *First Ladies of Gardening: Pioneers, Designers and Dreamers* (London: Frances Lincoln, 2015)

Howe, Bea, *Lady with Green Fingers: The Life of Jane Loudon* (London: Country Life, 1961)

Hyams, Edward, *Capability Brown and Humphry Repton* (London: J. M. Dent, 1971)

Jeffers, Robert H., *The Friends of John Gerard (1545-1612): Surgeon and Botanist* (Falls Village, Connecticut: Herb Grower Press, 1967)

Jenkins, Simon, *Newspapers: The Power and the Money* (London: Faber & Faber, 1979)

Jekyll, Francis, *Gertrude Jekyll: A Memoir* (London: Jonathan Cape, 1934)

Johnson, George W., *A History of English Gardening* (London: Baldwin & Craddock, & Longman & Co, 1829)

Jourdain, Margaret, *The Work of William Kent: Artist, Painter, Designer and Landscape Gardener* (London: Country Life, 1948)

Juniper, Barry, & Grootenboer, Hanneke, *The Tradescants' Orchard: The Mystery of a Seventeenth-Century Painted Fruit Book* (Oxford: Bodelian Library, 2013)

Kellaway, Deborah (ed.), *The Illustrated Virago Book of Women Gardeners* (London: Virago, 1995)

Kew, H. Wallis, & Powell, H. E., *Thomas Johnson: Botanist and Royalist* (London: Longmans, Green & Co, 1932)

Kingsbury Noel, 'Trentham stands triumphant', *The Garden*, 142:10 (October 2017), pp.30-37

Laird, Mark, 'John Claudius Loudon (1783-1843) and the field's identity', *Studies in the History of Gardens and Designed Landscapes*, 34:3 (2014), pp.248-253

Lane Fox, Robin, *Thoughtful Gardening: Great Plants, Great Gardens, Great Gardeners* (London: Particular Books, 2010; Penguin paperback, 2013)

Lane Fox, Robin, 'Box of tricks for killer pest', *Financial Times*, 2/3 December 2017, p.14

Langford, Paul, *A Polite and Commercial People: England 1727-1783* (Oxford: Clarendon Press, 1989)

Leach, Helen, *Cultivation Myths: Fiction, Fact & Fashion in Garden History* (Auckland, New Zealand: Godwit, 2000)
Leapman, Michael, *The Ingenious Mr Fairchild: The Story of the Father of the Modern Flower Garden* (London: Headline: 2000)
Lees-Milne, James, *The Bachelor Duke: A Life of William Spencer Cavendish 6th Duke of Devonshire 1790-1858* (London: John Murray, 1991)
Lees-Milne, James, *Earls of Creation: Five Great Patrons of Eighteenth-Century Art* (London: Classic Penguin, 2001)
Leith-Ross, Prudence, *The John Tradescants: Gardeners to the Rose and Lily Queen* (London: Peter Owen, 1984)
Le Rougetel, Hazel, *The Chelsea Gardener: Philip Miller 1691-1771* (London: Natural History Museum Publications, 1990)
Le Rougetel, Hazel, 'Philip Miller/John Bartram Botanical Exchange', *Garden History*, 14: 1 (Spring 1986), pp. 32-39
Lively, Penelope, *Life in the Garden* (London: Fig Tree, 2017)
Mansfield, Peter, 'An 18th-Century Landscape Restored: The Gardens of Claremont, Surrey', *Country Life*, CLXV: 4271 (17 May 1979), pp.1547-1550
Markham, Violet R., *Paxton and the Bachelor Duke* (London: Hodder & Stoughton, 1935)
Martin Robinson, John, *Temples of Delight: Stowe Landscape Gardens* (London: National Trust, 1990; 2nd edition, 1994, 2002)
Massingham, Betty, *Miss Jekyll: Portrait of a Great Gardener* (London: Country Life, 1966)
Massingham, Betty, *A Century of Gardeners* (London: Faber & Faber, 1982)
Mayer, Laura, *Humphry Repton* (Oxford: Shire Publications, 2014)
McKean, John, *Crystal Palace, Joseph Paxton and Charles Fox* (London: Phaidon, 1994)
Miller, John, *The Stuarts* (London: Hambledon Continuum, 2004; paperback, 2006)
Minter, Sue, *The Apothecaries' Garden: A History of the Chelsea Physic Garden* (Stroud, Gloucestershire: Sutton Publishing, 2000; Stroud, Gloucestershire: The History Press paperback, 2003)
Mowl, Timothy, *William Kent: Architect, Designer, Opportunist* (London: Jonathan Cape, 2006; Pimlico paperback, 2007)
Nicolson, Juliet, *A House Full of Daughters* (London: Chatto & Windus, 2016)
Nicolson, Nigel, *Portrait of a Marriage* (London: Weidenfeld & Nicolson, 1973)
Nicolson, Nigel, *Long Life: Memoirs* (London: Weidenfeld & Nicolson, 1997)
Paterson, Allen, 'Philip Miller: A Portrait', *Garden History*, 14: 1 (Spring 1986), pp. 40-41
Paterson, Allen, *The Gardens at Kew* (London: Frances Lincoln, 2008)
Pavord, Anna, *Hidcote Manor Garden, Gloucestershire* (London: National Trust, 1993)
Pavord, Anna, *The Naming of Names: The Search for Order in the World of Plants* (London: Bloomsbury Publishing, 2005)
Pearson, Graham S., *Hidcote* (London: National Trust Books, revised paperback, 2013)
Pearson, Graham S., *Lawrence Johnston: The Creator of Hidcote* (Hidcote Bartrim, Chipping Campden: Hidcote Books, 2013)
Plumptre, George, *Great Gardens, Great Designers* (London: Ward Lock, 1994)
Plumptre, George (ed.), *The Gardens of England: Treasures of the National Gardens Scheme* (London and New York: Merrell Publishers, 2013)

Potter, Jennifer, *The Curious Lives and Adventures of the John Tradescants* (London: Atlantic Books, 2006; paperback edition, 2007)

Quest-Ritson, Charles, *The English Garden Abroad* (London: Viking, 1992; Penguin paperback, 1996)

Quest-Ritson, Charles, *The English Garden: A Social History* (London: Viking, 2001)

Raven, Charles E., *English Naturalists from Neckham to Ray: A Study of the Making of the Modern World* (Cambridge: Cambridge University Press, 1947)

Raver, Anne, 'Cuttings; Gardening is so much more than, well, plants,' *New York Times*, 22 January 1995

Richardson, Tim, 'The Kit-Cat at Claremont', *Country Life*, CXCIX: 46 (17 November 2005), pp.56-59

Richardson, Tim, *The Arcadian Friends: Inventing the English Landscape* Garden (London: Bantam Press, 2007; paperback, 2008)

Richardson, Tim, *The New English Garden* (London: Frances Lincoln, 2013)

Ridgway, Christopher, 'William Andrews Nesfield: Between Uvedale Price and Isambard Kingdom Brunel', *Journal of Garden History*, 13: 1/2 (Spring/Summer 1993), pp.69-89

Ridgway, Christopher (ed.), *William Andrews Nesfield: Victorian Landscape Architect – Papers from the Bicentenary Conference, The King's Manor, York, 1994* (York: Institute of Advanced Architectural Studies, University of York, 1996)

Robinson, Barbara Paul, *Rosemary Verey: The Life & Lessons of a Legendary Gardener* (Boston: David R. Godine, 2012)

Ross, Diana, 'Beth Chatto, Nursery Woman', *Garden Museum Journal*, 21 (Winter 2008), pp.4-14

Rutherford, Sarah, *Capability Brown and His Landscape Gardens* (London: National Trust, 2016)

Schinz, Marina, and van Zuylen, Gabrielle, *The Gardens of Russell Page* (New York: Stewart, Tabori & Chang, 1991)

Scott-James, Anne, *Sissinghurst: The Making of a Garden* (London: Michael Joseph, 1975)

Shinn, Matt, *Croome* (Swindon, Wilts: National Trust guide, 2016)

Simms, Barbara, *John Brookes: Garden and Landscape Designer* (London: Conran Octopus, 2007)

Somerset, *Queen Anne: The Politics of Passion* (London: HarperPress, 2012)

Strong, Roy, *Royal Gardens* (London: BBC Books/Conran Octopus, 1992)

Stroud, Dorothy, *Humphry Repton* (London: Country Life, 1962)

Stroud, Dorothy, *Capability Brown* (London: Faber & Faber, 1975)

Symes, Michael, 'William Pitt the Elder: The Gran Mago of Landscape Gardening', *Garden History*, 24:1 (Summer 1996), pp.126-136

Tankard, Judith B., and Van Valkenburgh, Michael R. (eds.), *Gertrude Jekyll: A Vision of Garden and Wood* (London: John Murray, 1989)

Tankard, Judith B., and Wood, Martin A., *Gertrude Jekyll at Munstead Wood* (Stroud, Gloucestershire: Sutton Publishing 1996)

Tankard, Judith B., 'Sue Minter: The Well-Connected Gardener: A Biography Alicia Amherst, founder of Garden History', *Garden History*, 39:2 (Winter 2011), pp.284-285

Taylor, Geoffrey, *Some Nineteenth Century Gardeners* (London: Skeffington, 1951)

Taylor, Kristina, and Peel, Robert, *Passion, Plants and Patronage: 300 Years of the Bute Family Landscapes* (London: Artifice, 2012)

Thurley, Simon (ed.), *The King's Privy Garden at Hampton Court* (London: Apollo Magazine, 1995)

Tinniswood, Adrian, *The Long Weekend: Life in the English Country House Between the Wars* (London: Jonathan Cape, 2016)

Tooley, Michael J. (ed.), *William Andrews Nesfield 1794-1881: Essays to Mark the Bicentenary of His Birth* (Witton-le-Wear, Co Durham: Michaelmas Books, 1994)

Tooley, Michael J., *William Andrews Nesfield: Bicentenary Exhibition* (Witton-le-Wear, Co Durham: Michaelmas Books, 1994)

Tooley, Michael J., and Arnander, Primrose (eds.), *Gertrude Jekyll: Essays on the life of a working amateur* (Witton-le-Wear, Co Durham: Michaelmas Books, 1995)

Tooley, Michael J., 'Gertrude Jekyll and the Country House Garden: From the Archives of Country Life by Judith Tankard', *Garden History*, 39:2 (Winter 2011), pp.282-284

Uglow, Jenny, *A Little History of British Gardening* (London: Chatto & Windus, 2004; new edition with added material, 2017)

Way, Twigs, *A Passion for Gardening: How the British Became a Nation of Gardeners* (London: Prion, 2015)

Way, Twigs, *Gertrude Jekyll* (Oxford: Shire Publications, 2016)

Willes, Margaret, *The Making of the English Gardener: Plants, Books and Inspiration, 1560-1660* (New Haven & London: Yale University Press, 2001; paperback, 2013)

Williamson, Tom, *Polite Landscapes: Gardens and Society in Eighteenth-Century England* (Stroud: Alan Sutton, 1995)

Willis, Peter (ed.), *Furor Hortensis: Essays on the history of the English Landscape Garden in memory of H. F. Clark* (Edinburgh: Elysium Press, 1974)

Willis, Peter, *Charles Bridgeman and the English Landscape Garden* (London: A. Zwemmer, 1977)

Wilson, Andrew, *Influential Gardeners: The Designers Who Shaped 20th-Century Garden Style* (London: Mitchell Beazley, 2002)

Woodbridge, Kenneth, 'William Kent as Landscape Gardener: A Re-Appraisal', *Apollo*, C: 150 (New Series), (August 1974), pp.126-137

Woodbridge, Kenneth, 'William Kent's Gardening: The Rousham Letters', *Apollo*, C: 152 (New Series), (October 1974), pp.282-291

Woodward, Christopher, 'Chelsea Flower Show – tribute to garden designer Russell Page, *Financial Times*, 15 May 2015

Worsley, Lucy, *Courtiers: The Secret History of Kensington Palace* (London: Faber & Faber, 2010)

Wulf, Andrea, *The Brother Gardeners: Botany, Empire and the Birth of an Obsession* (London: William Heinemann, 2008; London: Windmill Books paperback, 2009)

Wulf, Andrea, *The Founding Gardeners: How the Revolutionary Generation created an American Eden* (London: William Heinemann, 2011)

NEWSPAPERS/ONLINE SOURCES

www.britannica.com/biography/Matthias-de-LObel. Accessed, 28 March 2017

www.rcpe.ac.uk/heritage/william-turner. Accessed, 28 March 2017

Curl, James Steven, 'John Claudius Loudon', *Oxford Art Online* (updated and revised 21 July 2004) http://www.oxfordartonline.com:80/subscriber/article/grove/art/T052089, accessed 18 July 2017]

Elliott, Brent, 'Loudon, John Claudius (1783-1843): landscape gardener and horticultural writer', *Oxford Dictionary of National Biography* (Oxford: Oxford University Press, 2004; online edn., May 2010) http://www.oxforddnb.com.ezproxy.londonlibrary.co.uk/view/article/17031, accessed 17 July 2017

Guinness, Bunny, 'Happy Birthday John Brookes, the king of garden design', *Daily Telegraph*, 30 October 2013 http://www.telegraph.co.uk/gardening/10409075/Happy-birthday-John-Brookes-the-king-of-garden-design.html, accessed 6 November 2017

Harris, John, 'London, George (d. 1714)', rev. *Oxford Dictionary of National Biography* (Oxford: Oxford University Press, 2004) http://www.oxforddnb.com.ezproxy2.londonlibrary.co.uk/view/article/37686, accessed 26 April 2017

Horwood, Catherine, 'Fish, Margery (1892–1969)', *Oxford Dictionary of National Biography*, Oxford University Press, Oct 2008 http://www.oxforddnb.com.ezproxy2.londonlibrary.co.uk/view/article/48830, accessed 29 August 2017

Keen, Mary, 'The life and legacy of Mrs Verey', *Daily Telegraph*, 19 January 2011 http://www.telegraph.co.uk/gardening/8264833/The-life-and-legacy-of-Mrs-Verey.html, accessed 17 October 2017

Kenworthy-Browne, John and Barton, Lin; bibliography updated by Lin Barton, 'Paxton, Sir Joseph', *Oxford Art Online* (2007-2017; bibliography updated 22 September 2015) http://www.oxfordartonline.com.ezproxy2.londonlibrary.co.uk/subscriber/article/grove/art/T065884

Marsh, Dr David, 'John Claudius Loudon and the rise of the amateur gardener http://www.feltonparkgreenhouse.org/history/john-claudius-loudon-an-appreciation, accessed 20 July 2017

Pimlott Baker, Anne, 'Wise, Henry (1653–1738)', *Oxford Dictionary of National Biography*, Oxford University Press, 2004; online edn., May 2010 http://www.oxforddnb.com.ezproxy2.londonlibrary.co.uk/view/article/29787, accessed 26 April 2017

Richardson, Tim, 'Tom Stuart-Smith: see the exhibition, read the book, visit the garden', *Daily Telegraph*, 23 May 2011 http://www.telegraph.co.uk/gardening/8525860/Tom-Stuart-Smith-see-the-exhibition-read-the-book-visit-the-garden.html, accessed 16 October 2017

Quest-Ritson, Charles, 'Great British Garden-makers: Russell Page', *Country Life*, 8 January 2011 http://www.countrylife.co.uk/gardens/great-british-garden-makers-russell-page-19453, accessed 5 October 2017

Thomas Seccombe, 'Nesfield, William Andrews (bap. 1794, d. 1881)', rev. Huon Mallalieu, *Oxford Dictionary of National Biography*, Oxford University Press, 2004 http://www.oxforddnb.com.ezproxy2.londonlibrary.co.uk/view/article/19901, accessed 18 July 2017

Tom Stuart-Smith, 'Trentham's Italian Renaissance', *Daily Telegraph*, 26 October 2007http://www.telegraph.co.uk/gardening/gardenstovisit/3345229/Trenthams-Italian-renaissance.html, accessed 28 November 2017

Tom Stuart-Smith website http://www.tomstuartsmith.co.uk/projects/show-gardens/chelsea-1998, 2000, 2003, 2006, accessed 27 November 2017

The Gentle Author http://spitalfieldslife.com/2011/07/02/thomas-fairchild-gardener-of-hoxton, accessed 6 February 2017

Uyterhoeven, Sonia, 'Tom Stuart-Smith: Finding a Language for the Modern Garden', *Plant Talk inside the New York Botanical Garden*, blog posted 5 February 2013 https://www.nybg.org/blogs/plant-talk/2013/02/learning/tom-stuart-smith-finding-a-language-for-the-modern-garden, accessed 16 October 2017

Acknowledgements

Any book is a collaborative process. I spent most of 2017 either in libraries or alone in my study at home in Gloucestershire, but I was supported throughout by many people, knowingly or unknowingly. The subject of this book is a broad canvas, so I have had perforce to stand on the shoulders of others. My first thanks go to all those authors whose work has helped me find my way, and who are credited in the notes and bibliography.

There are others, too, who have assisted my research. I want in particular to thank Beth Chatto's biographer, Dr Catherine Horwood, for giving me information on Beth's early life. I am very grateful to both Penelope Hobhouse and to Tom Stuart-Smith for talking to me about their life and work. I also had an enjoyable conversation with John Brookes in November 2017. Sadly, it was to be the last time we would meet: John died on 16 March 2018 as this book went to press.

A number of people have been generous in providing or helping me source images to illustrate this book: they include Dr Shirley Rose Evans, Graham S Pearson, Penelope Hobhouse, Peter Gillespie at John Brookes Landscape Design, Heather Power at Tom Stuart-Smith, Christopher Woodward and Emma House at The Garden Museum, Judith Ellis at the Chipping Campden History Society, Hazel Payne, Marguerite Bell at Mickleton WI, Sue Medway at the Chelsea Physic Garden, Anna McEvoy at Stowe House Preservation Trust, Wendy Bateson at Broughton Hall, Celine Leslie at Gravetye Manor, Mike Werkmeister at East Lambrook Manor and Susie Bulman at The Beth Chatto Gardens.

The librarians of both the London Library and the RHS Lindley Library have, as ever, been ceaselessly patient, seeking out and preparing material for me to work on in the libraries, and frequently supplying me with books by post.

I would also like to thank the team at Amberley: Jonathan Jackson for first suggesting I should write this book; Shaun Barrington and Alex Bennett for their work on the text and illustrations; and Sarah Greenwood and Hazel Kayes for their marketing and publicity support. I am grateful, too, to Katherine Hearst for compiling the index.

My mother died just before this book was commissioned, and I lost two of my oldest and dearest friends (Fe Robertson and Stephen Taylor) during its research and writing, so the past year and a quarter have been something of an emotional roller-coaster. I mention these three here for all of them have encouraged and sustained me over the years. I rely, too, on my sons, Nicholas and Matthew, and their partners, Sophie and Helena, but, as ever, my greatest debt of thanks goes to my husband, Chris Evans. He has read every chapter, and given me excellent, if not always welcome, advice. Without his help, I would never write a word.

Index